OUTER MONGOLIA

And Its International Position

LONDON: GEOFFREY CUMBERLEGE
OXFORD UNIVERSITY PRESS

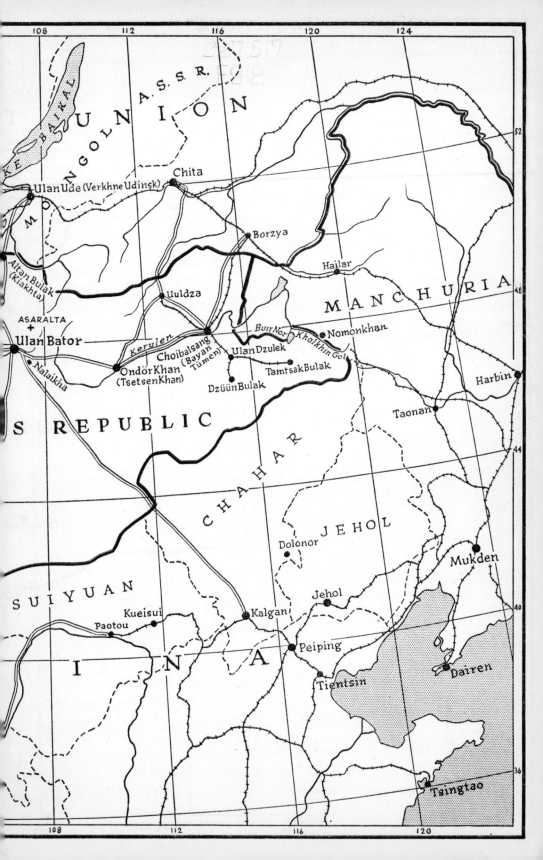

OUTER MONGOLIA
And Its International Position

By

GERARD M. FRITERS

Edited by Eleanor Lattimore

With an Introduction by Owen Lattimore

*Issued Under the Auspices of the International Secretariat,
Institute of Pacific Relations*

BALTIMORE

THE JOHNS HOPKINS PRESS

1949

PRINTED IN THE UNITED STATES OF AMERICA
BY J. H. FURST COMPANY, BALTIMORE, MARYLAND

The Institute of Pacific Relations is an unofficial and non-partisan body, founded in 1925 to facilitate the scientific study of the social, economic and political problems of the Pacific area. It is composed of National Councils in twelve countries.

The Institute as such and the National Councils of which it is composed are precluded from expressing an opinion on any aspect of national or international affairs; opinions expressed in this study are, therefore, entirely those of the author.

AUTHOR'S PREFACE

SOME YEARS ago Professor Manley O. Hudson of Harvard University suggested to me that it would be profitable to look into the question of the international position of Outer Mongolia, and out of this suggestion the present study has emerged. The book describes a little-known chapter of the diplomatic and colonial history of Central Asia. It is the first time that the story has been written in English, and, so far as I know, the first time that it has been arranged topically rather than chronologically. Though this method may present disadvantages in the writing of any general history, entailing as it does a certain amount of repetition, I have not hesitated to apply it to this study of a particular subject of political history; as it will, I hope, help to clarify the issues involved and the positions of the different countries concerned.

I have not been able to visit the Mongolian People's Republic, since no foreigner, except certain Soviet Russians, has been allowed to spend any useful length of time there for a considerable number of years. I cannot therefore write a descriptive book on Outer Mongolia similar to a number of interesting travel accounts published a good many years ago. I have therefore, except in the general introductory chapter, confined myself to the documentary material available. I am aware that material on recent developments, particularly statistics, cannot always be taken at its face value, and we are warned in the Soviet Siberian Encyclopaedia that statistics in Outer Mongolia are rudimentary.

In Russian material, we have a nearly continuous chain of documents at our disposal, including the much neglected *Orange Book* on Mongolian Affairs (1914), comprising the important negotiations of 1912-1913, and Russian books, both pre-war and post-war, have been consulted as far as they are accessible. Special mention should be made here of the great work of Grumm-Grzhimailo, " Western Mongolia and the Urianghai Region (1914, 1926, 1930) ," of the book of I. Maiskii,

"*Sovremennaya Mongoliya* " (Contemporary Mongolia), 1921, on which most writers, including Korostovets, base their story as to more recent times, and of the informative articles on the Mongolian People's Republic in the Soviet Siberian Encyclopaedia (Vol. 3, 1932) and in the Great Soviet Encyclopaedia (Vol. 40, 1938). Russian periodicals—and also Ukrainian— have been consulted as far as possible, though it has proved impossible to get hold of the periodical " Sovremennaya Mongoliya " to which Russian authors frequently refer. The same applies to the periodical " Khozyaistvo Mongolii " (The Economy of Mongolia), printed at Ulan Bator, though the very short summaries of articles which have appeared in it from 1926-31 have been consulted in " Bibliografiya Vostoka " (Bibliography of the East), 1, 1932, (pp. 119-124).

Whereas I have been able to give an adequate treatment of the Russian position from the Russian documents, and of the European powers and the United States on the basis of their published archives, I had also to rely to a great extent on the latter when analyzing the attitudes of China, Japan, and Mongolia itself. In a book written on Outer Mongolia it seems especially regrettable that the material from the Mongol side itself is so scarce or practically inaccessible. The Russian materials include, however, some documents from the Mongols themselves, and as to recent history we have the Russian translation of two reports made by a leading statesman of the Mongolian People's Republic.

As to the period treated in this book, the year 1911 suggests itself as a starting point, as it was then that Outer Mongolia declared its independence, and from then on the documentation is comparatively complete. The year 1911 is, however, not the birthday of the Mongolian problem, and it is necessary to describe certain developments which preceded it, going back sometimes to the middle of the nineteenth century or even earlier. My imagination has been stirred by reading tales of Chinggis Khan, but I have refrained from taking the story back so far, as this ground has been covered by many others.

My endeavor has been to give an impartial picture, as it

emerges from the evidence before me. And this picture, though not always completely satisfactory, is at least not obscured by prejudices due to a personal stake or national bias on the question of Outer Mongolia. I may, perhaps, be allowed to add that the conclusions arrived at have not been changed substantially to accord with the varying degrees of pro- and anti-Russian or pro- and anti-Chinese sentiments which have appeared since I published two articles in *Pacific Affairs*, the quarterly of the Institute of Pacific Relations, in 1937.

A good part of this book was completed—and some parts published—before or during 1939, when war broke out. The loss of part of the manuscript and of the notes, due to wartime conditions, for some time prevented the book from taking final form. The evacuation of a good many valuable library books to underground storage in the country or to inaccessible government departments has made it impossible to check certain points to my complete satisfaction.

I had the good fortune to win the interest of Mr. Owen Lattimore and I am much indebted for the encouragement which he gave me at the beginning of my study of this subject and for his continued interest and the important introduction which he has written to the book. I owe particular thanks to Mrs. Eleanor Lattimore for her long and careful work in editing and revising my manuscript during 1948, thus greatly improving its final form. Without the helpful collaboration of Mr. and Mrs. Lattimore it would not have been possible to publish the book at the present time.

Mr. Serge M. Wolff who was, in the second half of the twenties, Secretary to the Mongolian Trade Delegation and Educational Mission in Berlin, has put at my disposal valuable material which was in his hands and has been very helpful in many other ways. Dr. Ethel J. Lindgren, who spent some time in Ulan Bator (Urga), the capital of the Mongolian People's Republic, has also very kindly lent me material, has discussed a number of points with me and made a good many enquiries on my behalf. In difficult times her interest has meant a great deal to the continuation of the study. I am also much indebted to Miss Violet Conolly, O. B. E. for kindly assisting me in checking some material. The interest of the following friends should not go unmentioned: Mr. Boris Heiseler and Mr. Stanislav Kownacki, who have been of great assistance in the correct understanding of some difficult texts; Mrs. Hasel Popjak-Hammond and Mr. Howard Drake.

Finally I wish to express my appreciation for the patience with which the International Secretariat of the Institute of Pacific Relations, and particularly Mr. William L. Holland, its Secretary General, have waited for the arrival of the manuscript and assisted in making arrangements for editing and publication. Neither the Institute nor any of the persons mentioned above is in any way responsible for the presentation or for any part of the contents of the study, or for any of the opinions expressed. There remains the solace that the importance of the part of the world dealt with in this book is acknowledged today by many more than when I began the study.

G. F.

London

January, 1949

INTRODUCTION:

MONGOLIA'S PLACE IN THE WORLD

By Owen Lattimore

IN OUTER Mongolia—the Mongolian People's Republic—
there meet influences radiating from the Soviet Union, from
China, from America, and from such new centers of political
ferment and rivalry as Korea. We do not know enough about
this country. America based its vote against the admission of
the Mongolian People's Republic to the United Nations on the
statement that we know too little about the country or its
government.

We could know more than we do. In this book Mr. Friters
has painstakingly gathered more materials than have ever yet
been collected in one place on the history of the international
relations of Outer Mongolia since the Mongol and Chinese
Revolutions against the Manchu Dynasty in 1911. It is only
on the basis of such comparison of the sources that we can
begin to form intelligent opinion.

It is inevitable, in a period in which the main body of
material on an important question is still being gathered, that
opinions should differ. The significance of some of Mr. Friter's
material may be increased or lessened when further material
eventually becomes available. It is notable, for instance, that
while he has searched the files of international diplomacy, he
has been able to find far less in the way of statements of fact
and expressions of opinion by Mongol participants in the
events of Mongol politics than by the representatives of the
great powers interested in Mongolia. All students of both
Inner and Outer Mongolia are handicapped by this lack of
original Mongol material.

The Mongols are a people who are more often described in
the terms of folklore than in the careful definitions of political
science. Names and expressions like "Jenghis Khan," "Mongol
hordes," "savage horsemen," "primitive people," "the un-

sophisticated nomad " are scattered through the literature, and color the judgment of observers and commentators who are unaware that their thinking is being influenced more by handed-down clichés than by what they see with their own eyes.

There are two principal kinds of Mongol. The average Mongol, even in " revolutionary " Outer Mongolia, lives by his skill in the herding of sheep, horses, cattle, camels, and yaks. The proportions of the different kinds of livestock he owns differ according to the local conditions of soil, grazing, and climate. Contrary to the " folklore " of the social sciences, he is usually not a heavy eater of meat. He is a capitalist. Animals on the hoof are his capital. To butcher an animal is to cut into his capital. He therefore lives as far as he can on the interest of his capital—milk and cheese; or he exchanges surplus capital from the increase of his herds, or the sale of wool, for millet, wheat-flour, or other cereal foods.

This Mongol lives in a round felt tent. He moves his place of encampment to suit the grazing needs of his livestock. He does not, however, wander at haphazard. His use of wells, grazing grounds, and strips of country through which the stock is driven from one grazing ground to another is regulated by an intricate pattern of rights, customs, and interdependence on other Mongols; arrangements are often made, for instance, by which " you look after my sheep along with yours and I'll take charge of your horses and mine."

This Mongol is a devoted family man. The whole household works, and they are aware of their dependence on each other. He is a self-reliant man, and handy with tools: if a wheel breaks, there is no service station at which he can get it repaired. With the approach of winter, and in the dangerous season of spring blizzards, he must make his own decisions on moving his stock to shelter or in search of the young spring grass.

His loyalties are often more personal than institutional. His political thinking is more apt to be in terms of " our people " than in terms of " our ideology." He is deeply nationalistic in the sense of feeling that all Mongols are his own people, while all Chinese, Russians, and other strangers are " outsiders." He is convinced that the outsider rarely gives the Mongol a square deal if he can get away with giving him a shabby deal. He is religious; but he combines his personal religiousness with a racy stock of stories about the villainies and corruption of lama priests. He has a subtly graded scale of values in personal relationships and in such possessions as livestock, but very little sense of the value of money. Live animals are real values, to be guarded jealously; money is something with which to be profligate or generous. He admires physical strength (especially if it be combined with skill) and physical courage. A young Mongol likes to ride a hundred miles in a day, not because it is necessary, but for the pride of doing it.

There is also another kind of Mongol. An example in my mind is my friend Serat, now dead. Serat grew up a skilled handler of horses and camels. Then he became a skilled truck driver on the old Kalgan-Urga road. He spoke fluent Russian and perfect Chinese, in addition to his own language. He took photographs with a trained appreciation of the values of light and shade, and an artistic understanding of composition. On one occasion when a car had broken down far out in the desert, he made forced marches on a camel, in record time, back to the railway; travelled to Peiping, went to a repair shop and got the necessary spare parts and accessories, went back to his camel, and again by forced marches returned to the car, which he repaired. He was a better man with a motor car, as well as a better man with a camel, than the Europeans whose car he was driving.

Serat knew his way around in politics. He had his reservations about the Russians, and very deep reservations about the Chinese Government. Bred in an extremely conservative Banner of the Chahar Mongols, he did not believe that either princes or lamas were a source of strength to the Mongols of today. He worked for some years for Sven Hedin's Sino-Swedish Expedition. He had also, I believe, worked for Roy Chapman Andrews. His last big journey was when he acted as guide and chief mechanic for Sir Eric Teichman, a British diplomat who travelled through Mongolia and Sinkiang and then by caravan over the mountain barrier into India. Serat returned from India by sea.

Serat knew Russians, Chinese, and Westerners. He knew that Chinese and Westerners assume as a matter of course that the " real " Mongol has an unshaken feudal loyalty to princely nobles and church dignitaries. But I have sat listening while Serat talked in Mongol with other Mongols, and chuckled at the revelation of how much more Serat knew about foreigners than foreigners knew about the Mongols.

The Mongolia of today is a variable equation in which the " old " Mongol factor is dwindling and the " Serat " Mongol factor is growing; but at a jerky, changeable rate of speed and at different rates of speed in different parts of Mongolia. The rate of speed is no longer affected solely by " Russia " and " China," regarded as constants. Neither Russia nor China is a constant; both are themselves variables, and the rate of mutation in Mongolia is affected by the rate of mutation in China and Russia. It is also affected by the immensely in-creased importance of America as a power factor in Asia.

For these reasons, political changes in Mongolia must be regarded as part of a much wider general process of change both in the immediate zone of proximity to Mongolia and in the world as a whole. The most intimate linkage is with the accelerating process of revolution in China since 1911 and in Russia since 1917.

Mr. Friters has gathered for us the materials with which to study the phases of the process of change. The process as a whole has been governed by the fact that it took place in a geographical compartment enclosed on one side by China, on the other side by Russia, and cut off from the sea. When revolution broke out in China against the Manchu Dynasty in 1911, the Mongols also rebelled against the overlord rule of the government in Peking. From this time on through the succeeding decades the Mongol Revolution has run parallel with the Chinese Revolution, but has not been a part of it—still less a subordinate part.

The Mongols could not avoid being involved in and subordinated to events in China except by leaning against the other wall of the compartment in which they lived—which meant that they had to adjust themselves so closely not only to Russia but to events in Russia that Russia became the primary external factor in the process of internal change in Outer Mongolia. This necessity of adjustment was as inevitable for Living Buddhas and princely descendants of Jenghis Khan in the years after 1911 as it was for the more radical leaders in later years, especially after 1921.

One master thread, therefore, can be traced all through the maze of these confused years. That thread is the political question, in Mongol minds, of the degree of trust to be placed in Russia. It can first be picked up in the years when Mongolia was still under its hereditary princes and high clerical dignitaries, and when Russia was still under the rule of the Tsar. It is a thread which is always distinguishable from the differences between leftists and rightists, though it is involved in every conflict between left and right. By following this thread, moreover, it is possible to determine at any phase of development not only the orientation of Mongolia toward Russia, but the relative orientation toward Russia of Mongolia and other countries, such as Turkey or China.

Turkey, China, and Mongolia, in fact, represent three major types of relationship between Soviet Russia and adjoining countries in Asia. A comparison of these types of relationship helps to give a perspective and proportion which might be distorted if we were to narrow our attention too exclusively to Mongolia.

Between Turkey and Russia at the end of the first World War there arose a relationship of mutual interest. Britain and France were most unwilling to permit the success of the Russian Revolution and were also unwilling to see Turkey, under Kemal Atatürk, attain a higher degree of sovereignty and independence than it had enjoyed under the Sultans.

Kemal, for his part, represented a thorough-going political revolution but only a limited social revolution. His support came from a coalition between the landed gentry, who had always been powerful in the old Turkey, and a new middle class, interested in trade and industry, which had rapidly become wealthier and stronger in the closing decades of the old regime. Both classes resented the political and economic advantages which foreigners enjoyed through extraterritoriality, and the controls forced on their country by old treaties. Both wanted full political independence for their country, but the gentry did not want a degree of functioning democracy that would enable their tenants to outvote them, and the new middle class did not want to see any dangerous development of political rights linked with economic rights among their workers and employees.

The Russians did not want Turkey to be used as a base against them, and considered that a strengthened Turkey would be able to divert some of the pressure of Britain and France from them. They were therefore willing to make loans to Turkey, without interest, for purposes of economic development, even at a time when they themselves were economically very hard-pressed. Kemal was willing to accept help from Russia as a means of forcing the anti-Russian powers to bargain with Turkey.

The result was that Turkey attained the new and higher level of political independence at which Kemal and his associates aimed, but then hung at that level. Its economic progress did not equal its political progress. Economically, it remained on the fringe of the colonial world. Its rate of progress put it ahead of most other countries in the Near East, but it could not catch up with the advanced countries of the West; in fact the gap between Turkey and the advanced countries tended to become wider.

Between China and Russia there was also a community of interest at the end of the first World War. From the Asiatic side, the principal intervention aimed at preventing the success of the Russian Revolution came from Japan; but Britain, and to some extent America, were also involved (though America was also interested in preventing an undue expansion of Japanese control over continental Asia). The Russians were interested in any ability to distract the attention of the anti-Russian powers that China might manifest. Chinese nationalists, of the right as well as of the left, were interested in the possibility that dealing with Russia might improve their bargaining position against the Western powers.

China, however, was a vast and chaotic country as compared with Turkey. The best troops in Turkey were led by Kemal's closest adherents; most of the best troops in China were under the command of generals who were open to foreign political or economic influence. China's middle class also had more foreign connections than Turkey's. In Turkey the extraterritorial system had ceased to operate for a number of years during the war, because Turkey had been on the side of Germany; whereas in China, throughout the war, all the great powers except Germany had continued to exercise and profit by their extraterritorial privileges. In Turkey there was a united national interest in preventing the reimposition of the extraterritorial system; in China the system was still a going concern, and some of the Chinese who stood to profit if it could be abolished were unwilling to take extreme risks for fear that, if they failed, their position would be worse than it had been before.

In Turkey the most nationalistic group, with the widest popular support and the most troops, was able to take over the government. In the hands of Kemal, this government did more than claim recognition as a fully sovereign state; it acted like one. In China, the government which was internationally recognized was not the center of nationalism; it did not have full control of the country; and a great part of the revenue which sustained it was subject to foreign controls of various kinds. Another part of the national revenue passed through the hands of local militarists who could not be controlled by the government. These more than half-independent generals controlled most of the troops; and a number of the most important of them had " understandings " with foreign governments. The center of nationalism was among the followers of

Sun Yat-sen, who were not in power and could not come to power except through a combination of political revolution and military action.

In these two situations, the record of Russian policy toward Turkey in the early 1920's appears to indicate a fundamental decision not to gamble with vague theories of revolution, but to deal with a government that was nationalistic, had popular support, and seemed likely to be able to push away from the frontiers of Russia the strategic outposts of countries hostile to Russia. In China, the record of Russian policy in the same period indicates a fundamental decision to support the potentialities of a nationalist government which might come to power, rather than the actualities of the flabby government which was internationally recognized; because the legal government was incapable of defending its own interests, and therefore incapable of serving as a barrier to keep at a distance from Russia the outposts of countries hostile to Russia.

Thus Sun Yat-sen was able to deal with the Russians on a more nearly official footing than he had achieved in his attempts to deal with any other foreign country. Russian Communist advisors worked with him in China. Non-Communist Chinese, like Chiang Kai-shek, were sent to Russia for study and observation. Chinese Communists were admitted into the Kuomintang. A tremendous thrust of radically minded peasants in the countryside and industrial workers in the cities was mobilized behind the spearhead of the Kuomintang.

The spearhead was driven home to the target after the death of Sun Yat-sen. The Kuomintang took over the government of China. Then other forces came into play which had been inherent in the situation from the beginning. The Kuomintang, having used Russian aid to weaken the hold of the West on China, turned to the West not only to get enough help to dispense with Russian aid, but to check the social revolution which was a concomitant of political and military revolution.

The histories of the period are unanimous in describing this development as a great defeat for Russia. In the longer view, it would seem that the word " defeat," used in this context, has been made to carry too heavy a semantic load. Russian policy was " defeated " in the sense of not realizing the full potentials of the situation; but it was not defeated in the sense of not realizing any of the potentials. The government which came into power was not friendly to Russia; but it was better able to defend itself against Russia's enemy, Japan, than any previous government of China. Russian appreciation of the importance of a Chinese government able and willing to defend itself, in spite of its record of hostility to Russia and to social revolution, is proved by the fact that between 1937 and 1941 the Kuomintang Government, which had always been hostile to Russia and more friendly to America than to any other country, received far more aid against Japan from Russia than it did from America.

Mongolia represents a third situation and illustrates a third type of Russian policy. There is a definite continuity between this policy in Tsarist times and in Soviet times. The Tsarist policy, as Mr. Friters shows, was not to annex or absorb Mongolia. There were interests in Tsarist Russia which would have liked to exploit Mongolia, but on the whole they were held in check. In sum total, the Tsarist policy was to maintain Mongolia as a buffer, in the most old-fashioned sense of the word. The clearest indications that we have of Soviet policy also point to the use of Mongolia as a buffer. The Soviet policy, however, is much less static than that of the Tsars; it has from the beginning encouraged the Mongols to become able to look after themselves, whereas the Tsarist policy was to keep them inactive in a land of inaction.

From the Mongol point of view, even before 1911, the most pressing danger was not the " colonial " control of their country by a few foreigners representing a foreign government, but actual *colonizing* of the best part of their land by Chinese settlers; not subjection, but displacement; not the fate of India, but the fate of the American Indian. The Mongols of Outer Mongolia were fully aware that Mongols were being driven out of enormous areas of Inner Mongolia by Chinese colonization. In the decade before 1911 the Chinese (Manchu) government for the first time undertook an official promotion of Chinese colonization in Outer Mongolia; its intention was to " screen " the Russian frontier. Because Chinese farming took up the best land, pressure was caused by concentrating more Mongol herds in poorer pastures. The Mongol princes felt the effect in unrest among their feudal subjects. At the same time, both wealthy nobles and wealthy monasteries suffered a decrease in revenue, for the revenue from the newly settled farm lands was controlled not by them but by the Chinese authorities. There were scattered risings in Inner Mongolia which attempted to drive out the Chinese settlers, and some of these risings, especially in the lands of the Mongols in western Manchuria, began to affect the eastern fringes of Outer Mongolia. " Thus conditions were created in Outer Mongolia favorable to the development of a national movement of all classes for separation from China." [1]

For the Mongols, even in Tsarist times, there was never any real question of maneuvering between Russia and the great powers of the West. They could not play China against Russia as China itself and Turkey later played the Western powers against Russia, because the danger to them of being swamped by Chinese colonization was quite different from the danger to China or Turkey of being controlled by outside powers. Even Japan could not be played as an alternative to Russia, because Japan could not approach Mongolia except through territory inhabited by Chinese greatly outnumbering the Mongols. Japan could not take up a position which would make it " alternative " to Russia except by occupying this Chinese territory; but this kind of occupation would give the Japanese a much greater stake in Chinese territory than in Mongol territory, and would make their Mongol policy subordinate to their Chinese policy. It is not surprising therefore that Outer

---

[1] Anatolii Kallinikov, *Natsional'no-revolyutsionnoe dvizhenie v Mongolii* (The national-revolutionary movement in Mongolia), Moscow-Leningrad, 1926, pp. 23-25. The importance of the threat of colonization in touching off the nationalist movement in Outer Mongolia is confirmed by a statement which gives the point of view of the later Mongol revolutionaries; see p. 67 of Doksom's *Report* of 1936, which is cited in Mr. Friters' Bibliography.

Mongolian attempts to deal with the Japanese can only be traced to a few individuals here and there; no such thing ever existed as a social class or cohesive political group of Mongols identifying their interests with Japan. It was chiefly in Inner Mongolia that there was a tendency among some political leaders to turn to Japan when pressed to desperation by the crushing advance of Chinese colonization into their pastures.

Modern Mongol nationalism therefore developed in an atmosphere in which the primary question of foreign relations was the nature of the relationship with Russia—first Tsarist Russia and then Soviet Russia. Relations with China, Western countries, or Japan as " alternatives " to Russia, in any scale suggesting supersession of Russia in importance, could be thought of only by scattered individuals, usually for reasons of personal ambition. For all others, the problem has always been not whether to make Russia the most important country in foreign relations, but how to deal with the fact that Russia is the most important country in foreign relations. It naturally follows from this consideration that the tone of Russo-Mongol relations in any phase of development tends to be set by the relative degree of cordiality prevailing between those in whose hands power lies in Russia and Mongolia. A concomitant phenomenon is the tendency for power in Mongolia to gravitate into the hands of those Mongols who can get on best with the Russia of the time, whatever the time may be.

In the closing decade of Tsarist rule, when the Russian policy was to maintain Outer Mongolia as a buffer, with an internally stable and unchanging society, the only Mongol nationalism was that of the old ruling class of feudal aristocrats and clerical magnates. The outlook of this nationalism was as static as the Tsarist government could have desired. Thus in 1911 the Urga Hutukhtu called a session which named a delegation to go to St. Petersburg, and this delegation carried a letter which declared:

Formerly the Mongol Khans, Wangs, and Jassaks were rulers of their own subjects and, enjoying revenues from their lands, lived in tranquility. In recent times Chinese officials, taking power into their hands, and in every way interfering in Mongol affairs, and especially under pretext of reform colonizing Mongolia and changing its ancient customs, are diminishing local authority. This is truly sad.[2]

It would be hard to draft a better expression of a conservative, static nationalism which sought to prevent the extension of Chinese power into Mongolia, but not to transfer power from the Chinese state to the Mongol people.

In spite of a policy directed against change, however, the degree of autonomy enjoyed in Outer Mongolia for a few years after 1911 was a change, and a great one. The mere fact that, with the departure of Manchu and Chinese officials, new administrative duties had to be taken over and new personnel found was enough to stimulate a new political thinking, even if it was only among the few who took part in the new activities.

The following three paragraphs concerning the government of this period were sent by Mr. Friters too late to be included in the text.

When the princes of Khalkha declared their independence and proclaimed the Hutukhtu of Urga Khan of Mongolia in December 1911, no central state apparatus existed.[3] It is thus hardly surprising that sixteen months later the Russian Foreign Ministry could still speak of " the weak political consciousness " of the Mongols." [4] The Mongols were anxious to obtain Russia's recognition of their status as a government and were dissatisfied with the Russian representative's original intention to refer only to the princes in the proposed Russo-Mongolian agreement. Actually the final agreement of 1912 put the position quite correctly in its preamble in referring to " the Jebtsun Damba Hutukhtu, the Mongolian Government and the Mongol reigning princes." [5] Of these three, the Hutukhtu and the reigning princes already possessed prestige and controlled established administrative units in the aimaks and

---

[2] Cited in Doksom's *Report* of 1936, p. 82.

[3] According to W. N. Kokovtsov, in Korostovets, p. 133, " there are no elements even of the most primitive state . . . the whole apparatus must first be created."

[4] *IBZI*, I, 2, p. 362, No. 360, Special Journal of the Russian Council of Ministers, May 7/Apr. 24, 1914.

[5] *O. B.* No. 16.

hoshuns. But the weak link was the Mongolian Government, which was now supposed to have acquired all the functions formerly exercised by the Chinese Ambans and which had the task of establishing a uniform and centralized administration which had not existed before in modern times.

The new government consisted of five ministries: Foreign Affairs, Interior, Finance, Justice, and War, and by 1918 they had grown to the point where they employed from forty to fifty officials each.[6] Political rivalry continued to exist between the Lama Church and the princes. The Lama Church had obtained political power for the first time, and the fact that its spiritual ruler was at the same time the autocratic temporal ruler strengthened its position, especially in its opposition to reform, although the enactment of reforms was necessary if Mongolia was to have an efficient government.

A two chamber parliament was established in 1914. It consisted of an Upper House, which met every Sunday and consisted of the Ministers, the hoshun princes of first rank and the Ministers' assistants, although in practice only those princes attended who lived in Urga. The Prime Minister was the chairman. The Lower House, which met every Friday, consisted of the princes of second rank and the officials, and the chairman was one of the princes.[7] The motives of the Mongols in establishing these two chambers, according to Miller, the Russian diplomatic agent in Urga, were to divert the attention of the hoshun princes from the consequences of their light hearted policy of aggression, and to give the officials of the Mongolian Ministries the illusion that they participated in administrative affairs in accordance with the tradition of the old hurals of Chinggis Khan.[8] There is evidence, however, that little real discussion took place. Generally one of the " elders " would speak on a given subject and deliver an authoritative opinion. The lower ranks would then support him, and the matter would be settled. Anyone expressing a different opinion would do it

[6] Maiskii, p. 276.
[7] Maiskii, pp. 278, 279.
[8] *IBZI*, I, 2, p. 407, No. 420, Miller to Sazanov, May 13/Apr. 30, 1914.

only in the form of a question. In any case the two chambers were purely consultative in character and their exact powers were not defined.[9]

The first few years of autonomy were notably prosperous, and this fact, often overlooked, served as a stimulus to political thinking. The cancellation of debts to Chinese traders, and especially of the outrageous payment of interest on indebtedness, made possible a quick increase in the size of herds. The importance of this change can be judged by the fact that just before autonomy was achieved the average indebtedness to Chinese traders of a Mongol family was 540 Chinese ounces of silver—an enormous amount for poor shepherds—while one great Chinese firm alone collected yearly, in payment of interest, 70,000 horses and half a million sheep.[10] When this drain was halted for several years, the resulting increase of the national wealth " created, for the first time since the period of subjection of the Mongols to the Manchu Dynasty, something of a basis for the cultural and political development of the Mongol people." [11]

When revolt against the Manchus broke out in 1911, the ordinary people still " blindly followed " the nobles whom they regarded as their hereditary chiefs, and the lamas whom they regarded as the mediators between the people and Heaven. " But it was not of no consequence to the consciousness of the ordinary people that they took part in the movement. Along with the strengthening of national self-consciousness among the arats (the common people) there gradually developed a feeling of human dignity and of dissatisfaction with their subject condition . . . there began to form, among the most progressive elements of the arats, the younger lamas and the best representatives of the princely class, a thin layer of Mongol intelli-

---

[9] Maiskii, p. 279. *Tu Li P'ing Lun*, June 7, 1936, p. 10 and July 12, 1936, p. 12. In this long discussion between C. F. Chang and T. L. Hsü the question of the two houses of parliament was the " apple of discord " between the two. Hsü went so far as to say that since there was no discussion in the lower house " I assume it has never had any performances." See also CYB, 1921-22, p. 525.

[10] Kallinikov, *op. cit.*, p. 21.

[11] *Ibid.*, p. 32.

gentsia. Among a few of the most radical of this young Mongol intelligentsia there gradually dawned the thought of the injustice and the harmfulness to the regeneration of the Mongol people of class subdivision, and the necessity of a radical break with the whole feudal and theocratic structure of Mongolia." [12]

Military service was another stimulus both to nationalism and to a radical tendency within nationalism. Mr. Friters describes the force that was raised in Outer Mongolia and trained under Tsarist Russian officers. It was inevitable that, when the Russian Revolution began, the talk that was common among Russian soldiers should find its way into the barracks of the Mongol troops. Sukhe Bator, the first great leader of the Mongol Revolution, was one of the soldiers of this first national Mongol force, and it is not surprising that, even before he came in contact with avowed Communists, he had already declared himself both against the old social order and in favor of alliance with the Russian revolutionaries.

Sukhe Bator was a son of the people, who became a skilled soldier and a successful political organizer. Men of noble birth, however, also became revolutionaries. The prince who bore the title of Tsetsen Khan, hereditary ruler of Tsetsen Khan Aimak, one of the four great Aimaks of the old Outer Mongolia, renounced all his feudal rights, became a simple citizen, and served in the Revolutionary government after 1921 as Minister of the Interior.[13] Still more interesting was the career of Khatan Bator Maksorjab, a noble of Northwest Mongolia, whose fame as a warrior dated from the 1911 rising. Atlthough he had the title of prince (which he later renounced), he had known poverty in his youth and had worked with his hands. His trend toward radicalism, growing more marked and not less marked as he grew older, illustrates a type of political phenomenon which has been little studied by Western political scientists: the phenomenon of the traditional society, breaking

---

[12] *Ibid.*, p. 32.

[13] *Ibid.*, p. 55. It is significant that a man of such high aristocratic origin should have held the office of Minister of the Interior with, presumably, control of the police. The fact that he is mentioned with approval by this Soviet Russian author as late as 1926 indicates that he did not fall from power after a brief tenure.

down in the modern world, in which the man who has both high birth and great ability not infrequently finds that he has more to gain by relying on his ability in a new equalitarian social order than by trying to preserve his hereditary privileges and the social order of which they are a part.[14]

In the Mongol Revolution Sukhe Bator, as the primary architect of revolutionary thought and the primary organizer of revolutionary action, is to be compared with Lenin in Russia and Sun Yet-sen in China. Sun Yat-sen, born in 1866, and Lenin, born in 1870, were men of about the same age. Sukhe Bator, born in 1893, was a full generation younger. The lives of all three men came to a close at almost the same time, however. Sukhe Bator died in 1923, Lenin in 1924, and Sun Yat-sen in 1925.

In each of the three countries, preeminence both in party power and in government position is held today by a man who was a close associate of the revolutionary founder. Stalin worked with Lenin before and during the Russian Revolution. Chiang Kai-shek commanded the military forces of Sun Yat-sen and was sent by him to study both political and military organization in Russia. Choibalsang was a co-founder, with Sukhe Bator, of the Mongolian People's Revolutionary Party, formed in 1920 by the merger of the two secret revolutionary parties which had until then been led separately by Sukhe Bator and by Choibalsang. It is noteworthy, however, that it took Choibalsang much longer to succeed to preeminent power than it took either Stalin or Chiang Kai-shek.

While Stalin, Chiang Kai-shek, and Choibalsang are alike in representing the first political generation in succession from the founder, they differ in representing very different forms of succession. Stalin, though accused by dissident Marxists of perverting Lenin's ideas, is generally recognized throughout the

---

[14] *Ibid.*, pp. 49, 54. There is a biography of this extraordinary man (who had been named "Minister of War" by Ungern-Sternberg but who headed the rising in Northwestern Mongolia against Ungern-Sternberg), by Marshal Choibalsang, the present Premier: Kho. Choibalsang, *Arat-un Khatan Bagator Maksorjab-un Khoriyanggoi Teughe* (The People's Khatan Bator Maksorjab, Collected Volume), Ulan Bator, 1942, pp. 141. (Bagator is the written form of *bator*, ' hero ').

world as both the successor to Lenin and the continuator of his policies. Chiang Kai-shek, on the other hand, clearly stands far to the right of his predecessor, Sun Yat-sen. In analyzing the parallels and divergences between political developments in China and in Mongolia, it is especially important to note that Chiang Kai-shek repudiated cooperation with the Chinese Communists domestically and with Russia internationally, the two policies which had dominated the closing years of Sun Yat-sen's life. It is at this point that the widest divergence is to be noted between the recent political history of the Mongols and that of the Chinese: in Mongolia, Choibalsang continued and further developed the association with Communism and with Russia which in China was broken off by Chiang Kai-shek. (It is therefore to be expected that the Chinese Communists will emphasize a " restored continuity " between Sun Yat-sen and Mao Tze-tung.)

The details of revolutionary history in Mongolia are much more inaccessible than in either China or Russia; but further comparison with China does make it possible to fix relatively the position and character of the Mongol People's Republic as a revolutionary state. The relative position determined by this method can then be checked by comparing the Mongol Constitutions of 1924 and 1940 with various Russian and Soviet constitutions.[15]

Hazard states that " complete state ownership of the means of production was declared to be a principle of constitutional law in the constitutions of the R.S.F.S.R. and of the other Republics after they had joined in a Union of Soviet Socialist Republics in December 1922. The principle was not stated, however, in the first constitution of the U.S.S.R. This first federal document appears to have been conceived not as a statement of general principles but as a document establishing the

---

[15] For the Constitution of 1940, see Appendix. For a commentary on Soviet precedents and influences, see John N. Hazard, " The Constitution of the Mongol People's Republic and Soviet Influences," *Pacific Affairs*, New York, June 1948, pp. 162-170. Hazard does not mention the Mongol Constitution of 1924, a translation of which is printed in *China Year Book*, 1926-27, Tientsin, 1927, pp. 795-800.

structure of the new federal government." In this period the 1920 constitution of the Khorezm Soviet People's Republic, which replaced the Principality of Khiva, explained that for lack of the necessary industrial base, this Republic could not yet aim at a socialist structure. The 1922 constitution of the Bukhara People's Soviet Republic, which replaced the Principality of Bukhara, " made no comment on the subject," according to Hazard. (These two territories, formerly part of the Tsarist Empire, were subsequently incorporated in the Soviet Union.)

The Mongol constitution of 1924 falls within this general group. Its primary objective was clearly to establish a new, republican form of state, " without a President at the head of the State, all supreme power to be vested in the Great Assembly of the People and in the Government elected by the latter." Socialism is mentioned rather indirectly: " In view of the fact that the laboring masses of the whole world are striving to uproot capitalism and to attain socialism (communism), this Republic of laboring people must coordinate its foreign policy with the interests and fundamental aims of small oppressed nations and the revolutionary workers of the whole world." The direct aim, on the other hand, was " the abolition of the remains of the feudal theocratic regime and the strengthening of the foundations of the new republican order." To attain this aim, both feudal and clerical titles were abolished, and the right to vote and to be elected was restricted to " those who earn their means of livelihood by their own labor or are busy with their own establishments based on their personal labor," and soldiers. Traders, usurers, titled aristocrats, clerical dignitaries and lamas actually resident in monasteries were disfranchised.

On the economic side the constitution of 1924 nationalized land, mineral wealth, forests, and waters, and provided for a state monopoly of foreign trade, " to be introduced gradually, as circumstances will allow." Private property in livestock was not touched.

The constitution of 1940, at present in force, marks a step forward in evolution from the constitution of 1924. It continues to run parallel with Soviet development, but to lag behind it in important respects. Thus it imitates some of the features of the Soviet constitution of 1936, but retains other features from earlier Soviet practice. The difference is unmistakeably accounted for by the fact that Mongolia remains far behind the Soviet Union in economic development. As Hazard writes, "Marxists have believed that economic rights are empty phrases unless they can be made effective." Thus the current Mongol constitution, like the 1918 constitution of the R.S.F.S.R., contains no guarantee of the right to work. This right was written into the Soviet constitution of 1936, when the Russians believed that their socialism had become a going concern, able to guarantee that there would be no unemployment. The Mongols do not yet claim socialism, in spite of their many nationalized enterprises, and speak only of a successful abolition of the old feudal society, " ensuring a non-captialist approach to the development of the country to pave the way to socialism in the future."

On the other hand, the Mongols apparently do believe that their state now compares with the Soviet State in relative stability. In 1936 the Soviets restored the franchise to former priests, employers of labor, members of the former royal family, and tsarist police. In 1944 Mongolia took a similar step, through a special decree now printed with the 1940 constitution.

In several main features, however, the Mongol constitution still follows the pre-1936 Soviet model. The Mongols have not yet, like the Russians, written the principle of a direct and secret vote into their constitution. Instead, delegates to each higher level within the government structure are elected by voice vote of the delegates at the next lower level. Their Great Hural also resembles the pre-1936 Soviet Congress of Soviets. It meets normally every three years (the Congress of Soviets met every two years), and appoints a Central Executive Committee to maintain continuity between sessions. As in the Russian system before 1936, this Central Executive Committee appoints a still smaller body, the Praesidium; but the present Mongol Praesidium has the detailed, specific powers of the present Praesidium of the Supreme Soviet of the U.S.S.R. rather than the undefined, general powers of the Praesidium of the former Central Executive Committee of the pre-1936 Congress of Soviets.

Since the party organization of the Kuomintang and the structure of the Government in China, like the organization of the Mongol People's Revolutionary Party and the structure of the Government in Mongolia were strongly influenced by the study of Soviet models in the early 1920's, this method of comparison makes it possible both to define differences and resemblances between China, Mongolia, and Russia and to determine whether it is the differences or the resemblances that have been growing more important.

According to a biography of Sukhe Bator which was published in Mongol at Ulan Bator and may be regarded as official, the Mongolian People's Revolutionary Party was founded in 1920.[16] Of the two secret revolutionary groups which merged to found the Party, one had been led by Sukhe Bator, the other by Choibalsang. In this account, there is no mention of Russian or Marxist affiliations in the earlier thinking or political planning of Sukhe Bator. As the son of a poor family, he had learned Russian playing with children in the Russian quarter of Ulan Bator (then called Urga). Later he had served under Tsarist Russian instructors in the machine gun detachment whose organization is described by Mr. Friters in Chapter II.

There is thus a general parallel between Sukhe Bator and Sun Yat-sen. Both were born of poor families, both acquired a foreign language in youth, both began their political careers as nationalists, whose goal was national independence. To mark that independence, a new government was of course necessary. Independently of Communist urging both men became convinced that revolutionary changes would be required in the fabric of society itself, in order to maintain the new independent nation and sustain the new independent government.

[16] Sh. Nachokdorji, *Sukhebagator-un namtar* (Biography of Sukhe Bator), Ulan Bator, 1943, p. 39 and ff.

Lack of more detailed information makes it dangerous to carry speculation too far, but it seems legitimate to infer that at this stage the alliance between Sukhe Bator and Choibalsang, formed in 1920, ran parallel to the alliance between Sun Yat-sen and the Chinese Communists, which began formally in 1924, though Sun Yat-sen had sent a friendly message to Lenin as early as 1918, and had received an emissary from Lenin in 1921.

Sukhe Bator's original secret party of nationalist revolutionaries, like Sun Yat-sen's Kuomintang, contained a right wing and a left wing. In the right wing, some of whose members had official connections, the restoration of autonomy was thought of as both the primary and the ultimate goal. There was no thought of taking power away from the aristocratic and clerical officials who had always held power.

These nationalists may therefore be compared with those conservative members of the Kuomintang in Sun Yat-sen's lifetime who would have been office-holders under the Manchu Empire, had the Manchu Empire continued strong, and who as nationalists aspired merely to hold under a Republic the appointments and the kind of power that they would otherwise have held under the Empire. Both Mongol and Chinese conservative nationalists of this kind were, of course, prepared to remove certain individuals from power in order to make way for themselves, and part of their political program was to change the names of government bureaus and the titles of appointments; but essentially they believed that power was the prerogative of their " enlightened " group, and they did not believe in changing the structure of society in any way that might weaken their own position or place political controls in the hands of the " unenlightened " common people.

The left wing of Sukhe Bator's own party, led by Sukhe Bator himself, were already convinced that to drive out the Chinese troops and recover autonomy would not be enough. Like Sun Yat-sen, Sukhe Bator even before he came under Russian political influence had come to the conclusion that a social revolution was also necessary: " all the yellow (clerical) and black (lay) feudal aristocrats must be cast from off the backs of the common people." [17]

The complications that arise when revolution stirs under the feet of a foreign military occupation are well illustrated by this period of Mongol revolutionary history. Sukhe Bator himself was in favor of looking to Russia for help. " We are hearing news of the revolution which has broken out in Russia to the north of us. We need to see whether or not it can be of help to our Mongol nation at this turning point, and whether or not we can find a road on which to go forward together." [18]

This issue divided the party into a majority which followed Sukhe Bator and a minority which believed that the Mongols " should lean on one or another of the capitalist countries." Sukhe Bator believed that the Mongols could not turn to the capitalist countries without falling into their power; " this would be to escape from the maw of the wolf and fall into the maw of the tiger." As he put it, " internally our strength is the common people, and so in foreign affairs the Soviet country has become our prop and support." [19] In support of his belief, and with the encouragement of his dying father, Sukhe Bator made an attempt to go to Siberia to get in touch with the Russian revolutionaries, but was unable to penetrate the screen of Chinese troops along the frontier.[20]

The parallel between Sukhe Bator and Sun Yat-sen at this stage in the development of the revolutionary movements in Mongolia and China is important. Like Sukhe Bator, Sun Yat-sen took the initiative in showing interest in the Russian revolution, by sending a telegram of congratulation to Lenin when the Russian Revolution broke out. Like Sukhe Bator, he came to believe that the powerful non-revolutionary countries were fundamentally imperialist, though unlike Sukhe Bator he had tried for years to get support from them. By 1923—after his contacts with the Russians were well established—he declared to an American interviewer that " We have lost hope of help from America, England, France, or any other

---

[17] *Biography*, p. 34.
[19] *Ibid.*, p. 37.
[18] *Ibid.*, p. 36.
[20] *Ibid.*, pp. 37, 38.

of the great Powers. The only country that shows any signs of helping us . . . is the Soviet Government of Russia.[21] At the end of that year he phrased his opinion even more bluntly: " We no longer look to the Western Powers. Our faces are turned toward Russia." [22]

It was after his unsuccessful attempt to reach Siberia that Sukhe Bator came into touch with Choibalsang and the secret revolutionary group led by him. This group operated in the Russian quarter of Urga (Ulan Bator); Sukhe Bator already knew of them, but had been unable to unite with them because of the severity of the police control exercised by the Chinese forces occupying the city.

The parallel between the Mongol and Chinese revolutionary movements then developed a stage further; for Choibalsang's group resembled the Chinese Communists in the period when, with Sun Yat-sen's consent, they actually merged with the Kuomintang. Choibalsang was already in touch with two Russian Bolsheviks. Their names were Kucherenko and Gembarzhevskii, and it seems likely that they were not emissaries newly sent to Urga, but secret revolutionaries who had been in the Russian quarter of the city for some time. After their first meeting, Sukhe Bator is quoted by Choibalsang as having said: " We did not know where to go, but now, comrades, with your great help, we shall certainly be able to accomplish our task." [23] Through the cooperation of the two revolutionary groups, moreover, the two Russian Bolsheviks " for the first time penetrated among the young Mongol revolutionaries with Marxism and Leninism." [24]

---

[21] Sun Yat-sen, interview with Fletcher S. Brockman, *New York Times,* July 22, 1923, quoted in Lyon Sharman, *Sun Yat-sen, His Life and its Meaning,* New York, 1934, p. 252.

[22] Sun Yat-sen, addressing a meeting at the Y.M.C.A., Canton, December 1923, quoted in Sharman, *op. cit.,* p. 253.

[23] *Biography,* pp. 39-40. The spelling of the two Russian names, not clear in the Mongol account, is established on p. 38 of N. V. Tsapkin, *Mongolskaya Narodnaya Respublika* (The Mongolian People's Republic), Moscow, Ogiz, pp. 112, where they are described as " worker-revolutionaries."

[24] *Biography,* p. 40. On my first reading of this source, I missed one line of the text, and thus in an earlier article on Mongol politics I cautiously restricted myself

In the same crowded year of 1920 a Comintern representative named Sorokovikov (the transcription is again a little uncertain) reached Urga. His conferences with Sukhe Bator "laid the foundations" for creating a united party [25] out of the cooperation between the groups led by Sukhe Bator and by Choibalsang—thus carrying still further the parallel with the period when the Chinese Communists were actually taken into the organization of the Kuomintang.

This trend to the left—again as in China—did not mean that the conservative wing of Sukhe Bator's following ceased to exist. Although Choibalsang was already working closely with two secret Russian Communists, and a Comintern representative was able to reach Urga in the same year, there was still in the city a representative of the old Tsarist regime, named Orlov. Conservative members of Sukhe Bator's following, including men who continued to be important in later years like Doksom and Danzan,[26] applied secretly to Orlov for aid, in spite of the fact that " some people say that he had connections with the Chinese." Uncertain what to do, Orlov replied that he could not forward any communication unless it bore the seal of the Urga Hutukhtu.[27] The Mongols who had approached Orlov then went to the Hutukhtu, but he put them off, saying " the time is not yet."

In revolutionary crises there are always strange contacts and cross-connections. It is definitely stated that " the feudal faction headed by the Bogda (the Hutukhtu) were in contact with Sukhe Bator's secret group," but " because they did not entirely trust him, they were in search of other aid and support. Some of them wanted to rely on America, some to rely on Japan and the Russian White Guards." Even those who leaned toward America and Japan, however, " because they did not very

---

to the statement that " it is a fair inference, though there is no explicit statement in the record, that Choibalsang had already begun to draw on Marxist theory," etc.—Owen Lattimore, " The Outer Mongolian Horizon," *Foreign Affairs*, July 1946, p. 653.

[25] *Biography*, p. 43.

[26] This and the foregoing quotations are from p. 35 of the *Biography*.

[27] *Ibid.*, p. 48.

strongly believe " that help would be forthcoming, eventually " came to the point where they approved the propriety of the proposal to seek help from Soviet Russia."

Eventually, therefore, with all factions from the extreme left to the extreme right in search of foreign aid, and with all of them in touch with each other though not in alliance, a compromise was reached. Three appeals were sent out: to America, to Japan, and to Russia. It was as a result of this compromise that Sukhe Bator and Choibalsang were at last able to set out—still in the crowded year of 1920—on a mission to Soviet Russia, and to go not merely as the representatives of a small revolutionary party, but as the bearers of an official document stamped with the seal of the Urga Hutukhtu.[28]

The events which followed the granting of Russian aid are discussed by Mr. Friters. Sukhe Bator died prematurely in 1923; and he died, like Sun Yat-sen, before the alliance between his original followers and his new, Communist-influenced followers had settled into any long-term adjustment between Communist, pro-Communist, non-Communist and anti-Communist factions. Both men, moreover, died looking forward to policies of long-term alliance or friendly association with Russia, but before the conditions of such an association could be seen clearly in the framework of world politics.

After the deaths of Sukhe Bator and Sun Yat-sen, the parallels between the revolutionary history of Mongolia and China give way to a sharp divergence. There were bitter conflicts within the revolutionary coalition in both countries. In both countries some political leaders were purged from office and some were put to death. In Mongolia, however, the outcome was a continued coalition, under strong Communist or pro-Communist leadership, and a continued and strengthened association with Russia. In China, the coalition was broken up, the Communists were driven out of the ruling party, and the official policy became hostile both to domestic Communism and to Russia.

[28] *Ibid.*, p.49.

The Mongol Revolution was successful after 1921. It became still more firmly established after the death of the Urga Hutukhtu in 1924, which made possible the adoption of a republican government, closely modelled, like that of China, on the Soviet pattern. Like China, Mongolia also followed the Russian pattern in declaring only one party legal; but this party, unlike the Kuomintang, has been consistently Marxist in its aims. As early as October, 1925, the Mongolian People's Revolutionary Party stated that its ultimate aim was to pass " through the achievement of state capitalism and simultaneously of collective methods of construction, thus bypassing the capitalist stage of development, to the attainment of communism." [29]

The success of the nationalist revolution in Mongolia, the orientation toward Communism of the party which controls the country, and the close association of Mongolia with Russia both before and after the recognition of Mongol independence by China in 1945 are inseparable from each other, but they are not one and the same thing. A policy of turning to Russia for aid, if the Mongols were to be independent of China in fact rather than in legal definition, would have been a necessity for any Mongol government. Even if the Mongols had followed a line of development comparable to that of Kemalist Turkey, they would like Kemalist Turkey have had to appeal to Russia for support; and in view of their weaker bargaining position, they would have had to rely on Russia longer than Turkey did.

This aspect of the recent political history of Mongolia may best be defined by saying that while association with Russia was a foregone conclusion, the degree of cordiality in relations with Russia was not a foregone conclusion. The record shows, in fact, that Mongol politics have largely taken the form of competition between men who placed unquestioning confidence in Russia and men who, while recognizing the necessity of association with Russia, have attempted to avoid both com-

---

[29] Kallinikov, *op. cit.*, p. 82 citing the Party Program submitted to the Fourth Congress of the Mongol People's Revolutionary Party in 1925.

plete integration with the policies of Russia and involvement
with the policies of any country not friendly to Russia. For this
second type of policy, which falls between conventional classifi-
cations and is hard to define, there has until recently been no
convenient term; but a term has recently come into use which
describes it well: it is Titoism.

Both left-wing and right-wing factors have entered into
Mongolian tendencies toward Titoism. One Russian writer,
more than twenty years ago, describing the first big political
crisis after Sukhe Bator and his followers had come into power
after 1921, stated that a new Mongol " bourgeois " class began
to emerge, taking the place of the former Chinese and Russian
merchants. At the same time many of the nobles, who had supported the nationalist movement until the Chinese military
forces and the White Guard Russians of Ungern-Sternberg had
been cleared from the country, were now anxious to conserve
as much as possible of their old social preeminence. There was
a natural alliance between the new " bourgeois," anxious to
attain enough political power to protect their new interests,
and the old aristocracy, anxious to retain enough power to
protect its old interests, in face of the socializing pressure of the
Nationalist Party. This alliance was further bolstered by the
extreme leftist faction within the Youth League, which had
been organized to expand and train the future membership of
the Nationalist Party.[30] (There are a number of indications
that the Youth League, more than the Nationalist Party itself,
was the focus of Marxist thinking and Communist activity in
Mongolia after 1921).

It appears to be impossible to find in print a clear analysis
of the theories and motives which led these young leftists into
an alliance with right-wing interests. In terms of the 1920's,
it is probably not far-fetched to say that they were influenced
by at least the fringe of Trotskyist thinking; that is, they
believed in a cumulative world revolution which would eventually drown their right-wing allies and at the same time carry
the left wing to triumph over the more cautious socializing

[30] Kallinikov, op. cit., pp. 78-80.

program of the main body of the Nationalist Party. In terms of the 1940's, the suggestion may be hazarded that they wanted to push through the Mongol Revolution " on their own," without accommodating it to the pace or the needs of developments in Russia. Hence the similarity to Titoism.

The seriousness of this crisis was revealed when it came into the open at the Third Congress of the Nationalist Party in October, 1924, at a moment when the leader of the coalition, Danzan, was President of the Congress and Commander in Chief of the Mongol Army.[31] Danzan had been one of the original twenty followers of Sukhe Bator. In view of his prestige as one of the founding group of revolutionaries, his high political position, and his command of the Army, he should have been able to force through his policies if he had had any popular support worth mentioning. Yet before the Congress was over he had been arrested, convicted on charges of " economic counter-revolution " in collaborating in trade with Chinese merchants and helping them to collect their old debts, and executed—and there were no popular risings or manifestations to save him or to make his fall less disastrous.

The next major crisis was in 1931-32, when as a result of success in confiscating the properties of major princely families and ecclesiastical foundations, there developed an " extremely dangerous, harmful, and incorrect deviation to the left." [32] Encouraged by their success, the enthusiasts of the left attempted to push on beyond state capitalism in major economic enterprises and to enforce collectivization throughout the practices of livestock herding by which the overwhelming majority of the population lived. This attempt was made at a time when the Mongols did not have even the minimum backing of an industrial economy. With this kind of backing, the Russians had been able to enforce collectivization, though at terrible cost; without it, the Mongols failed.

The attempted forced march toward socialization and collectivization frightened and antagonized the herdsmen who

[31] *Ibid.*, p. 80. See also Doksom, *Report*, p. 86.
[32] Doksom, *Report*, p. 87.

formed the main bulk of the population and who owned its chief economic resource, the flocks and herds. They regarded collectivization not as a new form of ownership but as deprivation of ownership, and in resistance to it they slaughtered their cattle by the thousand. The whole attempt had to be abandoned, and the country returned to private ownership of livestock, modified by a strong emphasis on cooperative enterprises of all kinds as a means of turning the minds of the people toward the potential advantages of group enterprise in contrast with sole reliance on the enterprise of the individual or the household.

The importance of this crisis is that it indicates that the leftists undertook their program independently of the Russians; there is no evidence that the support of Russian industry and economic policy were thrown behind the drive for collectivization. The whole movement was one of " Titoism " in that it was an attempt to demonstrate, not rightist antagonism to Russia, but leftist independence of Russia, by showing that Mongol leftists could do the same things as Russian leftists, without gearing their outlying area of socialism to the main area of socialism in Russia.

Both after 1924 and after 1930-32, internal crisis was followed by a return to closer coordination with Russia and Russian policies, economic as well as political, and by public and strongly worded protestations of complete reliance on Russia and complete trust in Russian good faith, on the part of the Mongolian People's Revolutionary Party and its most important individual spokesmen.

The Western world does not have a complete enough record of the domestic politics of the Mongolian People's Republic to understand it in every detail or every change of phase. We do have enough evidence, however, to say that the tone or style of politics has been set by competition between nationalists, predominantly Marxist in their thinking, whose central principle is unquestioning faith in Russia, and nationalists, also predominantly Marxist in their thinking, who from time to time have endeavored to prove that the Mongols can move in the same direction as the Russians, but independently of them. (The difference can be defined as that between two columns moving on parallel lines. The " national " Marxists, not satisfied with advancing on a parallel line, from time to time attempt to push the head of their column forward until it is on a level with the head of the Russian column. The " fellow-travelling " Marxists are content to advance in echelon, parallel to the Russians but with the head of their column far behind that of the Russian column).

An economic consideration of overriding importance, and a question of psychological attitude toward it, combine to prevent this difference from remaining in the plane of theory or ideology and persistently intrude it into the plane of working politics. In the highly competitive world politics of today a Socialist state must, in order to have survival value, rest upon a well-rounded, diversified economy. It must either have industry already, or be able to industrialize rapidly or effectively. Industry in Mongolia is still at a very low stage of development. To have an " independent " Socialism, the Mongols must draw on industrial resources. Should their primary effort, therefore, be to force the pace of their own industrialization, or should their primary reliance be on the industry which already exists in the Soviet Union?

The first alternative would require psychological as well as political independence of the Russians. It would require years of heavy sacrifice from the prevailing livestock economy in order to finance " autonomous " industrialization. The second alternative—the one which hitherto has repeatedly prevailed—permits not only maintenance but increase of the prosperity of the herding economy, financing a much more gradual industrialization, accompanied step by step by the technological training of Mongols to man industry as it expands. It also involves, however, a psychological conviction that reliance on Russian industry in the long interim will not result in the Russians taking advantage of the Mongols—that the Russians will not profiteer on the political and economic margin between what they get from Mongolia in livestock, livestock products, and raw materials, and what they give to the Mongols in goods, services, industrial equipment, and technological and scientific training in Russian institutions.

A conviction of this kind places a great strain on nationalism. The exploitation of the margin of superiority is the essential characteristic of imperialism, whatever the political structure of the imperial country. The difference between suspecting that such a margin exists and phychological confidence that it does not exist, is what decides whether Mongols believe that the relationship between their country and Russia is still colonial, as it was in Tsarist days, or whether they genuinely believe that they enjoy that condition known as " real " equality—than which nothing in the whole field of politics more evasively eludes precise definition.

On the whole, it is clear that the suspicion that somehow the Russians get more out of Mongolia than the Mongols get out of Russia has never died. It is equally clear, however, that the controlling majority in the Mongolian People's Revolutionary Party has always staked its future on the belief that the innermost essence of the relationship with Russia is that " real " equality which it is so hard to define.

The outstanding personal symbol of this faith in Russia is the present Premier, Marshal Choibalsang. His rise to full power as the successor of Sukhe Bator has been much slower than that of Stalin as the successor of Lenin or that of Chiang Kai-shek (for twenty years at least) as the successor of Sun Yat-sen. The slowness of his emergence is indirect but suggestive evidence that the dying down of mental reservations about the Russians, in Mongol political life, has been slow. He is not, for instance, even mentioned in the Russian book on the Nationalist Revolutionary Movement, published in 1926, which has here been so often quoted.[33] There is a marked difference between the prominence of his name in the biography of Sukhe

---

[33] Kallinikov, *op. cit.*, Choibalsang is, however, mentioned in Tsapkin's recent book on the Mongolian People's Republic (p. 49) as having been president of the special commission which in 1929 finally broke feudal power by expropriating the 670 most powerful feudal nobles and ecclesiastical magnates.

Bator, published in 1942, and the lack of mention of him at times of crisis between 1931 and the middle 1930's. He appears to have come first into full power in the middle 1930's, when the Russians backed so strongly the resistance which the Mongols made against Japanese encroachments on their eastern frontier. While the Russians were fighting Hitler, he whole-heartedly carried out a policy of sending to Russia all the aid that Mongolia could provide, in full confidence that when the time came Russia in turn would strengthen Mongolia's position in Asia.

For the Western student of politics in Mongolia, and indeed throughout Asia, there are two important questions to be answered: Has the "real" independence of the Mongols increased or decreased through their association with Soviet Russia? And relatively, has Mongolia profited more by un-broken association with Russia than Turkey and Kuomintang China did by first associating with Russia and then breaking away from that association?

I do not feel that I have the materials on which to base a definitive answer. There are, however, certain things that must be taken into consideration in formulating any answer.

Mongolia came through the years of the rise of Hitler and Japanese militarism with less suffering, bloodshed, and eco-nomic loss than any country in Asia. This good fortune would have been impossible without the close association with Russia. Mongolia today has an army which, though small (since the total population is somewhere between 800,000 and a million and a half) is probably the best and the best-equipped in Asia; whereas the Turkish army has been described as having "the best preserved obsolete equipment in Europe." [34] The planes and tanks of the Mongol army are operated by Mongols. The speed and hitting power of the Mongol forces in the last days of the war against Japan were comparable to Russian standards of mobile warfare.

[34] Robert P. Martin, Overseas New Agency dispatch of Oct. 25, 1948, from Istanbul.

On the industrial side of the association with Russia, while the figures are scanty and often so veiled that it is impossible to state quantities, it is clear that industrialization has moved rather slowly. The gap between the Mongol level and the Russian level has certainly not been closed. In my opinion, it has been widened by the wartime industrialization of Siberia. On the other hand, the training of Mongol personnel appears to have kept pace with such industrialization as does exist, so that in industry and other new activities introduced into Mongolia the percentage of Russians tends to decrease rather than to increase—a point which is of psychological as well as technical importance. According to an account published in 1936,

The personnel of mechanized transport has been almost wholly Mongolized. The number of Mongol veterinaries has risen from 19 to 70, the number of Mongols in medical institutions from 30 percent of the total number of employees to 80 percent. All 237 teachers under the Ministry of Education are Mongols. In the cooperatives, Mongols constitute 94 percent of the total personnel. While formerly the Mongols were either herdsmen or lamas, we now have Mongol drivers, iron-workers, lathe operators, tanners, electrical workers, joiners, carpenters, miners, veterinaries, doctors, teachers, artists, writers, airmen, tank-drivers, artillerymen, etc. etc.

According to Tsapkin, in the handicraft cooperatives, which increased from 14 in 1931, with 694 workers to 198 in 1946 with 12,090 workers, the percentage of Mongols increased from 34 percent in 1937 to 91 percent in 1940.

Mr. Tsapkin's figures include 942 veterinaries in 1947, in the Ministry of Livestock alone, plus 5,439 " veterinary sanitarians "; an increase of medical stations from 20 in 1940 to 32 in 1947, and of hospitals from 17 to 31 in the same period, and of " feldsher stations " (health stations) from 157 to 316.

Education is stated to have developed even more rapidly. In 1923, according to the same source, 12 primary schools were opened. By 1947 the number had increased to 321, with 42,110 students. The increasing number of primary school graduates made it possible to increase middle schools and " not full "

[35] Report by Amor, prefixed to Doksom, *Report*, p. 66.

middle schools (equivalent to junior high schools) from 12 in 1940 to 39 in 1947, with 10,478 students. A Government University was opened in 1942, which in 1947 had 663 students and six faculties: zootechnic; veterinary; medical; physical and mathematical; philological; and social sciences.

These figures, together with those on the development of industry given in Chapter I, while they cannot support any categorical statements about the Mongolia of today, do indicate the increase of activities of a modern kind, without which mere political declaration would not make Mongolia a " modern " country. The list of modern occupations is impressive to any-one who has been acquainted for twenty years, as I have been, with the contrasting stagnation of life in Inner Mongolia. As for the traditional occupation of herding, I saw in 1944 several camps in the vicinity of Ulan Bator, where people were gather-ing for the annual national festival. Clothes and silver orna-ments were visible evidence of a more general prosperity than has existed anywhere in Inner Mongolia for many years. Per-haps even more striking was the readiness with which people answered questions about the amount of livestock they owned; throughout, Mongolia, as throughout China, vague or clear answers to such questions infallibly reveal whether people feel politically insecure or secure.

To carry development further, a five-year plan was an-nounced in 1948, to be completed in 1952. As in Russia, where the first five-year plan was undertaken when, a generation ago, more than half of all production was still in private hands, the Mongol five-year plan starts in a country in which the most important form of property is livestock, privately owned. The Mongol plan aims at a number of elementary improvements which could not rapidly be carried out by individuals. Among these are making more pastures available by the planned digging of wells, and protection against winter losses by a double program of growing hay for winter feed and building corrals as storm-shelters. Neither collectivization nor large scale agricultural settlement is aimed at under the plan. A doubling of industrial output is planned, however—especially in industries which process meat, hides, footwear, and other products and by-products of a pastoral economy.[36]

Relatively to such countries as China or Turkey, the position of Mongolia must be judged on the total evidence. The burden of this evidence is clear: there is no small country, and no economically backward or undeveloped country, that has "real" independence in the sense of being able to conduct either its political or its economic life in total disregard of whether other, more powerful countries are displeased. In this sense, Turkey and Kuomintang China, whose economies have not been integrated with America as that of Mongolia is integrated with Russia, are not as dependent on America as the Mongolian People's Republic is on Russia; but they can not be called independent.

The degree of relative independence, moreover, cannot be measured by the view that Americans hold of Turkey or China, or that Russia holds of Mongolia. There is a further degree of relativity to be considered, and that is whether the Mongols feel that they are better off than the Chinese, or whether the Chinese feel they are better off than the Mongols. A particularly sensitive index is the feeling of Mongols in Inner Mongolia, between China on the one side, and the Mongolian People's Republic on the other, who have been successively the victims of Chinese colonization policies, Japanese imperialism, and Chinese civil war.

On this outer edge of relative values, the feelings of the people who are themselves involved are subject to rather rapid change. There was an interesting revelation of attitude in the statements made by two Mongol officers who deserted in the summer of 1947 to join what they thought of as the American side. The fact that they deserted showed that there are areas of discontent. The form in which they expressed their discontent showed that they were not thinking of Mongolia as a satellite country in contrast to China as a free country. They declared that their country was overrun by Russians, but they

[36] N. V. Tsapkin, *Mongolskaya Narodnaya Respublika*, Moscow, 1948, p. 96 ff.

also revealed that they thought that China was " an American colony." [37] They were therefore trying to make comparisons between what they themselves thought of as less endurable and more endurable conditions of subject or satellite status.

This kind of comparison is made by some Mongols in Inner Mongolia as well as by some Mongols in Outer Mongolia. In 1946 I was told by an Inner Mongolian prince, living under Kuomintang jurisdiction in China, that he " hoped " that his son had succeeded in escaping across the frontier into the Mongolian People's Republic.

It is on this changeable fringe of opinion that the main competition is taking place in our time, in power politics, in nationalism and internationalism, and in adherence to ideologies. In this competition the Russians have in the Mongolian People's Republic an ally with weak spots—as is shown by the desertion of army officers—but on the whole a strong and loyal ally, and an ally whose neighbors probably look upon it more often with envy than with disdain. Whether such people continue to think that the Mongols are well off and the proportions in which they mix admiration and condemnation, will not depend solely on the future treatment of the Mongols by the Russians. They will be influenced at least as much by the treatment that they themselves get from America.

[37] Christopher Rand, unpublished notes of an interview with these two Mongols.

CONTENTS

ABBREVIATIONS USED IN FOOTNOTES.

For full titles see Bibliography.

B. D.	Gooch and Temperly, *British Documents on the Origin of the War.*
Benckendorff	*Graf Benckendorff's Diplomatischer Schriftwechsel*, edited by B. V. Siebert.
BPCMD	*British Parliamentary Command Papers.*
BSE	*Bolshaya Sovetskaya Entsiklopediya* (Great Soviet Encyclopedia) Vol. 40.
CYB	*China Year Book.*
DDF	*Documents Diplomatiques Françaises*, 3e série.
G. P.	*Die Grosse Politik*
Grimm	Collection of Agreements and other Documents from the History of International Relations in the Far East, 1844-1925, edited by Prof. E. D. Grimm.
Grumm-G.	G. Grumm—Grzhimailo, *Western Mongolia and the Urianghai Region.*
K. A.	Krasnyi Arkhiv (Red Archives).
Korostovets	I. J. Korostovets, *Von Chinggis Khan bis zur Sowjetrepublik.*
IBZI	*Die Internationale Beziehungen im Zeitalter des Imperialismus.*
Isvolski	*Der Diplomatische Schriftwechsel Isvolskis*, edited by Friedrich Stieve.
MacMurray	*Treaties and Agreements with China, 1894-1919*, edited by J. V. A. MacMurray.
Maiskii	I. Maiskii, *Sovremennaya Mongoliya* (Contemporary Mongolia).
MOEI	Mezhdunarodnye otnoshenya v epokhu imperializma (International Relations in the period of imperialism).
N. V.	*Novyi Vostok.*
O. B.	Orange Book, 1914, Imperial Ministry of Foreign Affairs, Collection of Diplomatic Documents concerning Mongolia.
Popov	Foreword by Popov to " Tsarist Russia and Mongolia, 1913-14." In *Krasnyi Arkhiv*, Vol. 37.
R. J.	*La Revue Jaune.*
SSE	*Sibirskaya Sovetskaya Entsiklopediya* (Siberian Soviet Encyclopedia) Vol. 3.
S. S.	*Skidny Svit* (World of the Orient).
T. O.	*Tikhii Okean* (Pacific Ocean).

CHAPTER I

GEOGRAPHY AND SOCIETY

A. PHYSICAL GEOGRAPHY

THE COUNTRY long known to China, and vaguely to the outside world, as Outer Mongolia is now the Mongolian People's Republic and appears on the new maps of Asia as an independent country lying between Siberia and China and occupying an area of 606,000 square miles, roughly seven times as large as Great Britain and nearly three times the size of France.

The name " Mongolian People's Republic " has been used by the Mongols since 1924 when after the death of the last Living Buddha the present government was established and the name of the capital changed from Da Khurie, known to Russians and Europeans as Urga, to Ulan Bator (Red Hero). Although the Mongols themselves have claimed independence since the fall of the Manchu Dynasty in 1911 their complete independence was never officially recognized by China until January 1946 and during most of the period covered by this study the territory under consideration was generally spoken of as " Outer Mongolia." In the period between 1911 and 1924 the Mongols referred to their country as " Autonomous Mongolia."

Until the twentieth century the general term " Mongolia " was commonly used to describe the country stretching from north of the Great Wall to the Altai region in the west, Siberia in the north and the Hsingan mountains to the east. The name Kalgan (Khalaga, from which the tribal name Khalkha also comes) which means in Mongol either " gate " or " barrier," that is, the gate in the Great Wall, the gate by which the Mongols entered China, expresses the idea that " the proper boundary between Mongolia and China should

1

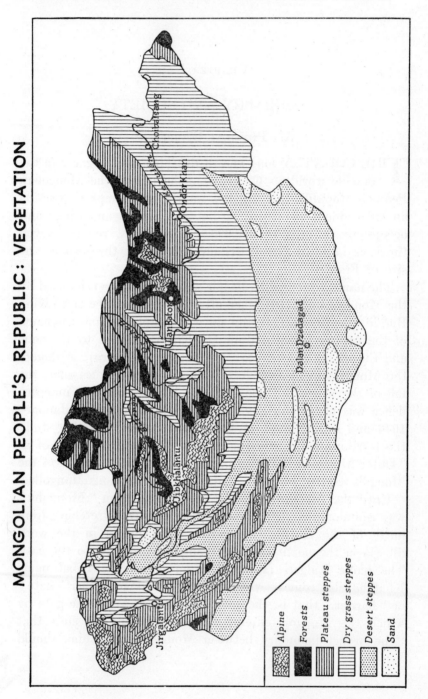

MONGOLIAN PEOPLE'S REPUBLIC: VEGETATION

Alpine
Forests
Plateau steppes
Dry grass steppes
Desert steppes
Sand

be the Great Wall." [1] But this lost its meaning in the ethnographical sense when the Chinese began to cultivate intensively the lands north of Kalgan. By the seventies of the last century Chinese agricultural settlements had advanced forty miles north of Kalgan and by 1930 Chinese settlers had progressed for more than another hundred miles. [2]

Geographically during this period the country north of the Gobi was spoken of as "Outer Mongolia" and the country south of the Gobi as "Inner Mongolia." Most authors explain "Outer Mongolia" as deriving its designation from the lesser degree of dependence in which it was placed under the Manchu Dynasty in comparison with "Inner" Mongolia. It seems obvious, however, that this lesser degree of control was partly due to the greater distance which separated Peking from the Outer Mongolian plateau. [3]

Inner Mongolia was never a political entity. Under the Manchus the territory referred to as Inner Mongolia was divided between tribes or groups of tribes which were separately tributary to the Manchu court. After intermediary stages between 1911 and 1927 the territory was divided in 1928 among four new Chinese provinces, Ninghsia, Suiyuan, Chahar and Jehol, each of which consisted partly of Mongol territory and partly of pieces carved from China's northern provinces of Kansu, Shensi, Shansi, Hopei and Liaoning (Fengt'ien). Important territories in Eastern Inner Mongolia were administratively absorbed into the already existing Northeastern or Manchurian provinces of Liaoning, Kirin, and Heilungkiang. Outer Mongolia, on the other hand, more or less in its present boundaries, had under the Manchus been largely the country of a single tribe, the Khalkha Mongols, whose princes were also vassals of the Manchu emperor.

---

[1] Hoines, "The Chinese in Mongolia" in *The Chinese Recorder*, Vol. 8, July-Aug. 1877, No. 4, p. 273.

[2] *Ibid.*, pp. 273-274; Owen Lattimore, *The Mongols of Manchuria*, New York, 1934; *The Times*, London, Aug. 8 and 9, 1930, p. 9.

[3] "Topography of Extra-provincial China," *The Chinese Repository*, Vol. XX, Feb. 1851, No. 2, Canton, p. 62.

As late as 1907 " Mongolia " was still used loosely as a political term. When Russia and Japan discussed their respective spheres of influence in 1907 Russia included Mongolia in hers, but Japan refused to allow a Russian claim on Inner as well as on Outer Mongolia. Thus it happened that as a sort of compromise " the special interests of Russia in Outer Mongolia " were mentioned in the Russo-Japanese Secret Convention of July 1907.[4] In November 1911 the Hutukhtu (Living Buddha) of Urga was proclaimed ruler of the Mongolian Nation though at first only a part of Outer Mongolia followed him. A year later Tsarist Russia, under repeated pressure from the Outer Mongols, with whom she desired a treaty, conceded to them the use of the term " Mongolia " in the treaty text but by November 1913, upon the insistence of the Chinese, with whom she also wished to come to terms, she allowed the insertion of the term " Outer Mongolia." [5]

Such play with words was more than a question of prestige. It signified the repeated attempts to delineate the geographical extent of Outer Mongolia, but in none of the above mentioned treaties were the boundaries exactly defined. Russia and Japan agreed in 1912 on a general definition, and in the Russo-Mongolian agreement of 1912 the Russian plenipotentiary reserved the right to define what territory Outer Mongolia was to embrace. In the Russo-Chinese agreement of 1913 Outer Mongolia was described as consisting of " the four Khalkha *aimaks* " (principalities), but no agreement was reached on the exact boundaries. The text alluded to the lack of adequate maps and stipulated that a joint commission should make up for this discrepancy. The Russo-Mongolian-Chinese agreement of 1915 determined the boundary between Outer and Inner Mongolia but left it to a future tripartite commission to demarcate the western frontiers. Subsequent events however, the Russian revolution and the reassertion of Chinese rule in Outer Mongolia, prevented the functioning of the boundary commission.

[4] Cf. Chap. IV A.
[5] Detailed references to these developments will be found in Chapters II and III.

In the following years there continued to be disputes over frontier questions and over the use of the term " Mongolia." During the Sino-Japanese war terminology became particularly confusing. There was a " Mongolian People's Republic " for the Outer Mongols, a government of Manchukuo which stated that it comprised the territories of " Manchuria and Mongolia " (referring to the Mongol-inhabited parts of Manchuria plus Jehol, which was added to Manchukuo by the Japanese in 1933), a " Mongolian Autonomous Government " proclaimed by the Japanese and consisting of parts of Inner Mongolia, and a " Mongolia " comprising Outer and Inner Mongolia over which China claimed sovereignty.

In an exchange of notes attached to the Sino-Soviet Treaty of August 14, 1945, the Chinese government's intention to " recognize the independence of Outer Mongolia in her existing boundaries " is acknowledged. Since no more specific definition of these boundaries was given they must have been generally understood at that time, although in recent disputes in the Baitik Bogda hills along the western border the Chinese have claimed that the Mongols are attempting to include somewhat more territory within their borders than they claimed either in the 1920's or in August 1945.[6]

The confusion as to boundaries and nomenclature is reflected in the maps of the early decades of this century. On some maps there was no boundary line between China and Mongolia. Others distinguished Outer Mongolia, Inner Mongolia and China. Only a few—a map printed for the Mongols in Germany, recent ones from Soviet Russia, a British War Office map and a new Swedish atlas—defined Outer Mongolia as a separate state under the name of the Mongolian People's Republic. Earlier maps sometimes called Outer Mongolia by its native (tribal) name Khalkha, which however should not have included the Khobdo district and the territory of Urian-ghai, which are not in the main inhabited by Khalkhas. Some older maps also include Kokonor and Tsaidam in Outer Mon-

---

[6] United Nations Security Council—*Report of the Committee on the Admission of New Members* S/479, Aug. 11, 1947, Annex VI.

golia although it is doubtful if they should ever have been so included and certainly not after 1911. In 1929 they were included in the new Chinese province of Ch'inghai. Other maps, even such recent ones as the Atlas of the Encyclopedia Britannica (14th ed., Vol. 24, 1936, p. 68), gave the Altai District and Jungaria to Outer Mongolia, though the Altai District was separated from the Khobdo District of Outer Mongolia in 1907 and Jungaria was united with Sinkiang province in 1878. After Inner Mongolia was divided between the provinces of Jehol, Chahar, Ninghsia and Suiyuan in 1928 most maps ceased to use the term Inner Mongolia.

The neighbors of the Mongolian People's Republic are: in the north (from west to east) the Oirat District of the U. S. S. R. (formerly the Province of Omsk of the Russian Empire), the Tuvinian Autonomous Region of the U. S. S. R. (formerly the People's Republic of Tannu Tuva and before that the Urianghai territory of Outer Mongolia), the Buriat Mongol Autonomous Republic of the U. S. S. R. (formerly the Siberian provinces of Yeniseisk and Irkutsk) and the Chita District of the U. S. S. R. (formerly Transbaikal); in the east the Manchurian province of Hsingan (formerly parts of the provinces of Heilungkiang and Liaoning (Fengt'ien); in the south (from east to west) the four Chinese provinces of Jehol, Chahar, Suiyuan and Ninghsia (formerly simply Inner Mongolia); followed in the southwest and west by Sinkiang Province of China (Chinese Turkistan).

High mountains provide natural frontiers in the northwest, part of the north, and the southwest. In the northwest the Sailyugem Mountains are a formidable barrier, their highest summit said to be 15,000 feet.[7] In the north the Tannu Ula and Ulan Taiga, forming a crest frontier about 385 miles long, separate Outer Mongolia from Tannu Tuva. Farther east the Sayan mountain chain forms a natural frontier between Outer Mongolia and Siberia.

From the eastern end of the Altai the southern boundary

[7] Cf. Chap. II, n. 278.

runs through the middle of the Mongolian Gobi. In the east
also no natural frontiers are to be found, the Great Hsingan
mountains touching Outer Mongolia at only one point. A
corner appears to have been cut from the northeast, due to
the fact that at the beginning of the twentieth century the
province of Heilungkiang was extended to include a large
slice (the Barga district) of what was formerly Mongolia.
Until 1924 an exact demarcation of frontiers was not undertaken and many disputes arose, but in 1924, when the Mongolian People's Republic was founded, frontier posts were
erected.

Thus in dealing historically with Outer Mongolia we must
bear in mind that the term did not at all times, and for all
authors, signify the same geographical territory which com-
prises the Mongolian People's Republic of today. It is essential
to insist on this point in order to avoid confusion as far as
possible, when trying to discuss the size and population of
Mongolia in different periods.

The Mongolian People's Republic of today is situated between 42′ and 52′ north latitude and 86′ and 120′ east longitude
and its area is officially given as 606,000 square miles. The
greatest distance from east to west is 1,620 miles and from
north to south is 620 miles.[8] It occupies the northern part of
the great Central Asiatic plateau, which is crossed by mountain
chains in between which there are green steppes and gravel
or sandy deserts. The plateau declines from northwest to
southeast, most of it being more than 3000 feet above sea level.
The mountains vary in appearance from alps with their characteristic snow peaks and glaciers in the Mongolian Altai to
mountains with smooth rolling contours and flat tops covered
with gravel, and mountain ridges and low flat hills gradually
sloping down to the plains. There are many lakes, streams
and rivers, particularly in the northwest and north, most of
the lakes being small and many of them salty. ·

The principal mountain ranges are the Mongolian (or Gobi)

[8] Detailed information on the physical geography of Outer Mongolia is contained
in E. M. Murzaev, *Mongolskaya Narodnaya Respublika*, Moscow, 1948.

Altai, which stretch for 1200 miles from the Russian Altai at the Russian frontier toward the southeast and east; the the Khanggai, consisting of a number of chains between the Khobdo lake basin in the west and the Orkhon in the east and covering about 117,000 square miles; and the Khentei chain, northeast of Ulan Bator, which are a continuation of the Yablonovoy and Stanovoy chains in Siberia which form the watershed between the Pacific and Arctic Oceans. The highest peak of the Mongolian Altai is Khüiten,, about 15,000 feet; of the Khanggai, Odkhon Tengri, 13,600 feet; and of the Khentei, Asaralta, 9340 feet. Traces of volcanic activity can be seen everywhere in the Khanggai. The Khentei are covered with alpine *taiga* (pine forest) such as are found in Siberia.

Another physical characteristic of Outer Mongolia is the depressions between the mountain chains, which reach their lowest point of about 2330 feet in the extreme east in the region of the Kerulen River. The Shara Muren depression stretches from the Mongolian Altai in the west to the Great Hsingan in the east, the lowest level being about 3500 feet.

The Mongolian plateau consists chiefly of the Mongolian Gobi, a desert which stretches from northeast to southwest for a distance of 625 miles. Its greatest width is about 340 miles. The Mongolian Gobi is about 3000 feet above sea level and is largely covered with gravel. Characteristic of the Gobi is a layer of red clay at considerable depth from the surface, in which underground streams enable people to get water from deep wells in the desert.

Sand deserts are found in many parts of Mongolia. Some of them are completely barren and shift with the winds and on others meager grass grows in summer. On many of the large grass covered steppes water is extremely scarce and for many miles there may be neither stream, spring nor lake.

Lakes, streams and rivers exist in great numbers in the north-western part of the country, and any map conveys this general fact although most maps are inaccurate in detail. Various expeditions sent at the end of the 1920's by the Mongolian Scientific Committee rectified many former mistakes, mainly in the less populated areas, but the results of their findings have not reached all non-Mongolian cartographers.

The chief rivers are the Kerulen, about 625 miles long, which is unfordable for some lengths of its lower reaches; and the Selengge (Selenga) about 750 miles long, which is formed by the junction of the Ider, whose source is in the Khanggai and the Delger Muren, whose source is in the Ulaan Taiga. Its chief tributaries are the Orkhan which flows into it near Kiakhta on the Russian frontier, and the Egiin, which comes from the Khöbsögol. Other rivers are the Tes, 437 miles long; the Khobdo, which originates in the glaciers of the Mongolian Altai and flows into the Khara Usu Nor; and the Dzabkhan, which originates in the Tarbagatai mountains near the town of Uliassutai and flows through the Airik Nor into the Kirghis Nor. The Dzabkhan is 375 miles long and dries up completely in a hot summer. In its lower reaches it flows through the Dürge Nor sands where it constantly changes its course, forming bogs which render its crossing difficult. Mongolian rivers reach their high water mark twice in the year, in spring when the snow melts and in summer during the rainy period, the latter being more important since little snow falls in Mongolia.

Most of the exceedingly numerous lakes both in the mountains and on the plains are small and many of them are salty. In the region of Khobdo in the extreme west there are big lakes such as the Ubsa Nor, 62 miles long and 47 miles wide; the Airik Nor, seven miles long and three miles wide; and the Dürge Nor, 44 miles long and 31 miles wide. The water in Ubsa Nor and Khirgis Nor is salty and undrinkable. That in Dürge Nor is salty at its southern and fresh at its northern end, due to the fresh water coming in from the rivers. Airik Nor gets its fresh water from the Dzabkhan. The water of some lakes, though bitter and somewhat salty, can be drunk by animals. The longest lake in Outer Mongolia is the Khöbsögol, near the Russian border east of Tannu Tuva. It is 75 miles long and 25 miles wide and its maximum depth is about 1700 feet. Surrounded by mountains, this alpine lake lies at about

5500 feet above sea level. Navigation is possible for only five months of the year, from June to October.

The development of Outer Mongolia is restricted not only by its mountains and sands but by its climate. Though in the same latitude as the Crimea, the average yearly temperature at certain important points is below freezing because of the high altitude. Many travelers have measured at various points of their journeys the abrupt changes which take place. A short summer, with temperatures up to 35° centigrade, gives way to a severe winter with temperatures which reach 40 to 50 degrees below zero centigrade. Only the month of July can be considered safe from frost, but even in this month a temperature below freezing has been registered at several places. Maiskii mentioned that in September of the year when he travelled from Khatkhal to Uliassutai ice had already formed along the banks of rivers and lakes and early in October there was ice on which a man could stand on a river about 50 kilometers northwest of Uliassutai. In winter the ice on rivers and lakes is as much as seven feet thick and it melts only in April or May. Cloudy days are rare, however, and the skies are generally bright and clear. Rain falls only in July and August and in winter the snowfalls are generally not enough to cover the ground. The average yearly precipitation is only about 200 millimeters and there are only about 60 days in the year when there is any precipitation at all.

In the course of the last fifteen years there has been much progress in meteorological observations in Outer Mongolia. Before this time observations had been made by various expeditions but they were generally limited to temperature tables and were usually made over short periods of time. There was a meteorological station at Ude in the Gobi but its findings were applicable only to a very limited area.

The population of Outer Mongolia is very small, published figures varying from 900,000 [9] and 850,000 [10] in 1938 and 1941

[9] *BSE*, Vol. 40, col. 74, article on "Mongolskaya Narodnaya Respublika," *Sputnik Agitatora*, No. 23, Dec. 1945. Tsapkin, p. 22.

[10] Murzaev, p. 213.

(Russian) to 905,000 [11] and 2,078,000 [12] in 1933 and 1944 (Chinese). On a visit to Ulan Bator in 1944 Mr. Henry Wallace was told that the population was then about 1,500,000.[14] It may be inferred that the population has increased somewhat in recent years, since both a lower death rate and a higher birth rate would have resulted from improved health measures and a great decrease in venereal disease, which was formerly very widespread and treatment for which is now reported to be compulsory.

B. ASPECTS OF THE NATIONAL ECONOMY

(1) *Livestock*

Livestock breeding has for centuries been the basis of Mongolia's economic life and the principle occupation of the Mongol nomad. All his essential needs—housing, clothing, and food— were provided by his herds. Hence, in spite of a severe climate and the outbreak of plagues with consequent reduction in the quantity of livestock, the Mongol economy had always something to fall back upon in times of political upheaval and wars. In the course of the nineteenth and twentieth centuries it also became the main factor of foreign trade. The problems of livestock breeding which faced the government of an autonomous or independent Mongolia were entirely different from those which arose in the very new branches of activity such as agriculture and industry. Actually, all factors of a political, social, religious, geographical and technical character which make up the complexity of Mongolian life converge here, and have been the millstone which long prevented the maximum development of this, the country's main resource.

Mongol livestock breeding is of a very extensive nomad type. Very little man power is used. The animals are generally left

[11] *CYB* 1935-36, p. 123.

[12] *Statistical Abstract of the Republic of China.* Directorate of Statistics, Chungking, 1945, pp. 6-7.

[14] Henry A. Wallace, *Soviet Asia Mission*, p. 164.

to graze in the open all the year round, only the calves, kids and lambs being tethered to the yurt during the first days. In the winter they obtain their food by digging under the snow and foraging for the old grass left from the summer. Indeed, one method used for clearing the pastures is first to drive out the horses whose hoofs loosen up the snow for the small animals which follow. When this is not possible and when the snow is deep many animals perish. In this way the law of natural selection eliminates all the old and the weak, though the Mongols immediately slaughter for meat any animals known to be defective before they lose weight. This frequently has to be done during a bad winter and is very wasteful because the animals are normally thinner during the winter.[15]

Building sheds for the protection of livestock and the storage of hay would improve this situation; but making hay for winter feeding was practically unknown among the Mongols in Outer Mongolia until the 1920's though it was practised there earlier by Russian and Chinese colonists and by a number of Buriats, and possibly, due to the influence of the latter, adopted in a small part of the northwest.[16] It has, however, been introduced by the Mongolian People's Republic government in their experimental agricultural stations and the example thus set has been copied with some success.[17] The storage of hay is particularly important for young animals in the most difficult months of the early spring, when in consequence of abrupt changes in the temperature hoarfrost is responsible for the loss of tens of thousands of them.[18] In the very prosperous district of Darigangga, for instance, the winter storms and frosts of 1923-24 destroyed in some regions all livestock down to the last head. Recovery from this blow took some time and was first noticeable among the sheep and goats which breed more quickly.[19]

In order to feed his herds, the Mongol moves them in search

---

[15] A description of these conditions will be found in Perry-Ayscough and Otter-Barry, *With the Russians in Mongolia*, pp. 132-133; in Maiskii; in *SSE*, p. 513; also in Otte, *China*, p. 42, and Weiske in *Osteuropa*, Dec. 1928, p. 127.

[16] Weiske, *op. cit.*, p. 157.

[17] *SSE*, Vol. 3, p. 514.   [18] Weiske, p. 157.

[19] V. N. Kazakevich, *Poyezdka v Darigangu*, Leningrad, 1930, p. 42.

of new pastures. Except for the *shabinar* (the lay subjects of monasteries) who were at liberty to graze their livestock anywhere, the radius of the movements of the *arats* (the ordinary laymen) was confined to the borders of their *hoshun* (administrative district). Under the new regime the radius has been unlimited, at least in theory. But in practice there are many obstacles to such unrestricted movements. There are the difficulties of moving to remote pastures; there is the fact that the animals get used to a certain food, and there is finally the herdsmen's knowledge of a particular district and its food resources. All these factors combine to limit their movement to new pastures and in fact they rarely cross their hoshun borders and they almost never cross the boundaries of their aimak, except during times of outstanding natural catastrophes. The number of pastures visited in a year varies from three to eight and depends upon the quality of food, the density of the population, and the size of the herd, etc. In summer, the Mongols stay with the herds in the valleys near rivers and streamlets in open areas; in winter in valleys and mountain passes sheltered from the winds and only lightly covered with snow.[20]

There are five kinds of livestock: camels, horses, cattle, sheep and goats. Their distribution is determined by geographical and climatic factors, cattle predominating in the north, sheep in the west, southwest and east, and camels in the south and southeast (i. e. in the south Gobi and east Gobi).[21]

According to the most recent figures, attributed to the year 1941, Mongolia had a total of 27.5 million head of livestock, more than twice the number at the time of the revolution and an average of 32 head per person and more than 120 head per family, including the town population. Of these, 15.9 million were sheep, 5.5 million goats, 2.8 million cattle, 2.6 million horses and 7 million camels.[22]

---

[20] *SSE*, p. 513. [21] *SSE*, p. 514.

[22] I. F. Shulzhenko, *Results of an Investigation into the Livestock Industry of Mongolia*. Works of the Committee of Sciences of the M. P. R. Ulan Bator, 1946, p. 18. Quoted in Murzaev, p. 28.

Cattle constitute about ten percent of the herds. Like the horses they are short of stature and are easily fed. Their meat is good in taste and nutritional value. Oxen are used for the transport of goods in carts and as pack animals in the mountainous regions.

In an average herd of cattle 70.3 percent are ordinary Mongolian cattle (so called " red " cattle), 27.5 percent are *sarliks* (yaks) and 2.1 percent are *Khainoks* (a cross between ordinary cattle and yak) and *otoms* (a cross between Khainok and either cattle or yak). The distribution of these different types is very uneven. In the Eastern, South Gobi and East Gobi Aimaks there are no sarliks at all, in the Khentei and Central Aimaks they are only two to four percent of the cattle herds, but in the Ubur Khangai and Dzabkhan Aimaks the average of sarliks, khainoks and otoms in the herd exceeds 50 percent, and in the Khobdo Aimak it reaches 70 percent.[23] An exact knowledge of the different kinds of cattle is important for improving the quality of the herds, but the simplest systems of stock breeding were formerly quite unknown to the Mongols.[24] Based on the Russian model, experimental stations for cross-breeding have been set up, but what progress has been achieved (apart from the initial successful cross-breeding of horses and sheep in about 1926-7) cannot be ascertained in detail.[25] The Five Year Plan of 1948 includes the establishment of two state farms for the improvement of pedigreed cattle.[26]

Since in cattle breeding, quantity rather than quality is the criterion, the milk production of a Mongolian cow is very low. It amounts to 85.8 gallons a year not counting the milk which is used to feed the calves. The sarlik cow gives a higher yield of 118.8 gallons annually and the highest yield, namely 157

---

[23] *SSE*, p. 515.

[24] Weiske, p. 158. Ryshik also writes, on p. 180, " In spite of the great success in the development of livestock breeding, it is necessary to stress that it is still very backward and that it pays little and is not productive."

[25] Weiske, p. 158; Wallace wrote in *Soviet Asian Mission*, p. 164, " They use yaks crossed with Mongol cows. The cross yields eight liters of milk, compared with six liters from the pure Mongol stock."

[26] *N. Y. Herald Tribune*, European Edition, Jan. 4, 1948 (Monthly Economic Review), p. 5.

gallons is obtained from the khainok cow. The fat content of the average cow's milk is four percent, although the milk of the khainok and sarlik cows contains up to eight percent. The milk is used largely for feeding the families of the encampment and very little is sold. The following products are obtained from it: butter, *urum* (dried cream), *tarak, arul, ejegei* and *byslak* (different kinds of cheese), and *airak* (a distilled liquor).

The average weight of the slaughtered Mongolian ox is 495 pounds, that of the khainok 550 pounds, and that of the sarlik 473 pounds. Eight percent of the weight of these slaughtered animals is fats.[27]

Even more than the horned cattle the sheep is the most important animal in Mongolia, not only because it exists in far greater numbers than any other animal but also because of the role it plays in the national economy. Sheep make up nearly sixty percent of the herds and provide the population with milk, meat and wool. In addition, they provide skins which, together with meat and wool, constitute the main items of export. The dead weight of a fully grown sheep (male) is about sixty pounds, but a good number of these animals are found to weigh up to eighty pounds, and ewes often weigh between forty and sixty pounds. The quality and taste of the mutton are up to normal standards though that obtained from the sheep in the steppe districts (which are rich in soluble salts) is considered better than that obtained from the wooded and humid areas. One characteristic of the meat which may tend to decrease its foreign market value is the unequal distribution of fat and lean in the carcass.[28]

The milk production of the Mongolian sheep is described by Maiskii in the following way: " A sheep is milked during about three months of the year and produces in this time about four pailfulls which are equally divided in consumption between lambs and human beings." [29] It is not known whether an exact calculation of the milk capacity of a Mongolian sheep and

---

[27] *SSE*, p. 519. [28] *Ibid.* [29] Maiskii, p. 137.

especially a chemical analysis of the fat content or other ingredients of the milk has now been undertaken. The milk has a *skin-urma* and is fairly thick in appearance. Sheep milk is generally used in the household and both cheese and dried milk are produced from it.

The skins of both sheep and lambs are essential for warm clothing which cannot be replaced by anything else during the severe and long winter. In addition, the wool is manufactured into felt material used for dwellings. The greatest importance of the wool is its value in the export market. The Mongolian sheep is a typical representative of the coarse wool species. This wool is composed of flock and long hair and its quality varies according to the district, the highest grade wool being obtained in the Uliassutai area, chiefly in the valley of the river Ider. Its quality and market value is dependent on the living conditions of the animals. Sheep which graze the whole year under an open sky, especially those which move frequently into new and clean pastures, give a better quality wool than those which are kept in special enclosures during the winter and whose wool becomes yellow and weighted with dirt, the mechanical shaking of which produces a loss in weight of between seven and ten percent. Formerly, the Mongols in their capacity as sellers, and the Chinese merchants in their capacity as buyers, did not wash the wool. Russian merchants, however, washed it by rather primitive methods. Hence the importance of the new installations of wool washing plants in many parts of the country. After being washed, the wool is said to lose 40 to 45 percent of its original weight. The sheep are generally shorn once a year with ordinary shears, though in some districts, with the exception of the year's addition to the flocks and of the ewes, they are shorn a second time in the autumn.[30] How far more modern methods of shearing have been introduced we cannot say.

Camels make up only 2.5 percent of all the herds. They are used mainly for transporting loads in the winter, both in

[30] *SSE*, p. 519.

harness and as pack animals. In 1932 the annual production of camel wool was 1,560 tons of which 1,400 tons were exported.[31]

Horses amount to almost ten percent of the herds. They are of a small breed (from twelve to fourteen hands) with a weak haulage power, but they have great endurance, and are not fastidious in their choice of food. Their economic importance is not great, as they are used exclusively for cattle herding and for transport. The importance of the horse herd increases during the period of heavy spring frost when the horses are driven in front of the herd to break the thin ice for the other animals who use the districts traversed by the horses as pastures. They are used only on rare occasions for the transport of goods. Mare's milk, fermented, is used as a drink, but horse meat is seldom eaten. Horse hides are of no great importance for export (30,000 big skins annually is the figure given in 1932). There remains to be mentioned the horse hair (mane and tail) and the foals which are chiefly used for export.[32]

The main endeavor of the Mongolian Government has been to increase the livestock breeding industry. But so many obstacles have had to be overcome that it is not surprising that the grandiose targets set have never been achieved. If one does not rely on only one statistical source, or selects the dates most suitable to prove one's case, one can easily despair of finding a reliable pattern. To some extent this is due to the fact that the technique of statistical compilation was admittedly unreliable until recently. An increase may therefore simply indicate that the statistical methods have been improved; there may be better coordination of the reports of the different administrative centers and the veterinary administration of the Ministry of Livestock Breeding. Furthermore, statistics from one source seem excessive if compared with another for the simple reason that one shows all cattle including the young cattle whereas the other does not include the young

[31] *SSE*, p. 518.   [32] *Ibid.*, pp. 516-518.

(or breed) cattle. This is clearly stated in one statistical table of 1932 for the years 1926-1932, but we do not know how figures have been computed since then.[33]

We have compiled a table which will give several statistics for some identical years. Those in brackets and italics were or are target figures. Details of the different categories are not available for recent years, the 1938 (Japanese) source being of doubtful origin.[34]

Years	Camels	Horses	Cattle	Sheep	Goats	Total
1918	300,000	1,300,000	1,400,000	9,500,000		12,500'000 [35]
1924	275,000	1,341,000	1,512,000	10,649,000		13,776,000 [36]
1925						16,451,000 [37]
1926	418,852	1,390,663	1,947,160	12,726,347	2,528,593	19,211,719 [38]
1927	452,613	1,627,951	1,755,639	13,501,540	2,846,054	20,183,797 [38]
1928	463,908	1,688,123	1,807,145	14,332,876	3,073,376	21,365,488 [38]
1929	472,120	1,575,087	1,859,464	14,704,079	3,339,299	21,950,057 [38]
1930	486,980	1,604,600	1,932,710	16,285,430	4,243,390	24,552,950 [38]
						23,676,000 [39]
1931	493,680	1,588,270	2,003,740	16,739,730	4,379,710	25,205,130 [38]
				21,897,400		
	461,250	*1,500,000*	*1,650,000*	*12,500,000*	*2,140,000*	*18,351,000* [40]
1932	501,010	1,588,220	2,080,310	17,321,200	4,576,200	26,066,940 [38]
	474,750	*1,530,000*	*1,720,000*	*13,482,000*	*2,240,000*	*19,447,000* [40]
	(					*16,002,000)* [41]
1933	*495,900*	*1,575,000*	*1,800,000*	*14,742,000*	*2,400,000*	*21,031,000* [40]
	(					*19,530,000)* [39]
1934	*516,250*	*1,638,000*	*1,820,000*	*16,216,000*	*2,600,000*	*22,860,000* [40]
	(531,900)	1,638,000	2,063,000	16,868,900		21,107,000) [42]
1935	*540,000*	*1,720,000*	*2,000,000*	*18,000,000*	*2,800,000*	*25,060,000* [40]
	557,320	1,770,290	2,351,220	17,693,650		22,327,480 [43]
1937	576,000	1,909,000	2,410,000	18,370,000		23,265,000 [44]
1938	915,766	4,008,096	6,214,853	12,560,195	1,416,516	25,115,376 [45]
1939						26,093,000 [46]
1941						27,000,000 [47]
1941	700,000	2,600,000	2,800,000	15,900,000	5,500,000	27,500,000 [48]
1945 (aim)						(50,000,000) [49]
1953 (aim)						(31,000,000) [50]
1957-58 (aim)						(200,000,000) [51]

[33] *SSE*, p. 515.

[34] Mishima and Goto, *A Japanese View of Outer Mongolia*, p. 24.

[35] Maiskii, p. 123; *BSE*, Ryshik, p. 180, gives 140,000 cattle which may be a misprint. Lower figures for 1918 are also given by W. Karamisheff, *Economic Map of Outer Mongolia*.

[36] Ryshik, p. 180; but according to S. M. Wolff, *Geopolitik,* Sept. 1928, p. 765, Mongols spoke of a total of 17,000,000 head for 1924. Weiske mentions the same figure, saying that it was obtained by an official addition of thirty percent to the statements obtained from various administrative units.

[37] A. Rish in *T. O.*, Oct.-Dec. 1935, p. 103.

[38] *SSE*, p. 515.   [39] Rish, p. 103.

[40] *SSE*, p. 532. Five Year Plan adopted in 1930.

In spite of the somewhat confusing picture, certain figures stand out and make sense if they are related to political and other events. The year 1930 shows roughly a doubling of the total number of animals since 1918, confirming Maiskii's statement of 1921 that the livestock could " easily " attain a figure of about twenty million.[52] But the year 1932 shows a decrease of thirty-two percent to about sixteen million. This is the aftermath of the reckless socialization policy inaugurated in 1929 which led to disturbances and the slaughter of many animals. In 1933, i. e. after the end of this disastrous policy, the livestock had increased again by 3,500,000 head to about 19,500,00. That the increase in 1934 was only just over one million is explained by the fact that in the spring great loss of animals was experienced due to the outbreak of disease in several aimaks.[53] The following years show a slow but steady rise, slow in so far as the target figure given in 1930 for 1935 was 25,000,000 and the last figure published at the end of 1945 for 1941 gives the figure of 27,500,000. But the 1945 source, though mentioning that the target for 1945 was 50,000,000, is silent as to what happened after 1941.

It is remarkable, however, how little progress was achieved in sheep raising. In 1930 the figure stood at over 16,000,000 and in 1941 it was 15,900,000, which means that any progress made in the intervening years had been lost again.

There may be many reasons for delay in reaching the 1945

[41] Rish, p. 103; Report of Amor (see Bibliography under Doksum), *T. O.*, July-Sept. 1936, p. 64.

[42] Rish, p. 103; Ryshik, p. 180.

[43] *Ibid.*; Amor, p. 64 gives 22.5 million.

[44] *BSE.*

[45] Mishima and Goto, p. 24, based on a report said to have been made by Choibalsang in April 1939.

[46] Perlin, *Mongolskaya Narodnaya Respublika*, p. 40.

[47] *Ibid.*; Edgar Snow, *People on Our Side*, p. 194, reports the remark made by the Mongols, " Today we have fifteen million cattle whereas we had only five million when the Republic was set up."

[48] Murzaev, p. 28.   [49] Perlin, p. 40.

[50] The Five Year Plan figure announced in January, 1948. *N. Y. Herald Tribune*, European Edition, Jan. 4, 1948 (Monthly Economic Review), p. 5.

[51] Perlin, p. 40.

[52] Maiskii, p. 233.

[53] Gendun's report in *T. O.*, Jan.-March, 1935, p. 259.

target for increasing the number of sheep; not only plagues and weather conditions but also preoccupation with the military defense of the Mongolian People's Republic, and extraordinary slaughtering and export measures for the supply of Soviet troops in Mongolia, in the Soviet Far East and for the all important western battlefields of the Soviet Union. The target figure of 50,000,000 comes near to Maiskii's figure in 1921, of 60,000,000 " if properly organized." [54] The target of 200,000,000 given for the period 1951-58 may not be reached in those years, but would be feasible in the long run if military priorities are reduced and if the veterinary and technical organization keeps in step. From the fact, however, that the Five Year Plan of January 1948 gives 31,000,000 as the target we can deduce that the 50,000,000 aim for 1945 was not reached and that there has been a very slow increase since 1941. [55].

If we had more detailed and up-to-date statistics as to the technical progress achieved we might be wiser as to the possible tempo of advance in the future. No observer has failed to use strong language concerning the heartbreaking difficulties in persuading the Mongols to adopt scientific methods for feeding and breeding livestock and to introduce vaccination. [56] The latter was practically impossible as long as Lamaism was still a force; Korostovets reports, for instance, that " such a progressive Mongol as Da Lama," in the Autonomous Government after 1912, " opposed the vaccination against epidemics of Mongol cattle which was undertaken by our (Russian) Veterinaries " on the grounds that " vaccination did not correspond with the spirit of Buddhism which forbids the introduction of foreign substances into the blood." [57] The influence of the Church having been only slowly broken, there remains the difficulty of finding sufficient men schooled in veterinary science; the size of the country is an additional handicap for making the maximum use of those available; and illiteracy sets additional limits to a rapid increase of indigenous experts.

[54] Maiskii, p. 233.
[55] See n. 50.
[56] Maiskii, p. 33.
[57] Korostovets, pp. 158, 159.

Epizootics are not infrequent; reference has already been made to one in the spring of 1934 and an earlier report of the autumn of 1926 speaks of a district near the Gobi where, in a few weeks, seventy-five percent of the horned cattle perished of cattle plague.[58] State veterinary stations have been set up all over the country, but they had a hard struggle to win the confidence of the Mongols; an additional obstacle may have been (at least originally) that they involved certain expenses.[59] 1931 is given as the first year in which it was possible to " get rid of the continuous epizootic in all districts—the pestilence of the horned cattle." In that year, however, there were only 22 veterinaries and 57 veterinary assistants in the whole country, which was an advance over the 24 veterinaries given for 1924.[60] In 1934 there were 91 veterinary experts available,[61] in 1936, 127.[62] The number of veterinary hospitals and aid stations increased from 13 in 1924 to 52 in 1934,[63] and 72 in 1936.[64] In 1939 there were 15 medical stations with veterinary surgeons, 166 semi-medical and 166 local veterinary stations.[65] Yet all these stations served only 3,000,000 odd head of livestock, which is an advance on the 808,883 [66] or 1,600,000 [67] head examined in 1935, or the 223,000 in 1932.[67] Prophylactic dipping against pest, pox, pneumonia, etc. has been carried out; here detailed statistics which would make a comparison useful are not obtainable—for 1934, 400,000 such dippings were recorded.[68] There exists now a local serum plant staffed with Mongol bacteriologists who were trained in Russia.[69]

Apart from veterinary help, other measures have been introduced to prevent the losses incurred from cold, hunger and storms. The Mongolian People's Republic government granted long term credits for the acquisition of haymaking tools, building of warm sheds, well digging, etc. In 1924-25 only 3,630 acres

---

[58] Weiske, p. 158, recording his personal observation.
[59] *SSE*, p. 516.
[60] *Ibid.*; *BSE*.
[61] Ryshik, p. 180.
[62] *BSE*.
[63] Ryshik, p. 180.
[64] *BSE*.
[65] Perlin, p. 40. The Five Year Plan for 1948-53 aims at 687 veterinary stations. (*Soviet News*, London, Feb. 5, 1948).
[66] Ryshik, p. 180.
[67] Amor, p. 64.
[68] Ryshik, p. 180.
[69] *BSE*.

of grassland were cut for hay, in 1930, 99,000 acres, in 1931, 154,000 acres and in 1932, 183,700 acres.[70] In 1935 there were 30,000 livestock holdings where hay was made for the winter [71] and in 1945, 100,000.[72] Haymaking stations were equipped with tractors and other machinery. In 1937 there existed 10 such stations with 40 tractors, with 124 trained specialists in charge. In 1938 the number of stations had increased to 24 with 107 tractors and other machinery.[73] The number of *hashiya* (corrals), some movable, had been increased from about 26,500 to 135,000 [74] and in 1945 there were 361,000.[75] The number of wells increased from 8,877 in 1932 to 11,500 (presumably in 1936).[76]

Though the progress made toward overcoming all these technical handicaps has by no means been breathtaking, the outlook for the future seems somewhat brighter. For the great political and social struggles directly connected with the organization of livestock breeding since the creation of the Mongolian People's Republic now appear to have been settled.

Fundamental changes in the ownership of livestock took some time to materialize. Distribution was very unequal. It was calculated in 1918 that a holding of a prince had on an average 2,400 head, a monastery 622 head, but a holding of an ordinary nomad (arat) only 60 head. Some feudal nobles possessed tens of thousands. Prince Durachi owned 1,000 horses, 8,000 head of cattle and 20,000 sheep. The Urga monastery Wang Khurie possessed 30,000 horses and 100,000 sheep.[77] Furthermore, in the holdings of the princes and those of the monasteries saleable animals (goats and sheep) and working animals (camels and oxen) prevailed.[78] In 1921 the monasteries are said to have owned fifteen percent of all the livestock, six percent of the goats, nine percent of the camels, eleven percent of the horses, eleven percent of the cattle and eighteen percent of the sheep.[79] Up to 1930 the monastery cattle were pastured

[70] *BSE; SSE*, p. 514.   [73] Perlin, p. 40.   [76] *BSE*.
[71] Amor, p. 64.   [74] Amor, p. 64; *BSE*.   [77] Ryshik, p. 171.
[72] Murzaev, p. 29.   [75] Murzaev, p. 29.   [78] *SSE*, p. 515.
[79] *SSE*, p. 520; Rish, p. 104, states that monastery herds formed twenty percent of the total livestock in 1918 and one percent in 1935.

by serfs of the monasteries. On the other hand, the poorer nomads had almost no working animals and few horses and could not sell their livestock since they provided the food for their households.

The following table shows the distribution of livestock among the groups of the population in 1921.[80] A *bodo* is a unit of livestock in Mongolia and is equal to one head of cattle, one horse, half a camel, seven sheep or fourteen goats. It can be seen that the majority of the Mongols were small or medium livestock holders.

Groups of the population possessing up to	Number of holdings	Percentage	Property in bodos	Percentage
1 bodo	7,839	4.71	1,628	0.04
1-10 "	59,210	35.37	335,690	7.25
11-20 "	39,224	23.43	609,301	13.15
21-40 "	30,910	18.46	876,954	19.36
41-100 "	22,379	13.37	1,387,598	29.82
101-200 "	5,984	3.59	736,606	15.90
201-500 "	1,581	0.93	451,259	9.74
over 500 "	254	0.14	219,795	4.74
TOTAL	167,381	100.00	4,618,831	100.00

In 1929 the livestock of 670 large feudal estates were confiscated and distributed among the arats and among those lamas who wished to leave the monasteries. We are told that in 1925 " twenty percent of the whole lot " (this referring presumably to the percentage of all animals belonging to the feudal nobles) was liquidated and in 1936 it had shrunk to one percent.[81] Monastery herds decreased from 2,649,000 head in 1925 to 224,000 head in 1935, the number of monasteries diminishing correspondingly from 7,614 to 2,625.[82] The inference, however, that the loss of the nobles and the monasteries was matched by a corresponding gain on the part of the arats is unwarranted since it does not take into account the mass slaughter of animals mentioned frequently in other connections

[80] *SSE*, p. 519.
[81] *BSE*; Rish, p. 104; Ryshik, p. 180; *Pravda*, Moscow, April 8, 1936.
[82] Ryshik, p. 181.

as sabotage; but it is possible that some of the animals confiscated from monasteries offset the self-inflicted losses during the " collectivization " drive of 1929-31. To give another figure, we are told that in 1930 of 3,300,000 head owned by the monasteries about 2,400,000 were transferred to the poor and middle arats (in addition to nearly 1,000,000 head to the collectives) .[83]

While the Government had soon begun to tax the livestock of the monasteries and princes as well as those of the arats, a special tax reduction amounting to from five to twenty percent was granted (from an unspecified date onwards) to those arats who proved to be good protectors of animals and pastures. Smallholders were relieved of any tax at all.[84] Co-operative undertakings were also encouraged, but details are not available.

The result of the liquidation of the ownership of livestock by princes and monasteries taken together with the increase of the number of livestock is revealed when comparing the number owned per household and per head from 1918 to 1941. While here also statistics are somewhat incomplete and erratic (some give only the household increase and here the number belonging to a household or yurt seems to vary between three and five; others only the increase per head) , the picture shows the following change (plain figures are taken from statistical sources; figures in italics have been calculated; they do not tally exactly with the steady increase in the detailed table on a previous page) :

Year	Number of animals per household	Number of animals per capita
1918	60	15 [85]
1935	*115*	*28.7* [86]
1936	*94.8*	23.7 [87]
1940	*115.2*	28.8 [88]
1941	130	32.6 [89]
1947	130	30 [89a]

[83] *SSE*, p. 520.
[84] *BSE*.
[85] Maiskii; *Sputnik Agitatora*, No. 23, 1945; *BSE*.
[86] Ryshik, p. 181.   [88] Perlin, p. 40.
[87] *BSE*.   [89] *Sputnik Agitatora; Murzaev*, p. 28.
[89a] Avdayev, " Lights in the Desert," *New Times*, Jan. 1, 1949, p. 23.

Thus the number per capita and per household has more than doubled between 1918 and 1941. It has now reached a figure which is the highest per capita in the world. One can, however, envisage the possibility that in the course of a further substantial increase and simultaneous improvements in the many technical aspects of livestock breeding, some kind of large state-controlled collectivization scheme may become the order of the day.

2. Hunting, Fishing and Forestry

Apart from livestock breeding, hunting has always been one of the main occupations of the Mongols, for the vast steppe, mountain and forest regions are rich in fur bearing animals which are an important source of income for many Mongols. Furs constituted about twenty percent of the total export trade in 1938, according to one source,[90] whereas according to a source in 1936 they amounted to only fifteen percent.[91] A source in 1932 mentioned that the "fur trade in spite of its great possibilities is insufficiently developed," which goes to show that the possibilities in this direction, characterized by Andrews in 1921 as "almost boundless" have not materialized.[92] Here again it was necessary for the Government to lead a campaign against the uneconomic methods of hunting which prevailed in former times. Measures against widespread poaching had to be taken and fixed periods and methods of hunting had to be prescribed.[93]

Seventy percent of all furs come from the marmots (*tarbagan*) which supply between 1,500,000 and 2,000,000 hides yearly.[94] The squirrel takes second place with up to 100,000 furs yearly, then the *korsuk* (or steppe fox) with over 60,000 furs, the fox 20,000 furs, the wolf about 13,000 and a number of others (lynx, panther, badger, hare, etc.) in lesser amounts.[95] Some rare kinds such as sable, ermine and the like can also be found.

[90] *BSE.* [91] Ryshik, p. 181.
[92] *SSE*, p. 525; Andrews, *Across Mongolian Plains*, London, 1921, p. 178.
[93] Ryshik, p. 181. [94] *BSE*; *SSE*, p. 525. [95] *Ibid.*; Ryshik, p. 181.

There is unfortunately no possibility of comparing export figures since recent statistics are not obtainable. All exports go now to the Soviet Union whence many must be re-exported. But whereas formerly the value of exports of furs depended on world prices, it is impossible to say whether today the Mongolian People's Republic would profit in any way from an increase in these prices. In 1927, before Mongolia became closed territory for direct export to foreign lands we were given the figure of 8,200,000 tughriks, in 1930 it had fallen to 2,600,00 and in 1931 it rose again to 3,500,000, but the amounts for 1934 and 1936 fall below this figure.[96] Thus Andrews' estimate that " within a few years Urga will become one of the greatest fur markets of the Orient " [97] falls short of realization; in any case it has not been an open market for many years. What technical improvements have been made, for instance, by introducing American steel traps, which in Andrews' opinion could double the number of marmot pelts, is not known to us.

The fishing industry was never very important.[98] The absence of any detailed reference to it in recent years makes one assume that no substantial advance has been made.

Forestry has also occupied the attention of the government. Seven percent of the territory is covered by forests, but they were on the way to being destroyed in former times. To protect them national forests have been organized. The forests are the property of the state and, according to a source of 1936, the arats have the right to use wood for their own needs and those of their holdings without paying for it.[99] What progress has been achieved and whether any reafforestation program has been undertaken we do not know, but again silence on these points makes us think that matters pertaining to forestry have not received any priority in recent years. The government of the Mongolian People's Republic has continued the law pro-

---

[96] *SSE*, p. 525.

[97] Andrews, p. 178.

[98] Most sources refer to it, if at all, only in passing; but see Maiskii, pp. 141 and 235; also Koslov's report in the Mongolian-Tibetan Expedition of the Russian State Geographical Society, 1923-26, Leningrad, 1928.

[99] Ryshik, p. 181.

hibiting hunting and the cutting of trees—in force since the eighteenth century—in the "magnificent Bogdo Ula, the true natural park of Mongolia," near the capital, and enforces it by maintaining "police posts in the numerous gorges in the mountain sides." [100]

3. *Farming*

"There is no scope for agriculture," Maiskii categorically stated in his survey on Outer Mongolia published in 1921.[101] Such a negative statement would not be in accord with the present policy of the Mongolian government. Yet the fact remains that the soil and the climate of Outer Mongolia are both unfavorable for farming. The soil is dry, and we find wide areas of sand and stony ground. There is a short growing season and rainfall is light, while there are periods of drought in summer and early frosts. Hence the few areas suitable for cultivation are chiefly in the valleys of the great rivers. Lack of irrigation limits the range of agriculture to narrow boundaries and only a rational system of artificial drainage has made farming possible in most districts. This, together with the necessity for a careful selection of seeds, puts a high premium on hard work.[102] Such drudgery was not to the taste of the Mongols who as horse-riding nomads looked askance at the attachment to a locality which farming demands.

Such farming as was done in the past was thus left to the Chinese, who were numerous in Mongolia before 1921 and who were the first to take up farming there on lands leased from the Mongols. At a later period, toward the eve of this century, the northern border of Mongolia was penetrated by Russian peasants. Some farming was done on the Kiachta-Urga Road, along the Selenga and Orkhon Rivers, also near the town of Khobdo, in the northern part of the Khobdo district around the Ubsa Nor and also near the mountain chain of Khan Khuchei. Here barley was cultivated almost exclusively, but

[100] Roerich, *Trails to Innermost Asia,* New Haven, 1931, p. 134.
[101] Maiskii, p. 230, also pp. 232 and 238.
[102] *SSE,* p. 524.

the method was inefficient. Along the Selenga River millet and wheat can be found in addition to barley.[103] There are vegetable gardens in Urga, Uliassutai and Khobdo which were mainly in the hands of the Chinese, but they did not exist in the north of the country. Roy Chapman Andrews reports with some feeling a mid-July visit to Urga, where he saw gardens cultivated by the Chinese which were full of " splendid radishes, beets, onions, carrots, cabbages, and beans, which were brought every day to market." North of the Bogdo Ula where there is considerable rain " vegetables grow so rapidly in the rich soil that they are deliciously sweet and tender, besides being of enormous size." [104]

But the Mongolian government wished to assert its " independence " from the Chinese in this field also, by trying to foster agriculture by what have been called " curious methods " during the reign of the Urga Hutukhtu. Thus in 1917 a decree was issued which forced the population to sow cereals. The hoshuns took this decree for a new tax and carried out the order from above in the following way. A certain number of families were compelled to sow a given amount of land. But because of the general disdain in which agriculture was held, in addition to its inherent difficulties, as many as possible tried to evade this work. Thus one could find serfs of the princes playing the part of dependent peasants. The main opposition to the decree of their temporal and ecclesiastical head came from the administrations of church domains. A special writ was sent to the Hutukhtu which said that agriculture was regarded as incompatible with the traditions of the great Holy Fathers of the Church and that it was not intended to spoil the beauty of the place by ugly digging of the soil. For disobedience the government imposed a fine on at least one ecclesiastical administration, and though the fine was paid during the subsequent years no cultivation of the land took place during that period.[105] The monasteries which, apart from the Chinese, were practically the only cultivators of land at

---

[103] Maiskii, p. 228. [104] Andrews, p. 142. [105] Maiskii, p. 229.

that time, did not improve their farming position under the Mongolian People's Republic; the reported decline from 8,800 acres in 1926 down to 154 acres in 1929 seems to tell its own story.[106]

It is probable that the monasteries stuck to the primitive methods generally used. It is only in quite recent years that up-to-date implements for the cultivation of the land and the harvesting of the crops have been employed. Here the initiative lay with the government of the Mongolian People's Republic which created some state experimental farms and also tried to prove the possibility of developing farming in the northern part of the country by new technical agricultural methods. Farm holdings were also created, and the existence of five state grain holdings was reported in 1932.[107]

Yet it remained difficult to get the native Mongolian population to take up farming, and it appears that there must have been considerable pressure to induce the arats to enlarge the small share which they held of cultivated land.[108] Preferential treatment was reserved for the development of private arat farming. Those who did farming well were freed for three years from taxes on their farm income. They were also given the best districts for farming, for which they did not pay. Additional assistance was provided by a system of privileged credit.[109] On the other hand, Chinese farming on a large scale of the highly intensive type was rapidly disappearing, and foreigners could make use of the land for purposes of cultivation only by renting it.[110] Technical methods which were of such a low standard were improved by some imports of new machinery from the U. S. S. R.[111] The figure given for 1931

[106] Ryshik, p. 181.

[107] *SSE*, p. 524.

[108] This is implied in the stress laid in all accounts on the passivity of the Mongols towards the problem.

[109] Ryshik, p. 181.

[110] Weiske, p. 159, mentions the difficulties which foreign farmers encountered in 1928 from the Mongolian government. Land could be rented for only a year or so, which was uneconomical, and as a result " two of the greater Russian colonizing villages in the Khentei mountains returned to Siberia."

[111] Ryshik, p. 181.

was 31,500 hectares (69,300 acres) sown, out of which the
state holdings included 7,300 hectares (16,060 acres) or 23.2
percent.[112] In 1943 the area under cultivation is reported to
have reached 74,000 hectares (162,800 acres). Meadow lands
amounted in 1941 to 742,000 hectares (1,632,400 acres)—for
1944 the ambitious plan of 1,330,000 hectares (2,926,000 acres)
was aimed at, but the Soviet source at the end of 1945 is silent
as to whether or not the figure had been reached.[113]

A trust of grain-growing state farms was created with a view
to encouraging the utilization of modern agricultural engi-
neering methods. The aim of the government was to increase
the state holdings and the cultivated areas in general with the
object of raising enough cereals so as to be free from importing
cereals from abroad.[114] Considering, however, the elementary
fact that farming could "never be the chief occupation of the
population except for a technical revolution in farming," [115]
it is not surprising to hear in 1936 that only 33⅓ percent of the
demand for cereals could be satisfied by the home market, the
remainder being imported from the U. S. S. R. In 1938 we
read that the net production of cereals still covered only about
forty percent of the internal consumption, amounting to from
15,000 to 16,000 tons. "The discontinuation of the import of
flour now constitutes an immediate task," we can read at the
end of 1945, but obviously the problem has not yet been
solved.[116] Maiskii estimated that the total area of suitable
farming land did not exceed four percent of the surface of
the whole country. According to him the area cultivated by
the Chinese before 1912 was between 162,000 and 189,000
acres.[117]

The main crops are wheat, oats, millet, spring rye, and
barley. It is significant that in a message sent by the Prime
Minister of the Mongolian People's Republic to Stalin at the
end of 1943, though exhaustive mention was made of different
articles sent in substantial quantities to the Red Army as a

[112] *SSE*, p. 524.
[113] *Sputnik Agitatora*, No. 23, 1945.
[114] *Ibid.*

[115] Maiskii, p. 230; Ryshik, p. 181.
[116] *Sputnik Agitatora.*
[117] Maiskii, pp. 230 and 226.

gift, no agricultural crops were included in the list, while products derived from fishing, hunting and cattle breeding were mentioned.[118] In considering the further outlook for farming, it must not be forgotten that concentration on its activities may, with the limited man power at hand, impair the success of Mongolia's main economic asset, livestock breeding.

4. *Industry*

Whereas Maiskii expressed a pessimistic attitude toward the prospects for agriculture, he foresaw in 1921 better tidings for the other neglected factor in nomad economy, industrial activity. In his words, in fifty to one hundred years enormous furnaces will be burning and one will hear the hammering of machines, and manufacturing cities will be animated with busy life.[119] Compared with the virtual non-existence of any factories in former times, apart from some home industries producing small items for domestic and religious use, some progress has certainly been made in the course of the last two decades. But the scope remains comparatively small and it appears doubtful whether, with the increased industrialization of neighboring Soviet Asia, Mongols and their advisers will feel the same urge to push ahead with a full program of industrialization. In any case there are two requirements for favorable development in this direction: first, the completion of a thorough investigation of the potential resources of raw materials, which demands time in such a vast country; and second, the availability of a sufficient number of workers. Such work does not come easily to a nomad people which tends to look down on such purely manual and stationary occupations. The little industry there was, chiefly in mining, before 1921 was almost entirely manned by Chinese, and such Mongols as were employed there were indifferent workers. It became rather a matter of prestige for the government of the Mongolian People's Republic to allow as few non-Mongols as possible to

[118] *Soviet Monitor,* Dec. 1943.
[119] Maiskii, p. 233.

work, with the result that a number of industrial activities came to an abrupt end for the time being.[120]

The Chinese were no longer allowed to immigrate and the Russians of the frontier districts had the greatest difficulty in obtaining Soviet permission to cross the frontier. This was possible only on a small scale for occasional work such as the building of roads.[121] At the time when these conditions obtained, namely in 1927, there could be found only sixty Mongol workers in all, and in the following years it was practically impossible to find any Mongol workers qualified for industrial labor.[122]

Mining might become an important factor in the development of Mongolia for there is coal in many parts of the country, generally brown coal of low quality and heavily mixed with fossils.[123] There can also be found gold, silver, iron ore, lead and a good deal of sulphur (utilized for medical purposes).[124] The gold mines lying in the Khentei mountains northeast of Urga were operated by a Russian company from 1901 to 1918. In consequence of the revolution and the devaluation of the ruble, work ceased and the concessionaires were deprived of their mining rights by the Mongolian Government. Other not yet exhausted sources are at the Khöbsögol, in the Altai and in the Gobi. Insufficient means and inefficient personnel forced the Mongolian Government, which had nationalized resources, to discontinue the work altogether in about 1927. At that time it desired to interest foreign capital in mining,[125] but nothing came of it.

A small beginning in the importing of machinery and the setting up of factories was made before 1928 with the aid of German and Swedish engineers, details of which are given in a later chapter.[126] There is no acknowledgement of this non-Russian help in Soviet sources, but when we are told that " the foundations for national industrialization were only laid

---

[120] See Chap. V, C and D.
[121] Weiske, p. 165.
[122] Ryshik, p. 183.
[123] *SSE*, p. 525.

[124] Ryshik, p. 182.
[125] Weiske, p. 164.
[126] See Chap. V, C and D.

down in 1927-28 " [127] and are given little information as to Soviet participation before 1934, there was obviously some non-Russian help in the early years.

The first coal mine was at Nalaikha, about 22 miles from Ulan Bator, where production began in 1915. Until 1932 it was mined by hand, but was later mechanized and a special electric power station was erected.[128] In 1927, 8,000 tons of coal were produced, and in 1931, 9,000.[128] A new shaft constructed in 1931 was said to make possible a production of 50,000 tons a year, and in 1936 we are told that production increased to 74,000 tons,[129] and in 1939 to 129,000 tons.[130]

In 1938 a narrow gauge railway, the first in Mongolia, was put into operation between Ulan Bator and Nalaikha, providing a direct link between the industries of Ulan Bator and the coal mines.[130]

Between 1938 and 1941 mines were opened at four other places, Bain Bulak, Undur Khan, Yugodsyr and Dzun Bulak, and the total output of coal in 1947 was said to be 290 times that in 1922.[131]

In 1934 an Industrial Combine was opened in Ulan Bator with the help of the U. S. S. R., consisting of a leather tannery treating 50,000 hides and 250,000 sheepskins a year; a shoe factory producing 90,000 pairs of high Mongol boots and 70,000 pairs of shoes a year; woollen mills, a steam wool washing plant; a felt pressing plant, an electric power plant; and the workers' village.[132] In 1936 this combine was said to employ 1,300 workers of whom 90 per cent were formerly nomads and shepherds.[133] In 1941, according to Perlin, there were 1,500 workers employed,[134] but Tsapkin, in 1948, says that in 1940 some 5,000 workers were employed.[135] The plants are almost entirely mechanized and produced in 1935 goods worth

[127] *BSE.*

[128] *SSE*, p. 525. *BSE.*

[129] *BSE.*

[130] Perlin, p. 46.

[131] N. V. Tsapkin, *Mongolskaya Narodnaya Respublika*, Moscow, 1948, p. 79. This book contains the most recent figures on Mongol industry as well as on other aspects of Mongol economy.

[132] Perlin, p. 46.

[133] Ryshik, p. 182.

[134] Perlin, p. 45.

[135] Tsapkin, p. 78.

7,100,00 tughriks and in 1936, 9,400,000 tughriks.[136] In 1947 its production was given as more than half again as great as in 1940.[137]

Other enterprises listed by Tsapkin include a modern meat packing plant built in 1946; a power station; a large machine shop; a wood working factory; lime and brick works; an auto and truck maintenance garage; and a large printing plant issuing four newspapers, five magazines and, between 1940 and 1947, two million school books. There are also a brewery; a distillery; a confectionery plant, and bakeries.

The chief industry outside Ulan Bator is dairy processing, there being 163 dairies in operation in 1947.[138]

Whereas in 1936 there were said to be 3,000 workers employed in industries,[139] and in 1938, 9,969,[140] by 1945 there were 50,000 wage and salary earners in industry, transport, communications, education, health and administration enterprises, most of which had not existed 25 years earlier.[141]

The value of manufactured goods jumped from 1,798,000 tughriks in 1929 to 12,200,000 tughriks in 1935.[142] According to another source industrial production increased to 64,000,000 tughriks in 1941.[143] In 1941 native industry and handicrafts supplied a quarter of the country's demand for manufactures, the rest coming from the Soviet Union. But by 1946 the country's production of felt boots had doubled, leather footwear increased 29 per cent, fur and sheepskin garments ninefold and textiles $2\frac{1}{2}$ times.[144]

Little is known of labor conditions, but we are told that in 1936 the fourteen or fifteen hour working day was replaced by an eight hour day. Labor laws provide for an annual two week holiday for all workers, and pregnant women receive an additional two or three months leave. A state financed social insurance scheme was also introduced.[145]

[136] *BSE*; Ryshik, p. 182.
[137] Tsapkin, p. 78.
[138] *Ibid.*
[139] Ryshik, p. 183.
[140] Perlin, p. 46.
[141] Tsapkin, p. 78.
[142] Ryshik, p. 183.
[143] *Sputnik Agitatora*, No. 23, 1945.
[144] Tsapkin, p. 78.
[145] Ryshik, p. 183.

Industry which is not owned by the state is owned by cooperative societies. There were 33 handicraft cooperatives in 1934, with over a thousand members, which produced felt and leather boots, clothing, saddles, doors for yurts, carts, baskets, ironware, etc.[146] Statistics published in 1936 give the value of production for 1934 as about 5,000,000 tughriks.[147] In 1945 we are told that the handicraft cooperatives produced a total of 19,000,000 tughriks worth of goods.[148] Our most recent source gives the handicraft cooperatives as employing 12,090 persons in 198 " artels " in 1946, with an output of 43,900,000 tughriks.[149]

C. The Effect of Lamaism on Mongol Society

At a time when Mongolia was a conglomeration of separate tribes with no national government the growing influence of the Lama Church introduced a new and stabilizing factor on a national scale. Buddhism had existed in Mongolia in former centuries and in the sixteenth century it was re-introduced by the Mongol chief, Altan-Khan who ruled as far as Tibet and defeated the Western Mongols.[150] It had a unifying effect, in addition to creating permanent monastery settlements and church property. It certainly did not result, as has been so often said, in sapping the vitality of the desert race.[151]

The continuous fierce struggles, mainly between the Western Mongols (Kalmuks), and the Northern Mongols (Khalkhas), in which the Lama Church took a leading part, show that the allegedly pacifying influence which followed the re-introduction of Lamaism was rather an afterthought, based mainly on developments in the nineteenth century, when the Manchus supported it in order to create a counter-balance against the princes. Originally the contact between church and princes was close and the first incumbent of the Jebtsun-damba " incar-

---

[146] *Ibid.*
[147] *Ibid.*
[148] *Sputnik Agitatora.*
[149] Tsapkin, p. 80.
[150] W. W. Rockhill, " The Dalai Lamas of Lhasa and their Relations with the Manchu Emperors of China " in T'ung Pao, Vol. XI, 1910, pp. 5, 6.
[151] John F. Baddeley, *Russia, Mongolia, China,* London, 1919, Vol. I, p. lxxxii.

nation " among the Khalkha tribes was a son of one of the greatest princes, namely, Tushetu-Khan.[152] Church offices had come to be looked upon as among the hereditary prerogatives of these ruling families. But as the Manchus feared this combination of temporal and ecclesiastical power, they made it a rule that the sons and nephews of ruling princes were not to be chosen in infancy as Living Buddhas. Henceforth Living Buddhas had to be selected quite arbitrarily by the drawing of lots, which was preceded by the establishment of a panel of candidates by the church authorities. The last attempt to declare the son of a prince the reincarnation of the Jebtsun-damba Hutukhtu of Urga was made in 1791. It was expected that the wife of a reigning prince would bring him forth, but the " incarnation " turned out to be a girl. An Imperial Edict of 1793 was issued against these practices.[153]

The first two of the eight incarnations of Jebtsun Damba, the Urga Hutukhtu, were born in Mongolia, after which a decree was issued by the Dalai Lama that the candidate must be born in Tibet. This decree was not accepted without protest by the princes of Khalkha. The latter decided to boycott the foreign incarnation. After a secret assembly they sent to the Manchu Emperor a report which stressed the unsuitability of Urga as a residence of a holy man—attacks by nomads, the presence of secular elements, and of women were mentioned as arguments—and proposed Dolon Nor as his residence. But their proposal was not accepted and the next Hutukhtu was born in Tibet and brought to Mongolia in 1763.

Since, in addition, the candidates were selected at an early age, there was a considerable safety margin against any political choice. In former times, when political motives dictated the selection of a candidate, Living Buddhas were known to die of poisoning previous to the age at which they might have attained some political maturity. With the choice confined to church circles and the education entirely in their

---

[152] A. Kallinikov, *Revolutsionnaya Mongoliya*, Moscow, 1925, p. 18.
[153] Rockhill, p. 55.

hands, such happenings became rarer and some Living Buddhas lived to grow up.[154]

The Urga Hutukhtu, the chief of the Living Buddhas in Outer Mongolia, gained increasing political importance through the centuries, based on the fact that, by the acquisition of so many shabinar and monks, he became one of the most powerful feudal leaders of Khalkha. In addition, pressure from outside, the decline of the great Mongolian Khan, and other internal reasons, helped to create a position in which the Kalkha princes, especially those from the two Eastern Khanates, began to look on their compatriot, the Urga Hutukhtu, as a sort of superior suzerain, almost as if he were an All-Khalkha Khan.[155] The princes even renounced some of their rights concering immunity to the advantage of the Hutukhtu. For example, the gathering of princes from three Eastern hoshuns (two Khanates) recognized the right of the Hutukhtu to give asylum to fugitives from their feudal territories.

In the beginning of the twentieth century his prestige might have seemed to grow further, when the Dalai Lama of Tibet took refuge from the British in Urga in 1904, but the Tibetan church authorties looked askance at the political activities of the Urga Pontiff. It is reported that the Dalai Lama gave frequent hints to the Urga Hutukhtu as to the desirability of his return to Tibet.[156] The successful prevention by the Manchu Dynasty of the emergence of a national leader who would have represented the interests of the church as well as of the princes, created, mainly in the nineteenth century, a kind of dyarchy, that is, a government exercised by the two independent authorities of the church and the princes. However, this process stands out in the long run as one bringing about the enlargement of the institutional interests of the church. It did not achieve complete separation of the actual influence exercised by the Living Buddha, on the one hand, and the

[154] Baddeley, Vol. II, pp. 235-36.

[155] B. V. Vladimirtsov, *Obshchestvenny stroi Mongolov* (Social Structure of the Mongols), Leningrad, 1934, p. 194.

[156] G. N. Roerich, *Trails to Inmost Asia*, p. 144.

princes, on the other. The seventh incarnation, for instance, who was born in 1815 in Lhasa and was of simple parentage, arriving as a child at Urga, came rapidly under the influence of a Mongolian prince (Tsetsen Khan Artasit). The latter was soon able to fill all court and ecclesiastical offices with the relatives of his Khanate. The consequent degeneration of the life at the palace of the Living Buddha went so far that a split in the monasteries was nearly brought about by those lamas who asked the Manchu Governor to eject and punish the degenerate lamas. Only the death of the Hutukhtu in 1860 cut short the strife.[157]

Yet the fundamental change in the social structure was probably accelerated during this period. There was first a great increase in the number of lamas. It is estimated that one-third of them lived permanently in monasteries.[158] Exact figures for the time are not available, but Maiskii gives for a later period the number of 40,000 out of a total of 150,000 lamas. Out of these 40,000, about 20,000 lived in the two Urga monasteries. All these permanent monastic " town dwellers," as well as many roaming lamas, were a dead loss to the country's wealth, since they lived as idle parasites doing little but repeating prayers—in the Tibetan tongue, which few of them understood. The higher lamas were rather busier since they had many administrative duties, including the task of accumulating wealth, for which holy purpose there were increased opportunities with the influx of Chinese traders to the towns which grew up close to the monasteries. For the privilege of trading there, and for the prestige with which this permission invested the traders, the lamas demanded and received a share in the profits. The fifth incarnation who, about 1815, asked the Chinese traders to leave the main part of the town for a more distant place, had to face the opposition of the lamas, since it entailed a decrease in non-ecclesiastical visitors and hence a loss of income. Chinese merchants and lamas, being equally dissatisfied, sent a complaint against the Hutukhtu to

---

[157] Korostovets, p. 40.   [158] Maiskii, p. 107 (footnote).

Peking while he was there. He had to pay a considerable sum in order to suppress the whole affair.[159]

Apart from the lamas, who at the end of the nineteenth century constituted about twenty-four percent of the population, church influence gradually increased through the growth of the number of shabinar who were serfs of the Lama Hutukhtus. These were people whom the princes gave to them as gifts. At times people also assumed voluntarily the status of shabi, in order to rid themselves of the protection of their feudal lords or because they preferred to live as simple Mongols attached to the monasteries. In the year 1750 the number of shabinar was estimated at 30,000.[160] The Manchus tried, even as early as 1754, to limit the powers of the Living Buddha over his serfs by introducing the office of Treasurer Administrator, with the comment that a holy man should not occupy himself with such worldly affairs, but the number of shabinar increased continuously and numbered 50,000 in about 1800, under the reign of the very stern and pious fourth " incarnation," Lobsang Tobden. The latter was directly related to the Dalai Lama of Tibet and was instrumental in issuing a new decree on the shabinar administration.[161] During the nineteenth century the shabinar increased up to 100,000, and they were variously reported as having numbered 150,000 in the first two decades of the twentieth century. This means that, together with the lamas, about fifty percent of the population was directly under the jurisdiction of the church. The shabinar were freed from state taxes, instead of which they paid a church tax and church duties and became thus one of the main economic foundations of the church in Mongolia, whose non-working members (i. e., the lamas) they supported by their contributions.

The Urga Hutukhtu had the largest number of shabinar.[162]

[159] Korostovets, pp. 39, 40.

[160] *Ibid.*, p. 37. In 1755 the Urga Hutukhtu was given the inhabitants of the Darchat territory as shabinar as a reward for his help in the pacification of Mongolia. Cf. Werner Leimbach, *Landeskunde von Tuwa*, Gotha, 1936, p. 100.

[161] Korostovets, p. 39.

[162] According to Doksom (cf. Bibliography) he had 90,000.

Other ecclesiastical dignitaries also had subjects of this kind, especially north of Uliassutai and toward Urianghai. Most of the shabinar (about 70,000 according to Maiskii)[163] lived scattered in various principalities. About 16,000 subjects of the Urga Hutukhtu lived on separate pastures which had been set aside for them east of Lake Khöbsögol, forming the Darkhat District. Shabinar were governed by special officials and were free from taxation by princes. After the death of the last Urga Hutukhtu in 1924 the adjustment of the special rights of the shabinar caused difficulties for the Mongolian People's Republic.[164]

D. DARIGANGGA

While such heritages from the old régime as the shabinar territories and the ownership of special grazing grounds by the Hutukhtus weakened the new régime by the problems they created, there was another district whose different administrative history strengthened the new régime.

Darigangga, in the southeastern part of Outer Mongolia, on the borders of Chahar in Inner Mongolia, was formerly administered by a number of appointed and elected officials who in their turn depended on and were controlled by the Chahar Banner administration, which claimed it as an appanage of Inner Mongolian Chahar. Apparently the institution of " taiji "—the nobility—never existed in Darigangga, for no legends to this effect have remained and there seem to be no references to it in the chronicles.[165]

The consequence of this different system was that Darigangga never experienced the hardships which were the lot of Khalkha. In Khalkha the power of the Prince and the division into classes carried with it the old institution of common responsibility of the entire hoshun for each of its members and in particular for the prince. This was exploited,

[163] Maiskii, p. 278.

[164] The number of shabinar given for 1924, in *Novyi Vostok*, No. 8-9, 1925, p. 226, was " roughly 85,000."

[165] V. N. Kazakevich, *Poyezdka v Dariganga* (Journey to Darigangga), Leningrad, 1930, p. 42, n. 2.

mainly by the Chinese, to the detriment of Mongolian economy. In Darigangga, however, cattle, the principal property of the nomad, was considered as state property and could be used for private purposes within definite limits. After the revolution of 1911 the cattle passed into private ownership, which placed the local rich in a leading position, but not to such an extent, in the comparatively few years of their power, as to affect the population decisively since Darigangga was rich in cattle because of good grazing lands. Not without reason was this district chosen by Chinese commanders in the fifteenth and seventeenth centuries as a natural base for one of the shortest roads from interior China to central Khalkha. After 1911 the population suffered less from the change in status of property than from military operations. The region always had the reputation of being infested with thieves, the Khalkhas having a tendency to look at any inhabitant of Darigangga as a thief. (This is similar to the part which ' baranta ' plays with the Kazakhs, who are more prosperous than the Mongols; here the driving away of cattle is explained by the need to show courage and skill.) Theft of money and goods was in later times also the consequence of economic deterioration brought about by wars.[166]

The material prosperity of Darigangga was severely impaired by the frost of 1923-1924, which destroyed all the cattle in some districts. Yet the fundamental conditions for its prosperity still remained, as well as the difference in administration. Under the new régime in 1924 and the subsequent renaming of aimaks Darigangga did not become part of the Khentei Aimak. The curious position arose that it was considered a separate hoshun, with an independent administration under the direct authority of the capital, Ulan Bator. At the hoshun session of 1927 the question of administrative union with the Khentei Aimak was again raised. But a negative resolution was adopted, the official explanation mentioning such factors as the remoteness of the Aimak administration, the additional

[166] *Ibid.*, p. 43.

administrative burden and the absence of a sufficient number of literate people for the Aimak administration. The absence of union did not mean however that Darigangga had an internal administrative structure different from any other hoshun in the Mongolian People's Republic.

Local self-government was introduced in Darigangga at some time toward the end of 1924 or the beginning of 1925. From 1911 to 1925 it was divided into five hoshuns, which were then united into one. The hoshun administration of Darigangga is situated approximately in the center of this territory.[167]

According to a description by the Russian explorer, V. N. Kazakevitch in 1930, besides the administration tents it had a prison consisting of two tents, a section of the State Interior Defense consisting of four tents, a school of three tents, and dwellings for employees of the administration amounting to about fifteen tents. The department of the Mongolian Central Cooperatives (Montsenkop) had tents near a small monastery. In one of the clay buildings of the monastery there was a shop selling liquor and other beverages. An interesting side light is thrown on self-government by the fact that all the members of the above named institutions were natives of Darigangga. Yet the exceptions were significant, for the natives took no part in the State Interior Defense, nor is the school teacher a native, but a Buriat.[168] Whether any conclusions as to the workings of the State Interior Defense can be drawn from the fact that Kazakevich, in search of experts in local literature, could find them only among the prison inmates, we do not know.[169]

Darigangga, being so much nearer to Inner Mongolia and China than other regions of Outer Mongolia, felt the disappearance of Chinese trading in two ways. First, the former buying up of goats, furs, mushrooms and other smaller items by Chinese was taken over by Russian organizations, such as

[167] *Ibid.*, p. 44.
[168] Cf. references to the influence of Buriats in other chapters. Cf. also Chapter VII, n. 43.
[169] *Ibid.*, p. 45.

Stormong and the wool shearing company interested in wool purchases and horned cattle and in selling Soviet goods such as cloth, iron wares, cigarettes, etc. Second, however, distant journeys by natives of Darigangga to Inner Mongolia, Chinese towns and farming colonies were severely curtailed and must now have stopped completely. The purpose of these expeditions had been the purchase of cereals of which Darigangga is as short as is the remainder of Outer Mongolia. These journeys were started in the summer and completed in autumn when the camels were fittest. They worked on a cooperative basis; some members offering their camels or money for purchase, some going as purchasers themselves, with others as their companions. Such expeditions were sometimes connected with pilgrimages to holy places such as Wutaishan, Dolonor, and Kuku Khoto. In former times such journeys encountered no serious obstacles, but since the frontiers of the Mongolian People's Republic were declared open only at certain places, namely, those where there were established offices of the Frontier Defense and of the Customs, such travels have been impeded by the necessity to produce documents giving permission to leave for abroad. Such permits to leave Darigangga were obtained from the hoshun administration on the basis of a recommendation issued by the somon authorities. Thereupon the traveller had to go to the nearest customs center and go through all the formalities with which the traveller in any part of the world of today is familiar. The journeys were never without risk, for it happened quite frequently that camels collapsed and this made the return journey full of hazard.[170] In the 1920's it was also quite possible to get involved in the Chinese civil war areas and to be carried away into interior China. Later on it might mean falling into the hands of the Japanese or their autonomous Mongolian Government. Today trade across the border is practically at a standstill.

[170] *Ibid.*, p. 46.

Chapter II

RELATIONS WITH RUSSIA

A. Policy of Tsarist Russia

RUSSIA'S FRONTIER with Mongolia has repeatedly been the subject of negotiations between the Russian and Chinese Governments since the 18th century. The treaty of Kiakhta in 1727, the treaty of Peking in 1860, the protocol of Chuguchak in 1864, the treaty of St. Petersburg in 1881 and the treaty of Tsitsihar in 1911 record the frontier agreements between the Russian Empire of the Romanovs and the Chinese Empire of the Manchus.[1] By the treaty of 1727 frontier marks were erected on both sides of the Russian border, except in Urianghai which remained a no-man's land.[2] Russian subjects had to pass through these posts when going for trade purposes to Mongolia or China, and the list enumerating the Russian posts and the nearest Mongolian posts was apt to raise many difficulties and many misunderstandings. Some parts of the frontier had no opposite posts whatsoever for long distances, in others they were far apart from each other.[3] About seventy-one posts were established along the Russo-Mongolian frontier in 1911, but they were abolished shortly afterward because of the new political relationship between Russia and Mongolia.[4]

The importance of these frontier posts in the 19th century

[1] Hertslet, Treaties, etc., between Great Britain and China, and between China and Foreign Powers, Vol. I (London, 1896), Part II, No. 49, Treaty of 1727; No. 54, Treaty of Peking; No. 55, Protocol of Conference between Russia and China defining the Boundary between the two countries, signed at Chuguchak, 1864; No. 56, Revised Convention for the Land Trade between Russia and China, Peking, 1869; No. 57, Treaty between Russia and China, St. Petersburg, 1881.

[2] Grumm-G., Vol. 2, Annex 2: "The Line of Mongolian Frontier Posts"; p. 821, cites N. Bauty-Kaminskii, "Diplomatic Collection of Affairs between Russia and the Chinese State, 1619-1792," p. 344.

[3] Ibid., p. 823; Grumm-G. gives many details especially concerning the failure of the Chinese to establish frontier posts along the Urianghai frontier. On pages 825-828 there is a complete list of frontier posts giving the different spellings of their names.

[4] Ibid., p. 828; Korostovets, p. 57; Baddeley, *Russia, Mongolia, China*, London, 1919, Vol. 1, p. XIX.

is evident from the fact that until the opening of Chinese sea ports to foreign powers by the treaty of Tientsin (1858), the opening of the Suez Canal, and, in particular, the building of the Trans-Siberian railway, Mongolia was the obvious route for any traffic from the East. It was the only tea route to Europe and the Russian tea traders who followed the caravan routes prospered.[5] But the opening of sea routes greatly reduced Russian through traffic via Mongolia, and the tea which still went by land was nearly all consumed in Mongolia.[6] St. Petersburg's official interest in Mongolia in the 19th century was strictly limited to the economic sphere. Muraviev, who in 1858 by the treaty of Aigun obtained from China without any military operations [7] the cession of a great part of the basin of the Amur (which earned him the title of Count Amurski), in 1854 as Governor General of Eastern Siberia desired to take advantage of the critical situation of the Peking Government caused by its dispute with Great Britain. He submitted a proposal to St. Petersburg that he should proclaim Mongolia a Russian Protectorate. A special committee decided to approach this question carefully and they reduced Muraviev's ambitions to a project for the acquisition of the sympathies of the Mongolian Hutukhtu and the creation of friendly ties with the more influential princes. Activities of the same Muraviev in 1860 were similarly neutralized by the cautious recommendations of the St. Petersburg Amur Committee of the same year.[8]

The economic interest of the Russian Government found expression in the opening in 1861 of the first Russian consulate in Urga, which had been preceded by the establishment of the first Russian trading firm in the same town a year earlier.[9]

[5] *Moskovskaya Torgvaya Expeditsia v Mongoliu* (Moscow Commercial Expedition to Mongolia), Moscow, 1912, p. 274; also *Larson, Duke of Mongolia*, pp. 233-34.

[6] *BPCMD* 3727-235-No. 4152, Annual Series, Diplomatic and Consular Reports. China Report for the Year 1907 on the Foreign Trade of China, October 1908, p. 16.

[7] George N. Curzon, *Problems of the Far East*, London, 1894, p. 222, n. 1: " Never was a fine Dominion so cheaply or more cleverly won."

[8] K. A., Vol. 37, " Tsarist Russia and Mongolia, 1913-14," introduction by A. Popov, p. 7, who also refers to B. M. Guriev, " Political Relations between Russia and Mongolia, 1911."

[9] *Ibid.*, p. 9. In 1883 there were ten firms, in 1910 over twenty.

The Peking agreement concerning trade of February 1862 stipulated that Russian merchants should, with the permission of their home authorities, be able to trade free of duty with small capital in Mongolia wherever there was a Chinese administration. But they were also allowed to penetrate into those parts of Mongolia where there was no such administration.[10]

The position achieved in the St. Petersburg treaty of 1881 was not so much an improvement on these rights of duty-free trade in Mongolia as on trade concessions in other parts of the Chinese Empire. Nevertheless, more detailed regulations were made as to the transit of goods from Russia via Mongolia to China, and points on the frontier at which Russian merchants must enter Mongolia were specified. In addition, Russia secured the right to open consulates in Khobdo, Uliassutai, Hami, Urumchi, and Kuch'engtze " accordingly as they are called for by the development of commerce, and after coming to an understanding with the Chinese Government." This additional clause obtained particular significance in 1911 when the Chinese obstinately refused to permit the opening of the Russian Consulate at Khobdo.[11]

When at the close of the nineteenth century the Russian Government tried to obtain from Great Britain and China the recognition of special trade and railway rights in China, Mongolia was a side-issue and the main object was Manchuria. The Foreign Minister, Count Michael Nikolaievich Muraviev, when defining the Russian sphere of influence left Mongolia out altogether and it was Count Witte, the Finance Minister, who demanded railway rights and a trade monopoly for Russia in all the three provinces of Manchuria and in Mongolia. Opposite the British suggestions referring to Manchuria as a Russian sphere of influence, Witte pencilled an " And Mongolia? " [12] The omission of Mongolia was later rectified

[10] Hertslet, *op. cit.*

[11] *Ibid.*, No. 57; Marten's Nouv. Rev. Gen. Traités, Deux. Sér., Tome VIII, 1883, pp. 221-234, especially p. 223, article X, and p. 224, article XII.

[12] B. A. Romanov, *Rossiya v Manchzhurii* (Russia in Manchuria), 1892-1906, Leningrad, 1928, pp. 192, 196, 215, 228.

by fixing the frontier of the Russian sphere along the Great
Wall, which included not only Manchuria but also Mongolia.
The Anglo-Russian agreement of April 1899, which took the
form of an exchange of identical notes between the British
ambassador and the Russian Foreign Minister, was confined
to railway concessions; Russia was promised British abstention
from competition for railway concessions in the region north
of the Great Wall and she in turn promised Great Britain the
same in the basin of the Yangtze.[13] But the inclusion of Mongolia as a Russian sphere of influence at that time was for
Russia only a matter of principle.[14] Witte had for instance
rejected the plan of Badmaev, a Buryat physician, who had
for some time worked in the Asiatic Section of the Ministry
of Foreign Affairs [15] and urged that a railway across Mongolia
from Kiakhta to Peking should be built. Witte himself hoped
that the Trans-Siberian railway would be continued to Vladivostok in which case it might possibly touch Mongolian
territory.[16]

In June 1899, a few months after this Anglo-Russian exchange of notes, Russia secured from China a reaffirmation of
her special rights by a promise that " if railroads are in future
built from Peking to the north or to the northeast towards
the Russian frontier," China, if not constructing them herself,
would not give the right of construction to any but the Russian
Government or a Russian syndicate.[17] Russia, however, was
not satisfied with this railway agreement and tried hard in the
succeeding years to obtain from Li Hung-chang, the Chinese

[13] MacMurray, Vol. I, p. 204; Grimm, No. 51, p. 137.
[14] Popov, p. 8; cf. also *IBZI.*, I, 1, No. 348, Sazonov to Krupenskii, February
28/15, 1914, p. 351: " We have insisted as a matter of principle that after the
agreement of 1899 any British railway construction north of the Great Wall violates
this agreement."
[15] *The Memoirs of Count Witte*, London, 1921, p. 86; for not altogether identical
details of Peter Aleksevich Badmaev (1849-1920) cf. editorial notes to *The Memoirs
of Count Kokovtsov*, Hoover War Library Publication, No. 6, edited by H. H.
Fisher, p. 590, and Editor's note in *IBZI.*, I, 2, p. 425, referring to the Russian
book *Behind the Scenes of Tsarism*; The Archive of the Tibetan Doctor Badmaev,
Leningrad, 1915, p. 117.
[16] Witte, *op. cit.*, pp. 86-87.
[17] MacMurray, Vol. I, pp. 207-08; Grimm, *Sbornik*, No. 52, p. 139.

4

statesman, mainly by offering him considerable sums as bribes, exclusive economic rights in the regions " north of Peking." Li thought it wise first to divert St. Petersburg's appetite to Mongolia and replied that China was prepared to agree to Russia's unconditional exploitation of the treasures of Mongolia and Kashgar which lay upon her borders; Russian settlers could go there, camouflaging the concessions to the Russian Government under the flag of a few pseudo-private companies.[18] From the Russian point of view this offer was inadequate in that it did not deal with the principal object of interest, which was Manchuria. But later Li included Manchuria within the scope of this proposal.[19]

These and other moves and countermoves did not lead far because Li was always anxious to postpone matters, in the meantime enlisting against the Russian pressure the influence of other powers who in their turn were strongly opposed to the active Russian policy. At the end of 1900, Witte demanded that China should engage not to build any railways herself in the Russian sphere of influence, i. e., the whole of China north of the Great Wall, Mongolia, the territory of Ili and Kashgar. Article 8 of the proposed convention read: " The Chinese Government shall not without the consent of Russia grant to any other Powers or to their subjects any concessions whatsoever for the construction of railroads, the working of mineral deposits or any other industrial enterprises in any of the districts adjacent to Russia, i. e. Manchuria and Mongolia, Tarbagatai, Ili, Kashgar, Yarkand, Khotan and Keriya. The Chinese Government shall not without the consent of the Russian Government build railways nor grant parcels of land for the use of foreigners without such consent, except in the free port of Newchwang.[20] The British Minister in Peking, Sir Eric Satow, warned the Chinese Government (i. e. the Viceroy and the Emperor) that this would have the effect

[18] Romanov, *op. cit.*, p. 263, referring to telegram of Ukhtomski to Witte from Shanghai, September 18/October 1, 1900.

[19] *Ibid.*, p. 275.

[20] *Ibid.*, p. 298; cf. also William L. Langer, *The Diplomacy of Imperialism,* New York-London, 1935, Vol. II, p. 715.

of depriving China of her sovereignty over Manchuria and that the prohibition against railway-building in Mongolia and Eastern Turkistan (Sinkiang) was equivalent to abandoning these regions also.[21] For the benefit of his own Government the British Minister remarked that Article 8 laid the foundation for future treatment of those districts in the same way as Manchuria and was prejudicial to possible interests of other Powers.[22]

Russia had finally to abandon the agreement in 1902-03, because of the opposition of the other powers and the death of Li; but what interests us here in connection with Mongolia is that following the demands of China—not of the other powers—the mention of Mongolia and other districts in addition to Manchuria had already been excluded from the text of February 1901,[23] so that Sir Eric Satow was referring, though he was ignorant of this fact, to a stipulation already obsolete.

While the activities of the Russian Government were concentrated on parts of China other than Mongolia, that semi-governmental institution, the Russo-Chinese Bank, was closely concerned with the foundation, in June 1897, of a syndicate for research into the mining resources of China (Syndicat pour l'exploration des richesses minières en Chine), which in its turn created, in the beginning of 1900, a limited company to exploit the concessions for mining gold in the districts of Tushetu Khan and Tsetsen Khan Aimaks in Outer Mongolia (along the river Orkhon and its tributaries) obtained from the Chinese Government. The original syndicate had been founded with a capital of 500,000 rubles, divided into 100 shares, the income to be shared as follows: 50 per cent to go to the members of the syndicate, who were mainly Belgians, 22½ per cent to the Russo-Chinese Bank, the same proportion to the Russian Gold-Mining Company and five per cent to members of the committee. The company for mining gold in Outer

---

[21] *B. D.*, Vol. II, No. 46, Sir E. Satow to the Marquess of Lansdowne, March 6, 1901, p. 37.
[22] *Ibid.*, No. 47, p. 39.
[23] Romanov, *op. cit.*, p. 303, n. 1.

Mongolia, called "*Mongolor*," was founded with a capital of three million rubles divided in 1200 shares (one third to be provided by the Belgian group). But only a year later—in 1901—the company was faced with the danger of bankruptcy and negotiations for its liquidation were begun, sponsored mainly by the Russo-Chinese Bank. The Russian Minister of Finance, Kokovtsov, however, intervened because he believed that from a political point of view it was not expedient to liquidate the only large Russian enterprise in Mongolia just at the time when the Dalai Lama was arriving in Urga. The company was therefore accorded a loan of 50,000 rubles which was supposed to afford it the possibility of continuing the work on a modest scale for about a year, in the expectation that during this time the political situation in the Far East would clear up and at the same time the attitude of the Belgian shareholders to the question of the company's continued activities would be finally determined.[24]

That "Mongolor," the only great enterprise in Mongolia, had to be given a small subsidy in order to keep up appearances is a clear indication of the limited extent to which the Russian Government was involved even economically in the destinies of Mongolia in the second half of the 19th century. Indeed, the characteristic of Russian trade in Mongolia was that it led a hopeless existence due to lack of capital, its representatives being small merchants from Siberian towns such as Biisk, Minnusinsk, Verkhneudinsk and Troitskosavsk and not big firms from St. Petersburg and Moscow, whose attention was concentrated on Manchuria. These Russian merchants started their trade in centers like Uliassutai, Urga and Khobdo, but soon sent their agents into the different Mongolian *hoshuns* and remote places. These *hoshun* representatives opened shops, but they had no capital with which to carry on business and had to take credit from the merchant firms, which gave it on difficult terms. Except for the Russo-Chinese Bank, which could not satisfy their demands, they

[24] *Ibid.*, Annex II, The Syndicate of 1897 & Mongolor, p. 599 and pp. 601-602 referring to full report of Minister of Finance, January 7, 1905.

had no other credit institutions. They could only have recourse
to the Chinese merchants, their competitors. Instead of silver,
the Chinese gave them tea and cloth and one of the main
reasons for the bad state of Russian trade was that Russian
merchants traded this with non-Russian goods.[25] Another
reason, adduced for instance by Boloban, Popov, and Consten
to account for the unsuccessful character of the business transactions of these Russians, is that they were the type of merchant who aimed at making as much money as possible in
the shortest possible period and employed primitive methods
of swindling. A net annual profit below 40 or 50 per cent was
generally considered by them as failure and goods imported
from Russia were sold at double their value.[26] Grumm-Grzhimailo, an impartial observer, whose works were published in
St. Petersburg before as well as after it became Leningrad,
cautions us not to take too critical a view of these merchants.
When they were sent to the distant parts of Mongolia they
often found an already well developed *hoshun* trade in the
hands of the Chinese and all they could do was to follow the
example of the latter, which was not too difficult a task as it
was only slightly different from the method of trade practised
in the Altai mountains. Grumm-Grzhimailo agrees that the
Russian merchants did not excel in intelligence, but he thinks
it a long step from such an admission to accusations that they
were in the habit of claiming payment of debts more than
once as alleged by S. Wildhaus on the basis of material found
in the archives of the Russian Diplomatic Mission in Peking.
He remarks ironically that he has of course not had the privilege of seeing this material, but that he thinks that one could
find many statements in the Russian mission's archives but
none referring to *hoshun* merchants.[27]

The position of the 200 or so Russian *hoshun* merchants
became worse when the Chinese began to sell American and

---

[25] *Mos. Comm. Exp., op. cit.,* p. 275, in the chapter of I. M. Morosov, " On the
development and strengthening of trade-economic and political influence of Russia
in Mongolia."

[26] Popov, p. 10.

[27] Grumm G., Vol. III, Pt. 2, Leningrad, 1930, pp. 671-73.

English cloth at much cheaper prices than that which was manufactured at Lodz or Moscow. The quality of the Russian product might have been better than the British and American cloth but the latter was dyed at Tientsin so as to make it attractive to the Mongols. The Russian cloth, moreover, had great difficulty in competing with this material in which the Chinese traded for, since the abolishment of the likin system, the transport tariff from Moscow to Urga was higher than that from Tientsin.[28]

Such were the conditions of Russian trade in the first decade of the 20th century. The average turnover of the largest Russian firm operating in Mongolia did not exceed 500,000 rubles and the capital of the average small firm was not above 20,000 rubles.[29] We are told that for six Russian shops there were as many as seventy-four Chinese.[30] The general turnover for Western Mongolia increased from 1,349,000 rubles in 1891 to 3,677,000 in 1908. But this increase was chiefly due to the increase of Russian imports from Mongolia. While the latter in the period 1891-1908 are said to have increased by 566 per cent, the import of Russian goods to Mongolia increased by only 22 per cent.[31] All trade figures reveal the clear tendency of the Russian trade balance with Mongolia to become increasingly passive because wool and cattle began to be imported on a large scale by Russia. Besides the total turnover between China and Mongolia, which amounted to about 50,000,000 rubles in 1908, Russia's 8,000,000 ruble turnover cut a poor figure.[32]

About that time (1908-1910) larger Russian firms at Moscow and Tomsk became interested in the economic possibilities of Mongolia. In 1909 a special " Departmental Committee " was created in the Ministry of Trade and Industry under the Presidency of Langovoi and its first meeting was held in April. Its

---

[28] *Mos. Comm. Exp.*, p. 277.

[29] Popov, p. 10.

[30] Hermann Consten, *Weideplätze der Mongolen, Im Reiche des Chalcha,* Vol. I, p. 126.

[31] Popov, p. 10. It is not quite clear how the author arrived at these figures.

[32] *Ibid.*, p. 10.

aim was to collect material in order to study the Mongolian market.[33]

In 1910 a Committee was set up in Irkutsk which aimed at the inauguration of measures to save Russian trade in Mongolia. A scheme was proposed for connecting Mongolia with the Trans-Siberian railway.[34]

Several trade expeditions were sent to Mongolia in the same year. One, sent by Moscow manufacturers, published in 1912 an extensive report.[35] It was emphasized at that time that these missions had a purely commercial interest in Mongolia.[36] There can be no doubt, however, judging from the general tone of the reports published, that the members of the expeditions as well as the agent of the Ministry of Trade and Industry, A. Boloban, were impressed by the necessity of influencing the Russian Government to evince more political interest in Mongolia. As the most important task, the creation there of a Russian Commercial Bank was suggested in order to help Russian merchants and also to compete with the Chinese credit system which made the Mongols economically completely dependent upon China.[37]

It has been frequently maintained that the unfavorable outcome for Russia of the Russo-Japanese War in 1905, while bringing the furtherance of her ambitions in Manchuria to a standstill, in compensation encouraged her activities in Mongolia. As far as we know, there is no evidence which would support this simplification of the facts. It is true that in a secret agreement with Japan Northern Manchuria and Outer Mongolia were designated as a Russian sphere of influence and thereby Russia was evincing a definite interest in Mongolia. Count Hayashi, the Japanese statesman, about that time

---

[33] *Ibid.*, p. 11.

[34] Maiskii, p. 253.

[35] *Mos. Comm. Exp., op. cit.*

[36] Prof. Sobolev and Prof. Bogolepov, of the University of Tomsk, published a long report. Cf. also Petermann's *Geographische Mitteilungen*, 1910, II, p. 195; Communication of Prof. Obruchev and *ibid.*, 1911, I, p. 194; also *The Economist*, Vol. LXXIII, November 4, 1911.

[37] *Mos. Comm. Exp.*, pp. 279-80; Popov, p. 11.

characterized Russia's right in Mongolia as incapable of definition.[38] During the negotiations for the Anglo-Russian agreement in 1906-07 Mongolia was again mentioned by the Russians, but was dropped when they had come to an understanding with Britain's ally, Japan.[39] For purely geographical reasons, moreover, it was inevitable for Russia always to consider Mongolia as vital. However, what counts is that while defining other powers' spheres of influence in China, about the time of the negotiations with Japan and Great Britain developments were taking place in China which made Russia increase her vigilance in regard to that region. China, motivated by various reasons [40] and encouraged by the defeat of Russia in 1905, suddenly began an active policy of political interference and economic penetration in Outer Mongolia. Until about 1907, although China's economic predominance in Mongolia was evident and although it was her territory, the internal administration of Outer Mongolia was not much interfered with and Chinese were forbidden to colonize there. The volte-face of the Chinese Government in Peking made it apparent to observers, including the Russian Minister in Peking and Russian Consuls in Mongolia, that in a few years China would have imposed her will in that region bordering Russia in such a way that it would not only become a barrier to any future Russian economic progress there but also a military threat to Russia herself.

From that time on, in particular after 1910, different tendencies can be discerned among the Russians. On the one hand the men on the spot and certain larger trading firms, as for instance the great " Russian Export Company," urged St. Petersburg to take measures to neutralize the Chinese plans. Some military strategists may also be included in this group.[41] On the other hand, the Ministry of Foreign Affairs

[38] *G.P.*, Vol. 25, p. 70, No. 8548, German Ambassador in Tokyo to Chancellor Prince Bulow, Augsut 5, 1907.

[39] Cf. Chapter V.

[40] Cf. Chapter III.

[41] V. Tomilin, *Mongoliya i yeyo sovremennoye znacheniye dlya Rossii* (Mongolia and its Contemporary Significance for Russia), Moscow, 1913; referring also (pp.

itself was very reluctant to seek new entanglements in the Far
East, burdened as it was by Near Eastern and European
anxieties and mindful of the debâcle of 1905. So it is necessary
when speaking of Russia's attitude, to keep these two currents
of opinion in mind.

Ivan J. Korostovets, Imperial Minister in Peking, one of
Tsarist Russia's ablest diplomats, may be considered the most
important supporter of an active Russian policy in Outer
Mongolia. In a long memorandum of November 1910, he
described China's attempts to reduce Outer Mongolia to the
status of a province and the increase of Chinese military
garrisons in all chief centers, which were menacing Russia's
security. He advised that some strong protest should be
launched in Peking and China forced to promise not to change
the status quo in Outer Mongolia. For such an action he
thought it necessary to enlist at least the tacit support of
Great Britain and Japan.[42] Sazonov, the Foreign Minister,
thereupon made some enquiries of the Russian diplomatic
representatives in Great Britain and in Japan, in which he
stressed that the whole question was very complicated and
went to the very root of Russia's relations with China.[43] The
replies were not too encouraging. Malevski-Malevich reported
from Tokyo that the Japanese Foreign Minister had pointed
out the dangers of carrying out strong measures against China
which would weaken her still more in her particular position
and drive her into the arms of the United States and Germany.[44]
Count Benckendorff from London commented first of all on
the traditional British policy, especially favored by a liberal
cabinet, of non-interference in the internal affairs of the countries of Asia. As to the wider aspect of the question, he thought
it unlikely that the British Government would consider the

361-2), to Duma speech by Cadet Deputy S. V. Vostrotin, criticizing policy of the
Government, especially the Ministry of Commerce and Industry, from a military
point of view; cf. text preceding n. 84.

[42] Popov, p. 9, Despatch of Korostovets of November 3, 1910, file No. 104. Full
text in Benckendorff, Vol. I, No. 302, pp. 378-83.

[43] Popov, p. 9.

[44] *Ibid.*, Letter of Malevski-Malevich December 3, 1910 (no file no. indicated).

moment opportune for supporting a strong protest in Peking as this particular question and the military operations of China did not affect or threaten British interests. He rejected the idea of making a bargain with Great Britain over Tibet, but thought that developments in the Near East were more likely to influence England's attitude in the near future.[45]

It must be remembered that important negotiations were in progress at that time for the renewal of the Russo-Chinese treaty of St. Petersburg (1881) and that China adopted a most intransigent attitude, withholding from Russia permission to open a consulate at Khobdo in accordance with the provisions of the treaty, denying that the development of commerce necessitated such a step.[46] Events of the later part of the year 1911 such as the Chinese revolution and the declaration of the independence of " Mongolia " by some Mongol princes of Khalkha have tended to overshadow the acuteness of the tension between Russia and China at the end of 1910 and in the beginning of 1911, as it emerges from press-reports and communiqués of that time and the diplomatic correspondence published after the Great War.[47] In spite of much provocation and war rumors, Sazonov's policy in the Far East remained one of moderation. He considered it his duty to advise most urgently, as long as there was still time, against a military engagement in the Far East. " All our Ambassadors are like myself of the opinion that, in view of the present international constellation in Europe, a one-sided engagement of the Russian military forces in the Far East must be avoided." [48]

Nevertheless, it seems obvious that a direct link exists

[45] *Ibid.*, Letter of Benckendorff, December 10, 1910 (ditto); also Benckendorff, Vol. I, pp. 401-2 (cf. Chapter V, n. 26), telegram of December 7/20, 1910.

[46] *G. P.*, Vol. 32, pp. 214-', Memorandum of Russian Government of February 1911, concerning Russo-Chinese differences; also *ibid.*, No. 11793, The German Ambassador in St. Petersburg to Chancellor Bethmann-Hollweg, March 15, 1911, p. 218; also Isvolski, Vol. I, p. 27, No. 18, Sazonov to diplomatic representatives in Paris, London, Tokyo, February 2/15, 1914.

[47] *R. J.*, 1911-12; also A. Strupp's thesis (see bibliography), chiefly based on this publication.

[48] *G. P.*, Vol. 32, No. 11792, Minister in Vienna to Chancellor Bethmann-Hollweg, February 20, 1911, p. 216.

between the threat to Russia's interest in Outer Mongolia in the first half of 1911, on the one hand, and the declaration of independence of that region in the later part of 1911 on the other. The latter must be attributed in part to the work of Russian agents,[49] although it is not possible for us to estimate the extent of their activities. A report of a special Far Eastern Committee of Ministers of August 1911 admits that " several of our agents in Mongolia have helped to a considerable extent to create among the Mongols the opinion that they can count upon Russia in case they should try to break with China." [50] The departure for St. Petersburg in July 1911 of a delegation of Mongol princes to ask the Russian Government to take Khalkha under its protection was partly a result of the work of these agents. This request was anything but welcomed and was considered very embarrassing by the officials of the Foreign Ministry. The policy of the latter was still the same as in 1905 when it was laid down and approved by the Tsar, that moral support should be given to the Mongol princes [51] but that actual intervention in the internal affairs of the Mongols was not desirable. It was only due to pressure exercised by Stolypin, the President of the Council of Ministers, that Neratov, who was at that time acting Minister of Foreign Affairs, decided not to raise any objection to the visit of the Mongolian delegation.[52]

This attitude of the Ministry of Foreign Affairs was also clearly reflected in its wire to Korostovets of July 27, 1911, which stated that " the internal situation in Khalkha does not in any way touch our vital interests." Its importance lay in its potential use in achieving " our political tasks in China." [53]

[49] Popov, p. 7.

[50] Report of Special Council of Ministers, August 4, 1911, as cited by S. Shoizhelov, " Mongoliya i Tsarkaya Rossiya (Mongolia and Tsarist Russia), in *N. V.*, Vol. 13-14, 1926, p. 255.

[51] Secret Report of Kuskinski of September 4, 1905, Tel. No. 1151 and the Tsar's note on it of October 1, 1905, as cited in Popov, p. 8.

[52] Letter of the President of the Council of Ministers to Neratov, July 21, 1911, No. 3529, Popov, p. 12.

[53] Wire of Sazonov to Korostovets, July 27, 1911, File No. 1046, as cited by Popov, p. 9.

In the middle of July 1911 Neratov had submitted a report
to the Tsar enclosing wires from Korostovets and the acting
Consul in Urga referring to the desire of the Mongol princes
and clergy to ask Russia for help against the Chinese Government's withholding of " those rights of relative independence
which they used to have until now." After suggesting, as he
did a few days later in the above mentioned wire to Korostovets, that the movement among the Mongols could be made
use of in Russia's negotiations with China, he proposed that
in view of the connection of this question with wider problems
of commercial and financial interests and with the military
situation in the Far East, it would be desirable to submit
the whole subject to a thorough examination by a special
Committee of Ministers as was customary in affairs of this
character.[54]

This report was approved by the Tsar and the meeting took
place on August 4, 1911 under the chairmanship of Stolypin.
It was attended by Kokovtsov, the Finance Minister, Grigoro-
vich, the Navy Minister, Timashev, the Minister of Commerce
and Industry, Polivanov, Assistant War Minister, Shilinsky,
the head of the General Administration of the General Staff
and, of course, by Neratov, acting for Sazonov, the absent
Minister of Foreign Affairs. The resolution produced by the
Council (there is no record available of the discussion itself)
clearly stated the Russian Ministry of Foreign Affairs' reluctance " to play an active part in the Mongolian question,"
because " in doing so to weaken our influence in the West
would be rather undesirable." On the other hand, certain
features of Chinese policy and plans in " the strip of land
bordering with us," such as " the linking up of the same by
railways, at points which would be situated close to this frontier
with centers of Chinese administration and the redistribution
of the Chinese army, and especially the appearance in the close
neighborhood of our possessions of considerable Chinese armed
forces, cannot fail to disturb us. Therefore," concluded the

---

[54] Neratov's report to the Tsar of July 11, 1911, in S. Shoyshelov, *op. cit.*, p. 354.

Special Committee, " the Mongolian question is for us of great importance, and support of the Mongols in their desire to counteract the above mentioned activities of the Chinese Government would fully correspond with our interests." [55]

However, as Neratov, after receiving the Mongol delegation on their arrival in the beginning of August, pointed out to Korostovets on August 6, 1911, it was not in the Russian interest " to assist the Mongols to separate from China, owing to the present political situation." But as the Mongol leaders whom he had seen had admitted discord among themselves and their inability to fight against the Chinese, it was desirable to promise the deputation Russian help for the preservation of the former state of affairs in Khalkha.[56] The delegates had also expressed fear for their personal safety when returning to Urga. The guards of the Russian Consulate in Urga were, therefore, to be increased by 200 Cossacks equipped with machine guns.

Korostovets in Peking was instructed to call on the Chinese Ministers and point out to them that the Russian Government " cannot be indifferent to the way which the Chinese Government has chosen for its Mongolian policy. We are very closely concerned to keep Mongolia quiet as it is bordering with our possessions for many thousands of versts and as we have large commercial interests in Mongolia. Plans for administrative and military reforms in Mongolia advanced by the Chinese Government cause excitement among the Mongols which can easily spread into our possessions. The experiment of Inner Mongolia shows that the introduction of reforms produces bands of robbers with whom Chinese officials admit themselves to be unable to cope. It follows that administrative and military reforms planned by China for Khalkha may necessitate our taking certain steps to safeguard our borders which might lead to further tension of the situation in Khalkha. Finally, and this is the most important point, we draw the attention

[55] *Ibid.*, pp. 454-55; see n. 50.
[56] *Ibid.*, Secret wire of Neratov to Korostovets on August 6, 1911, file No. 228-229, p. 356.

of the Chinese Government to the fact that the planned reforms and especially the creation of a Chinese army in Mongolia will lead to a disturbance of the balance of power at the frontier. If the Peking Government is interested in the continuation and development of Sino-Russian friendship, it should consider our demands! . . . According to the success of your conversation it is desirable that you should by some means make the Chinese understand that we shall not remain indifferent to the fate of the Mongolian deputies and of the persons who have sent them and that this delegation is considered by us as a somewhat naive demonstration against Chinese regression, which, however, on no account deserves punishment." [57]

Kokovtsov, the Finance Minister, was especially worried about the fate of the returning Mongol delegation and insisted that the Ministry of Foreign Affairs should send a letter to the Chinese Government demanding the recall of the Chinese Amban (Resident) from Urga.[58] A Captain Makushek was appointed by the staff of the Irkutsk military district for the secret convoy of the members of the Mongolian delegation home. This officer sent a memorandum to the Ministry of Foreign Affairs which he called " The prospect of rebellion in Mongolia and the measures necessary for its success." A network of arms magazines under the flag of trading firms was to be formed and partisan troops organized to seize power. One of the leading officials of the Ministry of Foreign Affairs at that time, Kozokov, condemned the plan put forward by the memorandum in a marginal comment which reads " What nonsense! " [59]

Subsequent developments revealed that Captain Makushek's suggestions were not completely fantastic. Some sort of action on the part of Russia was inevitable since the Russians had promised the Mongols their support. In addition, it was unlikely that Korostovets's negotiations with the Chinese Government would soon be brought to a successful conclusion.

[57] *Ibid.*, p. 355.
[58] Popov, p. 12.
[59] Popov, p. 13.

The Foreign Minister, in a wire to Korostovets on August 10, 1911, considered it " possible in principle in case of failure of our representations in Peking and unavoidability of a rebellion in Khalkha " to deliver arms to the Mongols.[60] Two months later, in the middle of October 1911, Sukhomlinov, the War Minister, ordered the delivery of 15,000 rifles and 7 million cartridges to the staff of the Irkutsk military district.[61] When the Living Buddha in Urga, acting on behalf of the princes, demanded arms in the beginning of November 1911, they were delivered to the Mongols under the description of " private business firearms " together with 15,000 sabres.[62] The administrator of the Russian consulate in Urga knew all about the insurrection plans and was active in the distribution of the arms. It was he who announced in a wire, on November 18, 1911, the " overthrow " of the Chinese Government in Urga with the help of Russian arms and proclamation of Mongolia's independence.[63]

The position of the Russian Foreign Office during the last three months before the declaration of independence was thus a difficult one. On the one hand, they were pressed by the Russian Minister in Peking who not only had knowledge of the considerable ambitions of the Chinese Government in Mongolia, but also warned them that a refusal of support to the Mongols would lead to an impairment of Russian prestige and to the " encouragement of Japan, who would not hesitate to take our place " in Khalkha.[64] In addition, there is evidence of an increased interest of the Ministry of Finance. Kokovtsov, the Minister, was himself interested in Mongolian affairs as was also the Director of the General Chancery of his Ministry, Lvov.[65] It must be remembered that the conflict with China on the opening of a new Russian consulate in Khobdo was within the sphere of this department and even more so were

[60] Popov, Secret wire of August 10, No. 1125.

[61] Popov, Letter of Sukhomlinov to Sazonov of August 17, 1911, File No. 340.

[62] Popov, Letter of Sukhomlinov to Neratov, November 3, 1911, File No. 340.

[63] Popov, p. 14, Wire of November 18, 1911, File No. 1102.

[64] Popov, p. 12, Wire of Korostovets of July 30, 1911. Cf. Chapter V.

[65] Popov, referring to report of Captain Makushek of August 12, 1911.

China's attempts to raise a loan from the Consortium of Four, with which it might help to finance its plans in Mongolia.[66] The Russian Minister of War, Sukhomlinov, was prepared to rattle the sabre frequently.[67] Sazonov, the Foreign Minister, was himself abroad during these months. Neratov and Kozakov were, it appears, the officials of the Ministry of Foreign Affairs most closely concerned with Mongolian affairs. Their endeavor was much more concentrated on coming to some written agreement with China than to any sort of agreement with the Mongol princes. "Difficulties," wired Kozakov at the end of September 1911 to Korostovets, "which the revolutionary movement in the South of China created for the Chinese Government could be utilized by us to secure confirmation by some written act of our position in relation to the question of Mongolia's future. . . ."[68]

The fear was always in the minds of these officials that the Mongols would definitely break with China, which would put Russia in the actual presence of " the danger which threatens us of being compelled to defend Mongolia from Chinese oppression with armed force," and it is for this reason also that they rejected the proposal that they should take " Mongolia " under Russia's protection. In the end, they came to the conclusion that some sort of autonomous régime which would guarantee " Mongolia's individual life " was the solution to aim at and for which to try to obtain the consent of the Chinese Government.[69] It is hardly possible to hold these officials directly responsible for fostering " the declaration of independence of Mongolia," which was not their aim, as was shown by the attitude which they subsequently took. It must be remem-

[66] This problem became pressing in the first half of 1912. Cf. Chapter V. See also *G. P.*, Vol. 32, No. 11883, Aide-mémoire of the Russian Government of April 24/ May 6, 1912, p. 304; . . . Le Gouvernement Russe doit devoir clairement indiquer des à présent que les conditions de l'emprunt de reorganization ne devront contenir rien qui soit de nature à porter atteinte aux droits et intérêts speciaux de la Russie dans la Mandchourie du Nord, en Mongolie et dans " l'ouest chinois." For later developments see No. 11899, June 11, 1912, p. 327.

[67] Cf. Kokovtsov, *Memoirs, op. cit.*

[68] Popov, p. 13, Wire of Kokovtsov, September 30, 1911, file No. 1482.

[69] Popov, Wire of Kokovtsov, November 9, 1911, No. 1853.

bered that the extent of the Mongolian revolution was very small at the beginning, being practically confined to Urga, the seat of the Living Buddha and of the Chinese Amban. The Amban, with his family and staff sought protection in the Russian Consulate, whereupon some of the Russian Cossacks stationed in Urga accompanied them to the Siberian frontier from where they travelled home by the Trans-Siberian.[70]

Shortly after these happenings, on December 8, 1911, Neratov commented on them to the French Chargé d'Affaires. He admitted that the events in Mongolia were not entirely unexpected but said that he had not thought them to be so near and that the actual circumstances caused him " some perplexity." He asked himself how such a vast territory, deprived of all means of communication, could be administered since the Chinese officials were already on their way home. Russia besides her Consular agents had only 200 Cossacks in Urga. If it were possible to anticipate the re-establishment of a strong government in Peking, Russia would probably intervene to conclude with the Chinese Government an agreement which would regulate the status of Mongolia and China's as well as Russia's relations with her. That is to say Russia would accord her moral support to the Mongols without being obliged to intervene directly in their affairs. Such an intervention might give rise to many difficulties, even to suspicion in the minds of other powers. The French Chargé d'Affaires replied that it was comprehensible that the Russian Government should show some reserve in expressing the satisfaction which it must feel " while so many other serious subjects claim her attention." [71]

In an official communiqué issued at the end of December 1911, the Russian Government explained its position thus: The Mongols on declaring their independence and having

[70] See Official communiqué from Ministry of Foreign Affairs, published in " Official Messenger," December 28, 1911 (January 11, 1912), in *BPCMD*, China No. 3, 1912, p. 68 (p. 440). Also in Grimm, No. 73, pp. 178-79; cf. also Neratov's conversation with French Chargé d'Affaires DDF, 3 serie, Tome I, No. 321, December 8, 1911, p. 310; Grimm, No. 73, p. 178.

[71] *DDF.*, Tome I, No. 321, etc., *op. cit.*, p. 311.

elected the Urga Living Buddha Khan of Mongolia appealed to the Russian Government for support. The Russian Government advised the Mongols to act with moderation and to find a basis for an agreement with China. The Russian Consul at Urga made his moderating influence felt by stopping the destruction of the Kalgan-Kiakhta telegraph line, preventing the plundering of the branch of the Ta Ch'ing (Chinese) Bank in Urga, and assisted the Chinese Amban to leave Mongolia. In the meantime the Peking Government had appointed a high official, Kueh Fan, to negotiate with the Mongols. This official inquired of the Russian Chargé d'Affaires whether he could rely on the friendly mediation of the Imperial consulate in Urga in these negotiations. At the same time the Russian Government was asked by the Mongols to mediate between them and the Chinese.

The Russian Government considered these two requests favorably. It was very desirable that the Chinese and the Mongols should come to an understanding which could be embodied in some act guaranteeing a new status to Mongolia. The acceptance of three conditions demanded by the Mongols was essential: they were directed against those measures which the Chinese had thought fit to introduce in Mongolia in recent years, i. e. the establishment of a Chinese administration, the formation of Chinese regular troops, and the colonization of Mongolia by Chinese. These three points could be taken as a basis for a possible agreeemnt. It was on this basis that the Russian Government, as it had declared to the Chinese Government through the Chargé d'Affaires in Peking, was prepared to act as mediator between the Chinese and the Mongols. If the Chinese Government would negotiate on this basis, Russian diplomacy would be directed towards inducing the Mongols not to sever their connection with China and to observe the obligations taken upon themselves. At the same time, the Russian Government expressed its readiness to give its friendly support to the carrying out in Mongolia of all necessary measures, whether administrative, or economic, or cultural.

At the end of the communiqué a warning voice added that Russia could not but be interested in the establishment of lasting order in the territory adjoining Siberia in which Russia had large commercial interests, and that an armed struggle between Mongols and Chinese was not desirable, " because our interests would inevitably suffer thereby." Moreover, " these large interests in Mongolia do not permit the Imperial Government to ignore the Government which has been practically established in that country. If Mongolia severs her connection with China, the Imperial Government, with every desire to see the Sino-Mongolian dispute ended, will be compelled by force of circumstances to enter into business relations with the Mongolian Government." [72]

Directly after the publication of this communiqué on Mongolia, Sazonov declared to the French Ambassador that Russia did not intend to take this immense country as she already had more than enough territory.[73] To the British Ambassador he remarked that the idea of annexing Mongolia would be " positively insane." [74] On the French diplomat's inquiring what Russia would do if the Mongols were not able to govern themselves, which Sazonov had admitted was " doubtful," the answer was forthcoming that Russia might increase the Consular Guard in Urga " and perhaps do something more . . . but not annexation." [75] The " something more " was described to the British Ambassador as consisting for instance in the sending of military instructors to the Mongols if a request were made. But it was also not Russia's intention to establish a protectorate as " she had no desire to take over administrative duties." He admitted, however, that it was doubtful whether the Mongols would recognize China's suzerainty if the Central Government in China were to assume a republican form, and

---

[72] Cf. n. 70.
[73] *DDF.*, Tome I, No. 462, M. Georges Louis to Minister of Foreign Affairs, January 12, 1912.
Edward Grey, January 14, 1912.
[75] Cf. n. 73.
[74] *BPCMD.*, China No. 3, 1912, p. 42 (p. 414'; No. 41, Sir G. Buchanan to Sir

that in such a contingency Russia would have to recognize Mongolia's independence if it were declared.[76]

In his speech in the Duma on April 13, 1912, however, Sazonov explained why Russia was not prepared to recognize or admit the independence of Khalkha or Outer Mongolia and the same reasons were repeatedly impressed on the Mongols themselves: " The Khalkhas are not prepared by their history for independent government. Being nomads, for centuries accustomed to obey the Peking Government, the Mongols of Khalkha possess neither a military nor a financial organization, nor leaders, without whom an independent state is impossible. To tear them away from China would, therefore, demand that we assume the task of organizing a state, a difficult task, which would cause great financial expense and enormous labor. At the same time Khalkha would be in permanent danger of being reconquered by the Chinese, and the duty would evolve upon us to defend her with the power of our arms. A complete breach between Khalkha and China would put us in a dilemma: either to occupy Khalkha or to retreat from it and to readmit the Chinese on the strength of the right of the conqueror. We have tried to avoid this dilemma and we have declared ourselves ready to undertake mediation between the Chinese and the Mongols for the conclusion of such a compromise as would, as far as possible, respect the wishes of the Mongols to preserve their peculiar customs, and the wish of China to reestablish her suzerainty over Mongolia. Peace could only be preserved in Khalkha if she knew that her two powerful neighbors, Russia and China, had come to an agreement about her future." [77]

On the whole we may discern in this speech a moderate tone especially if we consider that Russia was in an advantageous position in regard to a China in the midst of a revolution. Moreover, it was consistent with the Foreign Minister's aversion to an active policy in the Far East. In December 1911, i. e. about the time of the declaration of independence, on his way home from a holiday abroad, he had expressed to the

[76] *BPCMD., op. cit.,* n. 74, p. 43 (p. 415).
[77] Cited by Grumm-G., Vol. 2, pp. 748-49.

French Ambassador in Berne his dislike of a too rapid development of Russia's Asiatic policy and his regret of " the imprudent impulse towards the Far East, which was given to Russian foreign policy some years ago." [78] Korostovets, the Minister in Peking, then trying in a personal interview at the end of 1911 to persuade Sazonov to adopt a stronger policy in Mongolian affairs, was told point blank that " Russia must be a European and not an Asiatic Power," [79] and the German Chargé d'Affaires was told a year later that Russia did not wish " to increase its burdens along its long southern frontier." [80]

There was, of course, some opposition in Russia to this moderate policy. Korostovets, in later years, commented very unfavorably on the passive attitude of the Foreign Minister, while giving Kokovtsov, the Finance Minister credit, as " the principal promoter of our agreement with Mongolia." [81] Some newspapers were also not too well pleased. The much cited " Novoye Vremya " which, according to Count Witte, was a " powerful organ of the press . . . favored by the highest court circles including the Emperor," [82] though taking a moderate attitude in December 1911, two months later urged the Government to take immediate action in Mongolia (and Chinese Turkistan). Mongolia needed political advisers, and unrest in a country so near was a menace to Russia. Money advanced for administration and army organization was secured by the wealth the country had to offer. " Time presses. Russian diplomacy has no skill in creating conditions favorable to itself. In this case the conditions have arisen of themselves and all that remains to be done is to take advantage of them." The nationalist paper " Soviet " demanded a Russian protectorate for Mongolia. The opposition organ " Rech " emphatically rejected this scheme and thought the limit to which Russia

[78] *DDF.*, Tome I, p. 283, p. 297, French Minister in Berne to Minister of Foreign Affairs, December 5, 1911.

[79] Korostovets, p. 128.

[80] *GP.*, Vol. 32, No. 11996, p. 432, The German Chargé d'Affaires in St. Petersburg to Chancellor Bethmann-Hollweg.

[81] Korostovets, p. 268.

[82] Witte, *Memoirs, op. cit.*, pp. 176-77.

could go without violating the status quo in the Far East was to support Mongolia's endeavors to become an independent buffer-state between her and China.[83] In the course of the years following the events at the end of 1911, there were repeated criticisms from publicists and also from a few members of the Duma who urged an active policy for Mongolia, as much to increase the military security of the Russian frontier as for economic reasons.[84]

In the middle of 1912 Korostovets was sent as special envoy to Urga in order to negotiate an agreement with the Mongols. This decision was taken by the Ministry of Foreign Affairs not only because the Chinese Republic did not manifest any desire to come to terms with Russia on the Mongolian question but also out of apprehension that Chinese intrigues at Urga, or the influence of some pro-Chinese princes, might bring about a separate Sino-Mongol understanding in which Russia would have no voice. Such an understanding might have prejudiced the three conditions which were set out in the official communiqué of the end of November 1911 and in Sazonov's speech in the Duma in April, with the approval of the Tsar: (1) that the administration of Khalkha should be left to a national government. (2) that Chinese troops should not be permitted to enter this territory. (3) that the colonization of Mongolian land by Chinese should cease. From the Russian point of view these conditions could be guaranteed only if the Imperial Government received " the legal right of originating and carrying out such measures as shall in future be required in Khalkha."

Hence, " seeing clearly that it was impossible to agree with the Chinese who did not wish to recognize the change of the situation in Mongolia,, the Imperial Government have decided to get into touch with the Urga Government directly," and " By this we recognize Mongolia as a legal person and sanction its demand for autonomy." [85]

---

[83] *BPCMD.*, No. 66, Sir G. Buchanan to Sir Edward Grey, January 17, 1912, p. 96 (p. 468) and No. 144, the same, March 9, 1912, p. 20 (p. 572); see also *DDF.*, Tome I, No. 321, pp. 311-12.

[84] See n. 41.

[85] *O. B.*, No. 1, Letter of Sazonov to Korostovets, August 23, 1912, pp. 1-2.

The instructions of Korostovets remained rigorously confined to the recognition of the autonomy of the Mongols of Khalkha and not to meeting the aim of the leading men in Urga—the recognition of " the independence of Mongolia." [86] The latter would not only have meant complete separation from China, involving international complications because of violation of the principle of the integrity of China, but would have involved pressure to include in the new state other territory inhabited by Mongols, such as Inner Mongolia, Barga, Urianghai and Altai. This would have transcended the limits of Russian foreign policy, for Inner Mongolia would have infringed on the Japanese sphere of influence; to include Barga, at the northeastern corner of Khalkha, would have given rise to constant military friction with the Chinese; over Urianghai, northwest of Khalkha, Russia for various reasons (which we will examine later) preferred a protectorate; and in the Altai district, which up to 1907 had belonged to Mongolia, Prince Palta preferred Chinese rule to union with Khalkha.

Korostovets had a difficult task to perform. On the one hand he was bound by instructions which countenanced only an " internal autonomy " for Khalkha as against the " external independence of the Mongol State," which the Mongols demanded in order to be able to enter into relations with other states. On the other hand, he wanted to come to an agreement with the Mongols which confirmed the rights and privileges acquired for Russian trade and would continue to safeguard the interests of Russian subjects.[87] He also wished the Mongols to give assurances that they would not grant foreigners wider rights than those which Russians had.[88] The refusal of Russia to meet the repeated demands of the Mongols

---

[86] Cf. his speech in the Duma, n. 77. Russia stuck to this policy also in the treaty with the Mongols (see below). A letter sent by the nephew of Korostovets (Vladimir de Korostovetts) to Editor of Royal Central Asian Soc. Journal, Vol. XXIII, October 1936, Part IV, p. 721, claiming that " the treaty he (J. J. Korostovets) signed was that of recognition of ' Mongolian Independence " misses completely, therefore, this point of Russian policy."

[87] *O. B.*, No. 6, Korostovets to Sazonov, September 27, 1912, p. 5.

[88] *O. B.*, No. 1, p. 2.

to include Inner Mongolia in the new state increased the anti-Russian intrigues of the Chinese as well as of the pro-Chinese Mongol Ministers such as Da Lama, the Minister of the Interior. Sazonov instructed Korostovets to warn the Mongols that Russia would not recognize a Sino-Mongol agreement concluded without Russia's participation and would prefer to come to an agreement with the Chinese Government on Mongolia's fate. " Our interests in this country do not permit us to be satisfied with those promises which Chinese would give the Mongols as we do not doubt that they would be broken on the first possible occasion and we must provide a guarantee that such a breach of faith will not take place." [89] Mongolian demands for a Russian representative in Urga of the rank of Minister were rejected, a Diplomatic Agent being appointed by way of compromise. The counterpart, i. e. a Mongolian representative in Russia, was considered " undesirable," except in the form of a special mission which could depart for St. Petersburg after the signing of the Russo-Mongolian agreement. [90]

When the Princes had given up insisting on their " Mongol imperialism," as the Russian Foreign Ministry described it later [91] i. e. agitation for the inclusion of Inner Mongolia and other territories in the agreement, they asked Russia to agree to the substitution of the word " Mongolia " for " Outer Mongolia " in the treaty text. Russia was prepared to concede this, because it kept open the question of territorial limits, and without committing Russia was an overt threat to China of an extension of the agreement to other territories which might join Khalkha. [92] But Korostovets was instructed to specify in an

[89] *O.B.*, No. 10, Sazonov to Korostovets, September 1912, p. 8.

[90] *O.B.* For first draft of Russo-Mongol agreement see No. 16, p. 12, Art. 4; " The Russian Government appoints for permanent stay a Resident Minister to Urga. On the other hand, the Ruler of Mongolia and the Mongolian Government can, if required, send a Minister to the capital of Russia." And No. 21, Sazonov to Korostovets, October 18, 1912, p. 21, approves the signing of the agreement but for Art. 4, which was to be excluded.

[91] *K.A.*, Vol. 37, Draft of letter by Kokovzov to Minister of Finance, p. 34.

[92] *O.B.*, No. 12, Korostovets to Sazonov, October 1, 1912, No. 12; No. 13, Sazonov to Korostovets, October 3, 1912, p. 9.

exchange of notes or by unilateral declaration to what territories beside Khalkha itself Russia would extend the guaranteed autonomous rights given to Mongolia.[93] Korostovets
thereupon replied, " In declaring my consent to the replacement
of the words ' Outer Mongolia ' by the word ' Mongolia,' I have
the honor to declare that the Imperial Government reserves
the right to determine to what territories beside Khalkha the
guarantees of autonomous rights given to the Mongolian Government should apply." [94]

The Russians were so alive to the possibility that Mongols
might one day acquiesce in the Chinese demands that they
believed it necesary to add to the stipulated right of the
Mongols to be ruled by their princes, an obligation not to
renounce this form of government. This was, in Sazonov's
words, indispensable. " For our interests and for the Chinese
it will serve as a proof of our and the Mongols' determination
not to tolerate the transformation of Khalkha into a Chinese
province." Russia insisted also on special mention of the
inadmissibility of Chinese colonization in Khalkha, because,
though having no doubt about the present Mongolian Government's determination in this respect, " we must foresee the
possibility of a change in the point of view of their successors
in this matter." [95]

When the Russo-Mongol agreement was finally signed on
November 3, 1912, (October 21, old Russian calendar), Russia
had achieved those aims which Sazonov had sketched in his
original instructions. In a special protocol annexed to the
agreement Russia's trade rights in Mongolia were enumerated
in detail: her subjects could trade free of duty; they were
everywhere to have the right to hold allotments on lease or to
acquire them as their own property for the purpose of
organizing commercial and industrial establishments; they were
also allowed to lease vacant lands for cultivation. The Russian
Government was to have the right to appoint, in agreement

[93] *O.B.*, No. 13, Sazonov to Korostovets, October 3, 1912, p. 10.
[94] *O.B.*, No. 25, Korostovets to Sazonov, October 22, 1912, p. 31.
[95] *O.B.*, No. 13, *op. cit.*, p. 10, point 2.

with the Government of Mongolia, consuls in those parts of Mongolia it deemed necessary.[96] The consuls could avail themselves of postal establishments of the Mongolian Government, whereas Russian subjects retained the right to institute at their own cost a postal service for the transport of letters and wares. So Russia entered into " business relations " with Khalkha and recognized that, as the preamble of the agreement says, " the old relations between Mongolia and China thus came to an end." [97]

The only country from which the Mongols were able to obtain the recognition of their " independence " was Tibet with which they concluded a treaty shortly after the Russo-Mongolian agreement in Urga in January 1913. In this treaty Mongolia and Tibet recognized each other as independent states, mutually promised assistance against danger without and within, and support of Lama Buddhism. The Mongols signed this " rather harmless " agreement for the sake of prestige. They wanted to sign a treaty with a nation other than Russia which especially recognized their " independence " and whose position in relation to China was similar to their own.

While Korostovets had successfully concluded the negotiations with the Mongols, Krupenskii, the Russian Minister in Peking, had negotiated with the Chinese Government. It was pointed out to the Chinese Government that " we do not wish to recognize Mongolia as independent from China, but we cannot help but see that such independence has already existed de facto for over a year. It will depend on China as to how far we shall go in recognizing this fact." [98] The Chinese Government was also told that if, in spite of warnings, it should despatch troops against Western Mongolia (Kobdo), this " would force us to reexamine our attitude to Mongolia both from the point of view of her proclaimed independence as well as from that of the territorial extent of Autonomous Mongolia." [99]

[96] *O. B.*, point 3.
[97] MacMurray, Vol. II, pp. 992-96.
[97a] CYB 1914, p. 629.
[98] *O. B.*, No. 19, Sazonov to Krupenskii, October 16, 1912, p. 19.
[99] *O. B.*, p. 20; cf. also No. 2, p. 3, No. 4, p. 4.

A few days after the signature of the Russo-Mongol agreement Russia officially communicated the text to China, explaining that " our undefined position forces us to enter into de facto relations with the Government existing there." [100] The aim of Russia was now to get China's confirmation of the essential points of this agreement and especially of Outer Mongolia's status of autonomy and the prohibition of Chinese colonization. It was difficult to get the new Chinese Government's consent to these stipulations as the feelings of the new parliament of the Republic ran high when the text of the Russo-Mongol agreement became known, and when they heard that an official Mongol deputation had started for St. Petersburg to thank the Russian Government.[101] The Russian Consul in Kalgan reported military preparations and concentration of Chinese troops in districts bordering Outer Mongolia.[102] A despatch of these troops into Khalkha would be regarded, so the Chinese Government was informed, as tantamount to an act of war.[103]

The first treaty draft submitted by the Chinese in no way took account of the changed situation, since it insisted on China's sovereign (not suzerain) right in Khalkha, including the right of the Chinese Government to conclude all treaties, including those of a commercial character, on behalf of that territory.[104] Russia thereupon drew the attention of the Chinese Government to the fact that it was not Russia but the Chinese Government which was interested in a recognition by the Mongols of their link with China; that it was, therefore, not for China to put forward demands, but for the Russian Government to ask China to take upon herself certain obligations.[105]

---

[100] *O. B.*, No. 26, Sazonov to Krupenskii, October 24, 1912, p. 31.

[101] *O. B.*, No. 18, p. 18, No. 19, p. 20; No. 46, Sazonov to Krupenskii, December 5, 1912, p. 46: " You can tell the Chinese Foreign Minister that we do not consider it possible to prevent the departure of the Mongolian delegation from Urga."

[102] *O. B.*, No. 45, Krupenskii to Sazonov, No. 30, 1912, p. 45; also No. 35, p. 37 and No. 38, p. 38.

[103] *O. B.*, No. 48, Sazonov to Krupenskii, December 10, 1912, p. 48.

[104] *O. B.*, No. 41, Text in French, p. 42.

[105] *O. B.*, No. 48, pp. 48-9; cf. also No. 29, p. 33.

Though the next Chinese draft was more conciliatory, it aimed directly at the Russo-Mongolian commercial protocol when it stipulated that " all privileges accorded by the Mongols to foreign countries or to their nationals should not be valid unless approved by the Chinese Republic." [106] Sazonov's reply to this pretension was plain enough: " We consider it useless to sign an agreement with the Chinese Government concerning Mongolia which would not define the question of the commercial right of Russian subjects in this country." The Russo-Mongolian Urga Protocol was described as in essence merely confirming the Russo-Chinese agreement of St. Petersburg.[107]

At the end of April 1913, China was strongly warned that if she persisted in delaying and in the meantime agitated against Russia among the Mongol princes, Russia would " enter into new relations with the Mongolian Government, and then negotiate on a completely different basis with the Chinese Government." [108] It was not to be wondered that this threat was seized upon by anti-Russian agitators in Urga; and Korostovets in an interview with the Living Buddha at the end of August 1913 had to reassure him that Russia did not intend to establish a protectorate in Khalka, for if she had intended to do so, she had already had many opportunities. He emphasized, however, that Russia " never promised full independence to Mongolia as we have no reason to undertake such a task." The Hutukhtu saw difficulties in Mongolia's recognizing any ties with the Chinese Government by accepting its " suzerainty." [109] But shortly afterwards the Mongols pressed the Russians to permit them to participate in the negotiations with China and demanded that Russia should act as a mediator in a treaty of peace between Mongolia and China.[110]

Russia desired to have this rôle of mediator recognized by China, as it would give some definition to Russia's special

---

[106] *O. B.*, No. 47, Text in French, point 5, p. 48.

[107] *O. B.*, No. 60, Sazonov to Krupenskii, March 12, 1913, p. 51.

[108] *O. B.*, No. 66, April 24, 1913, p. 60.

[109] *O. B.*, No. 68, Korostovets to Sazonov, August 30, 1913, p. 61.

[110] *O. B.*, No. 81, Sazonov to Krupenskii, August 14, 1913, pp. 71-2; cf. also No. 84, Neratov to Krupenskii, September 11, 1913, p. 76.

position in Mongolia and would also prevent direct negotiations between China and Mongolia from which Russia would be excluded. Russia had really not much to offer to China except recognition of her suzerainty over Outer Mongolia. Even a demand for an acknowledgment that Mongolia was an integral part of China was not at first accepted; [111] but eventually Russia agreed in a special exchange of notes to recognize that the territory of Outer Mongolia formed a part of the territory of China.

Territory and political questions affecting Mongolia were not to be settled by the Chinese Government alone but were to be left for discussion by a tripartite conference. But in the exchange of notes already mentioned the territory of " Autonomous Outer Mongolia " was defined as including [112] the regions which had been under the jurisdiction of the Chinese Amban of Khobdo, which was a great advance on China's original proposal only to include the Urga district and perhaps the Tushetu Khan and Tsetsen Khan Aimaks. The exact boundaries of Outer Mongolia, however, as well as the boundary between the district of Khobdo and Altai were to be referred to the tripartite conference. [113]

In the declaration itself, which was finally signed on November 5, 1913, Russia recognized China's suzerainty over Outer Mongolia and in exchange received China's recognition of Outer Mongolia's autonomy. In addition, China recognized the Mongols' right to provide for their own internal administration and " to settle all questions of a commercial and industrial nature," and promised not to send troops to Outer Mongolia and to abstain from colonization. Russia was to keep no troops in Outer Mongolia except consular guards. Finally, China declared herself " ready to accept the good offices of Russia for the establishment of its relations with Outer Mongolia " in conformity with these principles and with the

---

[111] *O. B.*, No. 89, Neratov to Krupenskii, September 11, 1913, p. 76.

[112] *O. B.*, see for negotiations also No. 90, p. 77, and No. 91, pp. 78-9.

[113] *O. B.*, No. 93, Neratov to Krupenskii, September 22, 1913, p. 80; No. 94, Krupenskii to Neratov, September 25, 1912; No. 95, Neratov to Krupenskii, September 28, 1913, pp. 81, 82.

stipulations of the Russo-Mongolian Commercial Protocol of October 21, 1912 (November 3, 1912).[114]

Having thus successfully obtained a recognition of Outer Mongolia's autonomy from China, roughly one year after her own treaty with the Mongols and two years after Mongolia's own declaration of independence, Russia now directed her efforts to finding a stable basis for the status of Outer Mongolia by pressing the Mongols to participate in a tripartite conference. The diplomatic agent in Urga, A. Miller, who communicated the text of the declaration as well as the exchange of notes between Russia and China to the Mongolian Government, had again to explain to the Mongolian Ministers that full separation from China was impossible and that Russia was never willing to defend their full independence against China, nor to fight for the inclusion of Inner Mongolia in the territory of Outer Mongolia. But Russia would support the Mongols' demands within the limits which were fixed by the Russo-Chinese declaration.[115] The Russian policy toward the Mongols after the Russo-Chinese Declaration was, in Miller's words, to calm them with the hope of results from triple negotiations.[116]

An additional way to counteract any "shaking of Mongol faith" in the Russians was proposed by Miller. "Opportune financial assistance . . . especially at present . . . will strengthen their confidence in us." [117] Russia had given a loan of two million rubles in January 1913, but by November 1913 it was "almost totally spent." Therefore, when Sain Noyan Khan, the Mongolian Prime Minister, arrived in St. Petersburg in that month, his mission was aimed first of all at securing financial help from the Russian Government. It was necessary for the Russian Government, as a letter from the Minister of Foreign Affairs—drawn up by Kazakov—to Kokovtsov, the

[114] *O.B.*, No. 105, pp. 87-90, in Russian; in English in MacMurray, Vol. 2, pp. 1066-67.

[115] *O.B.*, No. 106, Sazonov to Miller, October 25, 1913 (Instructions), p. 91; No. 107, Miller to Sazonov, November 2, 1913, p. 91.

[116] *K.A.*, Vol. 37, Telegram of Miller, November 2/15, 1913, No. 303, p. 21.

[117] *K.A.*, Despatch of Miller, November 8/21, 1913, No. 312 (last paragraph), p. 27.

Finance Minister, pointed out, "to take advantage of Sain Noyan Khan's sojourn in St. Petersburg in order to attract him completely to our side and to have in his person a support for our activities in Mongolia. . . . It is very important to support Sain Noyan Khan and not to let him go back with empty hands. Therefore, we have to think over how we can satisfy his . . . request for a 'loan '." A credit amounting to two or three million rubles was envisaged although Sain Noyan Khan asked for five million rubles.[118] The Russians from the beginning of the negotiations laid stress on the condition that it could not be put at the disposal of the Mongolian Government without Russian control.[119] "There is no limit to the light-mindedness of the Mongols regarding the spending of money," was Miller's comment at the end of 1913.[120] But it was only after the Russian Government had refused to obtain an audience with the Tsar for Sain Noyan Khan and threatened not to recognize his position as a plenipotentiary equipped with full powers [121] that he signed, shortly before his return home early in 1914, a contract appointing Kosin, a Russian, adviser for the organization of the finances of the Mongolian Government, for the administration of state property and for the outlining of reforms.[122] He later took charge also of the administration of public revenues and of the treasury.[123] As to the details of the contract with Kosin, the project of making the loan dependent upon the prolongation of the original contract from three to thirty years was considered "disadvantageous to our political situation," because "this demand would convey"—to the Mongols—"a deep impression of long financial enslavement." The right of administration was considered a sufficient guarantee and "the Foreign Ministry firmly counted on the Russian Government possessing so much influence and importance in Mongolia that

[118] *K. A.*, Draft of letter of Minister of Foreign Affairs to Kokovzov, pp. 34, 35.
[119] *IBZI.*, Vol. I, 1, No. 91, Sazonov to Miller, January 11/24, 1914, p. 78.
[120] *K. A.*, Miller to Sazonov, December 16/29, No. 368, p. 47.
[121] *K. A.*, Letter of Sazonov to Miller, January 17/30, 1914, p. 66.
[122] *Ibid.*
[123] *IBZI.*, Vol. I, 1, p. 78, n. 2. Contract of December 25, 1913/January 7, 1914.

it would always be able to effect such prolongation of financial control as might appear necessary, without suddenly frightening the Mongols with the prospect of losing the right of free disposal of their revenues for decades." [124] As to the loan agreement itself, signed in July 1914, the new loan amounted to three million rubles, given without interest. It was to be used for the rehabilitation of finances, for internal reforms, the improvement of cattle-breeding and " for the maintenance and training of the army with the help of Russian and Mongolian instructors." Security for the loan was to be obtained by duties and the revenues of foreign trade. If the receipts of foreign trade should prove to be an insufficient guarantee, the Mongolian Government promised to give an additional one. Repeated unpunctuality in payment was to give the Russian Government the right to establish an effective control of the revenues which served as a guarantee for the loan and to administer them on the Mongolian Government's account.[125] In the negotiations for a loan as during the discussion of other points, the Russian Government was anxious to exclude the possibility of the Mongols' borrowing from foreign sources, especially from the Chinese, who by familiar methods might have been able to re-establish their influence. Rumors that China had offered to repay on the Mongols' behalf the loan given by Russia and had also offered credits to the Mongolian Government were denied by the Chinese Foreign Minister upon strong Russian diplomatic remonstrances to Peking. The Russians intimated that if the Chinese Government continued to disregard Mongolia's autonomy, Russia would have no reason to exert her moderating influence on Urga—which consisted chiefly in insistence that the Mongolian Government should give up its war-like designs upon China.[126]

[124] *IBZI.*, Vol. I, 4, Sazonov to Finance Minister Back, June 23/July 6, 1914, p. 102.

[125] *IBZI.*, Vol. I, 4, No. 315, Miller to Sazonov, July 8/21, 1914, pp. 284-85 (final text of loan agreement); cf. also original draft of First Councillor of Russian Ministry of Foreign Affairs, Vol. 1, 3, No. 242, p. 221.

[126] *IBZI.*, Vol. I, 1, No. 279, Sazonov to Krupenskii, February 6/19, 1914, p. 266; see also *ibid.*, n. 1, Answer of Krupenskii of February 10/23, 1914, No. 67, communicating denial of such Chinese action by Chinese Foreign Minister.—Original

Miller, the Russian Diplomatic Agent in Urga, believed that if, in addition to the appointment of a Russian Financial Adviser, a Russian bank were established in Urga, the two together would "help the Mongols to oppose Chinese and foreign economic pressure." [127] As early as October 1912 the Mongols had given the concession for a Mongolian National bank to financiers connected with the Russo-Asiatic bank and the International Commerce bank, as well as to a Swiss citizen. The Russians connected with this concession were the State-Councillor Juferov, a financier named Moskvitin, and a banker named Savaiko, and the concession of 1912 was always referred to as the Juferov concession.[128] It was not taken up, however, and only a threat from the Mongolian Government to the Russian Diplomatic agent that they would declare the concession void if no use were made of it and give it to some foreign concern or person, brought the matter before a special inter-ministerial conference in July 1914. The Tsar himself had on two occasions commented on this matter by putting " The matter needs despatch" on the bottom of Miller's reports.[129] The Finance Minister did not have much success however, in arousing any enthusiasm for the opening of a Russian bank in Mongolia by Russian private banks which insisted on guarantees from the Russian Government against possible losses due to political complications. Two offers were finally made, one from the Russo-Asiatic Bank and the other from the Siberian Commercial Bank; the latter was preferred by the Finance Ministry " as it requires less expenditure by the Imperial treasury." [130] As the political side of the question

news on Chinese offer transmitted by Miller in telegram, February 3/16, 1914, No. 35, *ibid.*, p. 265, n. 3. The Tsar annotated this report with a " Serious warning" on February 7/20, 1914.

[127] *K. A.*, Vol. 37, Despatch of Miller, November 8/21, 1913, No. 312, p. 27.

[128] *IBZI.*, Vol. I, 3, No. 148, Miller to Sazonov, May 20/June 2, 1914, p. 137, and *ibid.*, n. 2: Concession of Juferov on October 3/16, 1912; also Vol. I, 2, p. 425.

[129] *IBZI.*, p. 138, n. 3. Letter of Miller, May 24/June 6, 1914, No. 1361; Tsar's comment *ibid.*, Vol. I, 1, No. 137, Miller to Sazonov, January 16/29, 1914—comment of January 17/30, 1914, p. 443—comment of February 18/March 3, 1914; cf. n. 68 of Chapter V.

[130] *IBZI.*, Vol. I, 4, No. 241, Report of discussion of Inter-Ministerial Conference

was of great importance the interministerial conference considered all aspects of the organization of such a Russian credit institution. It could take the form either of an independent bank or of a branch of a bank operating in Russia itself; but it was found that neither the first form nor the second would give the bank the right to issue its own notes. The interministerial conference concluded, therefore, that it would be necessary to create a special form of bank in Mongolia which would be regarded by the Mongols as their National Bank which they themselves had intended to found by offering a concession for it to a private person. In addition, the advantage of a Mongolian National Bank instead of a private bank would be that it would be able " to accomplish certain other functions of political character which await the bank in the future." [131]

The plan for the Mongolian National Bank worked out by the Credit-Chancellory in collaboration with the Siberian Commercial Bank was based on the Juferov concession of 1912. It would have the sole right to issue banknotes and organize their circulation. The creation of such legal machinery of payment was also considered essential to facilitate the trade relations between Russia and Mongolia. The directorate of the bank was to be established in St. Petersburg, the administration in Urga. Two officials of the Mongolian Government were to be admitted as advisers and the Mongolian Government had the right to buy the whole of the bank after five years. If this right were not exercised the whole property of the bank would pass into the possession of the Mongolian Government after eighty years. The Mongolian Government would protect the bank against any losses and in emergencies recover amounts owed to it. In addition, the branches of the bank were to be under the protection of the Russian Government. The first share capital was fixed at a million rubles of which 200,000 rubles were to be paid for the transferred concession. The rest of the capital was to be divided among the founders of the

of July 2/15, 1914, p. 220; cf. *ibid.*, No. 108, Miller to Neratov, June 23, July 6, 1914.

[131] *IBZI.*, pp. 221, 222.

bank. Later capital could be raised with the authorization of the Russian Ministry of Finance. The bank could not begin to operate before 500,000 rubles had been paid in, excluding the costs of the concession, and not later than six months from the date on which the Tsar should give his assent to the statutes.[132] It was officially opened in May of 1915.[133]

The monopolistic character conferred on the bank gave Russia the right to object when the Chinese tried to establish a colonial bank in Urga in September 1915. Miller pointed out to them the undesirability of their giving permission for this undertaking. The Chinese bank intended not only to finance Chinese colonization, which was contrary to the St. Petersburg declaration, but also to issue its own notes, which would infringe the monopoly of the Mongolian National Bank.[134] The refusal of the Mongolian Government to give permission to the Chinese was, in the words of Sazonov, " a great success for us." The government also acknowledged the exclusive right of the Mongolian National Bank to issue notes and coins,[135] although it appears that the bank did not make use of the right to issue notes. Miller complained in a telegram to the Russian Foreign Minister in April 1916 that this fact made it more and more difficult to counter attempts to open Chinese banks, although no Chinese bank actually materialized during the Tsarist Russian period.[136]

Russia could also exercise her " moderating influence " by threatening to withhold supplies of arms from the Mongols. Another purpose of Sain Noyan Khan's visit to St. Petersburg had been to ask for a new arms supply. Nearly the whole amount of the first two million loan had been spent on the

---

[132] *IBZI.*, pp. 222-23; Vol. I, 5, No. 273, July 17/30, 1914, pp. 190-91, Council of Ministers agrees to proposal.

[133] *IBZI.*, Vol. II, 8, 2, p. 635, n. 2: Bank opened May 14/27, 1915. Telegram of Chionin of same date, No. 1318.

[134] *IBZI.*, p. 635, n. 1, Telegram of Miller, August 25/September 7, 1915, No. 186.

[135] *IBZI.*, No. 683, Sazonov to Miller, August 28/September 10, 1915, p. 635; *ibid.*, n. 3. Telegram of Miller, August 28/September 11.

[136] Telegram of Diplomatic Agent, April 5, 1916, No. 109, as cited in *S. S.*, No. 5, Prof. R. Gladstern, " The Mongolian Policy and the Russian Provisional Government," p. 167.

purchase of firearms from Russia, delivery of which, in the opinion of the Russian Ministry of Foreign Affairs, had been difficult for Russia to refuse " because we had required from the Mongols their participation in the defense of their territory against Chinese invasion." [137] But since Russia had come to an agreement with China, Sazonov found that " the supply of firearms to the Mongols gave us grave misgivings " as " it was evident that these arms were sought in order that the struggle against China might be continued." [138] He therefore pointed out to the Mongolian Prime Minister that since the Russo-Chinese declaration of St. Petersburg Mongolia " found herself in the fortunate position of a country which is not menaced by any of her neighbors." But inasmuch as the question became one of *amour propre* for Sain Noyan Khan and since it was essential to the Russian interest to strengthen his influence among the other Mongol Princes, Russia acquiesced in his demands for delivery of 20,000 rifles, 6 guns and 4 machine guns. As to payment for these arms, the Russian War Minister abandoned his usual routine and agreed to defer for one year payment of half the cost.[139]

Another reason for Russia's willingness to supply the Mongols with these arms was their threat that they would take up negotiations with foreign private persons or other governments in order to satisfy their demand. The Russian Minister in a note to Sain Noyan Khan warned him against falling into the clutches of these private persons who were trying to make large profits by deliveries of arms and, in addition, trying to secure for themselves rights which would turn out to be to the disadvantage of the Mongolian people and Government.[140] The Mongolian Prime Minster replied that the Mongolian Government would leave dealing with private persons out of consideration " if the Russian Government would continue to

---

[137] *K.A.*, Vol. 37, Draft of letter of Minister of Foreign Affairs to Kokoksov, pp. 34-5.

[138] *K.A.*, Letter of Sazonov to Miller, January 17/30, 1914, p. 66.

[139] *K.A.*, p. 67.

[140] *IBZI.*, Vol. I, 1, p. 128, n., Sazonov to Sain Noyan Khan, December 21, 1913/January 3, 1914.

supply them with arms in the desired quantities." [141] In July 1914 a Russo-Mongolian agreement was signed regulating the use of the arms and the method of payment. The arms were to be used for the equipment of the troops of the Mongolian Government which were to be organized by Russian and Mongolian instructors. The yearly payment in installments was to be secured by the Mongolian Government from internal duties. Up to the time of the payment in full for the arms the Mongolian Government engaged, if the delivery of arms were continued, not to give new orders for arms either to foreign governments or to foreign or Russian companies or to single persons without distinction of nationality.[142] The inclusion of Russian firms and private persons was an additional safeguard against foreign influences acting through them.

While the Russians were satisfying the Mongols' demand for money and arms in order to strengthen their influence in Outer Mongolia and also to forestall activities of the Chinese and possibly others, they refused categorically to sanction Sain Noyan Khan's claim to full independence for Mongolia. Sain Noyan Khan who became acquainted with the Russo-Chinese Protocol only after he arrived in St. Petersburg was especially disappointed about the stipulation in which Russia recognized China's suzerainty over Outer Mongolia. A most serious view was taken by the Minister of Foreign Affairs when Sain Noyan Khan addressed a note, similar to that sent to himself, to all diplomatic representatives in St. Petersburg, including the Chinese Minister, denouncing the Russo-Chinese declaration and averring that Mongolia had entirely broken with China.[143] When he also tried to obtain interviews with the diplomats in St. Petersburg, Sazonov pointed out to him that it was impossible for Mongolia to obtain recognition of her independence by the other powers. The majority of them

---

[141] *IBZI.*, Sain Noyan Khan to Sazonov, December 25, 1913/January 7, 1914.

[142] *IBZI.*, Vol. I, 4, No. 265, Miller to Sazonov, July 4/17, 1914 (full text of arms agreement).

[143] *K.A.*, Vol. 37, pp. 37-8. Letter of Mongol Prime Minister to Sazonov, December 3/16, 1913; copy of note presented by Mongol Prime Minister to Chinese Minister in St. Petersburg, pp. 39-40.

did not wish the disintegration of China nor the creation of an autonomous Mongolia, which owed her existence exclusively to the efforts made by Russia.[144] When the Mongolian Prime Minister, before his departure, informed the Russian Government that he would leave behind him a substitute who would be in charge of his seal and in permanent telegraphic connection with the Urga Government, this act was viewed by the Russians as " an attempt to establish a permanent diplomatic representation of the Mongolian Government in St. Petersburg." It was explained that the Russian Government did not wish such a relationship with Mongolia and that it would refuse to have official relations with his substitute.[145] Thus all possible danger of the personal contact of Mongols with foreign legations was prevented.

Russia never retreated from this position. Repeated attempts to make contact with other powers including Japan were all failures because Russian pressure prevented these powers from even answering the Mongolian requests. Russia's aim of isolating the Mongols from any diplomatic intercourse with other powers was inspired by the fear that they would enter into trade agreements with them. It is true that in the Russo-Chinese declaration Russia had recognized " the exclusive right of the Mongols of Outer Mongolia . . . to settle all questions of a commercial and industrial nature," but it was understood, as the blunt original version of Sazonov's commentary on this stipulation read, in October 1914, that " the right to conclude trade agreements remains likewise a dead letter if Russia and China agree to regard the conclusion of a trade treaty as a political act outside the limits laid down for the rights of the Mongol Government in the political field in the Declaration of November 5th, 1913." [146]

The trade relations of other powers with Mongolia caused the Russians much concern and in the first half of 1914 the

---

[144] *K. A.*, Vol. 37, pp. 63-4. Letter of Sazonov to Miller, January 17/30, 1914, pp. 63-4; also *IBZI.*, Vol. I, 1, No. 142, pp. 124-25.

[145] *K. A.*, pp. 67-8.

[146] *IBZI.*, Vol. II, 6, No. 415, p. 332. Sazonov to Krupenskii, October 15/28, 1914; also same page, n. 1.

matter was discussed in the course of an interministerial conference as well as before the Council of Ministers. Here again
the view of the Ministry of Foreign Affairs prevailed over those
of the Ministries of Finance and of Industry and Commerce.
It was against any system of trade in Outer Mongolia which
could bring Russia in conflict with other powers. The German
Government had already drawn the attention of the Russian
Government to the fact that as Outer Mongolia was an integral
part of China—as Russia herself had confirmed in the exchange
of notes with China—German trade treaties with China applied
also to Mongolia. The Council of Ministers followed, therefore,
the reasoning of the Ministry of Foreign Affairs: that the
introduction of duties at the Sino-Mongolian frontier would
not be legal and would only result in a not inconsiderable dissatisfaction among the other powers. In view of the fact that
Russia enjoyed trade free of duty as well as of any other form
of tax in Mongolia, whereas foreign goods which went via
China had in transit to pay an import and transit duty of $7\frac{1}{2}$
per cent, " the Foreign Ministry considers it dangerous to seek
to enlarge further the privileges which Russian trade possesses
at the moment." On the other hand, certain steps had to be
taken to impose some restrictions on Chinese and foreign trade
in Outer Mongolia. The way out seemed to be the introduction
of likin charges similar to the internal duties payable in China.
These were aimed not only at Chinese goods " which constitute
for our trade the most severe competition, but also at foreign
goods which are assembled in China and therefore come under
likin charges." Duties on other foreign goods would of course
be levied in accordance with the respective trade treaties with
China. In future negotiations with foreign powers concerning
Mongolia the view would be expressed that the exemption of
foreign goods imported into China from likin by the payment
of a $2\frac{1}{2}$ per cent duty was only valid inside China's frontiers
and could not be extended to Mongolia which must retain
the right to maintain likin for her own benefit.[147]

[147] *IBZ.*, Vol. I, 2, No. 368. Special Journal of Russian Council of Ministers,
April 24/May 7, 1914, pp. 361-3.

During the tripartite negotiations of 1915 much effort was needed to induce the Chinese to assent to the establishment of the likin system in Outer Mongolia. Likin [148] was explained as an administrative measure which an Autonomous Mongolia was fully entitled to employ as long as equality of rights between Chinese and Mongols was maintained.[149] In the tripartite treaty, Outer Mongolia's right " to conclude with foreign powers international treaties and agreements respecting all questions of a commercial and industrial character " was established, but this stipulation was only inserted in order to satisfy the Mongols and to give Russia a " legal right " to conclude such treaties with the Mongolian Government.

Boloban, the official of the Ministry of Trade and Industry whom we have mentioned before, who took this clause of the tripartite agreement at its face value, was soon put right by Sazonov. Boloban had conceived the idea that the transit certificates made out by the Chinese Maritime Customs were valid in Autonomous Mongolia only when the Mongolian Government had concluded trade treaties with the foreign powers. He therefore proposed to ask the Mongolian Government to impose on goods imported from China to Mongolia a higher duty than the prevalent rate until the conclusion of such treaties. Sazonov, however, rejected the proposal as based on false premises: it followed from the tripartite agreement that transit certificates of the Chinese Maritime Customs were ipso

---

[148] For an explanation of the *likin* system, see Grumm-G., Vol. III, 2, p. 498, n. 2, who gives the following details: There are in China internal customs authorities that collect likin (li-ehin), a tax that according to Parker, was introduced in 1849, according to Jameson, in 1853, and was originally due only for such goods as tea and salt, but was gradually extended to all goods of internal trade; still later, it was modified by a series of supplementary decrees so that nowadays " likin " connotes different taxes: (1) The real likin, originally equal to .1 of 1% of the value of the goods, i. e., one li from every liang (tael or ounce of silver), later raised by degrees to 6% and even 7%; (2) the local import tax (Lo-ti-shui), payable everywhere in China before likin was introduced; (3) the tax payable to the Provincial Government's treasury; (4) the tax to maintain guards . . . etc.; see also *IBZI.*, Vol. I, 1, p. 472: Likin in a proper sense: for a thousand—pro mille— . . . first introduced in 1853, extended to the whole Empire in 1861; cf. also *Encyclopedia Sinica*, by S. C. Gouling, Shanghai, 1917, p. 308; also Hosea Ballon Morse, *The Trade and Administration of China*, London-New York, 1920, pp. 120-22.

[149] *IBZI.*, Vol. II, 7, 1, No. 183, Sazonov to Miller, January 40/February 12, 1915, p. 170.

facto valid in autonomous Mongolia " which from the customs'
point of view is in the same position as any Chinese province—
a part of the united Chinese Empire." Therefore, subjects of
foreign powers could use the transit certificates for importing
into Mongolia without the conclusion for this purpose of a
treaty with the Mongolian Government.[150] Boloban was entirely mistaken even in conceiving the Mongolian Government
as capable of concluding trade treaties with other powers. Such
a possibility had already been spoken of favorably in the inter-
ministerial conference at the beginning of 1914 by the representative of the Ministry of Finance, but he, like Boloban in
1915, had been over-ruled for the reason that such treaties
would lead not only to the penetration into Mongolia of
foreign—and not always desirable—influences, but also to
claims of foreign powers for most-favored-nation treatment—
for the same right of trade free of duty there as Russian
nationals enjoyed. His proposal for the establishment of a
system of high duties between Mongolia and China was finally
considered by the Ministry of Foreign Affairs as involving " the
danger that foreign powers may be provoked to secure more
favorable conditions for their trade by direct negotiation with
the Mongolian Government. We would thereby drive them to
do what we want to prevent, for which action the Suzerain of
Autonomous Mongolia, the Chinese Government, who in this
matter is our natural ally, can have no sympathy." [151]

An additional argument adduced by the Ministry of Foreign
Affairs, in the beginning of 1914, was that it would be disadvantageous for Russia to shift the responsibilities for the activities
of the Mongolian Government from her shoulders. On the
contrary " we should accustom the powers to the thought that
they must speak on Mongolian affairs in St. Petersburg." [152]

On the question of communications Russia found herself of
course in serious opposition to the Chinese, who disputed the

---

[150] *IBZI.*, Vol. II, 8, 2, No. 796, Sazonov to Miller, September 14/27, 1915, p. 179.
[151] *Ibid.*
[152] *IBZI.*, Vol. I, 1, No. 406, Journal of a Ministers' Conference in Ministry of
Foreign Affairs, February 25/March 9, 1914, p. 405.

right of the Mongolian Government to conclude agreements concerning telegraphs or railways with the Russian Government as they were not treaties of an industrial and commercial character, which Mongolia was allowed to conclude, but treaties of a political and territorial character.[153] In actually concluding treaties of an industrial and commercial character with Outer Mongolia a much more solid opposition was encountered by the Russians from the Mongols themselves. Russia wanted telegraph and railway agreements from the Mongols and, as we have seen, had money and arms to offer in exchange. The chief Russian aim was therefore to exclude any possible concessions to foreign powers or their citizens. In May 1913 Russia had secured a telegraph concession in Western Mongolia (between Kosh Agach and Khobdo) in which the Mongolian Government bound itself to offer to the Russian Chief Administration of Posts and Telegraphs any concessions made " in any other direction whatsoever." [154] When, at the end of 1913, other telegraph lines were to be constructed negotiations for a new agreement to this effect were coupled with those for a railway agreement. Negotiations for the concession of the Mondy-Uliassutai telegraph line were constantly obstructed by the Mongolian Government who proposed changes which the Russians declared themselves unable to agree to because of technical and financial considerations.[155] To make the Mongolian Government more willing to sign this agreement Miller proposed that ten thousand rubles should be paid in advance. In addition, he suggested that the Russian Government should declare themselves prepared to share half of the expenses of a Khobdo-Uliassutai telegraph line to be built " when the state of Mongolian finances permits." [156] But in the end he succeeded

[153] *IBZI.*, see especially Vol. II, 6, 2, Miller to Sazonov, December 16/29, 1914, p. 605, Aide-Memoire of the Chinese Delegation at the Kiakhta Conference; also *ibid.*, p. 528, n. 1, Sazonov to Krupenskii, November 3/16, 1914, No. 3816, communicating protest of Chinese diplomatic representative in St. Petersburg against Russo-Mongolian Railway agreement.

[154] MacMurray, Vol. II, pp. 1038-9, Agreement of May 25, 1913, especially par. 4. conversation with Sain Noyan Khan; see also p. 44.

[155] *IBZI.*, Vol. I, 2, No. 57, Miller to Sazonov, March 7/20, 1914, reporting

[156] *IBZI.*, No. 130, Miller to Sazonov, March 18/31, 1914, p. 128.

in getting the agreement for the Mondy-Uliassutai telegraph line without any advance.[157]

The railway agreement had no significant connection with the frequent proposals of former years for a Russian railway through Mongolia; for instance Badmayev's, for the shortest route from St. Petersburg to Peking, advocated before the building of the Trans-Siberian and again in 1911; the plan of Rippos in 1915 for a new two-track railway through Mongolia; and the suggestion made in 1910 that a railway should be built from Mysovaya to Kiakhta and from there on to Urga.[158]

In 1905, Count Lamsdorff, the then Minister of Foreign Affairs, believed that the plan proposed to him contained " a lot of truth." . . . " But who will build the railway and who is to give the money? "[159] In 1913, the main objection of the Russians to the building of a Kiakhta-Urga railway was that it would not pay. " The time for such an undertaking has evidently not yet come," explained Sazonov to Khovzov at the end of 1913. " The foreign trade of Mongolia does not promise the necessary freight to the railways of the country, except in cases where they could be connected with the Chinese net of railways which we, however, do not consider desirable. In this case they would provide a means for the penetration of Chinese and foreign trade and their traffic would diminish the receipts of the Chinese Eastern Railway and the Trans-Siberian Railway."[160] For these reasons Russian policy was to prevent the building by private enterprise of a railway from Kiakhta to Urga, as well as from Kalgan to Urga, which the Chinese had contemplated for a long time. The attitude to be adopted towards the Mongols was to point out to them that railways in Mongolia should be constructed with a view to linking up with the Russian railway system. This was to be

---

[157] *IBZI.*, No. 101, Telegram of Miller of March 21/April 3, 1914.

[158] B. A. Romanov, *Russia in Manchuria*, pp. 192, 193, 196, 459, 460; also Popov, p. 8.

[159] Popov, p. 8, Ministry of Foreign Affairs, V. D. K., No. 687.

[160] *IBZI.*, Vol. I, 1, Letter of Sazonov to Finance Minister, Kokovtsov, December 20, 1913/January 2, 1914, No. 967, p. 11; also p. 10, n. 2. Telegram of Governor-General of Irkutsk, Kuyasev, of December 12/25, 1913.

laid down in a railway agreement which would prevent the construction of railways by Chinese or others and leave it to Russia to decide when to take advantage of the concession, postponing the date " on different pretexts." [161] It is obvious that such an agreement bestowed no favors whatever on the Mongols, and was, on the contrary, a one-sided engagement with no advantage to them of any sort.

The Mongols were quick to see that Russia wanted to " forbid them ever to construct railways " and seized the opportunity to put her in an embarrassing position by going so far as to threaten that they would never sign a railway agreement of any sort with Russia and by using their opposition adroitly to obtain more favorable terms in their demands for more credit and arms.[162] Indeed, they were so successful in their demands that Sazonov urged Sukhomlinov, the War Minister, " in view of the negotiation in Urga of a number of questions which are of very grave importance to us . . . not to delay the signing of the arms agreement nor the dispatch of the arms mentioned in Miller's telegram." [163] Russia signed the loan and arms convention in June 1914, and thought it " desirable " to sign the railway convention simultaneously, but agreement on the question was only reached in September.[164]

Russia had to a certain extent to abandon her original intention of obtaining a stipulation amounting to a Russian monopoly in railway-building in Mongolia. By his own admission, Miller's endeavors " to destroy the illusions " of Sain Noyan Khan, nourished during his stay in St. Petersburg by the discovery that his government would be able to sell railway

[161] *IBZI.*; also Vol. II, No. 216, Miller to Sazonov, March 31, 1914/April 13, 1914, p. 227.

[162] *IBZI.*, Vol. I, 2, No. 57. Miller to Sazonov, March 7/20, 1914, p. 43; Sain Noyan Khan communicated decision of Council of Ministers to reject the railway agreement in its entirety; also *ibid.*, n. 2, pp. 43-4. Telegram of Miller of March 8/21, 1914, No. 76; No. 90, Miller to Sazonov, March 12/25, 1914: Official note of Mongolian Government reiterating refusal, No. 420; Miller to Sazonov, April 30/May 13, 1914, p. 406: Reporting obstinate opposition of Da Lama and Sain Noyan Khan, p. 407, Finance Minister Tushetu Wang couples railway question with supply of arms and loan.

[163] *IBZI.*, Vol. I, 4, No. 306, Sazonov to Sukhomlinov, June 8/21, 1914.

[164] *IBZI.*, Vol. I, 5, Sazonov to Miller, July 16/29, 1914, p. 159.

concessions to foreign enterprises for considerable sums, were not very successful at first. He warned Sain Noyan Khan that if Mongolia after all the benefits which Russia had bestowed on her were to give a concession for a railway from Kalgan to Urga or in any other direction to any outsider, Russia would regard such a step as an obviously unfriendly act " against which she would know how to take adequate measures to safeguard her special interests in adjacent Mongolia." [165] When the Mongols were at least partly satisfied with a loan and arms it became easier to conclude the agreement, and the departure from the government of Da Lama, the anti-Russian Minister of the Interior, helped as well.[166] Nevertheless, the final draft presented by the Russians and the treaty actually concluded reveal some interesting differences. There was no mention in the draft of the first article of the treaty stipulating " the perpetual right of the Mongolian Government to build railroads within the confines of its territory." On the contrary, the draft considered it as " self-evident that the Mongolian Government will not undertake any railway construction itself, nor give concessions to private persons to build any," but the final treaty says that in view of the stipulation of the first article, " Russia will not interfere if the Mongolian Government should desire to construct a useful railroad out of its own resources." But the same article went on to reaffirm that, before the Mongols gave any such concessions, they were obliged to consult the Russian Government to find out whether the concessions were injurious to Russia's strategic and economic interests. This was what really mattered to Russia. In addition, the Russians considered the stipulation that the Mongolian Government has a right to construct a *useful* railroad itself (i. e., with its own means) as giving them " a right to intervene in case of the construction of a railway detrimental

---

[165] *IBZI.*, Vol. I, 3, No. 266, Miller to Neratov, June 2/15, 1914, pp. 236-8; Vol. I, 2, No. 57, Miller to Sazonov, March 7/20, 1914, p. 44.

[166] *IBZI.*, Vol. 4, No. 173. The Provisional Director of the Far Eastern Division to Miller, June 28/July 11, 1914, p. 169; for importance of agitation of Da Lama in this connection see Vol. I, 1, p. 267, n. 2. Telegram of February 3/16, 1914, No. 34.

to Russia's interests, i. e., by some other agency than the Mongolian Government." [167]

In yet another matter, Russia encountered opposition from the Mongols, and she was never able to cope satisfactorily with it. We have noticed that Sazonov had explained to a foreign diplomat that one of the things that Russia might at once do to assist those directing the new state of affairs in Outer Mongolia was to send some military instructors to Urga. Shortly after the conclusion of the Russo-Mongolian-Urga agreement a written understanding on the organization of a Mongolian brigade was reached. Part of the first loan which the Mongols received was to be spent on this brigade, but one clause, which annoyed the Mongols very much, stipulated that " for covering all expenses connected with the organization of military forces in Khalkha and with the invitation of Russian instructors, the Mongolian Government shall deposit with the Imperial Consulate the sum of 350,000 rubles, the expenditure of this sum being entrusted to the instructors by the Russian Government." The sum was to be reserved from the two million ruble loan to the Mongolian Government.[169] The Mongols complained about the establishment of control by the Russian Consulate and the high salaries of the Russian instructors who were probably not the best specimens of their profession but rather on a par with the inferior type of Russian merchant common in Mongolia, the final result being that on the expiration of this one year agreement with reference to instructors, the Mongols refused to renew it.[170]

It was originally agreed early in 1913 to train nineteen hundred men but early in 1914 Sazonov had to agree reluctantly that as Miller had " encountered difficulties in the negotiations with the Mongolian ministers . . . we shall not

---

[167] *Ibid.*, Vol. I, 1, No. 10, pp. 9-10. Draft of railway agreement in Sazonov's letter to Kokovtsov; also in *K. A.*, Vol. 37, p. 51; for final text see MacMurray, Vol. II, pp. 1178-9; re controversy " useful railroad " see *IBZI.*, Vol. I, 5, No. 565, Miller to Sazonov, July 22/August 4, 1914.

[168] See n. 76.

[169] *K. A.*, p. 62, n. 1. Russian-Mongolian (Brigade) Agreement of February 3/16, 1913; *ibid.*, p. 62, Telegram of Miller, January 16/29, 1914.

[170] *Ibid.*

raise any objections to the limitation of the strength of the brigade to 400 men including the battery and the machine-gun command." The Russian staff of instructors was to be decreased from 17 officers and 42 non-commissioned officers to one commander, seven or nine officers and 23 or 25 of lower rank; [171] shortly afterward Sazonov, with the consent of the War Ministry, agreed to a further decrease to only six officers and twelve non-commissioned officers. The Russian War Ministry, however, rejected the proposed period of three months military service as inadequate for the proper training of soldiers. Six months was considered the minimum, but half of the effective strength of the brigade could be furloughed every three months.[172] Moreover, " the further existence of a Mongolian brigade " was considered by the Foreign Minister, " as a necessary factor as well of our influence as also of the integrity of the Mongolian State," and in April 1914 Major-General Averganov, second Chief Quartermaster of the Russian General Staff, left for Urga to examine the activities of the Russian instructors and to discuss and work out with Miller the details of the new brigade agreement, which, in the end, was accepted by the Mongolian Government and provided for six Russian officers and sixteen Cossack officers.[173]

Having concluded this agreement the Russian War Minister agreed to supply 20,000 rifles with 20 million cartridges, as well as six guns with 3000 shells and four machine-guns with 400,000 cartridges. As agreed 400,000 rubles were to be retained from the loan, while demand for payment of the rest of the sum due, amounting to 60,000 rubles, was deferred for six months.[174] The Russian instructors, however, failed to win

---

[171] *IBZI.*, Vol. I, 1, No. 431, Sazonov to Miller, February 27/March 12, 1914.

[172] *IBZI.*, Vol. I, 2, No. 148, Miller to Sazonov, March 21/April 3, 1914, p. 149.

[173] *IBZI.*, Vol. I, 2, No. 261, Sazonov to Miller, April 9/22, 1914, p. 262; Vol. I, 3, p. 188, n. 2. Telegram of Miller of May 15/28, 1914, No. 130; No. 220, First Councillor of Foreign Ministry to Miller, May 30/June 12, 1914, p. 205.

[174] *IBZI.*, Vol. I, 3, No. 243, First Councillor of Foreign Ministry to Miller, June 2/15, 1914; also n. 1, Telegram of Miller, April 26/May 9, 1914: . . . The Mongolian Government's request that 400,000 rubles should be retained from the first payment for the promised arms, but this should not be mentioned in the loan agreement.

the sympathy of the Mongols who, two years later when Russia was completely absorbed in the Great War, put so many hindrances in their way that they were not able to carry out their duties.[175]

With the beginning of the world war, it became pressing for Russia to achieve a stabilization of the status of Mongolia, and this it was hoped to accomplish through the tripartite negotiations foreshadowed in the Russo-Chinese agreement of St. Petersburg at the end of 1913. Here also Russia's representatives in Urga had difficulty in securing the cooperation of the Mongolian Government. That the opening of negotiations was postponed until September 1914 was entirely due to the Mongols' reluctance to participate before having put pressure on China by means of a menacing attitude in the matter of Inner Mongolia, or without having secured beforehand Russian support against China.

The historical importance of Russia's categorical refusal of any such support may be mentioned in this connection. The years following the Chinese revolution of 1911-12 provided the greatest and possibly the last chance for some sort of union among the Mongol tribes. When Sazonov explained in his speech in April 1913 that " attempts to unite Inner and Outer Mongolia, disunited geographically and with the inhabitants having already lived a long time under completely different conditions, could hardly bring them any possibility of a united political life," [177] he was probably thinking more about the implications of a breach of the Russo-Japanese secret agreement of 1912 defining the two countries' respective zones of influence in Mongolia than about the value of his statement as an accurate description of the state of affairs.[178] When Sain Noyan

[175] Korostovets.

[176] *K.A.*, Vol. 37, p. 47, Miller to Sazonov, December 16/29, 1913.

[177] Duma Speech as cited by Grumm-G., Vol. II, Leningrad, 1926, pp. 746-7.

[178] In two footnotes, Grumm-G., takes Sazonov severely to task for this statement. Referring to Sazonov's phrase " disunited geographically," he remarks that if Sazonov includes in " Inner Mongolia " that part which is near the South Manchurian railway, then geographically it can hardly be considered disunited with Outer Mongolia. To the whole sentence he objects that it would have been much

Khan in St. Petersburg in his note to Sazonov insisted " on such fixing of the boundaries of the Mongolian state that within it there should be incorporated all the Mongols who would join it " it was explained to him that the inclusion of Inner Mongolia would mean a conflict with Japan and England whose intervention they had only prevented by an assurance that the Mongols' aspirations would not affect their interests in these regions.[179] (England's " region " being the territory of Kokonor and Tsaidam—now included in the province of Ch'inghai, bordering Tibet and largely inhabited by Western Mongols). Nevertheless, the Russians did suggest that some kind of tripartite arrangement between China, Mongolia and Russia might be made, which might be used by the Mongolian Government to restrain the Chinese in Inner Mongolia. The view taken in St. Petersburg was that Russia was not bound to say that the tripartite negotiations should not begin until China agreed to certain conditions regarding Inner Mongolia. Russia could only say to the Mongolian and Chinese Governments that in her opinion a certain goodwill over this question was desirable. Russia considered that concrete proposals, as for instance for the neutralization of a part of Inner Mongolia, could probably be made with advantage as a compromise solution during the tripartite negotiations, but that it would be premature to make them earlier.[180]

Sazonov pointed out to the Mongolian Minister, however, that any contemplated interference on the part of the Mongolian Government would require the establishment of a strong Mongolian power which could be produced only by many years of serious reform.[181] Miller in Urga was supported by Rockhill, the American diplomat and explorer, who while on a visit to Urga advised the Mongols to trust Russia, as " what

more cautious not to have mentioned it at all in a political speech, as nobody acquainted with Mongolia and the Mongols could subscribe to it.

[179] *K. A.*, Vol. 37, p. 37, Letter of Mongol Prime Minister to Sazonov, December 3/16, 1913; *ibid.*, p. 64, Sazonov to Miller, January 17/30, 1914.

[180] *IBZI.*, Vol. I, 3, No. 288, The First Councillor of the Foreign Ministry to Miller, June 4/17, 1914.

[181] *K. A.*, Vol. 37, p. 65, Sazonov to Miller, January 17/30, 1914.

has been practically a province cannot become a state all at once." [182] Indeed, the handful of Inner Mongols who had come to Outer Mongolia, either fleeing from Chinese persecutions or on the invitation of the Mongolian Government, also sought Russia's support—and purse. The Inner Mongols soon found out that the Mongolian Government was not strong enough to help them against the Chinese and addressed themselves to Russia. Prince Udai and Prince Arawan asked for the return of their *hoshuns* to them; the Tumets asked the Russian Government to secure for them from the Chinese Government a guarantee of the security of their persons and property and of freedom for the Yellow Church.

Miller tried to persuade the Tumets and the inhabitants of Inner Mongolia to wait for awhile and to write in the meantime to their followers asking them to be obedient subjects of the Chinese Government in order not to destroy any chance of a settlement assuring them of a peaceful existence being secured by the Russian and Mongolian Governments during the tripartite negotiations.[183] The Inner Mongols were bitter because of the lack of help from the Urga Government and when nine deputies sent by two thousand Chahar Mongols to negotiate with the Chinese were executed they decided to take the law into their own hands by raiding Chinese settlements, and for this they asked the blessing of the Living Buddha.[184] Miller, thereupon, intervened and begged that His Holiness should not give the benediction asked, but should give money to the Chahars and other Inner Mongols and advise them to wait for the tripartite negotiations. The Mongolian Foreign Minister enquired whence the money was to come as the Mongolian treasury was empty and the soldiers in Urga had

[182] *K. A.*, Vol. 37, p. 45, Mliler to Sazonov, December 16/29, 1913. Cf. Chapter V, text preceding and following n. 103.
[183] *IBZI.*, Vol. I, 3, p. 255, n. 1, Telegram of Miller of February 26/March 11, 1914, No. 57; n. 2, Telegram of Miller of May 30/June 12, 1914, No. 51; No. 332, Miller to Sazonov, June 9/22, 1914, pp. 278-88.
[184] *IBZI.*, Vol. I, 4, No. 107, pp. 111-13, Miller to Neratov, June 23/July 6, 1914, with copy of Note from Mongol Ministry of Foreign Affairs to Imperial Russian Consul General in Mongolia, dated 10th day of 4th moon of 4th year of the Mongol Government.

nothing to eat. Miller named Kosin, the Russian financial adviser to the Mongolian Government, who, he did not doubt, would advance the necessary sum. This Kosin did when Miller had explained the circumstances to him.[185] The predicament of the Mongolian Government in this matter gave Miller an additional opportunity of asking them to decide as quickly as possible on an early date for the beginning of the tripartite negotiations.[186]

Russia's refusal to support in any way the Outer Mongols' designs on Inner Mongolia was not the only discouragement she gave to their territorial aspirations. Miller, in July 1914, made it clear that under no circumstances could either Inner Mongolia or Barga and Urianghai be discussed during the tripartite conference.

Barga, the popular name of a part of the province of Heilungkiang, called Hulun Buir by the Chinese, now belonging to the province of Hsingan, was not mentioned in the Russo-Chinese declaration but might have been considered as belonging de facto to the new Mongolian state, as tribes of the Barga region had in 1912 submitted themselves to the Hutukhtu who had appointed a leading Buriat as his Viceroy and Amban in their territory. In the beginning of 1912 when the Barguts desired to follow the lead of Khalkha and to separate from China, they had first addressed themselves to Russia and were advised to compromise. Negotiations wth the Central Chinese Government were unsuccessful, and they then turned to the Urga Living Buddha.[187] In 1914, when Chinese military preparations threatened the Barga region, an assembly of elders resolved that in case they should fail to remain united with the Urga Government, which was their desire, they should ask the Russian Government to consent to Barga receiving an autonomous internal administration under the suzerainty of China.

---

[185] *IBZI.*, Vol. I, 4, No. 191, Miller to Neratov, June 29/July 3, 1914, p. 178.
[186] *IBZI.*, p. 177.
[187] For general remarks see Baddeley, *op. cit.*, Vol. I, p. XIIX; *IBZI.*, Vol. I, 1, p. 459 (notes of the Editor); *C. Y. B.*, 1914, p. 615, *IBZI.*, Vol. I, 2, p. 433 (notes of the Editor). For list of tribes in the Barga region see Lattimore, *The Mongols of Manchuria.*

Russia was uncertain what attitude she should take, for Barga was part of a Chinese province and therefore in a different position from the outer provinces like Mongolia, Tibet and Turkistan. On the other hand, it marched with Outer Mongolia and Russia and was a part of Manchuria, and influence there could be used to Russia's advantage as a means of exerting pressure on the Chinese Government in connection with the tripartite negotiations. This was the opinion of Sazonov, as expressed in a wire to Krupenskii, the Russian Minister in Peking, whom he advised to delay negotiations on the question of Barga until after the tripartite negotiations.[188] Krupenskii saw certain difficulties in using the Barga problem as a means of pressure as the Russian Government wanted to safeguard the interests of Russian industrialists and merchants in that region by demanding compensation from the Chinese Government, and also wished to connect it with the wider question of the limitation of armaments in Northern Manchuria. In addition, delay involved the danger of the Chinese coming to an understanding with Barga without Russia's participation.[189] He was thereupon charged to declare to the Chinese that Russia would not tolerate any decision on the destiny of Barga without her collaboration and would not recognize an agreement made directly between the Chinese Government and the Barga authorities.

Sazonov's conditions for the re-establishment of China's *sovereignty* (this term was used and not, as in the negotiations

---

[188] *IBZI.*, Vol. I, 1, p. 56, n. 2, Vice-Consul in Hailar to Russian Minister in Peking, December 29, 1913/January 11, 1914; *K. A.*, Vol. 37, Sazonov to Krupenskii, November 5/18, 1913, No. 3143, p. 23; " We did not include Barga in Autonomous Mongolia, and in principle we agree with the restoration of sovereignty of China in this Province. But this must be done through peace negotiations in which we might take upon ourselves the rôle of intermediaries. However, submission of Barga to China by armed force would affect Russian interests so much that we cannot regard it with indifference." (See wrong translation in *Chin. Soc. & Pol. Science Rev.*, Vol. XVI, 4, p. 663, which translates sovereignty of China as suzerainty— also n. 124, Chapter V); *IBZI.*, Vol. I, 4, No. 96, Sazonov to Chargé d'Affaires in Peking, Grave, June 22/July 6, 1914, p. 99. Vol. I, 1, p. 178, n. 1, Telegram of Sazonov, January 22/February 4, 1914, No. 174.

[189] *IBZI.*, Vol. I, 1, No. 191, Krupenskii to Sazonov, January 24/February 6, 1914, p. 178.

on Outer Mongolia, *suzerainty*) were, first of all that the Barga
tribes should be permitted to keep their local authorities;
second, that the Peking Government should confirm those
treaties made by Russian subjects with the authorities in Barga
" in the time of her de facto independence "; third, that Russian
subjects were to have preferential rights to build such roads
of approach to the Chinese Eastern Railway as should prove
necessary; fourth, that Russian gold mine proprietors who had
lost their concessions obtained before the Russo-Japanese war
were to be compensated by the Chinese Government.[190]
Krupenskii, who was not very pleased with the introduction of
such side issues as the compensation of the gold mine proprietors and found their demands " excessive and not sufficiently substantiated " and the Chinese Government's demands
for the submission of a complete list of the treaties between
Russian subjects and the local authorities in Barga " quite
natural," suggested that it might be advisable for the Russian
Government, before coming to any understanding with the
Chinese Government, to make inquiries of the Barga authorities
themselves as to the form of administration they desired.[191]
Sazonov agreed to this proposal and the answer of the Barga
authorities was that they would prefer to remain under the
power of the Bogdo Khan (Living Buddha in Urga); but that
if this were not possible they wished the same autonomous
status which had been achieved by Outer Mongolia. This
status in Barga was not to be interfered with by China, and
Russia was to assume responsibility for this.[192]

Krupenskii thought that the conditions of the Barga authorities were " in the main completely unrealizable as they
would place Barga in the same position as Khalka." [193] Sazonov,
on the other hand, considered that the transformation of Barga
into an autonomous territory on the basis proposed by the

[190] *IBZI.*, Vol. I, 1, No. 200, Sazonov to Krupenskii Febuary 6/19, 1914, p. 267.
[191] *IBZI.*, p. 306, n. 1, Telegram of Krupenskii, Febuary 15/28, 1914, No. 29.
[192] *IBZI.*, No. 357, Sazonov to Krupenskii, February 17/March 2, 1914, p. 359;
ibid., Vol. I, 2, p. 7, n. 2, Telegram of Consul in Hailar of February 22/March 12,
1914, transmitting demands of Barguts, especially see p. 8.
[193] *IBZI.*, Vol. I, 2, No. 10, Krupenskii to Sazonov, March 1/14, 1914, p. 8.

Barga authorities " would correspond with our interests." He was more or less sure that the Chinese would not accept this and thought that Russia's rôle as a mediator between the two opposing camps could then be established securely. He objected, however, to the special mention of Russia's guarantee for the inviolability of the constitution of the tribes in Barga as this would follow from the fact that she participated in its formation.[194] The Chinese, as a matter of fact, wished to reduce Barga's status to the order against which the tribes of the Barga region had originally revolted, whereas the Russians would have been satisfied with the reintroduction of the de facto autonomy as it existed before the Manchu dynasty engaged in its forward policy in 1907; in other words, non-colonization by the Chinese and no stationing of Chinese troops and officials. " The resident popoulation must be granted a legal status," was how Sazonov words it, " which permits it to develop peacefully in the customary traditional forms, and close economic relations, based on geographic proximity to the neighboring Russian territory, must be recognized, with all consequences resulting therefrom."

From the Russian point of view there was no object in hurrying the negotiations on this question and Chinese attempts in this direction were promptly rebuffed. Their suggestion that the conciliatory attitude which they had taken on the question of railway concessions in Northern Manchuria should be met by a similar attitude on the part of Russia over Barga, was considered by the Russian Foreign Minister as " completely wrong," as Russia was not willing to make " these negotiations which really have a technical character dependent upon the solution " of such complicated problems as that of Barga which would necessitate lengthy discussion. The question of railways related to the wider question of the economic development of Northern Manchuria in which China was as much interested as Russia, but the problem of Barga was that of securing for a territory of China a political structure by which its peaceful

[194] *IBZI.*, No. 16, Sazonov to Krupenskii, March 3/16, 1914, p. 12.

development would be assured " in which matter we cannot remain indifferent because of the Russian interests existing there." [195] This attitude kept the settlement of the Barga question pending until after the conclusion of the tripartite negotiations in June 1915, and an agreement on Barga was finally signed in November 1915, between Russia and China only, the authorities in Barga being excluded. The terms of the agreement reveal that nearly all Russia's original proposals were adopted: Barga (Hailar) was to form a special district, directly subject to the Central Government of the Chinese Republic, i. e., not to the governor of the province of Heilungkiang; only a local militia was to be kept, but in case the local authorities should be unable to keep order, troops of the Chinese Central Government might be sent " after notice thereof to the Russian Government "; after the re-establishment of order, these detachments were to be withdrawn; should a railway be constructed in Hailar and foreign capital be acquired, the Chinese Government would in the first instance look to Russia to find such capital; contracts made between Russian investors and the Barga authorities were to be confirmed by the Government of the Chinese Republic after examination by a Russo-Chinese mixed commission.[196]

Of Tsarist Russia's attitude towards Inner Mongolia, we may say that she succeeded in safeguarding her interests in that region without taking the responsibilities which she had assumed in Outer Mongolia, thus avoiding a conflict with other powers on the principle of the integrity of China and, at the same time, limiting the range of activity of the new Mongolian state. Russia was at this time—in the early years of the Great War—in no position to pursue further any active policy in this region, but her undisguised attempts to set bounds to

---

[195] *IBZI.*, Vol. I, 4, No. 96, Sazonov to Russian Chargé d'Affaires in Peking, Grave, June 22/July 6, 1914, pp. 99-100; *ibid.*, No. 281, The Provisional Director of the 4th Political Division of the Foreign Ministry to Grave, July 6/19, 1914, pp. 257-8.

[196] MacMurray, Vol. II, pp. 1247-49, Arrangement concerning the situation of Hulun Buir (Hailar), November 6, 1915. Cf. Korostovets, p. 128.

Mongolian aspirations had a bad effect on her relations with the leading Mongols.

The same is true of Russian policy toward Urianghai, where Russia assumed responsibilities prejudicial to the territorial aspirations of the new Mongolian state and to its attempts to have relations with other Mongol or allied tribes. In Urianghai as in Barga the leading men responded to the new régime in Outer Mongolia by addressing themselves to the Hutukthu in Urga—in the hope of uniting the five *hoshuns* of Urianghai in a special aimak under his leadership.

The clarification of Russian policy toward Urianghai took some time. In November 1911 the Council of Ministers agreed that the historical documents which went back to the 18th century and showed that some of the Urianghai tribes had paid tribute in furs, known as *yasak*, to both Russian and Manchu officials, could not serve as a firm basis to prove the allegiance of that territory to Russia. As for more recent agreements, the protocol of Chuguchak of 1864 demarcated a part of the frontier which had been moved northwards from the ridge of Tannu Ola and thus again refuted any possible Russian claim to the territory beyond the Sayansk mountains. The Journal of the Council of Ministers concluded that the only possible policy for Russia was one of peaceful penetration beyond the Sayansk mountains, and this was approved by the Tsar.[197] But in 1913 Russia began a more active policy and the Mongolian Amban, Gomborvi, turned to the Russians.[198]

Sazonov was convinced that it was necessary to tackle the question of the territory of Urianghai " carefully and gradually." As the main reason for such a policy he mentioned the lack of communication between Siberia and Urianghai, which cut the latter off from Russia during six or eight months of the year, when any intercourse between Minnusinsk and

---

[197] *IBZI.*, Vol. 1, 2, No. 167, p. 161, Sazonov to Russian Prime Minister, Goremykin, April 7/March 25, 1914, cites resolution of 1911; see also I, 1, p. 472 and p. 410(a).

[198] *IBZI.*, Vol. I, 4, p. 348, (Note of Editor). For general reference see Grumm-G. and Bibliography.

the territory of Usa-Urianghai was almost impossible.[199] The Governor-General of Irkutsk believed, however, in the necessity of strengthening Russian influence in that region, because he feared a possible affiliation of Urianghai with Autonomous Mongolia. In January 1914 he reported, therefore, that he had taken measures which resulted in the demand of the inhabitants of two *hoshuns* of Urianghai, Da and Beise, to be received as Russian subjects. In forwarding these demands to the Tsar, the Governor-General pointed out that, though it was perhaps not advisable to receive them formally as Russian subjects, it was most desirable to give them a definite answer to the effect that Russia would be willing to take them under her protection. A refusal " might cause them again to seek the protection of their spiritual sovereign, the Hutukthu of Urga." [200] Sazonov agreed with this proposal and in a memorandum to the Prime Minister he reaffirmed his belief in the righteousness of the policy toward Urianghai as laid down in the Journal of the Council of Ministers in 1911. " Now " he wrote at the end of March 1914, " the vacillation of the Urianghais between affiliation with Khalkha and subjection to Russian power compels us to give a definite answer to their petitions. These vacillations can be ended by the taking of the Urianghai under Russian protection. But there is no necessity to annex their territory and their waters for this purpose, because the aims which we pursue concerning the Urianghai question do not demand that we take these radical measures immediately. In connection with this question there would arise complicated and delicate problems in our relations with China and Mongolia." [201]

Before submitting the petition as interpreted by the Governor-General of Irkutsk to the Prime Minister and the Tsar,

[199] *IBZI.*, Vol. I, 1, No. 409, February 25/March 10, 1914, Sazonov to Minister of War, Sukhomlinov, Minister of the Interior, Maklakov and Assistant to the Head of the Chief Administration of Land Organization Ignatiev, p. 409; see also Korostovets, p. 12. 8. It was in this connection that Sazonov remarked to Korostovets that Russia must be a European, not an Asiatic power.

[200] *IBZI.*, Vol. I, 1, p. 408, Letter of Governor General of Irkutsk, January 14/27, 1914.

[201] *IBZI.*, Vol. I, 2, No. 167, Sazonov to Prime Minister, Goremykin, March 25/ April 7, 1914, p. 162.

Sazonov submitted his views to the Minister of War, the Minister of the Interior and the Assistant Minister for Land Organization and Agriculture. The last was the only one who favored a strong policy of immediate and complete annexation.[202] The War Minister agreed with Sazonov's policy provided that it was regarded as " the first step on the way toward the complete affiliation of the whole territory to our Empire." The advantage of such a policy would consist in achieving " a considerable shortening of the frontier of our Empire with Mongolia. If we could move the frontier over the Sayansk range toward the natural boundary, which is the range of the Tannu Ola, we should be able to cover that part of the Trans-Baikal railway which is open from the direction of the valley of the Irkut and to assure ourselves of the feasibility of making expeditions from Irkutsk and Tungka at the shortest distance from Uliassutai " (the chief town of Western Khalkha). This was important also, he added, from the purely military point of view. The Chinese troops in the district of Altai were 300 to 600 versts away, separated from Urianghai territory by autonomous Khalkha. If they were to march into Khalkha, in violation of the Russo-Chinese agreement, they would encounter resistance from Russian divisions stationed at Khobdo and Sha-Sume.[203] The Minister of the Interior also shared Sazonov's view that a cautious policy was the most advisable in the circumstances until the construction of the road from Usa was finished and a Russian steamship service on the Upper Yenisei possible, and until at least a small contingent of Russian troops had been transferred to Urianghai.[204] As Sazonov commented in his memorandum to the Prime Minister, these projects were still far from being completed and the military weakness of Russia in this region was apparent, as her only troops were the 45 men of the local guard at Usa. In a word, " annexation would not carry with it any practical

[202] *IBZI.*, Vol. I, 1, p. 410, n. 1, Answer of Ignatiev of February 29/March 12, 1914.
[203] *IBZI.*, Vol. I, 2, p. 161, n. 3, Letter of Sukhomlinov, of March 1/14, 1914, No. 4253.
[204] *IBZI.*, Letter of Maklahov, March 21/April 3, 1914, No. 363.

advantages. . . . Neither the colonization of this territory by Russians, nor its defence against the aspirations of the Mongolian Government would thereby be facilitated." [205]

Sazonov thought it prudent to limit the conditions to be put before the Urianghais for acceptance in exchange for their receiving Russian protection to one essential: " It is clear that the Urianghais must first of all give up the right of external relations and that they must pledge themselves to form connections with their neighbors only through the official stationed in the territory by the Governor-General at Irkutsk." [206] But in his communication to the Tsar, he mentioned another condition which in his former memorandum he had considered not very practical at the moment, i. e., submission of the inhabitants of Urianghai to the decision of the Russian official representative in disputes between different *hoshuns* of the territory.[207]

In July 1914 the text of these conditions was communicated by the Chief of Frontier Affairs, Zereni, to the Amban Noyan Gomborji and to all other leaders or officials of Urianghai together with the consent of the Tsar to take them and their subjects under his protection. " You have the duty of maintaining no relations of any kind with foreign states, including Mongolia. In case such relations should be necessary, they can only be conducted through me as the representative of the Russian Government in the territory of Urianghai or by a person deputizing for me." [208]

The Governor-General of Irkutsk was instructed by Sazonov not to make it public that Russia had extended protection to Urianghai, in order " to avoid a misrepresented and exaggerated interpretation." [209] Nothing could have come nearer to such

---

[205] *IBZI.*, Vol. I, 2, No. 167, p. 162.

[206] *IBZI.*, No. 203, Note of report of Sazonov to Nicholas II, March 29/April 11, 1914, p. 212; signed by the Tsar, April 4/17, 1914; " Agreed."

[207] *IBZI.*, Vol. I, 1, No. 409, p. 410.

[208] *IBZI.*, Vol. I, 4, Nos. 267-68, pp. 250-51, text of the Tsar's consent to a protectorate over Urianghai, as communicated to Gombodorji, together with Gombodorji's acceptance (original in Mongol), July 4/17, 1914, p. 250.

[209] *IBZI.*, Vol. I, 2, p. 212, n. 2, Telegram of Sazonov to Governor General of Irkutsk, April 5/18, 1914, No. 721.

an interpretation than that of Goremykin himself, the Russian Prime Minister, in his criticism of Sazonov's policy concerning Urianghai. While acknowledging Sazonov's prudence in not annexing the territory, he considered the establishment of a protectorate to be " a further step on the road which, it is my deep conviction, leads ultimately to complete and definite affiliation of the territory of Urianghai to a great and powerful Russia." [210]

When, therefore, Miller warned the Mongols in Urga in July 1914 that the question of Urianghai must under no circumstances be raised during the tripartite conference, it had already been settled by the Russians.[211]

Another problem which had been at least provisionally settled by Russia without the participation of the Mongols, but in agreement with China, was the delimitation of frontiers between the district of Khobdo—the western part of Outer Mongolia—and that of Altai; the latter had belonged administratively to Mongolia until 1907 and in 1911 it was due to the influence of Prince Palta, the Governor of this district, that it did not join the independence movement in Outer Mongolia. In December 1914, on the termination of hostilities between China and Mongolia, an agreement was made between the Russian Consul in Shara Sume and Prince Palta. Khobdo and Altai were to retain their old territorial limits and the inhabitants of each territory were not to penetrate into the other. In June 1914, shortly before the expiration of this provisional agreement, China proposed that it should not be renewed, as in an article in the Russo-Chinese declaration and

---

[210] *IBZI.*, Vol. I, 2, p. 212, Letter of Goremykin, April 9/22, No. 2283. The actual relations between Russia and Urianghai became known only much later from the texts of the documents cited only recently. In his article on the Treaty of Kiakhta of 1915, E. T. Williams writes in the *American Journal of International Law*, 1916, p. 800: " Inasmuch as Article XI of the tripartite agreement, which mentions the districts included in ' Autonomous Outer Mongolia,' omits all references to Urianghai, it seems not improbable that that district may become incorporated in Asiatic Russia. Baddeley, Vol. I, p. XIIX, comments in December 1917, that the Urianghai territory has for some years been undergoing a process of ' peaceful penetration ' or absorption by the Russians." That seems to be about all that was known at that time about Russo-Urianghai relations.

[211] *IBZI.*, Vol. I, 4, Miller to Sazonov, July 19/August 1, 1914, p. 273.

exchange of notes of Peking it was stipulated that this question should be subsequently regulated by means of conferences between the two signatories.[212] Russia agreed to this on condition that the stipulations of the old arrangement remained, i. e., that the two territories should keep their existing territorial limits and the prohibition against inter-penetration of the inhabitants still held. Russia could do this more easily as the main cause of difficulties in the Khobdo region, the ambitious Ja Lama who had made himself ruler there, disappeared when the " energetic steps " taken by Russia resulted in his arrest and deportation to Russia.[213]

In the tripartite agreement of Kiahkhta a compromise on the question of frontier delimitation was achieved with some difficulty; it consisted of a mere recital of the regions enumerated in the Russo-Chinese exchange of notes as constituting the territory of Autonomous Outer Mongolia. Exact demarcation was to be the task of a mixed commission which was to take up its duties within two years of the signing of the agreement. On Russian initiative a more exact agreement was reached between Russia and China over the frontier between Inner and Outer Mongolia, which was especially vague because it ran through desert regions. A frontier zone between the two was created which was to be entered only by the local nomad population, in order to prevent Chinese from crossing the frontier and settling in Outer Mongolia, and to avoid " frontier incidents and collisions between Autonomous Outer Mongolia and her Suzerain, China." This was provided for in an unpublished exchange of notes between the Russian Minister in Peking and the Chinese Foreign Minister.[214]

[212] *IBZI.*, Vol. I, p. 25, The Russian Chargé d'Affaires in Peking to Sazonov, June 16/29, 1914, and Annex thereto: Note of the Chinese Foreign Minister to Grave, same date, referring to the provisional agreement of December 8/21, 1913.

[213] *IBZI.*, No. 67, Sazonov to Grave, July 3/June 20, 1914, p. 77; No. 106, Aide-memoire of the Russian Minister in Peking to the Chinese Foreign Minister, June 23/July 6, 1914, p. 110.

[214] *IBZI.*, Vol. II, 7, 1, No. 310, Miller to Sazonov (from Kiakhta), February 19/March 4, 1915, pp. 286-7, and n. 1 on p. 287; Vol. II, 8, 1, No. 76, The Russian Minister in Peking to the Chinese Foreign Minister, May 25/June 7, 1915; Krupenskii to Sazonov, June 26/July 9, 1915, p. 259; see also Vol. II, 7, 2, No. 712, Krupenskii to Sazonov, April 25/May 8, 1915, pp. 699-700.

If we review Tsarist Russia's position when the tripartite agreement was signed in June 1915, we see that she had been able to circumscribe the activities of the Chinese as well as of the Outer Mongols themselves. In the political sphere she forced China to recognize her right to act as mediator in " questions of political and territorial nature " between China and Outer Mongolia. In the economic sphere we see that a likin tax was established between China and Mongolia whereas goods imported from Russia were free of duty, and Chinese banking enterprise in Outer Mongolia was frustrated while a Russian controlled Mongolian National Bank was established. The right of the Mongolian Government to conclude commercial and industrial agreements was limited in practice by Russia's determination not to tolerate any agreements which would be detrimental to her interests. In matters of arms, loans, railways and military instruction Outer Mongolia was to address herself first to Russia thus preventing any other foreign influence and any kind of bargain or understanding between Chinese and Mongols.

Tsarist Russia's control of Outer Mongolia after the tripartite agreement in 1915 would have been far more significant if the Great War had not cut short its development and diminished its possibilities. For from this date, Russia's energy was completely concentrated on war on the European front; her unsuccessful operations there as well as her inability to give any efficient support to her agents in Outer Mongolia soon diminished her hold over the Mongols and encouraged the Chinese to renew their activities. Shortly after the conclusion of the tripartite agreement the Chinese proposed to send an official mission of dignitaries to Urga in order to invest the Living Buddha with his official seal. " It does not matter," telegraphed the Russian Foreign Minister to the Minister in Peking in November 1915, " how long the mission will stay in Urga, but it matters that the ceremonies should not take the character of the normal investiture of foreign rulers dependent upon China. We cannot tolerate the return of the times when Mongolia was joined to China." [215] It appears also that Russian representatives were taken aback by the ingratitude shown by the Mongols toward the end of 1915, in passing " without taking advice from Russia " a resolution which characterized the relations of Mongolia with China in terms which ignored the position which Russia had tried to obtain for herself.[216]

The few years between the conclusion of the Russo-Mongolian agreement of Urga in 1912 and the tripartite agreement in Kiakhta in 1915 are also too short a time from which to judge Russia's economic hold on the country. Statistics between 1913 and 1915 show that the figures for Russia's exports into Mongolia rose in 1914 but fell sharply in 1915; her imports from Mongolia, on the other hand, remained stationary in 1914 but rose sharply in 1915, due entirely to the increased import of cattle during the Great War. The figures are:

Year	Imports from Mongolia	Exports to Mongolia	Total
1913	8,403,000 Rubles	2,689,000	11,092,000
1914	8,427,000 "	4,484,000	12,911,000
1915	11,461,000 "	2,429,000	13,890,000 [217]

The time was indeed too short for the advocated reorganization of Russian trade methods in Mongolia to be undertaken; Rockhill, who visited Urga at the end of 1913, on a study tour under the auspices of the American Asiatic Association (of which prominent American ' big business ' men are members) gave a very gloomy account of the prospects of Russian trade in Outer Mongolia, and his conclusions seem to be identical with those arrived at by the Russian Export Company in 1913. He wrote:

The general conclusion I have reached is that nothing short of the expulsion of most of the present Russian firms and small traders now

---

[215] Telegram of Foreign Minister, November 12, 1912, No. 5857, as cited in S. S., 1928, No. 5, p. 165; cf. *IBZI.*, Vol. II, 8, 1, p. 115, n. 1 and No. 124, Sazonov to Krupenskii, June 3/16, 1915.

[216] Telegram of Foreign Minister, December 30, 1915, No. 6038, as cited in S. S., 1928, No. 5.

[217] S. S., p. 160, Maiskii, p. 207.

engaged in the Outer Mongolian trade and the substitution of Moscow firms, the exclusion of all possible foreign competition, together with the maintenance of preferential treatment for home trade and the forcing of all Chinese imports to come by the Vladivostok-Verkhne-Udinsk-Kiakhta route, can secure to Russia the economic control of Outer Mongolia. With the right of this country to concede equally favorable trade conditions to other nationalities and the practical impossibility of excluding Chinese goods from the direct route the task seems quite an hopeless one.[218]

This seems to be a fair statement of the difficulties with which Russia was faced. We may say here that Tsarist Russia was not able to overcome them and we will leave it to a later stage to show how far Soviet Russia has been successful in the amelioration or elimination of those factors which Rockhill in 1914 considered it necessary to eliminate for the economic progress of Russia in Outer Mongolia.

The increasingly passive trade balance between Russia and Mongolia can to a great extent be explained, as we have mentioned, by the special needs which the war imposed on Russia. In this connection the creation in 1915 of a big state organization, called the " Mongolian Expedition " (Mongol-skaya Expeditsia), for the acquisition of livestock and live-stock products for the army is significant. It was not confined, however, to Outer Mongolia, but extended its activities to Siberia, Manchuria, China and even Australia. Up to 1917 the head of it was the explorer, P. K. Kozlov, who had travelled widely in Outer Mongolia. The business of the " M. E." was done chiefly by contracts with private merchants. Purchases of cattle and dairy produce were effected either by cash payments in silver or in exchange for goods (cloth, tea and the like) and the cattle were consigned to Russia through frontier stations (Katon-Karagay, Zaysan, Kosh Agach, Zheltukha and Kiakhta). Payments for these consignments (cattle, butter, fat, skins) amounted in 1915 to 3,438,000 rubles, in 1916 to 20,639,000 and in 1917 to 32,165,000 rubles. But the expendi-

---

[218] W. W. Rockkhill, " The Question of Outer Mongolia," *Journal of the American Asiatic Association*, May, 1914 (Vol. XIV, No. 4), p. 107; also in *The Far Eastern Review* (Shanghai), June, 1915, p. 9.

tures of the " M. E." were made without much supervision and in 1915 a special commission of the Senate was sent up to control it, but without result. The " M. E." had for a time almost a monopoly in the export of cattle, etc., from Mongolia to Russia.[219]

It is interesting to note the parallel efforts which Russian agents, the staff of the Urga Consulate General and the Russian financial adviser, made in inducing the Mongols to reform and organize their state. In the decrees of the Hutukhtu concerning compulsory land cultivation and the internal organization of the administration machinery, Russian influence can be discerned.[220] In 1915-16, Baron P. A. Witte, assistant to Kosin, the financial adviser, led an expedition to investigate the country geographically and statistically in order to find new sources of state income and objects for investment. The result was not as great as expected, but it was a starting point chiefly for statistical research. The report had not been completed when the Russian revolution broke out, and part of the material sent to Petrograd was probably lost on the way. The same Witte in 1916 created and assumed the head of a Special Administration of State Properties, which introduced new taxes, issued regulations for the renting of land for hay-making, pasture and cultivation, established statistical research institutes, and opened a type foundry, a machine shop, a telephone exchange, a brick factory, etc., in Urga.[221] But such a reform policy was strongly resented particularly by the Lama Church dignitaries, whose property (and this included the 125,000 Mongols called shabinar who were the direct personal subjects of the Living Buddha) had been exempted from taxes until that time. Miller was so impressed by the necessity of crushing the opposition of the Church that in 1916 he planned to stage a coup d'état in Urga with the assistance of armed forces, for the purpose of separating the Church

[219] Maiskii, pp. 212-17; special article in *SSA*, 1932, Vol. III, pp. 442-43, on Mongolskaya Expeditsiya.
[220] Maiskii, p. 96.
[221] *SSE*, 1932, Vol. III, op. cit.

6

from the State. St. Petersburg, however, did not approve of such drastic measures.[222]

It seems obvious from the details given above that Mongols owed many things to Russia—for instance, money and arms—but one should be on one's guard against over-emphasizing the effectiveness of her influence. The Mongols grew more and more sensitive to interference, especially since some of their influential leaders knew how little effective support from St. Petersburg the Russians on the spot could count on in the second and third years of the Great War. The Russian agents had to struggle against a tendency of the Mongols to force them into abandoning the position which they had reached by means of tenacious diplomacy and frequent threats. Russian merchants without substantial funds to do business on credit did not make any headway. On the other hand, the Chinese were preparing to re-occupy Mongolia at the first opportunity and reduce it to the status of a mere province again. After the fall of the Tsarist dynasty, the situation for the representative of the Provisional Government in Outer Mongolia became more and more critical.

B. Policy of the Provisional Government

The Provisional Government was too much absorbed with other questions—the internal situation and the European war front—to care much about Far Eastern or Mongolian policy. More than ever everything depended upon the ability of the Russian representatives in Outer Mongolia. The experienced, energetic and therefore much feared and respected A. Miller had left Urga in 1916. But the efforts of his successor, Orlov, to counter China's renewed attempts to regain her old position in Khalkha, were completely frustrated by events in the Russian colonies in Outer Mongolia, chiefly in that of Urga, which were the direct result of the Russian February Revolution.

[222] Report of Russian Diplomatic Agent in Mongolia to Russian Mission in Peking of April 12, 1919, as cited in Novy Vostok, Vol. II, Materials and Documents. Materials on the history of Intervention—Japan's part in the Mongolian Movement by A. F. S-ky, p. 598.

The Russian colony in Urga had at that time about 2500 inhabitants, that in Uliassutai about 100, and that in Kobdo 200-250. These were mostly small merchants and artisans with almost no laborers. Others belonged to the Consular service, and there were also the Cossack guard and the officers who had trained the Mongol brigade.[223] In the beginning of March 1917 the colony in Urga elected an Executive Committee which was to take care of its interests. It was meant as a sort of competing body to the Consulate, which was regarded as belonging to the old régime. But the consuls in China (including Mongolia) had by treaty more rights over Russian citizens than consuls normally had in Western countries. All administrative and judicial measures concerning Russian citizens were in their hands. When the members of the Executive Committee suddenly claimed these rights for themselves, the Diplomatic Agent and Consul General in Urga refused to recognize them or even to enter into correspondence on this matter.[224]

The dispute became more uncomfortable for Orlov when complaints about his political unreliability were forwarded to the Irkutsk Executive Committee and to the Foreign Ministry, and at the same time the unrest spread to the Cossack guard when one of its number became a member of the Executive Committee. Orlov thereupon forbade the guard any intercourse with the Executive Committee. By some indiscretion of an official of the Consulate, it became known to a higher officer of the guard that, in case of a " revolt " of the guard, Orlov planned to keep it in check by calling to his aid the Russian trained Mongolian machine-gun brigade. Whether he actually had such a plan, and if so whether he really meant the brigade

---

[223] See Korostovets, pp. 288-9; Prof. A. Gladstern, "Mongolska Politika timchasovoho rossiyskoho uriadu" (The Mongolian Policy and the Russian Provisional Government) in *S. S.*, 1928, No. 5, pp. 154-71; especially in this connection the same author's article: "1917 rik v Mongolii" (The year 1917 in Mongolia), *S. S.*, 1927, No. 1, pp. 91-119.

[224] *S. S.*, 1927, No. 1, p. 92; this material is based on the archives of the Diplomatic Chancellory of the Irkutsk Commissariat (which replaced the Governor General).

composed of Mongols or only those Russian officers who had instructed them, is not clear, but at any rate the report made the Executive Committee and some of the Cossacks think of arresting the Diplomatic Agent. Orlov gave the official who had been responsible for the story three days house-arrest.[225] In a report to the Foreign Ministry, this official complained of this step, quite unheard of in the diplomatic and consular service.[226]

At the end of March another incident complicated the situation. There was a considerable food shortage at that time in Urga, and in order to assess the existing stocks and to prevent any rise of prices, the Executive Committee required stocks of important commodities such as grain, sugar, salt, etc., which Russian merchants had stored, to be registered. Non-compliance with this order was to be regarded as an unpatriotic act and to be punished by such fines as the Committe should fix. A petty officer was charged with the execution of this order, but one of the bigger Russian merchants refused him access to his stocks. When other officers tried to adjust the difference, the Executive Committee accused them of hostile intentions against the interests of the " people," and of being still on the side of the Tsar. The officers indignantly repudiated such suggestions, recalling that they had sworn allegiance to the Provisional Government.[227] The dispute was finally submitted to a special commission presided over by a General from the Irkutsk Military district, and ended with the petty officer's recall from Urga.[228] But with this the tension between the Russian Consulate-General and the Executive Committee was by no means relaxed. At the end of April, the Executive Committee called upon the Commander-in-Chief at Irkutsk to

---

[225] *S. S.*, pp. 93-4, Protocol of the meeting of the Urga Executive Committee of April 5, 1917.

[226] *S. S.*, p. 95. Supplement to the report of Kuznetsov.

[227] *S. S.*, pp. 97-100, the Executive Order given in the name of Officer Malishov, March 17, 1917.

[228] *S. S.*, p. 102, Secret telegram of Orlov to the Foreign Minister, May 1, 1917. File No. 86.

forward to Petrograd their demand for the recall of Orlov and other diplomatic officials.[229]

In the meantime, the Chief of the Cossack Guard had become a member of the Executive Committee, but he took an attitude which displeased the Committee to such an extent that they complained about him to the military chief in Chita and asked for his immediate recall and replacement by an officer more loyal to " the new ideas of the new order." But they were informed that no replacement was possible.[230] At the same time a telegram reached the Commander-in-Chief in Irkutsk containing the resolution adopted at a meeting of the Cossack guard, in which vigorous protest was made against attempts to oust the diplomatic staff. The guard had decided to take the Consulate under its protection, and proposed to the officials that they should continue to discharge their duties until instructions were forthcoming from Petrograd. In a word, the guard recognized only the Petrograd authorities as competent to decide questions regarding the recall of officials.[231] At the same time, the Consul General, Lavdovski, who so far had tried to keep on good terms with the Executive Committee, wired to Petrograd referring to the extremely serious situation created by its attitude.[232] Orlov, who for a few days had left his duties to Lavdovski, now under pressure of the guard resumed them and reinstated the dismissed subordinate officials.[233] In the meantime, a reply from Petrograd stated simply that the actions of the Executive Committee were inadmissible, which was, however, not sufficient for Orlov, especially since he had to explain to the Mongols the attitude of the Provisional Government.[234]

" Our authority among the Mongols," he wired again in the beginning of May, " has fallen greatly, and to uphold it, it will be necessary to use methods which are not contemplated

[229] *S. S.*, p. 103. Telegram of Urga, Ex. Com. of April 28.
[230] *S. S.*, p. 103. Telegram of April 29, 1917.
[231] *S. S.*, p. 104.
[232] *S. S.*, Secret telegram of the Chief of the General Consulate, April 27, No. 87.
[233] *S. S.*, for telegram cf. above n. 228.
[234] *S. S.*, pp. 105-6.

in my instructions." [235] The head of the Irkutsk Executive Committee wired in the same sense to the Foreign Minister in Petrograd reporting the shocking state of relations between Mongols and Russians, which he attributed mainly to lack of instructions. He recommended a final adjustment of relations between the Russian Consulate and the Executive Committee.[236] The special interest of Irkutsk in this matter was that it was the headquarters of the Mongolian Expedition, the provisioning of which was rendered difficult by the dislocation of the cattle trade resulting from the confused conditions in Urga and also in Uliassutai.

Only when the Russian Minister in Peking reinforced these requests, however, was it possible to extract a fuller answer from the Petrograd authorities, preoccupied as they were with other questions. The wire of the Foreign Minister (Tereshenlov had succeeded Milyukov), was addressed directly to the Executive Committees in Urga and Uliassutai. After welcoming them as the proper organs of the Russian colonies, he added that he would examine all complaints forwarded through the Consul. "But I must warn the Committee against interfering with the administrative and judicial functions of the representative of the Provisional Government. This would create a dangerous state of anarchy and threaten to shake the position of Russia and the position of our citizens outside our frontiers, and that is the reason why it is inadmissible." "Only the Provisional Government or the judicial authorities are competent to decide whether these complaints necessitate the recall of officials." [237]

These warnings did not end the dispute. The Executive Committee in Irkutsk advised the Foreign Ministry that the only way to solve the problem would be to recall Orlov, Khonin and Bolaban, and put Lavdovski—the Consul General—at the head of the Consulate.[238] On the other hand, a meeting of

[235] *S. S.*, p. 106, for telegram cf. above 228.

[236] *S. S.*, Telegram of Kruglikov, head of Irkutsk Ex. Com. to Foreign Minister of May 6, 1917, No. 344.

[237] *S. S.*, p. 107; p. 108, telegram of Foreign Minister, May 8, 1917, No. 5974, and telegram of same date, No. 5973.

[238] *S. S.*, p. 109, telegram of Irkutsk Ex. Com. of May 10, 1917, No. 359.

Consuls, presided over by the Russian Minister in Peking, urged the Ministry to issue a decree reaffirming the Consular authority in all matters affecting administrative and judicial matters.[239] The answer of the Minister in Petrograd is not known, but towards the end of May the Russian Minister in Peking, Prince Kudashev, wired to Urga and other places that " the Foreign Minister requires you as the sole representative of the Provisional Government in your district to make known to all Russian citizens therein the telegram sent by the Foreign Minister to the Executive Committee." [240]

Prince Kudashev, as well as the Foreign Minister, seems to have been very optimistic about the effect of such a step. Yet the latter expressed his anxiety to the District Commissar of the Provisional Government at Irkutsk: " I am afraid that our authority in Mongolia declines further because of the social position of the whole of Russia, arising out of the change from the old order to the new. The result of this change is the situation in Urga." [241] The District Commissar agreed that there was a close connection between Russian authority in Mongolia and the situation in Russia itself " . . . taking into account that in the Russian colony in Urga there is the same democratic conviction upon which the internal order of the new Russian state organization is being based. The colony, which continually enters into relations with the Mongolian population and the governing class, undoubtedly has closer connections with Mongols than the official diplomatic agent. To give his voice power and authority, it is indispensable that he should have closer contact with the colony; and that is why in my opinion the attempt to support the authority of the official representatives by artificial means is futile." He thought it necessary to recall Orlov. Lavdovski was not proposed this time (it had become known in the meantime that he was on the side of Orlov, his friendly attitude towards the Executive Committee being only a tactical maneuver), but the head of

---

[239] S. S., telegram of Minister in Peking to Foreign Minister of May 12, No. 353.
[240] S. S., p. 110, telegram of Minister in Peking of May 18, 1917, No. 374.
[241] S. S., telegram of Minister of May 12 (or May 15), No. 2203.

the Mongolian Expedition, Dudokalov (successor of Kosin), was to be sent to Urga as mediator. " I am," concludes the District Commissar, " for the exchange of one agent of the Central Government by another, who according to the necessities of the political moment could represent Imperial interests and who would be supported by the understanding and help of the Russian colony, as well as by the commercial organizations of neighboring Siberia with which Mongolia is economically closely aligned. The presence of the commercial agent, Boloban, who lost his influence with the Russian colony, is also to be regretted as it brings about disorder and unauthorized interference." [242]

But the Foreign Minister did not act on this advice, and neither Orlov nor any other official was recalled. In June, the Urga Executive drafted a statute of its organization. But the Foreign Minister was of the opinion that " communal organizations which arise among colonies outside Russia under the name of Executive Committee, Security Committee, Municipal Council, etc., are not administrative organizations, and have exclusively the ' character of organs of communal opinion,' and the Government is always willing to proceed according to their suggestions." At the same time, however, he makes a 'concession in that he does not object " if the Executive Committees in those places which have not communal self-government assume the functions of self-governmental organs." [243]

We have no record of the outcome of the strained relations between the Consul and the Executive Committee in Urga, but we know that in Uliassutai the struggle came to an end because the Russian citizens became either indifferent or hostile toward the Committee and in the middle of July were able to dissolve it. In a public meeting it was decided that the Committee was useless, and a municipal council was to be elected

[242] S. S., pp. 111-2.
[243] S. S., p. 112, telegram of Foreign Minister to Khobdo of May 17, 1917; p. 115, telegram of Foreign Minister to Russian Consul in Kulja of June 10, 1917; telegram of the same to Ex. Consul in Khobdo, June 17.

which was to govern the community with the limits of the new statutes which the Foreign Minister had promised.[244]

Thus, those facts that we know show to what extent the effects of the February Revolution had paralyzed the activities of Russian official representatives in Mongolia, and even compromised their position toward Mongols, as well as toward Chinese. At least from March to June, 1917, the Russian representatives had, paradoxically, almost no protection from the Mongols against their own citizens, whereas the task assigned to them by the Kiakhta agreement was virtually one of protecting the Mongols. When in September 1917—the last month of the Provisional Government—the Mongol Government asked the Russian Government for the immediate dispatch of arms " to fight the bands of robbers which had appeared at all the frontiers of Mongolia," the Russian Government was unable to respond.[245] Only a few weeks later, the October Revolution deprived the Russian representatives of their official position, and the Chinese had little difficulty in completely isolating them.

The Provisional Government aimed at retaining the maximum of the authority inherited from the Tsar—with a minimum of effort. The new Soviet Government, however, refused the heritage of Tsarist Russia and denounced all " imperialist " treaties and rights secured by it. It thus left the Mongols to themselves—or, rather, handed them over to the Chinese.

C. POLICY OF SOVIET RUSSIA

In the first years of Soviet rule no direct participation in Outer Mongolian affairs is apparent. The Soviet Government, like the Tsarist régime in its last years and the Provisional Government, had its attention focussed on other problems such as the position on the western frontiers. For quite a considerable time—until the end of the Washington Conference

[244] *S. S.*, p. 118, telegram of Consul in Uliassutai to Diplomatic Agent in Urga of July 22, 1917, No. 31.

[245] *S. S.*, No. 5, 1928, p. 166, secret telegram of Diplomatic Agent in Urga to Foreign Minister of September 27, 1917, No. 205.

in 1922—Russia had to struggle to regain her position in Siberia and her Far Eastern region, and make it again an integral part of her territory. Unlike the Provisional Government which intended to profit from all Tsarist Russian achievements in foreign policy, the Soviet Government not only denounced all treaties made by the former governments, but also renounced all privileges accruing from them.

In July 1919, in a special declaration addressed to the Chinese Government, it surrendered all concessions made by China to the Tsarist Government. The right of consular jurisdiction in China, together with the right to have special foreign " settlements " was expressly abandoned.[246] But as this step was taken in the name of the right of every state to be free from foreign exploitation, it was only natural that in the same year the Soviet Government should issue a special message to the Mongolian people. " Mongolia is a free country," it read. " Russian advisers, Tsarist consuls, bankers and capitalists who have held the Mongolian nation in their hands by strength and by gold, and who have squeezed the last juice out of it, must be driven out of Mongolia. All power in this country must belong to the Mongolian nation. Not a single foreigner has the right to interfere with the domestic affairs of Mongolia. The Soviet Government loudly announcing this to the Mongolian nation offers immediate entry into diplomatic relations with the Russian people, and asks her to meet the representatives of the Red Army." [247]

Such a declaration could have no immediate effect, as the " Mongolian nation " was again in the firm grip of China, and Soviet Russia was not willing to intervene. Such activity as was displayed at that time was merely exploratory; the Irkutsk office of the All Russian Central Union of Cooperative Societies sent an expedition to Outer Mongolia to investigate economic possibilities. To its leader, I. Maiskii, we owe a masterly

[246] Cited by M. Galkovitch, " SSSR na Dalnyem Vostoke " (USSR in the Far East. A survey of Sino-Soviet and Soviet-Japanese relations 1917-1925, in *Meshdunarodnaya Letopis* (International Chronicle), No. 3, March 1925, p. 9.

[247] Cited by Doksom, *T. O.*, No. 3 (9), July-September, 1936, p. 72.

exposition of conditions in Outer Mongolia, published in Irkutsk in 1921.[248]

In the same year events in Outer Mongolia brought Soviet Russia back into the political scene. Partisan groups of Mongols were coming into being, mainly in those districts north of Urga which border Russia. Near Kiakhta, i. e., near the Russian-Mongolian frontier, partisan troops met in March 1921 and elected a temporary revolutionary government to liberate Outer Mongolia from its foreign rulers. "The overwhelming majority of the conference," reads the official Mongolian account of these events, decided to ask the Soviet Government for assistance in the coming struggle.[249] In the middle of March, the Chinese garrison stationed on the border was driven out. A much more dangerous enemy, however, was the white Russian Baron Ungern-Sternberg, who at that time was in control of Urga. He now moved his troops, said to have numbered eleven thousand horsemen, northward toward Kiakhta with the aim not only of crushing the Mongol detachments but also of realizing his ambition to conquer the whole of Transbaikalia.

This was a move which affected Russia directly and to which she could not remain indifferent, quite apart from the sympathy with which Communism greeted the revolutionary aspirations of the Mongols. Ungern-Sternberg moved into Russian territory, but was finally defeated and captured near Lake Gusinoe (which lies between Kiakhta and Verkhne Udinsk) on June 22, 1921. He was handed over to the Soviet Red Army and shot.[250] There still remained dispersed in Outer Mongolia a considerable number of White Russian detachments, those of General Bakitch, Colonel Kasagrandi, General Resvonkin, Colonel Kasantsev, Kitaigorodov, etc. The Mongolian People's Revolutionary Army entered Urga in July 1921, and in the following months they completed their task of liquidating the White Russian troops or driving them into Manchuria, assisted by Soviet troops.[251]

[248] Cf. Preface and Bibliography. [249] Cf. n. 247.
[250] *Ibid.*, p. 73. [251] *Ibid.*

In August 1921 the Provisional Revolutionary Government of Mongolia addressed an appeal to the Government of the Russian Socialist Federated Soviet Republics not to withdraw their troops " until the complete removal of the menace from the common enemy, who is now seeking reinforcements in the Eastern Steppes. . . . The presence of the Soviet troops is dictated by circumstances, its purpose being to preserve the security of the territory of Mongolia and of the frontiers of the R. S. F. S. R." Chicherin, the Commissar for Foreign Affairs, immediately replied welcoming collaboration between Soviet and Mongolian troops against those who tried to enslave the Mongolian people and were " at the same time threatening the security of Soviet Russia and the inviolability of the territory of the fraternal Far Eastern Republic." He emphasized two things; first, he promised to give to the Mongolian request " complete satisfaction," meaning apparently to reinforce considerably the Russian troops already in Outer Mongolia; second, he communicated the Russian Government's firm decision " to withdraw its troops from the territory of autonomous Mongolia . . . as soon as the menace to the free development of the Mongolian people and to the security of the Russian Republics and of the Far Eastern Republic should be removed." [252]

Such an emphatic reassurance is understandable if we take into account that the Soviet Foreign Minister was anxious to dispel any doubt as to the " unimperialistic " nature of such intervention, especially as the " imperialistic " Tsarist Government had never gone to such lengths of intervention in Mongolian territory. Indeed, this very piece of military intervention has been taken by many to prove that Soviet Russia's activities were from the outset a direct continuation of the Tsarist policy. But whatever the Government of the day or outsiders may read into the foreign policy of the country, the fact remains that the fundamental maxim of any government's strong policy is the preservation of the integrity of its territory.

[252] These notes are reprinted in full by Leo Pasvolsky in *Russia in the Far East*, New York, 1922, pp. 176-9.

This was menaced by Ungern-Sternberg's advance from Outer Mongolia into Russian territory more acutely than by any movement of Chinese troops in Tsarist days. Thus we cannot accept the contention that it was Soviet Russia's failure to establish her influence on her Western borders (i. e., her defeat in the Polish campaign in 1920) which made her turn to another field of activity.[253] This is a simplification which must be rejected, just as we rejected the statement that Russia's defeat in Manchuria in 1905 was the origin of her policy in Outer Mongolia. Of course, sooner or later Soviet Russia would have tried to establish political and economic contacts with Outer Mongolia—her neighbor along a long stretch of her frontier—but this would not have involved active military intervention while the Chinese were in power; and Ungern-Sternberg's victory absolved the Soviets from taking any active steps in the matter of the Chinese military occupation.

These events left the international position of Outer Mongolia still in suspense. In September 1921 Chicherin was asked by the Mongolian Provisional Government to act as intermediary in regard to China. Chicherin agreed with them concerning the " need of establishing peaceful and businesslike relations between Mongolia and China. More than once the Russian Government has approached the Government of China, both directly and through the representatives of the Far Eastern Republic who were in communication with the latter, with offers to begin negotiations on this question. In the near future the Russian Government hopes to enter into permanent relations with the Government of China by means of a trade delegation which is being sent to Peking." [254] Indeed, the Soviet Government was most anxious to establish diplomatic relations with the Chinese Government, but the latter insisted on the withdrawal of all Soviet troops from Outer Mongolia as a prerequisite to official negotiations. At the same time, it

---

[253] See for instance article in *The Times*, London, June 24, 1929, p. 15, " The Soviets in Asia." I. An Eurasian Movement. The Mongol Idea, by W. E. D. Allen, M. P.

[254] Cf. Pasvolsky, *op. cit.*, p. 181.

should not be forgotten that in the years 1921-22 there was still a strong possibility of a Chinese punitive expedition being sent to Urga, but the Chinese General Chang Tso-lin, who was charged by the Peking Government with the execution of this task, remained inactive.[255]

Soviet Russia, with troops in Outer Mongolia, naturally lent support to the new revolutionary movement there. In November 1921 an agreement establishing friendly relations between Soviet Russia and the People's Government of Mongolia was signed. The preamble recites that, in contrast to treaties made " by the cunning and predatory Tsarist Government, the agreement was one of " free friendship and collaboration between the two neighoring states." All Tsarist treaties were voided, and the buildings and equipment of the telegraph administration in Mongolia, formerly belonging to the Russian Government, were turned over to the Mongols. The parties recognized each other and agreed to arrange formal diplomatic representation through plenipotentiaries of equal status.[256] (We remember that Tsarist Russia had been very persistent in its refusal to admit a permanent Mongolian plenipotentiary). Such equality could not have been reconciled with the consular jurisdiction over its subjects in Mongolia formerly exercised by the Tsarist Government. On the other hand, there was no reason for the Soviet Union to expose its citizens to the barbarities of Mongol judicial procedure. It may have been for this reason that a clause was included stating that both countries were to be guided " by the high principles of civilization and humanity," and were to refrain from " any punitive or inquisitorial measures which might cause physical suffering and lower a person's moral condition." [257] Another obligation, stated to be reciprocal but applying in practice only to the Mongols, was that each state should prevent the " formation

---

[255] Cf. Chapter III.

[256] *Treaties and Agreements With and Concerning China*, 1919-29, Washington, pp. 53-4.

[257] E. Korovine, " La République des Soviets et le Droit International," in *Revue Générale du Droit International Public*, Vol. XXXII, 1925, p. 298; also in German, in book form, under the title, *Das Völkerrecht der Uebergangszeit*, Berlin, 1929.

or sojourn within its territory of governments, organizations, groups or individuals inimical to the other, or the importation into or carriage through its territory of arms belonging to such organizations." [258]

After ridding Outer Mongolia of the remnants of White Russian forces, the Russians had to face at Urga influences that were either pro-Chinese or anti-Soviet. It was only natural that the Church dignitaries—whose active participation in political life dated only from 1911—and some of the princes felt themselves increasingly menaced by the new and revolutionary wing of the Mongol National Party. The anti-clerical movement was guided by Buriats who, although racially related to the Mongols, lived in Russian territory adjacent to Outer Mongolia and were thus for the most part Russian subjects. [259] The Buriats had for some time been considered by the Russians as indispensable intermediaries between themselves and the Mongols. [260] Russian policy, unlike the Chinese, had not, as far back as the middle of the 19th century, favored the development of Lamaism. It is reported that Russia imposed upon the Buriats the regulation (whether by law or moral force could not be verified), that not more than twenty per cent of the male population should be Lamas. It is a fact that among the Buriats the Lamas are comparatively few. [261] In addition, a fair number of Buriats had some training for leadership as many of them had been educated in Russian schools and universities. [262] Some of them can thus be considered as the intellectual vanguard of the Mongols, and they were viewed with hostility by the Lama Church as having fallen under the influence of European civilization. [263] While many of them found a field of activity in the Japanese-influenced Pan-Mon-

[258] Cf. n. 256, Article 3, pars. 1 and 2 of the agreement.

[259] Maiskii, p. 93.

[260] Korostovets, p. 244. Referring to his report to the Foreign Ministry answering allegations that he favored the Buriats too much.

[261] See *The Chinese Recorder and Missionary Journal*, Vol. V (Shanghai, 1874), " Mongolia's Two Neighbors, Russia and China," by Hoinos, p. 71.

[262] See Baddeley, *op. cit.*, Vol. I, p. lii; *Bulletin de l'Ecole Française d'Extrême Orient*, Hanoi, Tome V, No. 3-4, July-December 1905, p. 459 (Bibliographical Note).

[263] Maiskii, p. 94.

golian movement in the twenties,[264] some of the most intelligent took a leading part in the new revolutionary movement in Outer Mongolia, since when they have been prominent in the direction of affairs there. When speaking, therefore, of Soviet Russia's influence in Outer Mongolia we have to take into account not only the Russian representatives themselves and the Red Army troops but also Russia's Buriat-Mongolian subjects. In 1923 a Buriat Mongol Autonomous Soviet Republic was established as part of the Soviet Union [265] with a common frontier with Outer Mongolia for approximately 450 miles.

These Buriats, few in number but of the utmost importance, have assisted Russia to a considerable extent in the past in the task of handling the situation in Outer Mongolia, which was far from settled in the first years of the new régime. Thus in April 1922, only a few months after Soviet recognition, the Prime Minister, Bodo, a Lama, and fifteen other officials were seized and shot. They were chiefly accused of connections and conspiracy with Chinese. Further revolts took place at the end of 1922.[266] Nevertheless, Soviet Russia being too weak during these years, and also strongly desiring to arrive at some agreement with China, at first took a cautious view of the international position of Outer Mongolia in spite of the Soviet-Mongolian agreement. For when Vasiliev, the Soviet Ambassador, presented his credentials to the Mongolian Government in January 1924 he stated that, as Soviet Russia was surrounded by reactionary states, it was sometimes necessary "to fall back on the second line of defense." [267] In an interview, he clarified his somewhat obscure phrases. When asked whether

[264] Cf. Chapter IV; also Korostovets, p. 32.

[265] For details see article on Buriat-Mongolia in *SSE*, Vol. 1; *Far Eastern Survey* (Institute of Pacific Relations), Vol. V, No. 10, New York, May 6, 1936, p. 97.

[266] Cf. n. 247, p. 86; also Maslennikov, "The Mongolian Problem," in *Mirovoe Khozaistvo i Mirovaya Politika* (World Politics and Economics), Moscow, May 5, 1936, p. 81. Also A. Rish, "Mongolia Guards its Independence," in *T. O.*, No. 4 (6), October-December, 1935, pp. 98-112. Also N. Khalkin, "The Stages of Development of the Mongolian People's Republic," in *Pravda*, Moscow, April 8, 1936, p. 2.

[267] *CYB*, 1924, p. 582.

Soviet Russia had now recognized Mongolian independence, he referred to the precarious situation of Soviet Russia in general. " I will say definitely that present conditions do not permit of our speaking or referring to the ' independence ' of Mongolia; the only thing referred to is ' autonomy ' for your country. But here it is important to emphasize that the difference between the two is more apparent than real." Too much stress was laid upon the external signs of independence, he concluded. " What should be considered are the actual conditions under which you live, and if you make the necessary preparations, you can live much more freely . . . with Autonomy than with Independence." He advised them to become strong financially, economically and militarily " so that you will be able to speak to all nationals as an equal. Then even if you have merely autonomy, your allegiance will be but nominal. You should be strong enough to insist on being allowed to go your own way along the road to progress and freedom." [268] These words are nearly identical with the advice offered to the Mongols by Sazonov, Korostovets, Miller, and the American diplomat Rockhill. Soviet policy was doubtless inspired in part by fear lest an open avowal of Mongol independence should impede negotiations with China. Partly also it was affected by a desire to prevent the Mongols from making political contact with other powers. But now, as in Tsarist days, the Russians were only speaking the truth; Mongolia was weak in every respect in which an independent state should be strong.

From this it followed naturally that the Soviet representative should announce, in his official speech, that he had brought with him from Moscow the ratification of the Russo-Mongolian bank project and the Russo-Mongolian telegraph agreement. These were to be " the first steps toward a prosperous future which would be to the mutual advantage " of both countries.[269]

[269] Cf. n. 267.
[268] *The North China Herald*, Shanghai, Vol. CL, No. 2953, March 15, 1924, p. 402,

In June 1924 the Mongolian Industrial and Commercial Bank was founded in Urga and branches were opened later in Uliassu-tai, Khobdo, Altan-Bulak (on the frontier opposite Kiakhta) and several other places. The Bank had a monopoly status; ownership was divided equally between the Mongolian Government on the one hand, and the Soviet State Bank and the People's Commissariat of Finance on the other. The directorate, however, as well as practically all the staff, was Russian. There was one Mongolian official on the directorate. The original capital was in Chinese silver dollars—$175,000 at first, raised later to $3,000,000. In spite of this, the notes issued were called *tughrik* (a Mongol word which is equivalent to the Chinese *yuan* and the Japanese *yen*); and in order to establish independence of Chinese currency, and also to replace the old Russian silver ruble, the tughrik was valued to begin with at the fixed exchange rate of 90 tughrik to 100 Chinese dollars. Parity between the tughrik and the Chinese dollar was later proclaimed, but this was not justified, as the tughrik contained only 20 grams of pure silver, as against 36 grams in the Chinese dollar. The tughrik was covered by silver deposits with the Minister of Finance, and was minted as a silver coin in Moscow, where the Mongol bank notes were also printed. The subsidiary coin is the *mungge*, of which there are 100 to the tughrik.[270]

In addition to the creation of this bank by Soviet Russians, the year 1924 threw light in other ways on Soviet Russia's attitude toward Outer Mongolia. First of all, in the "Agreement on general principles for the settlement of the questions between the Republic of China and the U.S.S.R.", finally signed on May 31, 1924, "the Government of the U.S.S.R. recognizes that Outer Mongolia is an integral part of the Republic of China and respects China's sovereignty therein."

---

[270] Diplom-Bergingenieur Fritz Weiske, "Die Wirtschaftlichen Verhältnisse in der Aeusseren Mongolei," in *Osteuropa*, December 1928, pp. 154-6; cf. also L. Zolotarev, "Denezhnaya Reforma v Mongolii" (The Bank reform in Mongolia) in *N. V.*, 1926, No. 13-14, pp. 234-6.

At the same time, the Soviet Government declared that as soon as the withdrawal of all Soviet troops should have been agreed upon at a subsequent Sino-Russian conference, " it will effect the complete withdrawal of all troops of the U.S.S.R. from Outer Mongolia." [271] Thus Soviet Russia reaffirmed that Mongolia was a Chinese possession in exactly that term— sovereignty—which Tsarist Russia had obstinately refused in 1912-1915 when conceding only " suzerainty." But as a matter of fact this was only an " agreement on general principles," and, apart from the promise of withdrawing troops, it contained no concrete proposal for reestablishment of direct contact between the Chinese Government and the Mongolian authorities. Evidently Soviet Russia was prepared to satisfy China's *amour propre*—for this was the condition of establishing official relations—but Chicherin, Commissar for Foreign Affairs, made it clear at the end of the same year that Russia did not intend to tolerate any interference by China in Outer Mongolian affairs: " We recognize the Mongolian People's Republic as part of the Chinese Republic, but we recognize also its autonomy in so far-reaching a sense that we regard it not only as independent of China in its internal affairs, but also as capable of pursuing its foreign policy independently." [272]

The second important event of the year 1924 was that just cited, the proclamation of the Mongolian People's Republic following the death of the Urga Living Buddha in July 1924 and the adoption of a Constitution in November. The first article of the Constitution declared Mongolia to be " an independent People's Republic," thus ignoring the terminology of the Soviet-Chinese agreement.[273] A Soviet writer has made a comparison between the Constitution of the R.S.F.S.F. of July 10, 1918, and the Constitution of the Mongolian People's Republic of November 26, 1924, as well as with the Consti-

[271] Cf. n. 256, p. 134, Article V; also League of Nations Treaty Series, No. 955, 1925, Vol. XXXVII, p. 176.

[272] Cited in A. Kallinnikov, *Revolyutsionnaya Mongoliya* (Revolutionary Mongolia), Moscow, 1925, p. 95. In the original Russian, the expression here rendered as " internal affairs " is " internal life."

[273] *CYB*, 1928, p. 383.

tution of Tannu Tuva of November 24, 1926.[274] While the names of the different national instiutions are naturally different, the preamble and the construction are nearly identical, so that it may be safely assumed that Soviet Russia's constitution provided the basis for that of the Mongolian People's Republic.

Certain passages of the Constitution seem, however, to show that the Mongols were as anxious as in the days of the Tsar to assert their right of " entering into relations with various foreign powers," which obviously meant other powers than Soviet Russia.[275] And that the Mongols, from the Soviet point of view, could not be relied upon entirely was shown when between the death of the Urga Living Buddha and the proclamation of the Mongolian People's Republic it was found necessary to execute Danzan, the Commander-in Chief of the Mongolian Army. For this act the same reasons were given as for the execution of Prime Minister Bodo in 1922. Danzan was executed during the third session of the Mongol People's Revolutionary Party, after he had made an anti-Russian speech.[276]

At the same Congress it became clear that the Mongols desired to include the territory of Urianghai in the Mongolian People's Republic.[277] Since 1921, when the Chinese were driven out of Urianghai, Soviet Russia had recognized its independence. To mark the new status, the name of Urianghai was changed to Tannu Tuva (Tangno Toba). But in 1924 the inhabitants of Urianghai declared their affiliation with Outer Mongolia.[278] Soviet Russia was intolerant of such a move as

[274] See Prof. V. Durdenevskii, " Narodni Respubliki Tsentralnoi Asii (Mongolska ta Tuvinska) " (The People's Republics of Central Asia-Mongolia and Tuva) in *S. S.*, 1929, No. 3 (9), 1929, p. 108.

[275] Cf. n. 273 and Chapter VI.

[276] Cf. n. 266.

[277] Cf. n. 274.

[278] Otto Mänchen-Helfen, *Reise ins Asiatische Tuva*, Berlin, 1931, p. 167. The author claims to have been virtually the only non-Soviet citizen to have travelled in Tannu Tuva.

Tsarist Russia would have been. Troops were sent which successfully suppressed the revolt. The Mongolian People's Party Congress was, therefore, faced in August with a *fait accompli,* but it adopted a resolution asking for a Russian Mongolian Commission to regulate the question of Urianghai.[279] Moscow met the desires of the Mongols on only one small point. A strip of territory, sparsely inhabited and small in size (about 16,000 sq. km.), called Darkhat—west of Khöbsögol—was given to Outer Mongolia.[280] In the course of 1925 a mission in Moscow prepared a treaty of friendship between the People's Republic of Tannu Tuva and the Mongolian People's Republic, which was modelled on the Soviet-Mongolian Agreement of 1921.[281] In this agreement, finally signed in August 1926, the two Governments recognized each other's independence and agreed to exchange representatives.[282]

Official Soviet pronouncements on Russia's policy toward Tannu Tuva are naturally scarce, but in a country with a state-controlled (and mosly state-owned) press, it seems fair to take the opinions of Soviet writers as almost equally good evidence. Prof. V. Durdenevsky wrote in 1928, " Mongolia and Tannu Tuva cannot join. The idea is clearly absolutely impossible." He instanced the different language (Turkish), and the fact that Tuva's economic development demanded conditions for farming similar to those in the Siberian districts. Moreover, the inhabitants " do not consider themselves at all as Mongols . . . the misuse of power by feudal lords who had all come from Mongolia made them not very friendly toward Mongols." Tuva's people and the Mongols, he concluded, will not become one nation.[283]

Soviet Russia's policy in Tuva has in fact been directed toward ensuring that a different national feeling is developed

---

[279] Korostovets, p. 340.

[280] Werner Leimbach, *Landeskunde von Tuva,* Gotha 1936, p. 101.

[281] G. Cleinow, *Neu-Siberian,* Berlin 1928, p. 98, gives references to *Pravda,* Moscow, in 1927. Unfortunately, the death of Geheimrat Cleinow has made it impossible for me to obtain supplementary information from him.

[282] Cf. V. Durdenevskii, *op. cit.,* p. 114, for an abbreviated outline of the agreement.

[283] *Ibid.,* p. 101.

there. Soviet agricultural policy has aimed at settling the inhabitants and thereby drawing them away from a nomad life like that of the Mongols. Intensive colonization by Russians, and the introduction of a national Tuvanic written language (which until 1931 had been Mongolian), have been other important means of separating Tuva from Outer Mongolia, and at the same time increasing Soviet Russia's hold on the country.

Strategically, Tuva is even more important to Russia now than formerly. For Soviet industrialization has brought into prominence the Kuznetsk coalfield, which lies northwest of Tuva, and it has become essential that Russia's frontier should be removed as far as possible from this vital center. The Tannu Ola, the mountain chain bordering Outer Mongolia, forms a frontier which could easily be defended, since it slopes more steeply to the south than to the north, and communications could be improved for such defense.[284]

While Soviet Russia set limits to the frontiers of the Mongolian People's Republic in the north, she experienced the same difficulty as Tsarist Russia in circumscribing the new state's aspiration with regard to Inner Mongolia. Here again we must refer to a Soviet writer, who in 1928 rebuked a prominent Mongol leader who advocated a "united Mongolia." Under the title of "How one should not put the question of the national self-administration of Mongolia," D. Shambolon asked Comrade Rinchino, "Is Outer Mongolia able to meet the demands of the economic and cultural deevlopment of a united Mongolia, when it is not able to solve its own problems? The reply to this question is clear to every person who has common sense."[285] We are reminded of Sazonov's explanation before the Duma, when the author goes on to mention that Inner Mongolia has a quite different culture from Outer Mongolia,

[284] See Werner Leimbach, *op. cit.*, pp. 106-7. A most vivid impression of the strategical importance of this industrial area is given by the map indicating the position of industries published in the Soviet atlas: *Bolshoi sovetskii atlas mira*, Moscow, 1937, pp. 131-2.

[285] D. Shambolon, "Kak ne sleduyet stavit vopros a natsionalnom samoopredelenii Mongolii" in *Revolyutsionny Vostok*, 1928, No. 3, p. 237 and p. 240.

and that by having had long connections with China it cannot be isolated from the problem of the Chinese revolution. Finally, Comrade Rinchino is told that his dream of a unification of all Mongols is a reactionary idea by no means guaranteeing a further development of the independence movement in Mongolia.

Mongol aspirations for a united Mongolia included, as in former times, the Barga district of the Chinese province of Heilungkiang. The Young Barga party made an attempt in August 1928 to revive the autonomy of Barga, possibly intending to affiliate with the Mongolian People's Republic. But this revolt was soon suppressed by Chinese troops, who were better armed and superior in number.[286] Soviet Russia actively intervened in Barga with troops over a year later, but though Chinese circles feared that Soviet Russia would insist on the autonomy of the district and its amalgamation with Outer Mongolia, events have shown that Barga was for Moscow, as formerly for St. Petersburg, a Russo-Chinese rather than a Russo-Mongol affair.[287] The raid into Barga toward the end of 1929 aimed mainly at forcing Marshall Chang Hsueh-liang of the Three Eastern Provinces to respect Russian rights on the Chinese Eastern Railway. It also provided a demonstration of Russia's strength and interest in these regions of the Far East.

With Mongol aspirations for Tannu Tuva, Inner Mongolia, and Barga successfully checked, there still remained for Soviet Russia the problem of what attitude she was to take toward the desire of the new state to establish relations with other countries. To some extent Soviet Russia's own economic conditions limited her capacity to help the Mongols to acquire the necessary equipment for improving the backward condition of their country; there was also a lack of Russian technical

---

[286] See " The Sino-Russo-Mongolian Struggle in Barga," by J. B. Powell, chiefly based on V. A. Koranasov's "' Barga," in *The China Weekly Review*, Shanghai, Vol. I, No. 13, November 30, 1929, pp. 486-8.

[287] *Ibid.*, see also " The Soviet Atrocities in Barga," J. B. Powell, *ibid.*, No. 9, November 2, 1929, pp. 337-40, especially p. 339. Also Otto Mossdorf, *Barga in Zeitschrift für Politik*, 1930, pp. 304-7.

experts who might have lent their assistance. During the years 1925 to 1928, which was a period of the revival of the feudal-capitalist ("right wing") forces in Mongolia, Soviet Russia did not object to the admission of a number of foreign (mostly German and Swedish) engineers to Outer Mongolia, and to the sending of a Mongolian trade delegation to Germany to engage these men and to buy machinery in European countries. But it can be said that too great an activity by this trade delegation was viewed with strong suspicion by the Moscow authorities, and when the Mongols tried in 1927 to establish a consulate in Berlin, the life of the trade delegation came suddenly to an end. It is not far-fetched to attribute its recall to the direct intervention of the Soviet Government.[288] After 1928 there were practically no non-Russian foreigners at work in Outer Mongolia, and no successful attempt was made by the government to send its representatives abroad, except to Moscow.

The period from 1929 to 1932 was one of violent socialization. The Russians helped considerably, chiefly in the sphere of veterinary medicine. They claimed to have saved a million head of cattle which would formerly have perished.[289] But collectivization, which involved depriving the monasteries and lamas of their cattle, was carried out too rapidly, and the resultant losses largely outweighed the benefits of Russian assistance. Government policy began to change in 1932, and a new period opened in 1934 with the visit of Prime Minister Gendung to Moscow. After this, it was recognized that the Mongolian People's Republic was not yet a Socialist state but was still in a period of transition.[290]

The texts of the different agreements concluded by Soviet Russia with the Mongolian People's Republic are not avail-

[288] Personal information; cf. Chapter V.

[289] Report by Doksom "Historic Lessons . . ." (cf. n. 247, p. 75); also speech of I. Maiskii on "Russian Foreign Policy—USSR and Outer Mongolia"—in The Challenge to Democracy, London 1936, p. 61: "But perhaps the most important thing of all was the assistance rendered by the Soviet Union in combating the plague which attacked the cattle."

[290] Report by Doksom . . . etc., *op. cit.*, pp. 91-3; cf. also references cited in n. 266.

able, but it is known that in 1930 conventions on the struggle against animal diseases, as well as a sanitary convention, were signed.[291] These, though of a technical character, are of political importance in the truest sense of the word, as they laid the foundation stones of a more healthy and efficient Mongolian state. Other agreements were concluded in 1934, during Gendung's visit to Moscow, on currency exchange rates, for the delivery of goods to Mongolia on preferential terms of gold, on joint companies, and on terms of employment of Soviet workers.[292] What kind of loan agreements were concluded is not revealed, but Doksom, the Chairman of the Little Hural (Central Executive Committee), left no doubt about the extent of Soviet Russia's assistance. He stated in a report in 1935: " Owing to the ruin of livestock breeding through wars, we could not export the quantity of livestock which would enable us to pay in full for goods purchased from the Soviet Union; but the Soviet Union again and again wrote off our indebtedness completely. Not only did the Soviet Union take no interest for the loans which we received, but it also postponed the date of payment for 25 years—again without interest." [293]

Furthermore, the Soviet Union helped in building up the commercial organizations of the country, constructed a big wool washing plant, a machine shop, a large printing press, and launched such enterprises as a Mongol Motor-Transport Company in which mainly Soviet drivers were at first employed. The " brotherly help of the Soviet Union " sent numerous instructors and experts to teach the Mongols the trades and occupations to which they were formerly unaccustomed, and " hundreds of doctors " (quite apart from the veterinary service) helped to improve health and to prevent the most serious diseases (syphilis, etc.) the incidence of which was formerly great.[294]

[291] See *Ostasiatische Rundschau,* 13. Jahrg. No. 3, February 1, 1932, p. 51, Col. 2.
[292] Gendung in his report to the Seventh Great Hural (see Bibliography) in *T. O.,* No. 1 (3), January-March 1935, p. 266, paragraph 32.
[293] Report by Doksom, *op. cit.,* p. 75.
[294] *Ibid.,* and Gendung, *op. cit.,* p. 266.

The growth of such active assistance is clearly reflected in the figures of trade between the Soviet Union and the Mongolian People's Republic. These statistics provide a mirror in which we can view once more the evolution of Soviet Russia's relations with Outer Mongolia. In the early twenties trade was practically at a standstill. Figures for the years 1922-1924 (calculated on the pre-war value of the ruble) show the catastrophic decline of Russian trade when compared with the years 1913 to 1915 (given on page 109).

Year	Imports from Mongolia	Exports to Mongolia	Total
1922	763,000	81,000	844,000
1923	418,000	346,000	764,000
1924	1,920,000	1,761,000	3,731,000

A Soviet author was to some extent justified when he wrote in 1922 that " no time must be lost," as otherwise the economic bonds between the two countries would be weakened by the establishment of American, Japanese, and other enterprises in Outer Mongolia. He saw in the Soviet-Mongolian agreement of 1921 a spring board toward a greater commercial activity for Russia, which in turn would insure increased political influence.[295] However, Soviet Russia's economic capacities were limited at that time, and the formidable Chinese competition which had not been driven out with the Chinese soldiers, was still firmly established.[296]

The period from 1924 to 1930 was characterized by a prolonged attempt on the part of Soviet Russia to diminish China's trade with Outer Mongolia, but purely economic pressure did not suffice. This was shown during the first Mongolian Fair in 1927, before the Mongolian Central Cooperative (Montsenkop) and the Soviet trade organizations, (Stormong) had obtained a position of predominance.[297] The figures for Soviet

[295] N. Pennskii, " Ekonomicheskive vzaimootnosheniya SSSR s Mongoliei " (Economic relations of the USSR with Mongolia), in *N. V.*, 1925, 10-11, p. 169.

[296] S. Kotlyarevskii, " Pravovye dostizheniya Rossii v Azii " (Legal rights attained by Russia in Asia), *ibid.*, Vol. I, 1922, p. 43.

[297] Summary of an article of Amuga, " First Mongolian Fair " in *Khozyaistvo Mongolii*, 1927, 1, 7, 3/5, as cited in *Bibliografiya Vostakai*, 1, 1932, p. 124.

Russia's and China's trade with Mongolia for the years 1924 to 1929 give us the following picture: [298]

Year	To USSR	Imports from Mongolia To China Proper (in 1000 tughriks)	From USSR	Exports to Mongolia From China Proper
1924	2,663	16,713	2,443	15,753
1925	4,743	14,992	3,789	15,858
1926	9,747	15,091	4,961	17,154
1927	16,900	12,080	4,000	27,600
1928	21,000	10,780	7,100	25,400
1929	21,500	6,000	2,300	8,700

Soviet Russia increasingly imported more from Mongolia than she sent to it, whereas China exported more to Mongolia than she received. For, quite apart from Soviet Russia's industrial weakness in these years, Chinese goods were in demand among the Mongols because they suited their tastes. Tea, tobacco, jewelry, silks, textiles, were the most important items, but they included also foreign goods transported through China such as rubber goods, textiles, and metal goods (electrical fittings, etc.).

The year 1929, however, was a turning point. The "left wing" came into power in Mongolia and the period of active socialization (collectivization) which followed not only stimulated Soviet-Mongolian trade relations, but brought with it a vehement anti-Chinese campaign which resulted in the expulsion of most Chinese merchants from Outer Mongolia. Such a policy, accompanied by a rupture of trade relations with countries other than China, greatly enlarged Soviet Russia's share of trade with Outer Mongolia. Whereas in 1927, Soviet Russia's share of Outer Mongolia's trade was only 34 per cent, the year 1934 saw her in possession of 91 per cent of all the external trade of the Mongolian People's Republic.[299]

The development from 1928 to 1937 is shown by the following Soviet Russian statistics:

[298] The figures for 1924-27, as cited by B. Nikitine, "La Mongolie," *Mémoires et et Documents*, October 1930, p. 18, and for 1928-29, as cited by Violet Conolly, *Soviet Economic Policy in the East*, London 1933, p. 103.

[299] B. Nikitine, *Les Relations Russo-Japonaises en Extrême-Orient*, April 1936, p. 23, citing a Russian journal.

	Imports from Mongolia	Exports to Mongolia
	(in 1000 rubles)	
1928 ⎱ 1929 ⎰	15,200	16,400
1930	19,745	17,819
1931	28,833	37,443
1932	19,278	41,395
1933	17,269	38,562
1934	20,561	44,896
1935	34,650	50,952
1936	32,120	50,433
1937	33,694	60,822

Reviewing statistics over a period of twelve years, from 1923-24 to 1936, the figures in tons are:

	Imports from Mongolia	Exports to Mongolia
1923-24	10,273	5,748
1925-26	9,668	9,332
1927-28	22,239	18,097
1933	17,269	69,493
1934	20,561	99,379
1936	42,635	105,039 [300]

These figures reveal a radical change in the structure of Russia's commercial relations with Mongolia. Not only has the volume of trade increased rapidly compared with Tsarist Russia's achievements or those of Soviet Russia in the twenties, but Russia's passive trade balance with Mongolia has developed into an active one. The percentage of Mongolian trade in the total foreign trade of the Soviet Union is now considerable, and in the peak year (compared with the period preceding it), 1934, imports from Mongolia as well as exports to Mongolia ranked third in importance, after those of Germany and Great Britain.[301] These are the figures of Russian trade with Mongolia in percentages:

[300] Figures from 1928-32, as cited by V. Connolly, *op. cit.*, p. 106, and by B. Nikitine, "La Mongolie," *op. cit.*; figures for 1933 to last date available are based on official statistical returns of external trade of the USSR. Cf. Bibliography, Official Documents, last two items of col. (b) Russia. Figures are also published in *Sowjetwirtschaft und Aussenhandel*, e. g., 15 Jahrg., No. 3, 1, Februarheft 1936, p. 22, 16. Jahrg., 1. u. 2, Märzheft 1937, p. 33. See also Galina Berkendorf, "Industrialisierung und Aussenhandel der Sowjetunion in ihrer wechselseitgen Abhängigkeit" in *Weltwirtschaftliches Archiv*, 43 Band, March 1936, Heft. 2, pp. 434-5. See also *Foreign Trade and Commerce Accounts* (Board of Trade), December 31, 1937, H. M. Stationery Office, London 1938, p. 126.

[301] Mongolia has not maintained this place and ranked eighth to tenth in Russia's foreign trade in 1937. A cartographic impression of Mongolia's importance is gained

	Imports from Mongolia	Exports to Mongolia
1927-28	1.3%	1.1%
1932	2.8	7.3
1933	5.0	7.8
1934	8.8	10.7
1935	2.3	3.2
1936	2.4	3.7
1937	2.5	3.8

The different items of which the trade is composed show all the characteristics of commercial intercourse between an industrial country and a country producing foodstuffs and raw materials. The Soviet Union imported cattle, meat, wool, etc., and exported finished goods, cloth, oil products, machines, etc. A detailed table for the peak year 1934, and for 1936 the last year for which detailed statistics are available, gives the following distribution for the most important items:

Imports from Mongolia			Exports to Mongolia		
(in 1000 rubles)					
	1934	1936		1934	1936
Livestock	6,393	12,640	Flour	5,218	8,038
Meat	1,459	380	Groats	833	1,247
Game	15	1,228	Tea	1,789	3,196
Furs	3,008	566	Sugar	881	1,594
Raw leather	3,559	4,778	Confectionery	1,563	2,445
Wool	2.715	7,036	Tobacco	2,281	2,394
Hair	2,405	4,666	Tanned leather	1,741	1,034
			Rubber goods	1,061	211
			Metal goods	1,390	1,893
			Naptha	1,347	2,383
			Motor transport goods	671	814
			Cloth	1,744	2,168
			Cotton goods	8,005	5,782
			Footwear	2,460	994
	19,546	20,894	Total Exports	44,810	50,433 [302]
Total Imports	20,561	32,120			

by reference to the new Soviet Atlas 1937 (Cf. Leimbach, *op. cit.*), pp. 166-7. As to the exports from the USSR, Mongolia occupied alone the second highest category—5-10%—following the first category—10-25%—occupied by Germany and Great Britain. As to imports to the USSR, Mongolia ranked in the same group as Iran and the United States.

[302] Detailed items for 1937 have not been issued. A comparison between the years 1934 and 1936 does not provide a completely satisfactory picture as the statistics for 1936 add new items to the existing list or subdivide original items. Thus for the item tobacco, the figure given in this book for 1936 has been obtained by adding up the several items which now replace the original item. A comparison

With the break-up of feudalism in Mongolia, her demand for industrial goods from the Soviet Union increased, while at the same time the import of goods from China for the use of the Lama Church (expensive cloth, silk goods, jewelry, etc.) steadily decreased. The only remaining import from China was tea, which reached Outer Mongolia via Vladivostok. Figures for 1932 give the value of this tea as amounting to 2,663,000 rubles, and for 1933 to as much as 4,389,000 rubles; but it is understood that such a high level has not been maintained and that it has decreased considerably since 1934.[303]

In the course of the development of trade with Outer Mongolia, Russia always had to struggle with the obstacle of inadequate trade routes. Much energy was therefore directed toward improving communications. In 1925 investigations into the possibility of steam navigation on the rivers Selenga and Orkhon were undertaken, and some dredging was done. Steam navigation (but only for small vessels) was then possible for 197 miles from the mouth of the Selenga (on Lake Baikal, i. e. in Russian territory), and for 194 miles from the mouth of the Orkhon (i. e., the point where the Orkhon flows into the Selenga on the Russian-Mongolian frontier). Agreements establishing steam navigation were concluded by the Soviet Union with Outer Mongolia in 1926, as well as for aerial, postal, and passenger communications between Mongolia's capital (Ulan Bator) and Verkhne Ulinsk.[304]

Most Soviet-Mongolian trade went via the Kiakhta road from Verkhne Udinsk (now Ulan Ude) to Kiakhta (on the Russo-Mongolian frontier) to Ulan Bator. Other routes had to overcome such natural difficulties as steep slopes, as for instance the Turkinsk road from Irkutsk via Kultuk (a railway

with the figures for 1935 might easily provide a pitfall, showing as they do a remarkable decrease in the volume of trade. This, however, is due to a revaluation of the ruble, and the low figures found in some statistics should be multiplied by 4.38.

[303] *Sowjetwirtschaft und Aussenhandel*, 14. Jahrg., No. 9, 1, Märzheft 1935, I, Markow, " Der Warentransit durch die USSR," pp. 6 and 9.

[304] *SSE*, Vol. 3, pp. 527-8; I. I. Serebrennikov, "A Soviet Satellite: Outer Mongolia Today " in *Foreign Affairs*, Vol. 9, No. 3, April 1931, p. 514

station on Lake Baikal) to Khöbsögol which was mainly used for cattle transport. There are two direct approaches from Russia to Khobdo and Uliassutai, the Usinsk and the Chuysk roads. The first runs from Minnusinsk via Usinskoe and Bulak to Dohoi Gol where the ways separate—one leading east to Uliassutai, the other west to Khobdo—both having to climb the crest of the Tannu Ola. It is of great importance for this route that the potentialities of navigation on the Upper Yenisei should be developed, for then wares could be shipped from Minnusinsk to Krasny.[305] The second road, the Chuysk route, is one of the oldest trade routes from Siberia via Urianghai (Tannu Tuva) to Mongolia, beginning in Biisk and going via Kosh Agach to Khobdo. It is a most hazardous way and during the civil war was the scene of many encounters which caused it to deteriorate still further. At one time the total abandonment of this route was contemplated, but it has in fact been retained and some improvements undertaken. Perhaps the decisive argument was non-economic. A Soviet writer stresses the route's " probable political role as the geographically nearest road to the East." From the economic point of view, however, the road has not been a success.[306]

Although reports have been current for many years that the Russians were building railways in Outer Mongolia,[307] they were apparently unable to break down the traditional Mongol hostility to railway building until 1945 when a line was constructed from Choibolsang (Bayantümen) to the Soviet frontier. A recent Soviet map (1947) shows that this line links up

[305] Cf. Erich Thiel, *Verkehrsgeographie von Russisch-Asien,* Königsberg/Pr.-Berlin 1934, pp. 197-201.

[306] D. Kashintsev, " Chuysky Trakt v Mongoliyu " (The Chuysk Highway in Mongolia) in *N. V.,* 1925, 8-9, pp. 133-43, especially p. 142. See also Y. V. Obrutchev, " Bolshe vimaniya tchuiskomu traktu " (More attention to the Chuysk Highway) in *N. V.,* 1925, 8-9, pp. 125-32.

[307] See articles of a Marine Correspondent in *Algemeen Handelsblad,* Amsterdam, January 12 and 13, 1938, with sketch of alleged railway routes. Also *CYB,* 1926, p. 800, Annex II, Alleged contents of the Railway agreement between the USSR and the Mongolian People's Republic (September 1925). Also B. Nikitine, " L'Asie Russe Economique." Extrait du *Bulletin du Comité de l'Asie Française,* Paris 1929, p. 20, n. 2. The alleged terms of this agreement are so drastically in favor of Russia that one can hardly believe that it ever existed.

with the Trans-Siberian Railway at Borzya. It also shows lines running from Choibolsang west to Uuldza and east to Tamtsak Bulak and to Dzün Bulak.[308] The only other railway in Outer Mongolia is only 40 kilometers long and runs from Ulan Bator to the Nalaikha coal fields.

Militarily there was a pause in Soviet Russia's activities in Outer Mongolia from 1925 to 1932 or 1933. This does not mean that Soviet Russia during these years did not tender to Mongolia, in the words of Doksom, the President of the Little Hural, "manifold assistance as regards technical equipment and military preparations of our army" during all these years.[309] But Soviet Russia withdrew her troops from Outer Mongolia at the beginning of 1925. A long exchange of notes took place between the Soviet and Mongolian Governments on the occasion of the fulfillment of the promise to do so made in 1921.[310] With the White Russian bands destroyed or disbanded, and no military action to fear from China, Soviet Russia could content herself with sending materials and instructors on a greater scale than were sent under the Tsarist régime.

After Japan's occupation of Manchuria in 1931 the position changed completely. From the Russian point of view, this Japanese advance not only entailed a direct threat to her remaining interests in Manchuria, but meant that for many miles she and Outer Mongolia were now confronted by a new neighbor in the form of the Japanese-controlled "Manchukuo." Barga, bordering Outer Mongolia, was incorporated into an autonomous Mongol province (Hsingan) of the new state and the problem of a united Mongolia came up again in a new form, the driving force emanating now from the other side of the frontier, backed and instigated by the Japanese headquarters in Kwantung. Soviet Russia soon withdrew from Manchuria (Manchukuo), sold her share in the Chinese Eastern Railway in 1934, and became feverishly engaged in strengthening her military position along the frontier of Manchuria. This frontier

---

[308] Shown on end paper map.
[309] Report of Doksom, *op. cit.*, p. 75.
[310] *Ibid.*, pp. 73-4, for text of notes.

region included the northeastern corner of Outer Mongolia, with which it soon became clear that Japan desired to establish direct relations. As border incidents began to extend from the Russia-Manchukuo to the Mongolia-Manchukuo frontier, Soviet Russia strengthened her relations with Outer Mongolia.

During the visit of Mongolia's Prime Minister in Moscow on November 27, 1934, Soviet Russia concluded with the Mongolian People's Republic a " gentleman's agreement " of mutual assistance, which amounted politically (though not legally) to a military alliance.[311] After that date fantastic reports were spread as to the strength of Soviet Russian forces stationed in Outer Mongolia, most of these reports coming either from Japanese sources or from sensational journalists who received their impressions while travelling on the Trans-Siberian railway.[312] Actually Soviet Russia probably sent such officers and troops to Outer Mongolia as she thought necessary in order to supplement the forces of the Mongolian People's Republic trained by her, and to be ready for the emergency foreseen in the Soviet-Mongolian Protocol of Mutual Assistance.

In this Protocol, signed by the Governments of the U.S.S.R. and the Mongolian People's Republic on March 12, 1936 in Ulan Bator, they engaged themselves " in the event of a threat of an attack on the part of a third state " at once to discuss jointly the situation created thereby and to adopt all those measures which might be necessary to safeguard the security of their territories." The two governments also undertook, " in the event of a military attack on one of the contracting parties to render each other every assistance, including military assistance." The last clause considered it " as self-evident that the troops of one of the parties finding themselves by mutual agreement on the territory of the other side in order to carry out the obligations " set out in the two preceding articles, " will be withdrawn from that territory as soon as the danger is over

---

[311] For text of Protocal, see *Pravda,* Moscow, April 8, 1936; *Moscow News,* April 15, 1936; *New York Times,* April 8, 1936.

[312] The American journalists, H. R. Knickerbocker and Karl H. von Wiegand, belong to the latter class.

7

just as took place in 1925 with respect to the withdrawal of Soviet troops from the territory of the Mongolian People's Republic." [313] This protocol, although it was drawn up in terms of complete equality, applied in reality only to military assistance to be given by the Soviet Union to Outer Mongolia. A few days before the signing of the protocol, on March 1, 1936, Stalin had expressed this in clear terms to an American interviewer, Mr. Roy Howard, who asked him:

> What will be the Soviet attitude should Japan launch the long predicted military drive against Outer Mongolia?
>
> Stalin: If Japan should venture to attack the Mongolian People's Republic and encroach upon its independence, we will have to help the Mongolian People's Republic. Stomonyakov, assistant to Litvinov (Commissariat for Foreign Affairs) recently informed the Japanese Ambassador in Moscow of this and pointed to the immutable friendly relations which the U. S. S. R. has been maintaining with the Mongolian People's Republic since 1921. We will help the Mongolian People's Republic just as we helped it in 1921.
>
> Howard: Would a Japanese attempt to seize Ulan Bator make positive action by the U. S. S. R. a necessity?
>
> Stalin: Yes.
>
> Howard: Have recent events developed any new Japanese activities in this region which are construed by the Soviets as of an aggressive nature?
>
> Stalin: The Japanese, I think, are continuing to concentrate troops on the frontiers of the Mongolian People's Republic, but no new attempts at frontier conflicts are so far observed.[314]

Indeed, while here and there a few incidents took place during the following year, they were less frequent on the Outer Mongolia-Manchukuo than on the Russia-Manchukuo frontier where a serious incident occurred on the river Amur in June 1937. Soviet Russia's attitude at that time seemed to indicate that she was not anxious to provoke serious conflict with Japan. Japan had become an ally of Germany in November

[313] Article 3 of the Protocol.
[314] See *The Soviet Union and the Path to Peace.* A collection of Statements and Documents, 1917-1936, London 1936, p. 15.

1936. Soviet-German relations had greatly deteriorated and the possibility of a two-front war became a nightmare to Moscow.

After the middle of 1937 events moved swiftly. Japan's war on China, which began in July 1937 near Peking had, by the beginning of 1938, made her master of the greater part of Inner Mongolia (Chahar and Suiyan), thus lengthening her frontier with Outer Mongolia, and cutting this line of communication between Russia and China. After hostilities started hardly a week passed without the circulation of some rumor or other concerning Soviet Russia's position in Outer Mongolia. At the end of August 1937 the newly arrived Soviet Ambassador in Tokyo was credited with confirming the story that General Blucher, the Commander-in-Chief of all Soviet Far Eastern forces, had gone to Outer Mongolia; but the Ambassador promptly denied that he had ever made such a statement.[315] When a Pact of Non-Aggression was signed between the U.S.S.R. and China in August 1937 it was said that Russia had thereby not only received the indirect acquiescence of the Chinese Government in the Soviet-Mongolian Protocol of Mutual Assistance (against which China had strongly protested in April 1936 as a violation of her sovereignty) but that the agreement contained secret clauses relating to Outer Mongolia. This was quickly denied by the Chinese Ambassador in Tokyo.[316] Later it was frequently rumored that the Chinese Government had tried to persuade the Russian Government to allow Outer Mongolia, which Russia had recognized to be an integral part of China, to intervene actively in the Sino-Japanese war, thus diverting Japanese troops to the north.[317]

Such overtures, however, if they were ever made, found no response in Moscow which, while sending some equipment to China, had carefully refrained from acting in a way which would involve her in hostilities. The Soviet-Mongolian Protocol

[315] *The Daily Telegraph,* August 23, 1937; *Neue Züricher Zeitung,* August 23, 1937, p. 2; denials in *Le Temps,* August 25, 1937, p. 2; *La Dépêche de Toulouse,* August 24, 1937, p. 4.

[316] *Le Temps,* September 3, 1937, p. 2.

[317] *The Osaka Mainichi,* October 20, 1937; *The Times,* London, October 21, 1937.

might have forced Russia to face a two-front war. If Japan had become established in parts of Mongolia the position of the Baikal region would have been extremely precarious so that it was in self-defense that Russia prepared for such eventualities.

Thus by force of circumstances Soviet Russia was driven to occupy the position which Sazonov had been anxious that Tsarist Russia should avoid. It is the main justification for his cautious policy that Tsarist Russia was never " compelled to defend Mongolia . . . with armed force." But the analogy is not complete. Sazonov had only to deal with Chinese oppression on Chinese territory. Litvinov was faced with the extension of Japanese military operations into territory which was virtually Russian. From a military point of view, Russia's increased strength around Vladivostok was offset by her liabilities in Outer Mongolia. On the other hand, in Outer Mongolia itself she had achieved what W. W. Rockhill considered in 1914 to be the indispensable condition of successful influence.[318] All former Russian firms and small traders had been expelled. In their place was one great Moscow firm, the state itself, possessing an exclusive trade monopoly. " All possible foreign competition " had been excluded and what remained of Chinese imports had to pass through Russia. She had carried through more reforms than were planned at the end of the Tsarist Russian period by Russia's political representatives there. This success had been aided by external factors, such as the White Russian threat in 1921 and the Japanese threat after 1932. It must also be remembered that Soviet Russia had greater opportunities than Tsarist Russia. Her relations with Outer Mongolia had time to develop, whereas Tsarist Russia dealt with an autonomous Mongolia for five years only, during three of which she was engaged in a European War.

In view of these different conditions and the divergent causes which brought them about, it seems rather ignorant to have

[318] Cf. n. 218.

recourse to the generalization that Tsarist and Soviet " imperialism " followed the same course in their policy toward Mongolia. It is indeed impossible to satisfy those who think that a complex historical development can be summarized in a slogan. Neither the assertion on the one hand that Soviet imperialism achieved a disguised annexation of Mongolia, nor the vigorous denial that Soviet Russia was prompted by anything but feelings of brotherly Socialist help toward Outer Mongolia on the other, is likely to lead to an understanding of the situation.[319] The " imperialist genius " of Soviet Russia, a phrase against which I. Maiskii, Soviet Ambassador in London, protested in a speech in the summer of 1936, certainly showed a greater ability in the treatment of the Mongols than Tsarist Russia. But she thought it wiser to give to the Mongols a breathing space in which to create for themselves with Russian help and protection an independent state, on the assumption that such a state, out of fear of an aggressive Japan and suspicion of non-revolutionary China, would necessarily remain friendly toward the Soviet Union.

The Soviet-Mongolian Protocol of Mutual Assistance of 1936 was first implemented by the Russians during the fighting which started on the Mongolian-Manchurian border in the Nomonkhan area in May 1939. Russia's position was clearly put by Foreign Minister Molotov in a report before the Supreme Soviet on May 31, 1939, i. e. at the beginning of the fighting: " I give warning that the borders of the Mongolian People's Republic, by virtue of the mutual assistance pact concluded between us, will be defended by us as vigorously as we shall defend our own frontier." [320] In a speech before the Supreme Soviet on October 31, 1939 Molotov drew a comparison between mutual assistance pacts " signed by some of the European great powers " with " luckless Poland " and " the value of pacts to which is appended the signature of the

---

[319] See for instnace, Court Sforza, " Imperialistic Russia in China " in *Foreign Affairs,* October 1927, p. 69, on the one side, and statements of Chicherin, Gendung, Doksom, Maiskii, on the other.

[320] V. Molotov, *The International Situation and Soviet Foreign Policy,* Foreign Languages Publications, Moscow 1939, p. 14.

Soviet Union." [321] The battles, which lasted from May to the middle of September 1939, were indeed " sometimes of a very sanguinary character "; Marshal Zhukov received in them his baptism of tank warfare, and " Japan's endeavour to appropriate part of the territory of the M. P. R. and thus forcibly to change the Mongolian Manchurian border in her own favor " met " with a resolute rebuff." [322] The truce which followed remained for some time an uncertain one, subject to all the vicissitudes of the world war situation and Soviet-Japanese relations in general, and it was only in May 1942 that the Mixed Border Commission, originally agreed upon toward the end of 1939, reached an agreement. It is only natural that during these years of uncertainty and danger, heightened as they were by the attack of Japan's ally Germany on Russia in 1941, Soviet influence in and solicitude for the Mongolian People's Republic increased considerably. The Declaration attached to the Soviet Japanese Neutrality Pact of April 13, 1941 in which Japan pledged herself " to respect the territorial integrity and inviolability of the Mongolian People's Republic " [323] was a positive achievement from the Soviet point of view if contrasted with Japan's previous intransigent attitude.

During the German war there were frequent visits by Mongolian Trade Delegations to Moscow, each time led either by the Mongolian Deputy Prime Minister or the Prime Minister himself. These delegations generally brought with them trainloads of food as presents and their arrival and departures in 1942, '43, '44, and '45 were each time mentioned in the Soviet press. [324] The meeting in July 1945 between Stalin and Marshal Choibalsang, which took place during the Sino-Russian nego-

---

[321] *Russia and the War.* Molotov's speech to the Supreme Soviet of the Soviet Union, October 31, 1939, London 1939, pp. 17-18.

[322] *Ibid.*, p. 17.

[323] Text in Harriet L. Moore, *Soviet Far Eastern Policy, 1931-1945*, Princeton, 1945, p. 201.

[324] Tass message of Dec. 7, 1942; *Times*, London, Dec. 8, 1942; Tass message of March 17, 1942, also Tass message of March 16, 1942 referring to a letter in *Pravda* by Lubsan, Vice-Chairman of the Council of Ministers of the M. P. R.; *Soviet Monitor*, Jan. 23, 1944; Tass message, Jan. 31, 1944; *Soviet News*, London, July 7, 1945; *Tass Information*, July 8, 1945.

tiations, resulted in a plan for Soviet-Mongolian military collaboration against Japan; for Russian participation against Japan
had been assured on February 11, 1945 at Yalta and was timed
" in two or three months after Germany has surrendered." The
secret clauses of the Yalta agrement, which enumerated the
conditions on which Russia would enter the Far Eastern war,
began with the statement that " The status quo in Outer
Mongolia (the Mongolian People's Republic), shall be preserved." [325] This rather ambiguous formula was interpreted by
the Russians during their negotiations with the Chinese in
July 1945 as a basis for a Chinese recognition of the independence of the M. P. R.; and this Russian view prevailed in the
final text of August 14, 1945 of the Russo-Chinese Treaty of
Friendship and Alliance through the face-saving compromise
of a plebiscite in Outer Mongolia (see Chapter III).

With the recognition of the independence of the M. P. R. by
China and the expiration of the Soviet-Mongolian Protocol of
Mutual Assistance of 1936, a new agreement, officially called a
" Treaty of Friendship and Mutual Assistance," was concluded
between the USSR and the MPR on February 27, 1946.[326] The
treaty is in every particular a repetition of the 1936 Protocol,
incorporating also the assurance " that the troops of one of
the Parties stationed by mutual agreement on the territory of
the other Party . . . will be withdrawn from the territory in
question without delay when the necessity for this is over. . . ."

Since Japan's defeat the only threat to the territory of the
M. P. R. has come, according to Soviet sources, from the
Sinkiang border. Whatever may be the rights or wrongs of

[325] Full text of the Yalta agreement including those parts not published in the
communiqué of February 12, 1945, was released by the Department of State,
Washington, March 24, 1947 and appeared in *The New York Times*, March 25,
1947.

[326] Full text in *Soviet News*, London, March 1, 1946, p. 1. To this treaty was
added an " agreement on Economic and Cultural Collaboration between the Government of the USSR and the Government of the MPR," *ibid.*, p. 2. It envisaged in
Art. II " separate agreements and contracts . . . between corresponding economic,
scientific and cultural-educational intstitutions and organizations." Such collaboration has, of course, existed previous to the new agreement. E. g. the Central
Railwaymen's Theater visited Mongolia for three months in 1942. There is also a
Soviet Mongolian film studio. *Moscow News*, Jan. 12, 1943.

the case, these incidents cannot be compared with the thirteen years of border incidents along the Japanese controlled Manchurian border. Though Soviet troops have been withdrawn from Northern Korea, no announcement as to the withdrawal of Soviet troops from Outer Mongolia has been made so far, though a Soviet-trained Mongolian army has existed for some time. Strategically, the Mongolian People's Republic belongs to the "chain of strong points, from the Kuriles to Outer Mongolia" by which Russia wants to guard its Far Eastern territory, and "to neutralize as far as possible the presence of American power in Japan, Korea, and China," as an American commentator put it in 1947.[327] Politically, the withdrawal of Soviet troops would make it more difficult for Russia to exercise her restraining influence on "Pan-Mongolian" ambitions.

[327] John C. Campbell, *The United States in World Affairs, 1945-47*, New York, 1947, p. 298.

CHAPTER III

RELATIONS WITH CHINA

A. POLICY OF THE MANCHUS 1636-1911

IT IS ESSENTIAL to note that here we are not concerned with the relation between " China " and " Mongolia," but with that between the Manchu Emperors and the Mongol chiefs. The Manchu conquerors and some of the Mongols were for a time allies. In the course of the seventeenth century, the Manchus subjugated first the Inner Mongols and—at the end of the century—the Outer Mongols. The first document dealing with relations between the Manchu Emperor and the Inner Mongolian tribes seems to be one dated 1636, and in it the suzerainty of the Manchu Emperor is recognized. It was stipulated, however, that should the Dynasty fall, all the laws previously existing should come into force again.[1] In 1688, an assembly of Mongol princes at Dolon Nor decided to submit to the Manchu Emperor. The Chinese later considered this event as marking the formal annexation of Mongolia, but the Mongols claimed that the assembly only paid homage to the Emperor personally. In 1691 this " annexation " was solemnly " ratified." [2] The Emperor K'ang Hsi accompanied by all his guard and many followers came to Dolon Nor, where 24 regional princes of Khalkha swore an oath of allegiance.[3]

The policy of the Manchus was to treat the Mongol nobles as feudal vassals who did not have to serve them as did the subject Chinese, but in the same way as they had formerly served their Great Khans. To legitimize the succession of the Manchu Emperors a legend was invented that the seal of the

[1] Herbert A. Giles, *China and the Manchus*, Cambridge, 1912, p. 20.
[2] Grumm-G., Vol. II, pp. 683-684; Korostovets, p. 22.
[3] *Ibid.*; see also Maurice Courant, " L'Asie Centrale aux XVIIe et XVIIIe. Siècles. Empire Kalmouk ou Empire Mantchou? " *Annales de l'Uniersité de Loyn*, Loyn-Paris, 1912, pp. 57-58.

last emperor of the Mongol (Yüan) Dynasty had descended to them from the son of Ligdan, Khan of the Chahar Mongols. The Manchu Emperor in finding the Yüan emperor's jasper seal and in ascending to the throne in Daidu (Peking), where the Khans of the Yüan Dynasty had resided, had become the successor to the throne of Chingghis.[4]

The Manchus were ethnologically akin to the Mongols and their nobility had for some time used the Mongolian literary language. Furthermore, the Manchu Court and the Mongolian nobility were both followers of Tibetan Buddhism. The relations between the two were especially strengthened by the Manchus' policy of marrying their princesses to Mongolian nobles. For the Mongolian princes this brought certain pecuniary advantages, as well as the title " Hosho Fu " (Son-in-law of the Emperor).[5]

Many other titles were conferred on Mongolian princes, thus introducing a great differentiation among them, and strengthening their link with the Dynasty. When Emperor K'ang Hsi increased the number of hoshun rulers from twenty-four to thirty-seven in 1691, this was only the beginning of a policy aiming at dividing the Mongols into the smallest possible units. At the end of his reign the number of hoshun was seventy-two, later to be increased to eighty-six, for which definite territories were fixed.[6]

The Manchus were thus observing the old maxim of " divide et impera," for they feared the possibility of the re-emergence of a great Khan, who by uniting the Mongols, might become a danger to their rule. While leaving the fundamental scheme of the administrative and political organization of Outer Mongolia on the whole untouched, they created a non-Mongol institution, the leagues (in Chinese, *meng*), to pave the way for the gradual passage of power into the hands of

---

[4] B. V. Vladimirtsov, *Obshchestvenny stroi Mongolov* (The Social Structure of the Mongols), Leningrad, 1934, p. 194.

[5] *Ibid.*

[6] Grumm-G., Vol. 2, p. 686; A. Kallinikov, *Revolyutsionnaya Mongoliya* (Revolutionary Mongolia), Moscow, 1925, p. 18.

officials nominated by themselves. These coincided, however, in Outer Mongolia (Khalkha) with the four existing aimaks (groups of hoshuns), whereas in Inner Mongolia the twenty-four aimaks were irregularly grouped into six leagues.

The condition of vassalage of the Mongol lords was reflected in the payment of an annual tribute to the Emperor like the homage paid to their Suzerain by the Emperor of Annam or the King of Korea. The time and manner of presenting gifts was prescribed in regulations of the Tribunal of Outside (foreign) Affairs in the Department of Rights. Therein were set out the number and value of the horses to be presented to the Emperor by Mongol princes. For instance, the Mongolian High Priest, the Jeptsun Damba Hutukhtu, living permanently in Urga, the Tushetu and the Tsetsen Khans of Khalkha, had each to send to the annual festival at the Court a present of a white camel and eight horses of the same color—the tax of " nine whites." [7]

The Chinese reforms of 1691 were practically limited to those we have mentioned; the Jasaks were not deprived of former rights. But soon these were restricted to some extent and in the first half of the eighteenth century—about 1719—decrees were issued depriving them of their rights to have independent relations with the governments of neighboring powers: a limitation was likewise placed upon their powers in civil affairs of great importance and in criminal affairs involving the death penalty. The Manchu language was made obligatory in those Mongol affairs which demanded communication with Peking, and military service was introduced. [8]

Administratively, the Mongols came under the Li Fan Yuan, or Department of Territories, also sometimes translated as the Colonial Office or High Court of the Administration of Vassals, or Board of Control for Dependencies. None of these translations provides a satisfactory rendering of the Chinese term

[7] Stefan Lipovtsov, *Ulozhenie Kitaiskoi Palaty vneshnykh snoshenii* (The Regulations of the Chinese Board of Foreign Relations), St. Petersburg, 1828, Vol. 1, pp. 208, 345 (In the original misprinted as 245); Grumm-G., Vol. 11, p. 684, n. 1.

[8] Grumm-G., pp. 684-685.

"*fan*," which means 'frontiers.' This Department was divided into several offices, a Bureau of Inner Mongolia, a Bureau for Receiving Princes from Inner Mongolia, a Bureau of Outer Mongolia, a Bureau for Receiving Princes from Outer Mongolia, a Bureau of Eastern Turkistan, and a Bureau of Justice. The last had charge of the civil and criminal cases in Inner and Outer Mongolia. The Bureau of Outer Mongolia (Tien Hsu Ssu) dealt with relay communications and trade in Mongolia between Chinese and Mongols, the nomadic tribes, and Tibetan lamas.

The special relation between the Manchu Dynasty and Mongols was reflected in the fact that this was the only Department where Chinese held no official positions, as these were divided between Manchus and Mongols. The ninety Mongol officials outnumbered the sixty-five Manchus, but the latter had taken care to secure for themselves the most important posts—the Supervising Ministership, the Ministership, two Vice Ministerships, the Directorships of the Translation Office, and all the positions in the Treasury. To the Mongols an extra Vice-Minister was conceded, and it depended strictly on his personal ability how far he succeeded in neutralizing the majority position of his two Manchu colleagues. The functions of Vice-Ministers might be compared with those of British Permanent Under-Secretaries of State, i. e., virtually heads of their respective departments. By allowing only a Mongol of the rank of a Prince to occupy the extra Vice-Ministership, the Manchu Dynasty further consolidated its relations with the Mongol nobles, already cleverly fostered by marrying them to Manchu princesses.[9]

As to the administration in Outer Mongolia itself, the Chinese official appointed from Peking was the Military Governor of Uliassutai, who was first appointed in the middle of the eighteenth century during the rebellion of the Jungars in Western Mongolia. His authority, originally confined to mili-

---

[9] See W. F. Mayers, *The Chinese Government*, Shanghai, etc., 1897, p. 23 (183); P. Huang. *Mélanges sur l'administration*, Shanghai, 1902, p. 18; Pao Chao Hsieh, *The Government of China*, Baltimore, pp. 322-324.

tary matters, was after the suppression of the rebellion extended
to civil matters, and all four aimaks were under his authority.
He administered them with the assistance of an Imperial
Councillor, usually a civilian. There was also an Imperial
Agent (Resident or Amban) at Urga in charge of civil matters,
who acted originally as assistant Military Governor of Uliassutai. He, together with an Assistant Imperial Agent who was
appointed by the Mongols, were—as the translation of their
titles from Mongol signifies—" officials deputed by Imperial
will and directing affairs at Urga." The Imperial Agent at Urga
soon, however, extended his influence to the two aimaks east
of Urga, the Tushetu-Khanate and the Tsetsen Khanate,
leaving to the Military Governor at Uliassutai the remaining
two aimaks west of Urga (and east and west of Uliassutai)
the Jasaktu Khanate and the Sain Noyan Khanate.

The remaining territory on the west, the Khobdo district,
was at first administered by a deputy military governor from
Uliassutai, but he soon became independent of the latter and
the title of Imperial Resident at Khobdo was conferred upon
him. All these officials were appointed by the Emperor and
were generally Manchus, and the Imperial Residents in Urga
had the privilege of making direct reports to the Emperor.[10]

The Imperial Resident in Urga had to rely for the maintenance of his authority over the Khalkha chiefs on the
spiritual influence of the Living Buddha at Urga, the Jeptsum
Damba Hutukhtu. But this was not the only advantage
which accrued to the Manchus from supporting the Yellow
Religion. By supporting the spread of Lamaism, they intended
to support the transformation of an aggressive race which had
once conquered China into a non-militant people. This was
admitted in very frank terms by a Manchu official about 1840:
" The weakness of the Mongols is China's strength. To tame
the Mongols with the Yellow Religion is China's best policy;
and, indeed, from the point of view of Mongol interests, it is
much better for them to live quietly, and multiply, with no

[10] H. S. Brunnert and V. V. Hagelstrom, *Present Day Political Organisation of China*, pp. 453-454.

other cares than those of finding pasture and water, than to swoop down upon the frontiers as the Huns and Turks used to do, keep China under perpetual arms, and drench the plains with human gore. This policy, in fact, is what may be called dispelling ferocity through charity, and guiding untameable men with the doctrine of rewards and punishments. . . ." [11]

Up to the eve of the nineteenth century, the Chinese Government left the Outer Mongols to themselves, apart from the restrictions above-mentioned. While in the second half of the nineteenth century Chinese colonization advanced from Kalgan towards the north, colonization by Chinese in Outer Mongolia was strictly forbidden. Detailed regulations were laid down as to the routes by which Chinese traders could enter and trade in Outer Mongolia. The Chinese were forbidden to marry Mongolian women or to take their families to Outer Mongolia, and were thus prevented from settling there. [12]

Again in accordance with the policy of the Manchus of keeping on good terms with the Mongols, they also tried to protect them from exploitation by Chinese traders. Chinese traders in Outer Mongolia were forbidden to give credit to Mongols, but this regulation had to be modified eventually as credit operations could not be avoided because of the very nature of Mongol economic life. The Chinese brought brick tea, tobacco, sugar, flour, rice, and cotton materials, which were exchanged for sheep's wool, camel hair, chamois skins, horse and cattle hides, horsehair, furs, and even cattle. But most of these Mongol products could only be brought into the market during certain periods of the year, and not, for instance, in spring, when the main commercial business was done. The Chinese merchants advanced the necessaries of everyday life, such as tea, tobacco, and cloth, and the Mongols, when the time came to pay back with their own goods, such as furs,

[11] *Journal of the China Branch of the Royal Asiatic Society,* 1887, New Ser., Vol. XXII, Shanghai, 1888, p. 101: "Wei Yüan on the Mongols." Wai-Yun or Wei Yüan is defined as "an officer of any rank deputed to perform certain duties" by Herbert A. Giles in *A Glossary of Reference on Subjects connected with the Far East,* Shanghai, 1900, p. 312.

[12] Stefan Lipovtsov, *op. cit.,* Vol. II, pp. 67-71 (74-83).

skins, etc., found either that they had bought too much or that their goods did not come up to the value of those they had received. Unfavorable hunting, a cattle epidemic, or a severe winter which would kill many cattle, might bring them into heavy debt to the Chinese traders, who, in addition, being shrewd merchants, had all the advantage over the unbusiness-like nomads in a bargain.

The profits of the Chinese were further increased by their use of short weight or false measures. The Government had, by force of circumstances, to allow its merchants to give credit to hoshuns, and from this the granting of credit to individuals was only a short step. While by reason of the economic structure of the country it was impossible to bar all credit operations, the Manchu Government was also too weak or unwilling to set up any adequate control of the credit operations, and the more " Chinese " the Manchu dynasty became, the less probable were any effective measures in this direction.[13] Not much imagination is needed to picture the extent of Mongolian indebtedness to Chinese merchants, since thirty per cent per month was the prevailing rate of interest.[14]

With the turn of the century, a definite change in the official policy of the Chinese Government towards Outer Mongolia became apparent. Several reasons may be adduced for this, such as pressure of Chinese population and the success of Chinese colonization in Inner Mongolia, but still more important was the attempt of the Dynasty, after the humiliation endured in its dealings with Western powers and in the Sino-Japanese War, to save Outer Mongolia from the fate of Manchuria and other frontier territories. The laws against immigration and intermarriage were repealed, special endowments were given for mixed marriages, and an active policy of colonization in Outer Mongolia was inaugurated. For this purpose two new Government bureaus were established, in accordance with a memorial presented to the Emperor in

[13] *Ibid.*, pp. 72, 85; Grumm-G., Vol. 3, Part 2, pp. 478-479.
[14] Cf. also *The Chinese Recorder*, Vol. 8, July-August 1877, No. 4, " The Chinese in Mongolia," by Hoinos, pp. 273-95, esp. pp. 275-77.

January 1901. First, the Bureau of Territorial Development—
or of Colonization—(Chi Tsan Ssu), which was in charge of
the inhabitants of Mongolia, the preservation of wild animals,
fur curing, and railway construction; and secondly, the Bureau
of Frontier Defence (Pien Wei Ssu), which was charged with
the training of Mongolian and Tibetan troops, education, and
trade expansion.[15]

Such a policy found encouragement in the defeat of Russia
in the Russo-Japanese War, which made it unlikely that
Russia would intervene effectively. Already in 1905 the pres-
sure exercised by the new Chinese policy was so strongly felt
by the Mongols that they addressed themselves to the Russian
Consul in Urga for help and assistance, which, however, was
not forthcoming. "It is the determined aim of the Chinese
Government," says a memorandum of the Russian Consul-
General in Urga in 1907, " to subject Mongolia to general
Chinese administration, and to settle on Mongolian lands
Chinese colonists who would interfere with the nomad life and
the cattle farming which is the chief means of existence " of
the Mongols.[16]

In retrospect, it looks as if the Manchu Dynasty in its last
years was running a race with time by employing all means
at its disposal to get Outer Mongolia completely in its political
and economic grip. The inherent weakness of the Chinese
Government was, however, also very obvious. It had not
sufficient means to finance its grandiose schemes, which included the projects of building a railway between Kalgan and
Urga, developing a mining industry in Mongolia, and also the
opening of schools. This last scheme was intended for the
teaching of Chinese to the Mongols (its use had formerly been
forbidden to them), and for the purpose of military training.[17]

---

[15] See Brunnert, *op. cit.*, pp. 163-64; Pao Chao Hsieh, *op. cit.*, p. 324.

[16] Popov, p. 4, Memorandum of General Consul Shishmarev of Oct. 24, 1907.

[17] As to railway schemes see J. Kushelov, *Mongolia i mongolski vopros* (Mongolia and the Mongolian Question), St. Petersburg, 1912, p. 56; *R. J.*, 1 Année,
No. 4, March 15, 1911, p. 205, from Peking May 22, 1909, and June 15, 1909; *ibid.*,
2 Année, Nos. 8-9, August 15-September 15, 1912, pp. 378-79. As to schools and
military training, cf. above cited numbers of *R. J.*, especially number of March 15,
1911, p. 204.

It was also proposed to establish, with Government support, a Chinese commercial bank in Urga, which should assist the private Chinese bank already established there. (This was opened in Urga in the summer of 1911, i. e., only a few months before Chinese rule there ceased altogether).[18] In an explanatory note attached to the report on this subject, submitted to the Chinese Government by the Bureau of Outer Mongolia, it is stated that in founding this bank the Government hoped that it would assist and increase colonization, and regulate and improve Mongolia's finances. Then " there need be no fear of foreigners " (Russians) " who dream of conquering Mongolian lands." [19]

The Chinese Government realized that the intensified application of its new policy might encounter the opposition of the Mongolian princes, and of the Lama Church. In 1908, therefore, they ordered the Chinese Resident (Amban) in Urga to enquire from the Mongols as to their attitude toward the participation of Mongols in a Chinese representative body, and toward the railway projects. He was also charged to find out the cause of possible opposition to the projected reforms.[20]

An assembly of Mongol princes, which gathered at Urga, resolved that it was their desire that Khalkha should be left in its former state, but the opposition to the question of railways was met with the answer that a categorical order from Peking had already been issued that they should be built in any case.[21]

Such statements were not conducive to better relations between the Chinese Resident (San Tao, a Manchu, and a very energetic man), and the Living Buddha (Hutukhtu) in Urga, who in these years became increasingly the leader of the Mongolian nobles in their opposition to the Chinese policy. Relations became extremely strained and a crisis was reached in 1910. A brawl between three drunken Lamas and an em-

---

[18] J. Kushelov, *op. cit.,* p. 55.

[19] *Ibid.*

[20] Popov, p. 5, telegram of Consul General in Urga Shishmarev of March 24, 1909, No. 374.

[21] Popov, Report of the same of May 2, 1909, No. 531.

ployee of a Chinese shop, which ended in a Mongolian crowd plundering the shop, and a clash with Chinese soldiers as well as the stoning of the Amban when he arrived on the spot, resulted in the arrest of several Lamas who stood close to the Living Buddha. Among these was his first assistant, who was the administrator of the property of the monasteries, and who had been the ringleader in the disorders. The Hutukhtu tried by correspondence with the Peking authorities to achieve the reinstatement of the persons dismissed, but without avail.[22]

Soon afterwards the Amban ordered that the market place for Chinese, Mongol and Russian merchants in Urga, which was in the main square of the Lama monastery, should be transferred to a site near the Yamen (Amban's residence). San Tao, with the permission of the Peking Government, granted the Chinese traders a large area. Then he gave orders that a fence should be put around it, a flag hoisted, and money collected from the traders. At the same time he proposed to erect Chinese leather, soap-making, and wool factories, and also a wool washing plant. When the Chinese and Mongolian market was transferred to the new site, the Hutukhtu sent a Mongolian prince to the place to tell the Mongols that they should remain and trade on the square of the lama monastery. The Chinese Amban reported to Peking that the Hutukhtu and the Shabi administration had openly defied the order of the Bogdo Khan (the Emperor of China).[23]

Such incidents as these, and the resultant increased tension between the Chinese authorities and the Mongols together with the latter's renewed desire to seek help from Russia, hastened the decision of the Chinese to strengthen their military position in Outer Mongolia, especially in Urga, and in the frontier districts close to Siberia. In 1910, in a secret report, the Chinese War Minister, General Yü Ch'ang, proposed to add to the formation of the already planned divisions another fourteen, whose special duty would have been the protection of the fron-

---

[22] Popov, p. 5.
[23] Popov, p. 6, based on Memorandum of Shishmarev, from 1910, his reports of March 29 and 31, 1910, No. 328, 344 and report of Lavdovski from Urga of November 20, 1910.

tier districts. Among other places, Uliassutai, Khobdo, Altai, Tarbagatai, Urga, as well as the Tibetan frontier province of Kokonor were each to receive one division.[24] In September 1910 the Chinese Foreign Minister ordered a delegation of officials to investigate the extent of Russian influence in Outer Mongolia, taking into account mainly economic aspects such as loans given in connection with business contracted by Russians, the amount of Russian money in circulation, the general commercial situation of the Russians, and statistics of all Mongols who had become naturalized Russians.[25] Evidently, the Chinese Government intended to check the progress of Russian commercial influence in Outer Mongolia, and was prepared to carry this so far as to provoke an open conflict with the Russian Government.

By the Treaty of St. Petersburg of 1881, Russia had the right to open consulates in Mongolia at certain defined places; but it was stipulated that this was to take place only if the development of commerce necessitated such a measure. The Chinese Government, clinging obstinately to the restrictive stipulation, denied that the development of Russian commerce was sufficiently advanced to warrant the opening of a consulate in Khobdo in western Mongolia.[26] The Chinese War Minister, in a conversation with the German Minister in Peking, expressed his indignation at the firm attitude which Russia took in this matter. He expressed his anxiety about Russian war preparations. " I know for certain," he said, " that all the Russian measures tend toward depriving us of Mongolia." He himself was prepared to make war against Russia, but had to submit that China was completely incapable of such action, as " my countrymen do not understand the situation of China and have not yet granted means for the modernization of the equipment of the army." [27]

[24] Benckendorff, Vol. I, report of Korostovets to Sazonov of November 3/16, 1910, No. 104, pp. 379-80.

[25] *R. J.*, of March 15, 1911, pp. 208-209, from Peking, September 15, 1910.

[26] For details see different numbers of *R. J.* and thesis of K. Strupp (cf. Bibliography).

[27] *G. P.*, Vol. 32, No. 11797, p. 221, The Minister in Peking to Bethmann-Hollweg, March 30, 1911.

The Chinese Government was thus too weak to put into effect the many plans which were evolved in the last two years of the Manchu dynasty for the military as well as political reorganization of Mongolia. It was also intended to split up the whole of Mongolia into five provinces.[28] Such a policy needed strong and capable men, but when in September 1911, a very short time before the final overthrow of the dynasty, Prince Su became Minister of the Department of Territories (" Colonial Office "), he dismissed nearly all the officials for incompetence.[29] It is clear that, although because of his close relations with Mongol princes he displayed special interest in Mongolia, circumstances made it impossible for him to realize any of those plans which might have strengthened China's influence in Mongolia.

On the other hand, the very firm but not very wise Chinese (Manchu) resident in Urga, San Tao, while in 1911 forbidding the Mongols to take loans from Russians or to have any intercourse with them, was backed only by 250 Chinese soldiers stationed in Urga, and was in June 1911 incapable of preventing the departure of the Mongolian Delegation to St. Petersburg.[30] Finally in November 1911 the Mongols, encouraged by news of the increasing disorder in China, and helped by Russian agents on the spot, declared the Living Buddha in Urga Ruler of the Mongolian nation. The Chinese Amban, deprived as he was of any possible reinforcement from China on account of the political situation there, had to seek refuge in the Russian Consulate, whence he was soon afterwards escorted by Russian Cossacks to the Siberian frontier. Whereas the Chinese were able to hold out longer in Khobdo, the chief town of Western Mongolia, Manchu rule over Khalkha came thus to an end, before the abdication of the Emperor of China and the proclamation of a Chinese Republic.

---

[28] Cf. n. 24.

[29] *R. J.*, 1 Année, No. 10, October 15, 1911, p. 632, from Peking, September 15, 1911.

[30] Popov, p. 6; Kushelov, *op. cit.*, pp. 61-62, and pp. 66-68.

B. Republican China; Negotiations, 1911-1915

For the prestige of a new regime like the Chinese Republic, it was a serious matter that it had no control over a territory the inhabitants of which had until recently professed allegiance to the Manchu Emperor. Of no avail was any legal argument that, because Outer Mongolia was a part of the Chinese Empire under the Manchu Dynasty, it should remain an integral part of the territory of the government which succeeded the Empire.[31]

For it was impossible to deny that the Mongol princes stood in a special relation to the former dynasty. The first President of the Republic, Yuan Shih-k'ai, recognized the special position of the Mongol princes and tried by rather primitive methods to gain their allegiance to the Republic. He asked the former Emperor to issue an appeal in the form of an edict to the Mongols, in which it was to be stated that a union of the five races in the Republic—Chinese, Manchus, Mongols, Tibetans, and Mohammedans—should take place, and that his last edict concerning the new regime should be respected.[32] Furthermore, Mongol princes were not only to retain their titles but the rank of each holder was raised a degree, and when nobles were already princes, the title of prince would be given to one of their sons.[33] This, however, applied in practice only to those princes, mainly living in Peking, who were willing to help the Chinese Government to regain control over the dissenting princes.

Several policies were available to the Chinese Government. First of all, negotiations with the Outer Mongols themselves, which, however, failed completely, as the intermediaries who were sent either did not reach their destination or were prevented from establishing contact with the Living Buddha in

[31] Tsi Chu Chen, in this thesis (cf. bibliography), p. 60, still maintains this view and cites " Professor H. Smith, one of the leading authorities in International Law " who concurs with his views.

[32] *R. J.*, 2e Année, No. 11, November 15, 1912, p. 471, from Peking, October 5, 1912.

[33] *Ibid.*, p. 469, from Peking, August 30, 1912.

Urga. Telegrams sent by the President to the latter remained unanswered.[34] Moreover, it soon became evident that the leading Outer Mongols aimed at inducing the Inner Mongol nobles to adhere to the new " Mongolian State," and that their ambition carried them as far as sending armed bands of Mongols beyond the territory of Khalkha. An immediate necessity arose, therefore, for the Chinese Government to counter these acts of aggression, spare Inner Mongolia the fate of Khalkha, and retain control in Western Mongolia (Khobdo) and the Altai district, and the adjoining area of Turkistan. It is not quite clear whether Chinese troops ever reached Khobdo, but 2000 were reported to have been still stationed there in December 1912; moreover, it was admitted by Yuan Shih-k'ai that reinforcements were sent to Altai and Turkistan.[35] At the same time, whether with special approval from the Peking Government or independently, we do not know, the troops in Inner Mongolia and Manchuria took extremely brutal measures against any opposition encountered among the Inner Mongols, so that several Inner Mongol leaders fled to Urga.[36]

Another possibility was for China to enter into negotiations with Russia, and to accept her good offices in reestablishing relations with Urga. Such a policy was urged by the Russian Minister in Peking, but however willing the President might have been to agree to this, public indignation thwarted it. At the end of September 1912, the Assistant to the Minister of Foreign Affairs repudiated the Russian Minister's protest against the sending of troops to Altai and Khobdo, told him that " the present state of affairs in Mongolia had become intolerable," that " up to the present time the Chinese Government paid great attention to the wishes of the Russian Govern-

[34] *G. P.*, Vol. 32, No. 11993, p. 429. The Minister in Peking to Bethmann-Hollweg, November 13, 1912.

[35] *DDF*, Tom IV, No. 609, The French Minister in Peking to M. Poincaré, December 2, 1912, p. 629. *O. B.*, No. 19, Sazonov to Krupenskii, October 16, 1912, p. 20; No. 35, Sazonov to Krupenskii, November 11, 1912, p. 37, referring to a wire by The Russian Consul in Uliassutai. No. 40, Krupenskii to Sazonov, November 17, 1912, p. 41; *The Times*, London, December 7, 1912, p. 5.

[36] *K. A.*, p. 19, Miller to Sazonov, October 28/November 10, 1913, No. 290.

ment, but that it must now ask the latter to abstain from neutralizing measures which were necessary to establish law and order in Outer Mongolia." [37] He proposed that a third power should be asked to mediate between China and Russia. Which this third power was to be was not specified, but a month later, in a debate in the National Council, a delegate proposed Japan. Submission of the case to the Hague Tribunal was considered useless as weak states got no justice there. [38]

The Government was of course aware of its weak position as against Russia, who threatened to enter into direct relations with the Outer Mongols without taking China's position into account. The sending of the former Minister in Peking, M. Korostovets, on a mission to Urga, clearly showed that Russia meant business. [39] It may have been that the Chinese Foreign Minister privately agreed with the argument of the Russian Minister that an understanding with Russia on Mongolia would better than anything else serve the real interests of China. But he and the President could not ignore the violent outburst in leading political circles against what was regarded as a weak Mongolian policy. All possible pressure was brought to bear on the President to prevent him from coming to terms with Russia, and to entangle him in an openly hostile policy toward her. Four of the great political parties sent telegrams to all provincial Governments, protesting against the President's attitude. [40]

Vice-President General Li Yuan-hung submitted a memorandum to the President urging him to punish severely those Mongolian princes who had declared independence, and suggesting the despatch of an expeditionary force of Manchurian and Shansi troops. [41] But, as the Minister of War explained to

[37] *O. B.*, No. 2, Krupenskii to Sazonov, September 23, 1912, p. 3.

[38] *The Times*, London, December 3, 1912, p. 5, from Peking, November 15.

[39] *O. B.*, No. 15, Sazonov to Krupenskii. October 9, 1912, p. 11; the Chinese Chargé d'Affaires in St. Petersburg, on inquiring whether it was true that Korostovets had recognized the independence of Mongolia, received the answer that for such inquiries the Minister in Peking was the competent authority.

[40] *G. P.*, Vol. 32, No. 11993, *op. cit.*, p. 428.

[41] *The Literary Digest*, February 22, 1913, p. 392, *Revue Indo-Chinoise*, XVI Année, No. 1, January 1913, p. 81.

the Cabinet, such an expedition was doomed to failure from the outset, from the military point of view. Communications were difficult; the temperature was low and especially unsuitable for Chinese soldiers; the Gobi Desert, where there was no water, had to be crossed; and there were great obstacles in the way of feeding an expedition. Even supposing that it could reach Urga easily, this would not mean that the large territory of Outer Mongolia would come under Chinese control. On the contrary, bands of Mongols would threaten the position of the Chinese, and the Mongol Government would simply move to another place. Such a result would not justify the necessary cost. In fact, such an expedition would not only cost the lives of many thousands of Chinese, but by engaging soldiers stationed in Manchuria might lead to complete domination by bandits in that region and its possible complete loss to China.

The main thing was therefore for China to concentrate on the defense of Inner Mongolia against all invasion.[42] In the middle of November it was reported that 10,000 Chinese troops were stationed at Kalgan, which was also the headquarters of a Division, and that arrangements had been undertaken for other Divisions to proceed to Inner Mongolia by way of the Peking-Kalgan railway.[43]

The Government had to take these measures to save its face when the agitation reached its climax at the beginning of November 1912. Then it became known that Russia had concluded an agreement with the Living Buddha in Urga and the Outer Mongolian princes, in which she recognized that the old relations between China and Mongolia had come to an end. " If Young China had its way," wrote the Peking correspondent of the London *Times* in the middle of November, " the whole of the army would now be marching upon Urga in spite of knowledge that behind the meager forces of the

[42] *R. J.*, 2e Année, No. 11, November 15, 1912, p. 475; cf. also article in *North China Daily News*, as cited in *Revue Indo-Chinoise*, XVI Année, No. 2, February 1913, p. 219.

[43] *The Times*, London, November 19, 1912, p. 7, " China and Mongolia—A Military Demonstration."

Hutukhtu stand the armed hosts of Russia." [44] The news that Russia had obtained special trade privileges in the Treaty aroused the indignation of Chinese merchants in Manchuria and in Kalgan, and since the contents of the treaty were not made public until later, wild rumors were circulated and several protest meetings were held at which the military Governors of Mukden and Kirin and President Yuan were urged to prepare a military expedition into Mongolia.[45]

Feelings in the Kuomintang party also ran high, and discussions in the National Council were extremely heated. The first victim of all this agitation was the Minister of Foreign Affairs himself, Liang Yu-hao, who resigned on November 13.[46] The fact that he was made a scapegoat was useful to President Yuan, whose position would otherwise have been imperilled. However, he confessed to the French Minister that " all my enemies . . . now profit from the Mongolian difficulty in order to raise their heads." [47] Quite conscious of the limits beyond which China could not go in dealing with Russia, he found an ingenious way of calming the belligerent passions of his compatriots. On November 24th a decree was issued for the launching of a war loan. Thereupon the zeal of many abated to some extent, and although the atmosphere was by no means calm, the President gained a breathing space.[48]

Apart from direct negotiations with Russia into which it was difficult to enter because of public unrest and Russia's firm attitude, a third possible policy was to enlist the opinion of other powers against Russian violation of China's territorial integrity. Here, however, the position was anything but hopeful. The German Minister was sympathetic and while admitting the danger to China of taking forcible measures, remarked that by a formal protest she would at least give expression to the legal point of view.[49] The Wai Chiao Pu

---

[44] *The Times*, London, December 3, 1912, p. 5.
[45] Consten, Vol. II, p. 9.
[46] *G. P.*, Vol. 32, No. 11993, *op. cit.*, p. 430, and note.
[47] *DDF*, Tom IV, No. 609, p. 629.
[48] *Ibid.*
[49] *G. P.*, Vol. 32, No. 11993, p. 429.

(Chinese Foreign Office) in fact sent instructions to its diplomatic representatives abroad to protest against the Russo-Mongolian agreement.[50] As to the other powers, no support whatever and not even sympathy could be expected from Great Britain, with whom the Chinese Government was in conflict over Tibet. The Peking correspondent of the London *Times* at that time drew a close parallel between Anglo-Chinese and Russo-Chinese differences in Tibet and Mongolia respectively.[51] The French could, from China's standpoint, be no more than useful intermediaries between her and Russia.

Toward the end of November, President Yuan asked the French Minister to come to see him, obviously to discover from him the attitude of France's ally, Russia, concerning the future. Again he was told that any agreement between China and Russia had to be based on the acceptance by China of three conditions: no occupation, no administration, no colonization by Chinese in Outer Mongolia. He declared himself opposed to Chinese colonization in Outer Mongolia, but that he did not agree with the two other stipulations was evident from his insistence that what China wanted was real Chinese sovereignty; the term ' suzerainty ' did not appear sufficient to him.[52] One of his closest confidants, Sun Pao-ch'i, the former Governor of Shantung, who in September 1913 became Foreign Minister, had already a short time before repudiated the three conditions by admitting that their acceptance by China would be tantamount to her having no voice whatever in Outer Mongolia, and to her giving up the territory altogether. There seemed, therefore, nothing about which one couldd possibly negotiate.[53] Furthermore, there was always the consideration of *amour propre*—that it was beneath the dignity of China to negotiate with Russia about a territory which could only be considered as belonging to China.

In spite of this failure to establish direct contact with the

---

[50] *DDF*, Tom IV, No. 459, M. Poincaré to M. George Louis, November 14, 1912, p. 471 and note.

[51] *The Times*, London, December 3, 1912.

[52] *DDF*, Tom IV, No. 609, p. 62.   [53] *G.P.*, Vol. 32, No. 11993, p. 429.

Mongol authorities in Urga, Yuan tried again and again in etxensive telegrams to impress on them China's determination to consider the whole of Mongolia as belonging to China, and warned them that by their attitude they would ultimately suffer the same fate as Korea and Formosa.[54] It is impossible to say to what extent he had knowledge of the anti-Russian attitude of a few of the Outer Mongol nobles, such as Da Lama, the Mongolian Minister of the Interior. He seemed to have relied mainly on offering the Urga " rebels " pecuniary facilities, especially shortly before the final signing of the Russo-Mongolian agreement.[55] When all these many communications to Urga were at last indirectly answered at the end of November 1912, in a telegram from the Mongolian Prime Minister and in another from the Living Buddha himself, announcing Outer Mongolia's declaration of independence, he took the opportunity to stress that all five races were united on equal terms in the new Republic, and proposed to the Living Buddha to send a special envoy to Urga to discuss this matter with him. This offer was promptly refused by the Living Buddha, who proposed the mediation of Russia instead.[56]

It was of no avail for the Chinese Government to confine itself exclusively to an insistence on its sovereign rights in Mongolia. The Russian threats that further delay in coming to an agreement with her on the status of Mongolia might be followed by the territorial increase of the Hutukhtu's power were not to be taken lightly. The Chinese Government was aware of the fact that the question of the extent of territory to which the Russo-Mongolian agreement applied had been

[54] Cited by Korostovets, p. 228. President Yüan was specially qualified to speak of the case of Korea, because for twelve years, from 1883 to 1894, he had been agent in Korea and occupied the position of Resident at the Korean Court in Seoul. His task there was to urge the King " to rely solely on the help of China which alone can protect Korea from the insulting treatment of foreign nations." See *United States Foreign Relations*, 1887, Mr. W. W. Rockhill to Mr. Bayard, Seoul, January 28, 1887.

[55] *O. B.*, No. 22, October 19, 1912, p. 22; No. 37, November 12, 1912, p. 38; *ibid.*, No. 52, Korostovets to Sazonov, January 5, 1913, p. 53.

[56] E. T. Williams, in *American Journal of International Law*, 1916, pp. 804-805; see also for text of telegrams *Revue Indo-Chinoise*, XVI Année 3, March 1912, pp. 334-335.

left open. The inhabitants of Barga, in the northwestern corner of Manchuria, had already asked the Living Buddha in Urga to take them under his protection. Mongol bands repeatedly attacked lands lying in Inner Mongolia, and it was only a question of time before the Chinese would have to give up their position in Western Mongolia (the Khobdo district). No illusions could be entertained as to the Mongols' close relations with Russia, especially when it became known at the beginning of December 1912 that a Mongolian delegation had departed for St. Petersburg. The news of this made a bad impression on public opinion, and the Chinese Foreign Minister asked Russia to postpone the visit of the Mongols until after the conclusion of Sino-Russian negotiations; the refusal of Russia only intensified the already strong campaign against her in the Chinese press.[57]

In the negotiations with Russia which were finally begun in December 1912, the Chinese submitted treaty drafts of their own. The term 'sovereignty' again replaced 'suzerainty' verbally proposed by Russia; 'Mongolia' was belittled by the use of the term 'Urga,' which revealed the intention of China to restrict the territory of an "autonomous Mongolia" to Urga and its district, to be extended at most to the Tushetu Khan and Tsetsen Khan Aimaks. Nothing was said of the three conditions on which Russia had constantly insisted.[58] It must have been obvious to the Chinese from the beginning that such terms could not provide a sound basis for agreement with Russia, which categorically rejected them, and threatened China that any actions which she might wish to undertake against Outer Mongolia itself would be regarded by Russia as an act of war.[59] In a further draft the condition—no Chinese troops—remained still unfulfilled.[60]

[57] *O. B.*, No. 44, Krupenskii to Sazonov, November 28, 1912, pp. 44-45; No. 45, Krupenskii to Sazonov, November 13, 1912, pp. 45-46; No. 46, Sazonov to Krupenskii, December 5, 1912, p. 46.

[58] *O. B.*, No. 47, Krupenskii to Sazonov, December 5, 1912, pp. 46-47, with Chinese treaty draft in French on p. 47.

[59] *O. B.*, No. 48, Sazonov to Krupenskii, December 10, 1912, p. 49.

[60] *O. B.*, No. 50, Krupenskii to Sazonov, December 29, 1912, pp. 50-51, treaty in French.

Demands on Russia for a promise not to send troops were refused, as were those for new Chinese consulates in Siberia, and a change in passport regulations.[61] Russia, however, was willing to meet the request (it would mean " giving in formally," wrote Sazonov) that the Russo-Mongolian commercial protocol should be considered as a separate act from Russia's political agreement with the Living Buddha.[62] Encouraged by this success, which meant that any mention of the especially hated political treaty between Russia and—from the Chinese point of view—one of China's territories was to be excluded from any Sino-Russian agreement, the Chinese proposed to replace in the Urga protocol—which according to Russia included not much more than China had conceded to Russia in the treaty of St. Petersburg in 1881—the word ' Mongolia ' by the word ' China.'[63] Such ignoring of the changed circumstances was unacceptable. The Chinese Minister of Commerce opposed the special recognition of the Urga protocol in a Sino-Russian agreement, but the Russians responded that they considered it useless to enter into an agreement with the Chinese Government which did not define the position of the commercial rights of Russian subjects in Mongolia.[64] The mention of the Central Government was conceded by Russia only in so far as it recognized the historical character of the local Government in Mongolia as a part of the Chinese Empire.[65]

The Chinese Government had great difficulty in coming to a swift decision, as it had to reckon with the constant opposition of the newly set-up Parliament. The deputies proposed many changes in the articles of the draft submitted to them, including a prohibition of colonization in Mongolia by anybody

[61] *O. B.*, No. 51, Sazonov to Krupenskkii, January 3, 1913, p. 52; No. 45, Krupenskii to Sazonov, January 16, 1913, p. 54.

[62] *O. B.*, No. 56, Sazonov to Krupenskii, January 23, 1913, p. 55.

[63] *O. B.*, No. 57, Krupenskii to Sazonov, February 4, 1913, p. 56; No. 58, Sazonov to Krupenskii, February 6, 1930, p. 56.

[64] *O. B.*, No. 59, Krupenskii to Sazonov, March 10, 1913, p. 56; No. 60, Sazonov to Krupenskii, March 12, 1913, p. 51.

[65] *O. B.*, No. 63, Sazonov to Krupenskii, April 9, 1913, p. 58; No. 56, Krupenskii to Sazonov, April 21, 1913, p. 59; No. 66, Sazonov to Krupenskii, April 24, 1913, p. 60.

except Mongols and Chinese, a limitation of the privileges of the Mongols to those granted to them in a decree issued in 1912, and of the trade privileges of the Russians to ten years.[66] The Government was well aware of the danger inherent in these delaying tactics and in the official Press blamed the deputies for a very serious situation.[67] Especially violent was the opposition coming from the deputies of the Kuomintang, which had its stronghold in the south of China and took advantages of the opportunity to attack the Government. One of their demands included the renunciation of the title of Emperor of Mongolia (Bogdo Khan) by the Living Buddha in Urga, and the replacement of the word 'Mongolia' by the term 'Outer Mongolia' in the treaty text. To this Russia subsequently agreed, for it was again a matter of form.[68] But the Chinese claim that questions of a political and territorial order in Mongolia fell within the authority of their suzerainty was rejected by Russia.[69]

Such control on the part of China was irreconcilable with the three Russian conditions for negotiation, and the resignation of the Chinese Foreign Minister in July 1913 may be taken as a sign of his despair of reconciling these with the opposition to them emanating from the Parliament.[70]

Agreement between the two governments could at last be reached only on the basis of a Russian draft which took the form of a joint declaration and left open many questions. On the one hand, the basis of this draft was Russia's recognition of China's suzerainty over Outer Mongolia. Special mention that this designated Outer Mongolia as a part of China was first rejected by the Russians as tautology, but later admitted in a separate exchange of notes, as China insisted on its vital

[66] *O. B.*, No. 69, Krupenskii to Sazonov, May 22, 1913, p. 62; No. 72, the same, June 4, 1913, p. 63.

[67] *O. B.*, p. 64.

[68] *O. B.*, No. 71, Krupenskii to Sazonov, March 29, 1913, p. 63; No. 73, the same, June 6, 1913, p. 64.

[69] *O. B.*, No. 74, Sazonov to Krupenskii, June 20, 1913, p. 65; No. 75, the same, June 28, 1913, p. 66; No. 76, Krupenskii to Sazonov, June 30, 1913, p. 68.

[70] *O. B.*, No. 80, Krupenskii to Sazonov, July 11, 1913, p. 71.

importance to her.[71] On the other hand, China recognized the autonomous regime of Outer Mongolia in all questions of internal administration, trade, and industry, and engaged herself not to send troops to Outer Mongolia nor to colonize its lands. A Chinese official in Urga was to take charge of the interests of Chinese there. Russia engaged not to send more troops to Outer Mongolia than were necessary for the protection of her consuls. China also accepted Russian mediation for reestablishing her relations with Outer Mongolia, and it was agreed that questions of political and territorial character concerning Outer Mongolia were to be shelved until negotiations between the Russian, Chinese, and Mongolian Governments, which were to begin as soon as possible and were to be based on the Russo-Chinese declaration, and on the Russo-Mongolian trade protocol of 1912, should take place. The boundaries of Outer Mongolia were then to be fixed.[72] But it was agreed that in the above mentioned separate notes the different territories which composed Outer Mongolia were to be enumerated.[73]

In order to facilitate the consent of its parliament to this, the Chinese Government insisted on its presentation with the exchange of notes, and in the beginning of November the two instruments were finally signed, nearly one year after the negotiations had begun.[74] President Yuan was, however, fully alive to the fact that he would be unable to obtain the consent of Parliament, and therefore before allowing his Foreign Min-

[71] Russian draft in French, *ibid.*, pp. 67-68; No. 89, Neratov to Krupenskii, September 11, 1913, pp. 76-77.

[72] *O. B.*, No. 28, Krupenskii to Sazonov, August 15, 1913, p. 72; No. 83, Sazonov to Krupenskii, August 23, 1913, p. 72; No. 91, Krupenskii to Neratov, September 16, 1913, pp. 78-79.

[73] *O. B.*, No. 93, Neratov to Krupenskii, September 22, 1913, p. 80; No. 94, Krupenskii to Neratov, September 25, 1913, p. 81; No. 95, Neratov to Krupenskii, September 28, 1913, pp. 81-82.

[74] *O. B.*, No. 96, Krupenskii to Neratov, October 2, 1913, p. 82; No. 98, Krupenskii to Neratov, October 10, 1913, p. 84; No. 100, Krupenskii to Sazonov, October 14, 1913, p. 85; No. 101, Sazonov to Krupenskii, October 15, 1913, p. 85; No. 102, Krupenskii to Sazonov, October 16, 1913, pp. 85-86; No. 105, Krupenskii to Sazonov, October 23, 1913, pp. 87-90; text of agreement in Russian. For text in English see MacMurray, Vol. II, pp. 1066-67.

ister to sign, he published an edict liquidating the Kuomintang; members of Parliament who were members of the Kuomintang were deprived of their right of representation, and banished from the capital.[75]

China's hopes that the immediate effect of the agreement would be the reestablishment of contact with the Outer Mongols themselves were soon disappointed. The Mongols postponed the commencement of the tripartite negotiations which China had proposed and Russia had agreed to hold at Kiakhta. The Russo-Chinese agreement had deeply disturbed them, and when in December 1913 the Mongolian Prime Minister arrived in St. Petersburg he took the opportunity to send to the Chinese Minister a note protesting against it, announcing that his Government considered its relations with China severed forever.[76] Towards the end of March 1914, the Chinese Foreign Office submitted an aide-memoire to the Russian Minister in Peking, calling attention to the clause of the declaration which said that China would take advantage of the mediation of Russia and repudiating the allegation that she had allowed irresponsible persons to establish direct contact with the Mongols. " In my opinion," concluded the Chinese Foreign Minister, " there has elapsed a considerable time since the moment of signature of the declaration, during which China has not yet entered into formal relations with Outer Mongolia." [77]

Indeed, developments in Outer Mongolia were anything but encouraging for China. The entry of Chinese goods into Outer

---

[75] *K. A.*, p. 18, Telegram of Krupenskii of October 23/November 5, 1913, No. 703. *DDF*, Tom VIII, No. 461, p. 581, M. Gérard, Ambassador in Tokyo to M. Pichon, Minister of Foreign Affairs, November 8, 1913.

[76] As to Chinese proposal of Kiakhta, see *O. B.*, No. 92, Krupenskii to Neratov, September 18, 1913, p. 79; Russian acceptance *ibid.*, No. 93, Neratov to Krupenskii, September 22, 1913, p. 80. But cf. also *K. A.*, p. 61, Sazonov's note to the Tsar of January 12/25, 1914: " Kiakhta . . . has the advantage that the Chinese and Mongolian representatives delegated to the conference will not be exposed to any foreign influence which would unavoidably happen if the conference were held either at St. Petersburg or at Peking." As to note of Mongolian Prime Minister see *K. A.*, pp. 39-40.

[77] *IBZI*, Vol. I, 2, No. 83, Aide-memoire of March 11/24, 1914, pp. 73-74.

Mongolia, whether through Russian or Chinese merchants, suffered severely from the imposition of *likin* charges and various other collections and fees. Debts owed to Chinese merchants by the Mongols were not paid, but were considered as having been cancelled by the declaration of independence. The Chinese bank in Urga, to which the leading princes and the Living Buddha owed about one million roubles, was not able to collect the considerable interest due to it.[78] In every respect a delay was disadvantageous to China. Fears of Outer Mongolian intrusions into Inner Mongolia were not allayed, and Russian influence especially in the financial and commercial field was able to make headway without the slightest resistance from China. It appears, however, that, as was reported in June 1914, Chinese settlers had again begun an influx into Outer Mongolia, to some extent taking advantage of the fact that its exact boundaries were not yet settled.[79] Anxieties in China were increased when rumors spread that Russia had fortified her position by several agreements with Outer Mongolia, of which one on railways was made public after its conclusion in September 1914.

When the tripartite negotiations at last opened in the beginning of September 1914, the Chinese delegation thought itself in a more advantageous position as Russia was deeply involved in the European war. The attitude of the Chinese delegation was therefore from the beginning an aggressive one, and this rendered negotiation extremely difficult. The Chinese delegates, the chief of whom were General Pi Kuei-pang and Chen Lu, immediately asked that the Living Buddha should renounce his title of Bogdo Khan, and that the Mongolian national calendar should be replaced by the Chinese; they demanded recognition by the Mongols of the Sino-Russian declaration and notes, and a special admission that Mongolia

[78] *K.A.*, pp. 28-29, Telegram of Miller of November 18/December 2, 1913, No. 333, and copy of report of the agent of the Ministry of Trade and Industry in Mongolia of November 8/21, 1913, No. 317.
[79] *IBZI*, Vol. I, 4, No. 155, Miller to Sazonov, June 26/July 9, 1914, p. 150.

8

" has never been independent." [80] Miller, the Russian delegate, considered that their ambitions were nothing short of reducing Khalkha once more to the status of a Chinese colony,[81] in opposition to his demand that the Chinese Government agree not to transform Outer Mongolia into a Chinese province. In return Russia would engage herself not to annex Outer Mongolia or any part of it.[82] Such terms as " Autonomous State " or " Autonomous Government " were stubbornly rejected by the Chinese, the motive being their comprehensible anxiety that from such a status it would be only a short step toward either the creation of an independent state, or a state under Russian protection, with subsequent annexation by Russia in either case.[83]

The Chinese were thus employing the same tactics to which they had resorted with so little success during the Sino-Russian negotiations. Their reasoning was very simple. If instead of the terms " Autonomous State " or " Government " the terms " Country " or " Authorities " were employed, it followed that such regions or persons could not maintain troops, contract loans, or conclude treaties of a commercial and industrial character, such as telegraph or railway agreements, or even accept the Russian diplomatic agent in their capital. It was as Sazonov said " a play on words," in order to belittle " the extent of the political rights of autonomous Mongolia." [84] In Peking, the Government's attention was drawn by the Russian Minister to the need of recognizing that Outer Mongolia was restricted in its rights only by Chinese suzerainty as regards political and territorial questions. China was assured that, together with Russia, she could always prevent the intercourse

[80] *IBZI*, Vol. II, 6, 1, n. 4, pp. 330 31, telegrams of Miller of August 30/September 12, 1914, No. 18, September 2/15, No. 23, September 7/20, No. 29, September 10/23, No. 38.

[81] *IBZI*, telegram of Miller of September 17/30, 1914, No. 51.

[82] *IBZI*, Vol. I, 5, p. 275 (art. 2), Miller to Sazonov, July 19/August 1, 1914.

[83] *IBZI*, Vol. II, 6, 1, pp. 330-31, telegrams of Miller, September 27/October 10, 1914, No. 81, and of October 3/16, No. 96.

[84] *IBZI*, telegrams of Miller, October 4/17, No. 98, and of October 7/20, No. 106; telegram of Sazonov to Krupenskii, October 5/18, No. 3340.

of Mongols with any other power, even in merely economic or industrial matters, but that it would be unwise to insist on any such specific prohibition, which would unnecessarily hurt the *amour propre* of the Mongols.[85] But China contested Russia's right to enter into railway, post, and telegraph agreements, as she had actually done, and claimed in an official protest against the Russo-Mongolian railway agreement as well as in a memorandum handed to the Russian delegation at Kiakhta, that such agreements were of a political character and therefore fell within the authority of the suzerain.[86]

In this matter, the feelings of the Chinese were so strong, on the one hand, and the willingness of the Russians to compromise was so slight, on the other, that negotiations were broken off for some time. When they were resumed in the beginning of 1915, it was only with a view to an agreement on a matter which was still more difficult to solve. The Sino-Russian declaration and Peking's Notes represented the maximum of possible compromise to be attained by the two powers on questions of principles and definition. All concrete points, however, had been shelved for consideration in the tripartite negotiations. Among them was one which preoccupied business circles in China especially—trade rights in Outer Mongolia. It was the aim of the Chinese delegates to obtain for their merchants the same privileges that Russia had secured for her merchants in the Russo-Mongolian protocol of 1912. In fact, they seem even to have aimed at obtaining stipulations that would have enabled them in due time to reestablish their economic domination over the Outer Mongols; they had, however, to be reminded by the Russians that precisely this policy had been one of the main reasons for the creation of an autonomous Mongolia.[87]

Equality with Russian merchants, who could import goods

---

[85] *IBZI*, telegram of Sazonov to Krupenskii, October 9/22, No. 3412; No. 415, Sazonov to Krupenskii, October 15/28, 1914, p. 332.

[86] *IBZI*, Vol. II, 6, 2, p. 528, n. 1, telegram of Krupenskii of November 3/16, 1914, No. 201, and of November 25/December 8, No. 224.

[87] *IBZI*, Vol. II, 7, 1, pp. 48-49, telegram of Miller January 6/19, No. 317; No. 376, Neratov to Miller, March 2/15, 1915, p. 344.

free of duty, was to be attained by the abolition of the five per cent import and transit duty. Some approval of this proposal was at first expressed by the Russian delegate who, however, wished to exclude from it all luxury articles such as silk cloth, gold, silver, and other ornaments, silk embroidered boots, spirits, and tobacco, all of which, he claimed, should be subject to the duty of ten per cent already in force on spirits and tobacco.[88] But soon the amenable attitude of the Russian delegate changed, on instructions from St. Petersburg, to a refusal, chiefly because the Russians feared the competition of Chinese tea and tobacco with their own.[89]

The Chinese did not abandon their resolve to obtain for their subjects equality of treatment with Russians, which meant not only the import of Chinese goods free of duty, but the rights of Chinese to lease or buy commercial and industrial establishments.[90] If the Mongols insisted on retaining a kind of duty in the form of likin, the Chinese demanded the right to administer the Mongolian likin offices and the payments were to be made, as formerly, to the Peking Government, which would also decide what part of the payment was to be returned to autonomous Mongolia.[91] Such proposals could only result in a complete deadlock in the negotiations, and the Chinese finally modified this demand to read that goods imported from China into Outer Mongolia were not to pay any duty, but would pay likin to the value of 2.5 per cent, the tariff to be worked out by the Mongolian Government with the consent of the Chinese dignitary in Urga.[92]

The Russians countered that such participation by the Chinese representative in the internal administration of Outer Mongolia could not be permitted, as the autonomy of Outer

[88] *IBZI*, No. 50, Miller to Sazonov, January 7/20, 1915, pp. 48-49, and p. 49, n. 1, telegram of Miller January 8/21, No. 332.

[89] *IBZI*, No. 54, Sazonov to Miller, January 8/21, 1915, p. 51; No. 63, Sazonov to Miller, January 9/22, 1915, p. 59.

[90] *IBZI*, No. 65, Miller to Sazonov, January 9/22, 1915, p. 60.

[91] *IBZI* and p. 95, n. 1, telegram of Miller, January 16/29, No. 339.

[92] *IBZI*, p. 109, n. 2, telegram of Miller, January 17/30, 1915, No. 343; p. 169, n. 2, telegram of Miller, January 29/February 11, 1915, No. 361; p. 344, n. 4, telegram of Miller, February 23/March 8, 1915, No. 413.

Mongolia involved its right to control independently all matters concerning trade and customs.[93]

Soon the Chinese delegates received orders from Peking to adopt a more conciliatory attitude, as those advantages which they might possibly have possessed on account of Russia's preoccupation with the European war were offset by China's own preoccupation with Japan's aggressive policy.[94] However, this did not mean that the delegates changed their tactics immediately. On the contrary, they insisted on obtaining extraterritorial rights for Chinese workmen and craftsmen, who were to be exempted from all taxes. No Chinese were to be placed under Mongolian jurisdiction. Telegraph lines were to be restored to the administration of the Chinese Government.[95] This provoked the Russian Minister in Peking to a new protest and the Chinese Government was again threatened with the complete rupture of all negotiations.[96] In the end the Chinese agreed to pay five per cent duty on goods, of whatever origin, imported by Chinese merchants into Outer Mongolia. They also consented to the payment of double duty on spirits and tobacco on condition that this stipulation should not be specially mentioned in the treaty.

The Chinese continued to insist on the exemption from taxes demanded for Chinese workmen and craftsmen,[97] but since neither Russians nor Mongols could possibly concede this, since it would have put Chinese in a more favorable position than Mongols themselves, Russia was willing to meet three other Chinese demands: first, merchants and craftsmen of

[93] *IBZI*, No. 106, Sazonov to Miller, January 17/30, 1915, p. 95; No. 183, Sazonov to Miller, January 30/February 12, 1915, pp. 169-170.

[94] *IBZI*, No. 118, Sazonov to Miller, January 20/February 2, 1915, p. 109.

[95] *IBZI*, p. 333, n. 1, telegram of Miller, Febuary 27/March 12, 1915, No. 425. For Chinese attitude in regard to telegraphic lines cf. also *ibid.*, Vol. II, 6, 2, p. 528, n. 1, telegram of Miller, November 20/December 23, No. 201, and of November 25/December 8, No. 224.

[96] *IBZI*, Vol. II, 7, 1, No. 364, Krupenskii to Sazonov, February 28/March 13, 1915, p. 333; *ibid.*, n. 2, telegram of Neratov to Krupenskii of March 2/15, No. 1161; for instructions see No. 376, Neratov to Miller, pp. 344-45.

[97] *IBZI*, p. 359, n. 1, telegrams of Miller of March 2/15, and 3/16, Nos. 426 and 428.

autonomous Mongolia and of China were to have the reciprocal right of free movement in the other's country; second, Mongolian goods imported into China were to be subject to all duties payable there; third, a special system of judicial procedure was to be established for Chinese in Outer Mongolia.[98] This last concession had been held back by the Russians until the last moment, with the argument that if—as China attached so much importance to asserting—Mongolia was Chinese territory, it followed logically that Mongolian law courts were Chinese law courts and that therefore no extraterritorial rights could be claimed by the Chinese in this or any other respect.[99] The Chinese dignitary and his assistants were from now on to have exclusive jurisdiction in disputes between Chinese, and a Mongolian official was to participate in any dispute between Chinese and Mongols. The Russians also agreed to the omission of similar provisions for the Mongols in China itself, though they did not admit that the Mongols had in principle no right to demand it.[100]

Similar provisions were made for civil or criminal cases between Chinese and Russians; should the defendant be a Chinese, the proceedings were to be held under the auspices of the Chinese dignitary with the cooperation of the Russian Consul; in the case of a Russian defendant, the proceedings would take place in the Russian Consulate, with the cooperation of the Chinese dignitary.[101]

[98] *IBZI*, No. 413, Sazonov to Miller, March 10/23, 1915, p. 383; Vol. II, 7, 2, No. 447, Krupenskii to Sazonov, March 16/29, 1915, pp. 455-6 and Sazonov's consent in telegram of March 17/30, No. 1455, p. 456, n. 1.

[99] *IBZI*, Vol. II, 7, 1, No. 10, Sazonov to Miller, January 2/15, 1915, p. 10; for original proposals by Chinese delegates, *ibid.*, telegram of Miller, December 28, 1914/January 10, 1915; No. 301; also No. 413, in n. 98.

[100] *IBZI*, for final treaty text see MacMurray, Vol. II, pp. 1241-42, article XIII and XIV.

[101] The Chinese first proposed simply to apply article 7 of the Treaty of Tientsin of June 13, 1858, to Sino-Russian civil or criminal cases. But, as there was a difference of opinion between China and Russia as to the interpretation of this article, the Russians preferred to lay down new and detailed stipulations in the tripartite agreement of Kiakhta. See *IBZI*, Vol. II, 7, 1, No. 17, Sazonov to Miller, January 3/16, 1915, p. 19; pp. 237-8, n. 1, telegram of Miller, February 10/23, 1915, No. 384; No. 257, Miller to Sazonov, February 13/26, 1915, pp. 237-8; MacMurray, p. 1242, article XVI.

In exchange for these concessions, the Chinese had to renounce their insistence that the Kiakhta-Urga-Kalgan telegraph line should be placed under their supervision. It was agreed that that part of the line which crossed the territory of autonomous Mongolia would become the exclusive property of the Mongol Government, and that at the frontier between the two countries a station should be erected which was to be administered by Chinese and Mongol officials. The rates of telegrams and the distribution of the income were to be fixed at a conference to be held by the contracting parties at a later date.[102] Another demand to which the Chinese finally acceded after long reluctance was the creation of a neutral zone between Inner and Outer Mongolia, where Chinese were to be forbidden to colonize. The plea that in order to avoid complications at home this concession should not be included in the tripartite agreement, but should be left to an exchange of notes between Russia and China, gained Russian consent. Furthermore, China was to give amnesty to all Mongols who had given their allegiance to Outer Mongolia, and was not to prevent those Mongols who lived in China from proceeding on religious pilgrimage to Urga; this was also left to an exchange of notes between China and Russia.[103]

To the satisfaction of the Chinese, no mention was made in the tripartite agreement finally signed at the beginning of June 1915, in Kiakhta, of the Russo-Mongolian political treaty of November 1912, from which they concluded that it had been dropped. China recognized only the Sino-Russian agreement

---

[102] *IBZI*, Vol. II, 7, 2, No. 467, Sazonov to Miller, March 21/April 3, 1915, p. 475; MacMurray, article XVII, and detailed arrangements in Tripartite Agreement concerning the Outer Mongolian telegraph line of January 24, 1916, pp. 1259-63, and pp. 1263-65.

[103] *IBZI*, Vol. II, 7, 2, p. 578, n. 1, telegram of Sazonov to Krupenskii of April 2/15, No. 1693/4; No. 578, Krupenskii to Sazonov, April 8/21, 1915, p. 578; No. 596, Sazonov to Krupenskii, April 10/23, 1915, pp. 893-4; No. 712, Krupenskii to Sazonov, April 25/May 8, 1915, pp. 699-700: Acceptance by Chinese Government; p. 699, n. 2, telegram of Krupenskii of April 22/May 5, No. 228; Chinese request for special exchange of notes; for amnesty No. 776, Miller to Sazonov, May 4/17, 1915, p. 757-8; Vol. II, 8, 1, No. 75, Miller to Sazonov, May 25/June 7, 1915; MacMurray, pp. 1243-4.

of November 1913, which in turn had recognized the Russo-Mongolian trade agreement of 1912. The political provisions concerning China's suzerainty in the Kiakhta agreement were however more precise than those of the Peking agreement. China together with Russia was in charge of the foreign relations of Outer Mongolia. As Suzerain the President of the Republic had the right to invest the Living Buddha with the title of Bogdo Jeptsun Damba Hutukhtu Khan of Outer Mongolia; a Chinese dignitary was to take up his duties as representative of the suzerain in Urga; and on all ceremonial or official occasions the first place of honor was due to him. In addition, he was allowed to keep a bodyguard of 200 men, the Russian Consul having one of 150 men.[104]

The agreement was no sooner signed than it became apparent that the Chinese Government desired to read into it as much as possible of the rights of suzerainty. The President immediately issued four decrees. In the first, it was announced that a Russo-Chinese agreement had been concluded recognizing that Outer Mongolia was a part of Chinese territory and China its suzerain, that the independence of Urga had been abolished, and that an amnesty in Mongolia was to be declared. In the second decree two special envoys were nominated to communicate officially to the Living Buddha his elevation in title—conferred by a third decree. By a fourth, all titles and honorary designations which Mongol princes and lamas had received from the Manchu dynasty or from Outer Mongolia, were confirmed.[105] The Russians immediately protested against these decrees, which seemed to them to serve two purposes; first, to mislead Chinese public opinion in avoiding any mention of the part played by the Mongols themselves in the negotiations, or of the new status of Outer Mongolia, and second, to promote the establishment by the two special Chinese Envoys of more Chinese influence than was conceded to the Chinese dignitary in Urga. In the bestowal of title on all Mongol princes and

[104] *IBZI*, pp. 1239-43.
[105] *IBZI*, Vol. II, 8, 1, p. 115, n. 1, telegram of Krupenskkii of June 1/14, 1915.

lamas an attempt was seen to ignore completely the fact that this power was vested in the Living Buddha himself, as head of Autonomous Mongolia, with its right of internal administration, who would particularly resent the withdrawal from him of a privilege so important in the East. The Chinese Foreign Minister denied that China had any sinister motives. The despatch of envoys to Urga aimed exclusively at conformance with Chinese etiquette in regard to the investiture of a high personage. As to the bestowal of titles on other Mongols, it appeared only natural to the Chinese Government that if the President of the Republic could invest the Living Buddha with a title, such a procedure should even more apply a fortiori to the persons beneath him.[106]

When, in June 1915, the Russians warned the Chinese that their misleading of Chinese public opinion on the actual status of Outer Mongolia, i. e., ignoring the limits set to Chinese suzerainty, would in future lead to complications,[107] the Chinese could not yet foresee that this prophecy would not be fulfilled. But only twelve to eighteen months later the war situation as well as internal troubles became so disastrous for Russia, that like a gift a new opportunity came for China to reassert her influence in Outer Mongolia.

C. Reassertion of Influence, 1916-1918, and Rule, 1919-1921

In 1915 the first Chinese dignitary in Urga, Cheng Lu, one of the chief delegates to the tripartite conference, confined himself more or less to those rights and duties granted to him by the Kiakhta agreement. At the same time Chinese merchants took steps to recover lost economic ground. Attempts to open a Chinese bank in Urga were, because of the monopolistic character of the Russian-controlled Mongolian National

---

[106] *IBZI*, No. 124, Sazonov to Krupenskii, June 3/16, 1915, p. 115; pp. 115-6, n. 2, telegram of Krupenskii of June 5/18, 1915, No. 333.
[107] *IBZI*, No. 124.

Bank, at first unsuccessful,[108] but were resumed at the beginning of 1917 when Tsarist Russia collapsed. Chinese banks raised the rate for Russian credit rubles, and Chinese merchants in Outer Mongolia spread the news that Russian credit bank notes were not being accepted and that therefore the money circulated by the Mongolian National Bank or by individual Russians had lost its value.[109] In May 1917 the Chinese succeeded in opening a branch of a Chinese bank in Urga.[110] Strong protests lodged with the Chinese Government by the Russian Minister in Peking, the Russian diplomatic agent in Urga, and the Mongolian Government itself, were of no avail.

To the Russian protest that the opening of a bank ran contrary to Article Five of the tripartite agreement, which recognized the exclusive right of the autonomous Government of Outer Mongolia to attend to all affairs of its internal administration, the Chinese retorted that the establishment of a new firm of a purely economic character such as a bank, did not violate this stipulation, and that in any event it was clear that if nothing was said about credit establishments in the text of the treaty this did not mean that such institutions were forbidden. The Russian reply to this argument was that Russian credit institutions in Outer Mongolia were specifically mentioned in the Russo-Mongolian trade protocol of October 1912, the stipulations of which had been recognized by China, but that no analogous statements on Chinese banks could be found in any of the agreements concluded between 1912 and 1915.[111]

The Mongolian Government tried to counter the opening of the Chinese bank by issuing a decree forbidding the circulation of Chinese bank notes and imposing a fine on all on whom notes of this bank were found. In June 1917 the Chinese

---

[108] Korostovets, p. 287; A. Gladstern, " The Mongolian Policy and the Russian Provisional Government " in *S. S.*, 1928, No. 5, p. 167.   ,

[109] *Ibid.*, pp. 167-68, telegram of Diplomatic Agent in Urga of March 24, 1917, No. 61; Korostovets, p. 288.

[110] *S. S.*, 1928, No. 5, p. 168.

[111] *S. S.*, telegram of Russian Minister in Peking, May 6, 1917, No. 418; telegram of Diplomatic Agent in Urga of June 7, 1917, No. 116.

dignitary in Urga received an official note of protest against the violation of the rights given to the Mongolian National Bank; but it seems doubtful whether he ever forwarded it to Peking as he returned it immediately to the Mongols.[112] A still stronger note was presented a short time later by the Mongolian Foreign Minister, probably on advice from the Russian diplomatic agent, stating that as the Chinese Government was not fulfilling its normal duties, he considered that the normal relations between his Government and China were broken off.[113]

These protests, as well as a third in the middle of July, could however be ignored by the Chinese who felt sure that neither the Mongols nor the Russians were in a position to take active measures. On the contrary, the new Chinese dignitary, Cheng Yi, carried the policy a step further. He insisted on cancellation of the Russian concession for the Mongolian National Bank, and also on abrogation of duties disadvantageous to China, as well as on restoration of Chinese post offices in Urga, Khobdo, and other places.[114] In demands for payment of Mongolian debts, however, the Chinese were less successful, and only in 1919, with the backing of armed forces, were they able to obtain the promise of the Government of Urga that all private debts should be repaid in the course of the next three years.[115]

By the end of 1918, the Chinese dignitary had reinforced his guard in Urga, in defiance of the specific stipulation of the Kiakhta agreement, and it was obvious that the Chinese aimed at getting rid altogether of the restrictions placed on them by that agreement. So much was plainly admitted in December 1918 by the Chinese Foreign Office in a statement in answer to an enquiry by the American Government, addressed to the Chinese Ambassador, Dr. Wellington Koo: " With regard to Outer Mongolian affairs, the Chinese Government, for the sake

---

[112] *S. S.,* No. 117, p. 169, telegram of Diplomatic Agent of May 9, 1917; p. 170, telegram of Minister of Foreign Affairs to Diplomatic Agent, May 10, 1917.

[113] *Ibid.,* telegram of Diplomatic Agent, May 10, 1917, No. 119.

[114] Korostovets, p. 288.   [115] *CYB.*

of the relations between China and Outer Mongolia, does not want to abolish the autonomous Government without due consideration, but it is the policy of the Chinese Government to terminate the treaty between China and Mongolia." [116]

Even more explicit was a statement made by the Foreign Minister at the end of 1919 to Reuter, in which he claimed that "the recognition of Chinese sovereignty (sic) of Outer Mongolia by Russia, with the corresponding recognition of so-called autonomous Mongolia by China, was at that time nothing but a diplomatic trick of a temporary character. An essential element in the situation was that Russian agents accompanied by armed forces had openly made Urga their base, and had persuaded the Mongolian officials to create a so-called Cabinet of Ministers, furnished them with a considerable sum of money, and in doing so with ' mala fides ' have disrupted the traditional relations between two friendly nations. The fact that it would be impossible ever to fix even approximately the frontiers of Outer Mongolia with the exception of that part along which run the century-old Russo-Mongolian frontiers, shows clearly the ephemeral and non-permanent character of the agreement, which was painfully felt by the whole Chinese people as a violation of its sovereignty." [117]

In January 1919, the Chinese Foreign Office charged the Chinese dignitary in Urga, Cheng Yi, to try to come to a new agreement with Outer Mongolia, which should take the place of the tripartite agreement, and should serve as a bargaining point for the recognition by China of the new Soviet Government. The Chinese dignitary thereupon started secret negotiations with the Mongols.[118] He found support from a few Mongolian princes, whose relations with the politically powerful lamas were at that time strained. But Cheng Yi's report of the middle of August 1919 reveals that the desire of the Outer Mongols to come under the control of the Chinese

---

[116] Cited by C. F. Chang, " Recollections of the Outer Mongolian Question " in *Tu Li P'ing* (Independent Critic), April 26, 1936, p. 5.

[117] Maiskii, p. 263.

[118] C. F. Chang, in *Tu Li P'ing Lun, op. cit.*, p. 5.

Government could not have been as strong as he had claimed, for he advised the sending of " the East and West Route Armies to Outer Mongolia for national defence and the preservation of peace." [119]

In answer, the Chinese Government stressed its anxiety to avoid national complications in Outer Mongolia. On the other hand, they could not forget that " at the present time, in regard to Outer Mongolia's situation, there are a great number of people anxious to succeed to Russia's previous special position. . . . If this should happen, the northern border of China would never be peaceful again. That is why we must pay due attention to this question." Furthermore, its inability to grant help to Outer Mongolia would make that country doubt the ability of the Chinese Government to deal with Mongolian affairs and consequently might decrease respect toward China. Therefore Cheng Yi was charged to obtain proof from the Mongols of their willingness to return to Chinese sovereignty, and was asked to obtain a petition from them expressing their willingness to give up their autonomy. " Then our Government, using this petition as a basis, could discuss terms with them." [120]

At that time Cheng Yi had a brigade of 4000 men, and this, combined with the complete impotence of Tsarist Russia's former official representatives in Outer Mongolia, may have been a reason for the Living Buddha's eventually promising to abolish the autonomous Government after he had agreed with Cheng Yi on a draft of sixty-three articles, enumerating the special privileges which the Mongols would retain. Cheng Yi's secretary went to Peking to obtain the Government's approval for this draft. [121]

Relations however became worse with the arrival of General Hsü Shu-tseng (commonly known as " Little Hsü ") in Urga in October 1919, after his appointment in June as special Envoy to the Northwestern frontier (Defense Commissioner for the Northwestern frontiers or Commander-in-Chief of the Northwestern Wing).

---

[119] *Ibid.* [120] *Ibid.*, pp. 5-6. [121] *Ibid.*, p. 6.

The evidence before us for the following months is not complete, and to some extent contradictory. Two facts however stand out clearly: first, that General Hsü took a much stronger attitude towards the Mongols than Cheng Yi. The most favorable opinion we have is that of his son, who likens his policy to " the enlightened autocracy of the Emperors, although sometimes he had to apply presure by force." [122] Second, the relations between General Hsü and Cheng Yi were extremely strained, so that there was no collaboration between these two representatives of China. It appears that General Hsü was not acquainted by Cheng Yi with the details of the sixty-three articles, and that General Hsü was not only in favor of a drastic revision of the many privileges enumerated in them, but also pressed for the abolition of the autonomous government before agreement had been reached on the extent of these privileges. Finally, Hsü reduced the articles to eight—far more stringent than those elaborated by Cheng Yi and the Mongols. He presented them to the Outer Mongolian Government and gave them thirty-six hours to answer his demand for the abolition of autonomy, threatening that otherwise he would escort the Living Buddha and the Premier to Kalgan.[123]

The Living Buddha refused to sign the petition, and referred the question to the Parliament. The members, the leading princes and lamas, supported his refusal, but with increasing pressure and threats from General Hsü, they finally agreed to the petition being signed by the various ministers and vice-ministers of the government departments. With this General Hsü was satisfied, and he proceeded to Peking, explaining to his Government that the Living Buddha never personally signed a document. At the same time, he persuaded the Government to charge him with the whole administration of Outer Mongolia and to withdraw Cheng Yi altogether from Urga.[124] In previous telegrams he had already defended his

[122] T. L. Hsü, " Some doubtful points concerning ' The Recollections of the Outer Mongolian Question '," in *Tu Li P'ing Lun,* May 31, 1936, p. 17.

[123] C. F. Chang, *op. cit.,* p. 6; T. L. Hsü, *op. cit.,* p. 11, citing telegram of General Hsü to Chinese Cabinet of November 14, 1919.

[124] C. F. Chang, *op. cit.,* p. 6; T. L. Hsü, *op. cit.,* p. 18.

policy against that of Cheng Yi, claiming that the latter's proposals to the Mongols did not include plans for the reconsideration of tariffs, the reconstruction of financial administration, or the development of agriculture and mining. Cheng Yi, he maintained, had confined himself to fixing salaries for the princes and lamas which apparently were to be levied in Outer Mongolia itself, thus increasing the charges on the already overburdened population. Hsü, on the contrary, seems to have favored a policy of bribes among the princes and lamas, by which, with an adequate force in the background, he hoped " to keep the balance from above." He was against a detailed agreement with the Mongols, which might give rise to many misunderstandings.[125]

Following the Mongols' petition for the abolition of autonomy, the President of the Chinese Republic issued a mandate, dated November 22, 1919, in which the " most sincerely expressed " request was " granted and the desires of the people of Outer Mongolia hereby complied with." The dignity of the Bogdo-Jeptsun-Damba-Hutukhtu Khan of Outer Mongolia was hereafter to be preserved and the rights and privileges of the chiefs of the four leagues and the Shabinar administration were to be respected. The old system obtaining under the late Manchu dynasty was restored, and especially favorable treatment given to Outer Mongolia. The President hoped that peace and good relations might forever be maintained between the Central Government and Outer Mongolia. An honorary title was at the same time conferred upon the Living Buddha.[126] Concerning foreign relations it was stated that since the Outer Mongols had renounced their autonomy, all treaties or agreements concluded between Russia and Mongolia as also the Kiakhta agreement " become null and void automatically." [127]

---

[125] T. L. Hsü, *op. cit.*, pp.12-14, telegram of General Hsü to Chinese Government of November 1, 1919.

[126] *CYB*, 1921-22, p. 577.

[127] Chesney Hill, " The Doctrine of ' Rebus Sic Stantibus ' in International Law," *The University of Missouri Studies*, Vol. IX, July 1, 1934, No. 3, 25: E. A. Korowin, " The Termination of the Autonomy of Outer Mongolia," pp. 61-63 in *Das Völkerrecht der Uebergangzeit*, Berlin, 1929 (cf. n. 257, Chapter II), p. 108, calls this

General Hsü's rule in Urga was not however of long duration. He was one of the leaders of the Anfu party and it appears that already before the summer of 1920, i. e., before events in North China finally destroyed this organization, he left Urga and assigned his duties to his subordinate.[128] In the short time in which he ruled, he had nevertheless not failed to strengthen Chinese influence considerably and to thrust the Mongols back again into their former attitude of hostility.

The Mongols were disarmed, a branch of the Frontier Development Bank opened in Urga, and Russian currency finally prohibited. The Mongols were held responsible for the provisioning of the greater part of the Chinese army, and Chinese firms which had operated in Outer Mongolia before its autonomy returned, not only asking for the repayment of the old debts but also for all the interest which had accumulated during the eight years of autonomy, as well as for recompense for the loss which they had suffered during the Revolution in 1911-1912. In the Khobdo district, where fighting had been fiercest in three years, the inhabitants had now to pay 50,000 camels in repayment of their old debts.[129]

Following the Anfu party's defeat and General Hsü's departure from Urga, the Chinese Government, at the end of July 1920, abolished the Frontier Defense Bureau and put the troops which had formerly been under its authority at the immediate disposition of the War Office. General Hsü was replaced by Li Yuan, who had been the first Chinese dignitary in Urga after the Kiakhta agreement in 1915 (and had been in charge of the Ministry of Foreign Affairs since 1918); but he did not long remain, and soon Cheng Yi returned to the office from which General Hsü had forced him.[130]

decree of the Chinese President very peculiar (" sehr eigenartig "). Equally " peculiar " is, perhaps, the question, " Worauf konnte sich China bei diesem Schritt stützen? " set in an examination paper for the diplomatic service—see *Jahrbuch 1934 der Konsular-Akademie zu Wien*, p. 46.

[128] His subordinate was Mr. H. Lee; see C. F. Chang, *op. cit.*, p. 6.

[129] See Doksom, " Historic lessons . . ." etc., in *T. O.*, No. 3 (9), July-Sept. 1936, p. 71.

[130] Cheng Yi was reappointed on August 14, 1920, see C. F. Chang, *op. cit.*, p. 6.

The Government was obviously anxious not to alienate the Mongols any further. To this feeling expression was given in two presidential mandates of August 1920. In the first, Chinese officials were warned not to fall back into those old mistakes which had been the cause of earlier Mongol dissatisfaction with Chinese rule and to pay special respect to Lamaism. In the second mandate, honorific title or higher rank were conferred upon all Outer Mongolian princes and lama dignitaries.[131] Finally, on September 9, 1920, a Presidential mandate regulated provisionally " the organizing of the administrative system of the Pacification Commissioner of the Urga, Uliassutai, Khobdo, and Tannu-Urianghai regions, and the institutions subordinate to him. The Pacification Commissioner was in full charge of the military administration, of the supervision of finance, and of justice. Offices of Counsellors in the different regions were instituted, and Chinese as well as Mongols were eligible for these posts. A Mongol could also be elected as Chief of the Civil Administration, or as one of the special officers attached to this post.[132]

This scheme of administration was however never put into effect, as events from outside again endangered Chinese rule in Outer Mongolia. In October 1920, Baron Ungern Sternberg, a follower of Semenov, suddenly appeared near Urga in command of 2000 soldiers, and an attack by him was successfully repulsed. General Ch'u Ch'ih-hsiang, who was in command of the Chinese troops, seized this opportunity to demonstrate his anti-foreign feelings by allowing his soldiers to plunder and shoot the foreign population, chiefly Russians, under circumstances which have been described as reminiscent of the Boxer Rebellion. Furthermore, he infuriated the Mongols by surrounding the Living Buddha's palace with soldiers and thus making him virtually a prisoner.[133] In the meantime, Ungern Sternberg had assembled more soldiers, and had inscribed on his banner the idea of Pan-Mongolism which, in view of the

[131] CYB, 1921-22, p. 579.   [132] Ibid., for text, pp. 598-600.
[133] Ibid., p. 579 and Robert T. Polard, China's Foreign Relations 1917-1931, New York, 1933, p. 162.

experiences of the Mongols during General Hsü's rule and
General Ch'u's activities, had a new appeal for them. Soon
fighting began in the vicinity of Urga and with the help of a
mixed force of 5000 Russians, Buriats, Mongols, and Tibetans,
Ungern Sternberg, in the beginning of Febuary 1921, was successful in capturing Urga.[134] Sections of the Chinese garrison
escaped to Kiakhta, but many others were massacred. Thus,
as in 1911, Chinese control over Outer Mongolia ceased
abruptly.

But already in April 1921 it looked as if the Chinese would
have another chance to recapture their position. The Living
Buddha, dismayed by the oppressive measures of Ungern
Sternberg over all of Outer Mongolia, sent an emissary to
Peking asking for Chinese help to terminate the hostilities on
the basis of Mongolian autonomy under Chinese suzerainty.
As in 1912 and the following years, the Chinese Government
was unable to finance an expedition. A decision on the policy
to be adopted was referred to a conference of the Super-
Tuchuns (Chang Tso-lin, Tsao Kun and Wang Chan-yuan)
which met in Tientsin in April 1921. Here it was agreed that
Chang Tso-lin, the Inspector General of Chinese forces in
Northern Manchuria, should send troops into Outer Mongolia
in order to regain control. A Presidential mandate of May 30,
1921, gave him full powers for the subjugation of the insur-
gents.[135] But he never carried out these instructions and preferred to take a completely passive attitude. This, apart from
the fact that Chinese troops could by no means be sure of
success, was probably due to the fact that relations between
Chang Tso-lin and Ungern Sternberg were more friendly than
hostile. It had even been suggested that Ungern Sternberg's
plans were carried out with the approval of Chang Tso-lin,
who worked at that time for the restoration of the Manchus
and the defeat of the revolutionary forces in China.[136]

---

[134] *Ibid.*, p. 580 and Pollard, p. 162.
[135] *The North China Herald*, Shanghai, Vol. CXXXIX, No. 2808, June 4, 1921,
p. 650.
[136] Tsi Chu Chen, p. 131.

Summing up the period of Chinese policy in Outer Mongolia from 1916 to 1921, we may say that the chance given to China by Tsarist Russia's preoccupation with the Great War and its subsequent collapse at the beginning of 1917, was seized upon by her with such military and financial means as were at her disposal, but that her official representatives in Outer Mongolia displayed no vision whatsoever in trying expedients other than force and bribery for the reestablishment of relations. Furthermore, friction was increased by the greed manifested by the returning Chinese merchants, whose approach to the Mongols was naturally purely commercial in character. The Chinese might, however, have preserved their rule for some time if the destruction of their army of occupation in 1921, an incidental result of the Russian Revolution (Ungern Sternberg had been driven from Siberia with a small force of Russian White Guards), had not completely defeated their prospects.

D. Protests, Assertions, and Recognition, 1922-1946

Ungern Sternberg's reign in Outer Mongolia was of short duration. His defeat had nothing to do with efforts displayed by Chinese soldiers, but was due to Soviet Russian troops, who had been asked by the Mongols to liberate them. Not many details were known in Peking for some time as to Soviet Russia's relation with Outer Mongolia except that Russian troops were stationed in several parts of the country. In unofficial negotiations, begun at the end of 1921 between the Peking Government and a Soviet representative, the latter declared that the Soviet occupation of Outer Mongolia was of a purely temporary character and that no Russo-Mongolian agreement had been concluded.[137] But when the Russo-Mongolian agreement of the 5th November 1921, which treated Outer Mongolia as an independent state and omitted all mention of her relations with China, was published soon afterwards, the Peking Government on May 1, 1922 lodged a protest with the Soviet representative, Parkes, against this agreement,

[137] Pollard, *op. cit.*, p. 166.

declaring that Outer Mongolia was Chinese territory and that
Soviet Russian policy in that region, in spite of all contradictory statements from the Soviets themselves, was following
in the footsteps of Tsardom.[138]

When in August 1922 a new Soviet representative, Joffe,
arived in Peking, the position of Outer Mongolia and of the
Chinese Eastern Railway were the two main points of his
discussions with the Foreign Minister, Dr. Wellington Koo.
The latter insisted on the evacuation of all Soviet troops from
Outer Mongolia as the condition for beginning official negotiations.[139] Joffe's *pourparlers* were therefore unsuccessful. He
did, however, in the beginning of February 1923, agree with
the leader of the revolutionary South of China, Dr. Sun Yat-
sen, on a joint declaration in which the latter, after being
assured that " it is not and has never been the intention or
purpose of the present Russian Government to pursue an
imperialistic policy in Outer Mongolia or to cause it to secede
from China," agreed that he " does not view an immediate
evacuation of Russian troops from Outer Mongolia as either
imperative or in the real interest of China, the more so on
account of the inability of the present Government of Peking
to prevent such an evacuation being followed by a recrudes-
cence of intrigues and hostile activities by White Guardists
against Russia, and the creation of a graver situation than
that which now exists." [140] But the " imperialists " of the
Peking Government were not willing to play the game of the
" revolutionary " Russians to the same extent as Dr. Sun
Yat-sen.

[138] Text in Alfred Dennis, *The Foreign Policies of Soviet Russia*, London, 1924,
pp. 323-4.
[139] Pollard, *op. cit.*, pp. 169-70.
[140] Alfred Dennis, *op. cit.*, p. 327. Cf. also speech of Zinoviev at the First Conference of the Revolutionary Organisations of the Far East in 1922: " It seems to
me that it would be sad if amongst the active leaders, for instance amongst those
of revolutionary South China, there were people who would consider the Mongolian
question in a dogmatic way, and say that Mongolia should be returned to China.
I think that the final decision of the Mongolian question will be found only in
that moment when the Chinese free themselves from the yoke of their oppressors
. .", cited by T. Ryskulov, " Veliky Khuruldan Mongolii " (The Great Huruldan
of Mongolia), in *N.V.*, 1925, 8-9, p. 218.

When a new Soviet-Russian delegate, Karakhan, arrived in Peking in September 1923, the Government insisted on a discussion on the status of Outer Mongolia, and refused to agree to the Russian proposal to make the beginning of official negotiations dependent on the previous recognition of the Soviet Government by China. The unofficial negotiations pursued during the following months ended in the middle of March 1924 with the signing of a treaty draft which contained in Article Five a stipulation concerning Outer Mongolia, recognizing it as an integral part of the Republic of China, and Soviet Russia engaged herself to respect China's sovereignty therein. She also promised to withdraw all her troops as soon as feasible. The Peking Cabinet however was not prepared to agree to this draft, and repudiated its negotiator by accusing him of having exceeded his instructions.[141] In a circular telegram sent out by the Cabinet with reference to the talks with Russia, it was emphasized in March 1924 that " there still remain in dispute the following important questions: (1) In the opinion of the Government the treaties made between Russia and Outer Mongolia should immediately be cancelled . . . in view of the fact that these treaties consider Outer Mongolia as an independent country, and that a Minister has been sent there by the Russian Government, this is quite contrary to the sentence ' respecting the sovereignty of China,' and this of course is of great importance; (2) The Chinese Government is of the opinion that the Russian troops in Mongolia should be withdrawn immediately . . . without any conditions, so that no hindrance may be created." [142] In a manner recalling the Russo-Chinese negotiations between 1912-1915, Karakhan, in the middle of March 1924, demanded that the Chinese Government should agree to the draft within three days; otherwise he would not consider himself bound by its stipulations, and the Chinese Government would have to bear the consequences of its refusal.[143]

[141] Pollard, *op. cit.*, pp. 181-2; for text see *CYB*, 1924-25, p. 881.
[142] *Ibid.*, p. 883.
[143] Pollard, *op. cit.*, p. 186; for a memorandum of Karakkhan of March 29, forwarded April 1, 1924, see *CYB*, 1924, p. 886.

In spite of the strained atmosphere, negotiations were not broken off. Dr. Wellington Koo and Karakhan finally agreed on a treaty text and on several declarations at the end of May 1924. Stipulations with regard to Outer Mongolia were contained in the " Agreement concerning general principles for the settlement of pending questions between the Chinese Republic and the U. S. S. R." Article Five of this agreement corresponds word for word with Article Five of the draft, i. e., the recognition of China's sovereignty in Outer Mongolia. A change was however made in regard to the withdrawal of Soviet troops by the substitution of the words " questions " for " conditions." [144] According to the draft China and Russia were to discuss at a subsequent conference the " conditions " for the withdrawal of the troops. But the final text eliminates any preliminary " conditions " and stipulates that the projected conference should solve only the " questions " arising out of the withdrawal of troops—a small point, but more satisfactory to a " sovereign " China.

It is interesting to note that while it was stipulated that all treaties, agreements, etc., concluded between the former Tsarist Government and any third party or parties affecting the sovereign rights or interests of China were null and void, and that the two Governments agreed that in the future neither of them would conclude any treaties or agreements prejudicial to the sovereign rights or interests of either, no mention was made of any treaty concluded by Soviet Russia. Thus, in contrast to the stipulations of the treaty draft wherein China repudiated also all treaties affecting her sovereign rights concluded by Soviet Russia, the final agreement made no mention of this, and the Soviet-Mongolian agreement of 1921 was not repudiated. It would be going too far to say that the Chinese Government had thereby indirectly recognized the Soviet-Mongolian agreement, as such an interpretation cannot be reconciled with the Soviet recognition of China's sovereignty

---

[144] *Ibid.*, p. 881; for text see *Treaties and Agreements Concerning China*, 1919-29, Washington, 1929.

of Outer Mongolia, which was more than the suzerainty conceded to China by Tsarist Russia at Kiakhta in 1915.[145]

Soviet Russian recognition of her sovereignty over Outer
Mongolia in May 1924 contained for China nothing more than
a principle. When in August 1924 a group of members of
Parliament sent a communication to the Peking Government
pointing out that as the formal negotiations on pending questions between China and Soviet Russia were shortly to begin,
it was in their opinion necessary to appoint a special commission to study questions connected with Outer Mongolia
and the actual restoration of China's sovereignty over that
region, the Cabinet decided to refer the matter to the Ministries of Foreign Affairs, War and Interior, for consideration,
with instructions to these Ministries to appoint the Commission
if they deemed it necessary.[146] The Chinese Government was
in fact compelled to stop short of concrete realisation of
sovereignty over Outer Mongolia, as home affairs, the Civil
War of 1926-1928, as well as the actual circumstances in Outer
Mongolia eliminated any possibility of establishing control
there. Only a month after the agreement of May 1924, Outer
Mongolia, upon the death of the Living Buddha, had declared
itself a Mongolian People's Republic. This showed clearly
the extent of Soviet Russian influence there, as well as the unwillingness of the Outer Mongols to accept China's sovereignty.

The value of the recognition of the principle of China's
sovereignty over Outer Mongolia by Soviet Russia was diminished when in 1927 Sino-Soviet diplomatic relations were
interrupted, to be resumed only in 1932, thus preventing the
conference on outstanding questions mentioned in the 1924
agreement from completing its labors. The Chinese Government was far too much absorbed with internal troubles to be
able to occupy itself effectively with Outer Mongolian affairs.
The Manchurian authorities under General Tsou Tso-hua were.
however, not idle and were endeavoring to advance the railway

---

[145] Cf. text and treaty draft in *CYB*, 1924, p. 881.
[146] *The North China Herald*, Vol. CLII, No. 2978, August 16, 1924, p. 242.

system to keep pace with colonization toward the Outer Mongolian frontier. These plans found encouragement in a short-lived intrusion of Soviet troops into Barga (Heilungkiang) in 1929.[147]

The rapid advance of such a railway line, wrote a correspondent in Manchuria to the London *Times* in the middle of 1930, would drive a wedge between the Barga Mongols and those of Outer Mongolia, and provide direct access and transport for Chinese colonization on the most vulnerable frontier of Outer Mongolia. " Such a positive forward movement is the most important event in the relations between Chinese and Mongols since the rout of Chinese forces at Urga in 1920." With the aid of a Colonization Bureau which was in the hands of General Tsou Tso-hua, who was " one of the most ambitious, energetic, and talented of the followers of Marshal Chang Hsueh-liang " (son of Chang Tso-lin), colonization was speeded up. Whereas in the past the method had been to acquire Mongol land by purchase through the princes, who generally acquiesced because of the profit made by them on these transactions, the new method was much more radical in the whole area being occupied by the troops of General Tsou in advance of the colonists. General Tsou's main object was neither the creation of a commercial railway nor commercial land speculation, but the planting of a solid self-supporting Chinese population along a strategically selected portion of the Mongolian frontier. To attain this object conditions imposed upon buyers of these lands were much more stringent. They had to have enough capital to develop the property, and had to plough their land and occupy it, or provide tenants within three years, failing which they lost their title.

Thus, with a Chinese population brought to the border of the most fertile parts of Outer Mongolia, a new possibility would have been opened up to the Chinese authorities for slowly regaining control of Outer Mongolia. The new railway, in which no other foreign power had any interest, would have

[147] Cf. notes 286 and 287 of Chapter II.

changed completely the strategic aspect of a Chinese advance into Outer Mongolia, as the main obstacle to a successful Chinese occupation and control of Outer Mongolia—the march through the Gobi Desert—would have been overcome. At the same time it would have meant an increased influence of the Manchurian Government in the affairs of North China.[148] Here again, however, Chinese endeavors were defeated by an exterior factor—the occupation of Manchuria, including the territories adjacent to Outer Mongolia, by the Japanese army in 1931 to 1932.

Whereas the Manchurian authorities' Mongolian policy involved comprehensive economic and military measures, the Central Government, whose seat had been moved from Peking to Nanking in 1928, had not had similar possibilities. Nevertheless, it brought into force political and administrative measures in order to strengthen its hold on Inner Mongolia, bordering Outer Mongolia along the Gobi Desert. This territory was in 1928 divided into three provinces, Chahar, Suiyuan, and Ningshia.

In May 1930, the Chinese Government called together a Mongolian Affairs Conference, which was not however attended by any delegates from Outer Mongolia. On the occasion of the formal inauguration of this Conference, the Ministry of Foreign Affairs addressed a statement to the peoples of Mongolia and Tibet which reaffirmed that Mongolia was Chinese territory. A direct appeal was addressed to Outer Mongolia. The Mongolian problem was not a question of a simple relation of vassalage in the eyes of the Chinese Government for ". . . inasmuch as both Mongolia and Tibet are integral parts of the Chinese Republic, the local authorities there should take care to avoid establishing direct diplomatic relations with any foreign Government. . . . The peoples of Mongolia and Tibet being citizens of the Republic of China are entitled to protection by the Central Government against foreign oppression,

---

[148] *The Times*, London, August 8, 1930, p. 9, and August 9, 1930, p. 9: " Chinese Aims in Mongolia. I. Penetration by Colonies; II. Creation of a Province."

while at the same time the local authorities should never allow themselves to be misled and taken advantage of by foreign neighbors. . . . The Ministry is seeking an appropriate and satisfactory solution of various outstanding issues between China and Russia, especially those affecting Mongolia."

The statement refers then to the fact that Russia, in the Sino-Soviet agreement of 1924, had formally recognized Mongolia as an integral part of China, as well as China's complete sovereignty over the territory. " It is therefore obvious that Russia had renounced and does not now possess any special interest in Mongolia. The Mongolian people must guard against being intimidated by their Soviet neighbors, and should strive under the leadership of the Central Government for the solidarity of the entire country. The authority for dealing with the foreign relations of Mongolia and Tibet rests with the Central Government; local authorities in these districts may act only through the Ministry of Foreign Affairs." [149]

In October 1931, a Mongol League, Tribe and Banner Organic Law was promulgated, Article Nine of which states that " military matters and foreign affairs and other national executive questions in Mongolia shall all be in the hands of the National Government." [150] Before that, the Provisional Constitution for the Period of Political Tutelage of the Republic of China of May 12, 1931 again reaffirmed in its first article that " the territory of the Republic of China consists of the various provinces and Mongolia and Tibet." The Constitution provides, under the " Executive Yuan," for a " Commission on Mongolian and Tibetan Affairs," which consists again of three divisions: (a) Division of General Affairs; (b) Division of Mongolian Affairs; (c) Division of Tibetan Affairs. This Commission is considered by China to be the competent organ for Outer Mongolian affairs.[151]

---

[149] *Chinese Affairs*, Nos. 82-83, International Relations Committee, Nanking, May 31, 1930, pp. 1-2 (reproducing Chinese official documents in English).

[150] *British and Foreign State Papers*, 1931, Vol. CXXXIV, London, 1936, pp. 1215-1219, esp. p. 1216.

[151] *Ibid.*, p. 1208, 1214; also *CYB*, 1934, p. 466; 1935, p. 60. See also J. Escarra,

Actually, this Commission never had any communication with Outer Mongolia. Direct postal communication between China and Urga no longer existed and was possible only by way of Siberia (Verkhne Udinsk). Furthermore, after 1925 Chinese merchants were virtually excluded from Outer Mongolia.[152] The only possible way for China to have reestablished contact with Outer Mongolia would have been by negotiation with Soviet Russia. Thus, with the resumption of Sino-Soviet diplomatic relations in 1932, an influential Chinese newspaper, the Hsin Wen Pao, suggested that the Chinese Government should immediately take up with the Soviet Union the question of Outer Mongolia. "As the present regime in Outer Mongolia is virtually independent of China, the Government should negotiate with Russia for the restoration of that territory. Such a step, if realized, would not only defeat the reported Japanese scheme to set up a so-called Manchurian-Mongolian State, but would also facilitate our national defense." [153]

The speed of the Japanese advance in Manchuria and the impotence of the Chinese Government to check it, condemned such a suggestion to utter futility. But still worse for the Chinese Government, with the loss of Manchuria and Jehol with their many Mongolian inhabitants, the danger arose that those Mongols who still remained under her rule would wish to join the Mongols of " Manchukuo " who had received an " autonomous " regime in the province of Hsingan. That would have been tantamount to China's complete loss of those regions which are called Inner Mongolia. China, having wished to prevent the Inner Mongols from following the example of the " independent " Outer Mongols by applying an extensive policy

La Chine et le Droit International, Paris, 1931, p. 229: " Ainsi, le Gouvernement national affirme nettement que la Mongolie fait partie du territoire (ling t'ou) de la Republique. Il n'est plus question d'un simple lien de vassalité. Mais les faits sont là."

[152] See Ostasiatische Runschau, 12 Jahrg., No. 12, May 16, 1931, pp. 271-73, citing Ta Kung Pao, Tientsin, February 27, 1931; also 13 Jahrg., No. 3, February 1, 1932, pp. 50-51, " Chinas entfremdete Aussenländer," by Otto Mossdorf.

[153] Chinese Affairs, Vol. 4, No. 24-26. December 15, 1932, p. 302.

of colonization and penetration in these regions, had now to pay for a policy which had alienated the Mongols from her.

A Mongolian Political Council created by the Inner Mongol, Prince Teh, was soon under the influence of Japanese officers. To counteract this Council the Chinese Government, in March 1936, formed the Suiyuan Mongolian Political Council, which gave to the Mongol princes and nobles a certain degree of autonomy.[154] The last meeting of the Mongols who were included in this Council seems to have been held in the form of a conference in Kueihua, on the Peking-Suiyuan railway, in March 1937, in the presence of the Vice-Chairman of the Mongolian and Tibetan Affairs Committee and under the guidance of the Directing Commissioner of the Council, General Yen Hsi-shan (who was also Pacification Commissioner for Shansi and Suiyuan). General Yen Hsi-shan is reported to have stated on this occasion that local autonomy was a desirable thing, and no sensible person should object to it. But, he added, " only to acknowledge the desirability of autonomy is not courage. The Chinese should help the Mongols to achieve self-government, and there is no better way than to assist in promoting education and developing production." He saw no reason why the different races under the Chinese flag should not cooperate for the welfare of the country.[155]

In fact, from the military point of view, it was important for the Chinese to gain the assistance of these Mongols against Prince Teh's aggressive acts. And to some extent they were at first successful in repulsing his advance, but any possible Chinese success was cut short by the hostilities between Japan and China which started only a few months later. In a few months the greater part of Chahar and also of Suiyuan (with the Chinese railway from Kalgan into Suiyuan), fell under the control of the combined Japanese and Mongol (Prince Teh's) forces, thus leaving to China only the province of Ninghsia of all the territories inhabited by Mongols.

[154] For Chinese point of view cf. Dr. Shuhsi Hsü, *The North China Problem*, Shanghai, 1937, pp. 41-59: " The Inner Mongolian Phase."

[155] *The North China Herald*, Vol. CCII, No. 3631, March 10, 1937, p. 398; No. 3633, March 24, 1937, p. 495.

The hostilities with Japan made China seek closer relations with Soviet Russia, and a pact of non-aggression was concluded between the two powers in the autumn of 1937. It became obvious that the Chinese Government, by force of circumstances, was bound now to look differently at the Protocol of Mutual Assistance concluded between the U. S. S. R. and the Mongolian People's Republic in the beginning of 1936 from the way it did at that time. When the terms of the Soviet-Mongolian Protocol of Mutual Assistance became known, the Chinese Minister of Foreign Affairs had sent two notes of protest to the Soviet Ambassador, the first on April 7, the second on April 14, 1936. The first recalled the recognition of Chinese sovereignty over Outer Mongolia by the Sino-Russian agreement of 1924, and reasserted that " in so far as Outer Mongolia is an integral part of the Chinese Republic, no foreign state may conclude with it any treaties or agreements. The actions of the Government of the U. S. S. R. which concluded with Outer Mongolia the above-mentioned protocol in violation of its obligations towards the Chinese Government, form undoubtedly a violation of the sovereignty of China and the terms of the Sino-Soviet agreement of 1924. It is, therefore, my duty to declare a strong protest to Your Excellency, and to state that the conclusion of the above-mentioned protocol by the Government of the U. S. S. R. is illegal and the Chinese Government cannot, under any circumstances, recognize such a protocol and is in no way bound by it." [156]

The second note was a reply to the answer given by the Soviet Government to the first note of protest: " I have taken cognizance of the pledge," states the Chinese Foreign Minister, " thus given by the Government of the U. S. S. R. that it recognizes Outer Mongolia as an integral part of the Republic of China and respects China's sovereignty therein." But he protests against the argument in the Soviet Note that the Chinese Government did not protest at the time when the Soviet

[156] For text see *CYB*, 1938, pp. 31-32; also in *The Chinese Year Book*, 1936-37, second issue, pp. 425-428.

Government concluded a separate agreement with the authorities in Mukden in 1924. Two protests were made by the Chinese Government at that time, and it was not until the agreement had been approved by the Central Government and all legal procedure had been complied with, that a notification was sent to the Soviet Government in March 1925, to the effect that the Mukden-Soviet agreement was to be considered as an annex to the Sino-Soviet agreement of 1924. " Thus, the signing of the Mukden-Soviet agreement, which was originally an illegal act contrary to international practice, was only rectified subsequently by the Chinese Government. In no sense can it be referred to as a precedent for the Government of the U. S. S. R. to enter into any agreement with Chinese local authorities." [157]

These notes added another protest to the many made by China to Russia concerning the status of Outer Mongolia. Japanese accusations at that time, that China's protests were just a means to hide an understanding with Russia on Outer Mongolia, hardly correspond with the facts, as Russia had no need to come to an agreement with China on the question. But they contain some truth in so far as knowledge of the existence of a Russo-Mongol Protocol of Mutual Assistance was the only effective means to stem the advance of Japanese troops into Outer Mongolia, and at the same time it imposed upon Japan the heavy obligation of keeping a considerable number of troops in the regions of Manchukuo bordering Outer Mongolia, thereby at least delaying her advance into Inner Mongolia and North China; such a situation was certainly not to the disadvantage of China which as formal sovereign of Outer Mon-

[157] For original protests see *The North China Herald*, Vol. CLIII, No. 2984, October 18, 1924, p. 203; and Vol. CLIV, No. 3004, March 7, 1925, p. 378; and No. 3006, March 21, 1925, p. 466. But see Editorial Comment *ibid.*, Vol. CXCIX, No. 2584, April 15, 1936, p. 93: ". . . Whatever may be the rights and wrongs of this contention it does not seem to be a happy reminder. On the day that the Mukden agreement was signed hostilities broke out between Marshal Chang Tso-lin and General Wu Pei-fu, who at that time was at the head of the Chinese Government. Moreover the Foreign Office at Peking lodged an emphatic protest, although the almost immediate collapse of the Wu Pei-fu regime threw the incident into obscurity."

golia, was quite unable to give her the help which is to be expected from sovereign and suzerain alike.

Another rumor emanating from Japan which the facts do not justify was that, after hostilities between Japan and China started in the summer of 1937, Russia had offered Outer Mongolia back to China.[158] Apart from the obscure meaning of this " offer " (there was nothing to offer back, unless the Russians could persuade the Mongols to acknowledge China's suzerainty, as in 1915), the idea behind this suggestion was that thereupon Outer Mongolian troops would have been able to intervene openly on China's side against the Japanese, putting them in a delicate position, engaged as they were in Inner Mongolia and North China. For Outer Mongolia had lost for China much of its value as a channel for arms from Russia, since Japan had been successful in occupying a great part of those territories of China (Chahar and Suiyuan) which separate China from Outer Mongolia.

The occupation of large parts of Inner Mongolia by the Japanese in 1937-1938 meant that China had lost the greater part of Inner Mongolia, in addition to Outer Mongolia, and the creation of a sort of " Manchukuo " in the form of the Autonomous Mongol Government [159] meant that it was lost to China for the time being as completely as Manchuria and Jehol were in " Manchukuo."

Mongolia meant many things for China. Strategically, in the words of a Chinese, " this region constitutes for China the first line of defense in the Northwest. If the Chinese lose Mongolia, all the region in the Northwest is immediately placed in danger." [160] Economically, it meant a field for colonization and for Chinese trade not only for exports but also for imports. For a long time the Chinese had obtained their horses from Mongolia. It was even prophesied that Mongolia would come to occupy a place in China's economic system similar to that

---

[158] *China Weekly Review*, Vol. 82, No. 8, October 23, 1937, p. 153.
[159] Chapter IV, n. 80.
[160] Article in *Kuo Wen* (weekly) by Chang Tso-hua, cited in *Bulletin de Documentation Coloniale* (Ministère des Colonies), No. 119, October 1-15, 1937, p. 22.

of Denmark (or Switzerland) in Europe's—a reservoir of dairy products.[161]

Though ultimately China's retreat from Outer as well as from Inner Mongolia was due to her inability to undertake the military defense of these territories this explanation does not take into account the fact that the Chinese had failed to make the Mongols their friends. It was only when it was too late, as for instance in 1920 in Outer Mongolia, and in 1936 in Inner Mongolia, that they were prepared to make concessions to the Mongols' strong desire for " self-government." For geographical reasons also Outer Mongolia could never have been subject to complete control by China or to intensive colonization by the Chinese.

Before the defeat of Japan and the withdrawal of her troops from Inner Mongolia the question was how the vacuum would be filled. Since the days of the pro-Japanese collaborators among the Inner Mongolian princes were numbered, who would take their place? A glance at the map will show that it is the Chinese Communist zone in Shansi and Shensi which borders directly on Inner Mongolia to the north and that it is less than 300 miles from Shensi to the Mongolian People's Republic. Whereas it may be Chiang Kai-shek's policy to keep Russian influence as far away as possible, such ideas are unlikely to guide the Chinese Communist leaders. This is not the place to investigate the presence or absence of Soviet Russian patronage of the latter at any period, but the fact stands out that the Chinese Communist Party is not far behind the Communist parties in other parts of the world in backing any policy which the U. S. S. R. pursues.

The Chinese Communist Party, after the conclusion of the Soviet-Japanese neutrality pact of April 13, 1941, and the special declaration about reciprocal respect for the territorial integrity and inviolability of " Manchukuo " and of the Mon-

---

[161] See Dr. Friedrich Otte, *China: Wirtschaftspolitische Landeskunde* (cf. Bibliography), Gotha 1927, p. 41-42. See also " The Agricultural Methods of Chinese Colonists in Mongolia," by Paul Wilm in *The Chinese Economic Journal*, Vol. I, No. 12, December 1927, pp. 1923-43.

golian People's Republic, issued a long statement on April 21, 1941.[162] The Chungking Minister of Foreign Affairs, Dr. Wang Chung-hui had, a week earlier, on April 14, 1941, reiterated in an official protest that " it is an indisputable fact that the four Northeastern Provinces and Outer Mongolia (so-called Manchukuo and the so-called People's Republic of Mongolia respectively) are an integral part of the Republic of China and will always remain Chinese territory," and that therefore " the Chinese Government and people cannot recognize any engagements entered into between third parties which are derogatory to China's territorial and administrative integrity, and thus considers the Soviet-Japanese declaration as having " no binding force whatsoever on China." [163]

The Chinese Communist Party, however, in its statement on April 21, 1941, jumped to the defense of Soviet diplomacy. The Soviet-Japanese arrangement did not mean, it said, that the U. S. S. R. would " restrict its just aid to oppressed peoples in the interests of imperialists. The hope of the Chinese people for aid from abroad rests, above all, on the U. S. S. R., and by this treaty the U. S. S. R. has not disappointed and will never disappoint China." " Now the Soviet-Japanese Declaration guarantees that Outer Mongolia will not be subjected to aggression. This is not only of positive significance for Outer Mongolia, it will also benefit the cause of liberation of the whole of China. Individuals who maintained that Russia had acted incorrectly in declaring that it would not attack Man-churia were, to say the least, craven tricksters," since it was " the sacred task of the whole Chinese people to win back all the lost lands of China." [164]

The lost lands of China apparently, in the Chinese Com-munists' eyes did not include Outer Mongolia. However, Edgar Snow reports a conversation which he had in 1936 with Mao Tse-tung, the Communist leader, in which the latter

---

[162] Full text given in Anna Louise Strong, *China's New Crisis*, Key Books No. 14, London, n. d., pp. 49-51.

[163] Full text in *China Handbook 1937-1943*, New York, p. 170.

[164] Strong, *op. cit.*, p. 50.

expressed the expectation that " when the Peoples' revolution
has been victorious in China the Outer Mongolian Republic
will automatically become a part of the Chinese federation,
at their own will." [165] Mao Tse-tung's idea of 1936 would
have found little response from the Mongols of the Mongolian
People's Republic interviewed in Moscow in 1943 by Edgar
Snow.[166] The possibility of China and Mongolia cooperating
" as friendly neighboring States " was to be based on China
sanctioning a Mongol claim to the restoration of Mongolian
boundaries formerly recognized by the Manchu Dynasty—
which in fact would mean the recognition of an independent
federation of Outer and Inner Mongolia. It may well be that
the Chinese Communists—as neighbors of Inner Mongolia, and
an influential element in North China and actual controllers
of Manchuria—would be primarily affected by the first signs
of a realization of such aims. But so far neither Soviet Russia
nor the Chinese Communists have backed these Mongolian
aspirations.

Soviet Russia's withdrawal from Sinkiang in 1943 may have
fostered among some the hope that Russia would pursue a
similar course in Mongolia. Be that as it may, there is no
evidence whatever that circles near to Chiang Kai-shek had
changed by one iota their legal claim to Outer Mongolia as
an integral part of China until 1945. Official, semi-official and
private spokesmen did not tire of bringing up this point on
all possible occasions. The official China Handbook 1937-1943
begins on page one with a statement that " the frontier of
China marches with . . . Siberia . . ." [167] Generalissimo Chiang
Kai-shek's book *China's Destiny*, published in Chungking in
March 1943 in Chinese, is reported to contain a map including
Outer Mongolia (as well as Tibet and Hong Kong) as Chinese
territory.[168] Professor H. D. Fong, author of *The Post-War*

[165] Edgar Snow, *Scorched Earth, London,* 1941, p. 289.
[166] Edgar Snow, *People on Our Side,* New York, 1944, pp. 196-197.
[167] *Op. cit.* Cf. also publications by the Chinese Ministry of Information such as
Introducing China, October 1944, The Australian Office, Sydney, pp. 15-16.
[168] Cited by Wilfred Fleisher in *What to do with Japan,* New York, 1945, p. 76.

Industrialization of China (Washington, June 1942), in an article, refers to the war as having made Outer Mongolia (and Tibet) "increasingly important to China's national defense." [169] S. R. Chow in his *Winning the Peace in the Pacific* (New York, 1944), after pressing for the withdrawal of Soviet troops from Outer Mongolia, once Russia has "no longer any fear of the Japanese menace on the Siberian border," asserts that if this contingency were realized " China would deem it wise and safe to grant the Outer Mongolian people, if they desire, a regime of self-government compatible with Chinese sovereignty." [170] A similar implied doubt was voiced by two Chinese members, speaking from a personal point of view, at the Ninth Conference of the Institute of Pacific Relations in January 1945, when they saw no objections to the independent membership of Outer Mongolia in a future world security organization " provided the people really wanted independence without being pressed from outside and provided that the people in that region were capable of growth and self-government." For China, they added, " it is largely a question of maintaining these regions free from foreign control and in general it was security that China chiefly desired." [171]

The manifesto issued by the Sixth National Congress of the Kuomintang held at Chungking, May 5-21, 1945, promised to what are called "the frontier racial groups" respect for their languages, religions and customs, and the promotion of self-government. The authors of the manifesto seemed to be under the impression that they reinforced this general formula by giving special mention to Outer Mongolia and Tibet, which would be granted " a high degree of autonomy." [172] However this formula can hardly be called an advance over the many similar ones since 1912 which we have studied.

These details may appear irrelevant after January 5, 1946,

[169] See " Post-War Needs of China " in *Asia*, September 1942, p. 546.
[170] P. 90.   ,
[171] See *Security in the Pacific*. A Preliminary Report of the Ninth Conference of the I. P. R., Hot Springs, Virginia, January 6-17, 1945, New York, 1945, p. 122.
[172] See *China Newsweek* (London), No. 139, May 31, 1945, p. 9.

the date on which the Chinese Republic officially recognized the independence of the Mongolian People's Republic. But they make it possible to evaluate the *volte-face* of China and to seek an explanation for it in events outside the control of the Chinese Government. No actual proof could be obtained at the time as to the secret arrangements made between the United States, Britain and the U.S.S.R. at the Yalta Conference without the participation of or consultation with China. Certain stipulations regarding the results of Russia's eventual participation in the war against Japan did become known, however, such as the transfer of the Kurile Islands. It was assumed that it included an understanding as to the recognition of Outer Mongolia's independent status. The main argument favoring this view was the fact that, after Premier T. V. Soong's visit to Moscow following the San Francisco Conference, the face-saving formula was evolved by the Sino-Russian negotiators of organizing a plebiscite in Outer Mongolia. This was laid down in an exchange of Notes regarding Outer Mongolia on August 14, 1945 between the Chinese Minister of Foreign Affairs, Dr. Wang Shih-chieh and the Peoples' Commissar of Foreign Affairs, Mr. Molotov. The translation of the Chinese texts reads as follows:

In view of the desire for independence repeatedly expressed by the people of Outer Mongolia, the Chinese Government declares that after Japan's defeat, if a plebiscite of the people of Outer Mongolia confirms the desire, the Chinese Government recognize the independence of Outer Mongolia in her existing boundaries.[173]

It was only ten days afterward that Generalissimo Chiang Kai-shek, in an address to the Joint Session of the Supreme National Defense Council and the Kuomintang Central Executive Committee, on August 24, 1945, made a general statement on China's relations with Outer Mongolia which contrasts strongly with former far less generous declarations. He said then:

[173] Full text in *Soviet News*, London, August 28, 1945, p. 5.

. . . Our people should realize that if we ignore the aspirations of these racial groups for freedom and restrain their urge for independence and self-government, it will not only be contrary to the spirit of our National Revolution, but will also tend to increase friction between the racial groups and jeopardize our entire program of national reconstruction. This in turn will adversely affect world peace and security.

The racial group of Outer Mongolia had, in effect, declared its independence from the mother country (*sic*) as early as 1922 when the Peking Government was in existence. That was almost a quarter of a century ago. The world is undergoing rapid changes and this is a propitious time for renewing old friendships. Therefore, we should, in accordance with our revolutionary principles and the Kuomintang's consistent policy, recognize with bold determination and through legal procedure, the independence of Outer Mongolia and establish friendly relations with it. We must seek a satisfactory solution of this question. If we fail, happy relations between China and Mongolia will be impossible and not only our own domestic tranquility but also the peace of the world will be seriously jeopardized . . . if frontier racial groups situated in regions outside the provinces have the capacity for self-government and a strong determination to attain independence, and are politically and economically ready for both, our Government should, in a friendly spirit, voluntarily help them to realize their freedom and forever treat them as brotherly nations, and as equals of China we should entertain no ill will or prejudices against them because of their choice to leave the mother country. Our frontier racial groups should in a friendly spirit and through legal channels, make known their wishes to the Government of the mother country. In this way they may be able to realize their aspirations. They should not defy the mother country and stir up mutual hatred.[174]

This declaration has been given at length in order that we may judge whether the somewhat paternal and condescending undertone of the statement taken together with the unsatisfactory history which preceded it justified the opinion that it "will rank as one of the most important state papers of Chiang Kai-shek, and a major contribution to the modern statesmanship of Asia." [175] It looks to us rather like the amplification of a "better late than never" policy. Whether it really involves an actual change of attitude and is more

[174] *The Collected War-time Messages of Generalissimo Chiang Kai-shek,* Vol. II, New York, 1946, pp. 855-57.

[175] Owen Lattimore, "Outer Mongolian Horizon" in *Foreign Affairs,* July 1946, p. 657.

than a lofty afterthought it will be possible to estimate only after watching China's attitude toward Inner Mongolia. For at the end of his speech Chiang Kai-shek not only referred to the "frontier racial groups situated in regions *outside* the provinces," but also the "the large and small racial groups *inside* the provinces." The latter should receive "legal and political equality, and unhindered economic and religious freedom, so that a warm community spirit and friendly collaboration may develop among all the groups."

The plebiscite by which the people of Outer Mongolia confirmed their desire for independence took place on October 20, 1945, based on a decision of the Little Hural Praesidium made on September 25. According to Article 71 of the Constitution "all citizens over eighteen years can take part, irrespective of sex, race, religion, education, nomadic or sendentary way of life, property status, social origin, past or present activities, except for those disfranchised by law and mentally deficient and certified as such on a legal basis." [176] By a decree of the Little Hural Praesidium of October 5, 1945, the following voting formula was laid down:

"The question put to the vote deals with the political independence of the Mongolian People's Republic. Please indicate on the ballot form in the space opposite your name whether you are for or against it, and affix your signature, or, if illiterate, the imprint of your right thumb." [177]

Thus, it was an open vote and the number of voters whose thumb was guided to the right column (the two columns being "For" or "Against") by some official's hand must have been considerable, since sixty percent of the population are illiterate. Guidance was provided by 304 local commissions consisting of 20,138 persons who established 4,251 polling booths all over the country. The task of the local commissions was to explain to the citizens "the purpose and aims of the plebiscite, the decrees of the Small Hural Praesidium, the voting formula and the instructions on the voting procedure."

[176] Moscow Radio, Nov. 21, 1945 and *Soviet News,* Nov. 23, 1945, p. 1.
[177] *Ibid.*

For this purpose, we are told, 10,282 meetings were held which were attended by 586,122 persons. There were also 3,178 women's meeting attended in all by 176,081 women.[178]

Voting took place all over the country on October 20, 1945 between six o'clock in the morning and midnight. 494,960 persons were registered by the local commissions as entitled to take part in the plebiscite. Of this number 7,551 persons failed to take part for various reasons such as travelling or grave illness, so that 487,409 citizens took part in the plebiscite, that is, 98.4 percent of all citizens entitled to take part [179] and roughly half of the total population,[180] and no single vote was entered in the column " against."

The day of the election was made into a day of " spontaneous mass demonstrations," mainly in Ulan Bator, where out of 26,658 citizens 24,683 cast their votes.[181] The final results in thirteen aimaks were known one or two days later and amounted to 381,243 affirmative votes. The remaining five aimaks were too remote and the results were received with some delay.[182] A special corps of riders was organized for this purpose, we can read, " new post stations were set up, and 20,000 of the fleetest horses were employed." [183] Many speeches exalting the result were made on the day of the election and the day following by many leading personalities including " the Head of the Buddhist Church in the Mongolian People's Republic, Erdenibal, on behalf of the believers." [184] Following

---

[178] All these details can be found in *Soviet News, op. cit.,* p. 2; also Moscow Radio, *op. cit.*

[179] *Ibid. Soviet News, op. cit.* The *S. N.,* Oct. 24, 1945, p. 4 gave 483,291, or 97.8 per cent of 494,074 persons eligible to vote.

[180] An interesting comparison may be made with the figures given for Soviet elections. On Feb. 12, 1946, out of a population of 193,198,000 there were 101,717,686 i. e. 52.6 per cent who voted. On Dec. 12, 1937, out of a population of 170,467,572 there were 91,113,153 i. e. 53.5 per cent who voted. In the United States there were on Jan. 1, 1944, 88,666,355 of voting age out of a population of 131,669,275, i. e. 67.4 per cent (1940 statistics). In the United Kingdom there was in 1945 a potential electorate amounting to 32,827,624 out of a population of 43,845,745, i. e. 79 per cent.

[181] *Soviet Monitor* (Tass), Oct. 22, 1945.

[182] *Ibid.* Moscow Radio (in German), Nov. 22, 1945.

[183] *Soviet Monitor, op. cit.*

[184] *Soviet Monitor,* Oct. 22, 1945; Moscow Radio, Oct. 21, 1945.

this 83,789 letters and gifts, we are told, were sent to Marshal Choibalsang including one communication from an old woman saying: " On this day of independence, and in keeping with the ancient custom, I present white lambs as gifts to old partisan—now President of the Little Hural-Buma Tsende, to Yanchima—wife of the founder of our Republic, Sukhe Bator— and to fighting General Gundub Surung, who led our regiments to victory over the last enemy of our independence, the Japanese Samurai." [185]

All these messages and letters were presented to the Sukhe Bator Museum. In addition, in the center of one aimak an obelisk ten meters high was built, and " in a solemn ceremony the state flag of the Mongolian People's Republic was raised." [186]

Thus the " legal procedure " referred to by Chiang Kai-shek was legal farce, but that would be looking at the matter through Western eyes; and, after all, it may be a matter of taste whether a legal farce carried through to the, to all appearances, harmonious end is not somewhat more dignified than continuously erratic and frequently empty protestations such as the United States and Britain have indulged in concerning elections in Bulgaria, Poland and Rumania, taken in conjunction with the doubtful Greek situation. Be that as it may, Mr. Lei Fa-chang, Vice-Minister of the Interior of the Chinese Republic, was sent to Ulan Bator as an observer of the plebiscite and did not fail, in a long declaration, to welcome its outcome whole-heartedly. Actually it appears from his statement that " the granting of freedom and equal rights to all peoples of the Chinese Republic " had been obstructed by " fifty years of Japanese aggression in China." He continued, and his words are given here at length, since, in our opinion, it would be a pity not to record this example of modern Oriental diplomacy:

Now that the war against the Fascist aggressors has been brought to a victorious conclusion, the time has come to settle all relations between the

---

[185] *Soviet Monitor,* Nov. 9, 1945.
[186] *Soviet News,* Nov. 23, 1945, p. 2; Moscow Radio (in German) Nov. 22, 1945.

nations and to bring about a normal situation so as to insure a peaceful life for the peoples and peace throughout the world. . . . The overwhelming majority of the Mongolian people voted for independence. I am convinced that when Mongolian representatives arrive in Chungking to report the results of the plebiscite, the Chinese National Government will make a binding official pronouncement about Mongolia's independence. After this plebiscite, Mongolia's position will at last be legally defined. I am extremely pleased at this development. All the material at my disposal, the explanations given by Marshal Choibalsang and our observation of the plebiscite procedure confirm that the plebiscite was well prepared. The persons in charge of the preparations carried out their task very conscientiously, fully aware of their responsibilities. On October 20, accompanied by the Mongolian Minister of Cattle Breeding, Surunjab, and the Vice-Minister for Foreign Affairs, Namsarai, I visited two polling districts in Ulan Bator. I witnessed the voting procedure. I saw Mongolian citizens casting their votes in a single-hearted, free, voluntary and sincere way for Mongolia's national independence. One saw that they were acquainted with the purpose and procedure of voting.[187]

This was followed by a highly complimentary description of Ulan Bator as a modern town and ended with "Everywhere we saw the great progress achieved by the Mongolian people who will know how to carry on with building up their country." We may add here as a matter of interest that after the plebiscite 200 Chinese workers residing in the Dzabkan Aimak are reported to have sent a Mongolian flag accompanied by a letter to the Mongolian Government. "We have been living in the Mongolian People's Republic since 1921. We live prosperously and happily as full-fledged citizens of the Republic," they said, and "We regard Mongolia as our second Motherland."[188]

Nevertheless, the Chinese representative on the Security Council of the United Nations at its meeting on August 29, 1946, criticized the memorandum on Mongolian development submitted by the Government of the Mongolian People's

[187] *Tass*, October 24, 1945; also *Soviet Monitor*, October 25, 1945. The Chinese Minister does not mention in his statement, as alleged by Moscow Radio on October 22, 1945, that he visited also " the rural districts of Zulun-Somon, 130 km. from Ulan Bator " (in addition to two districts of Ulan Bator).
[188] *Soviet Monitor*, November 9, 1945.

Republic: " I think it is rather oversimplified history which is not acceptable to us. My Government has the right to make further observations when the appropriate occasion arises." [189] The establishment of diplomatic relations with the Mongolian People's Republic agreed upon on February 13, 1946 [190] will, for the time being, be hardly more than a formal gesture. But future developments in Sinkiang, Inner Mongolia and Barga, especially the Chinese Communists' influence in the two latter areas, may one day put the Mongolian problem back on the Chinese agenda, ". . . like sweet bells jangled, out of tune and harsh."

---

[189] United Nations Security Council, Official Records, First Year: Second Series, No. 5, p. 90.

[190] Even the date of the formal recognition of the independence of the Mongolian People's Republic seems to be uncertain. The memorandum presented by the Mongolian People's Republic to the Security Council of the U. N. gives January 5, 1946, but a Chinese source gives February 13, 1946, adding that, " arrangements for the exchange of diplomatic envoys will be made in due course." (Foreign Office spokesman at a press conference in June 1946: *China Newsweek*, August 29. 1946.)

Chapter IV

RELATIONS WITH JAPAN

A. Relative neutrality before World War I

IN THE SECRET convention with Russia of July 1907 " the Imperial Government of Japan, recognizing the special interests of Russia in Outer Mongolia," undertook " to refrain from any interference which might prejudice those interests." In return, the Japanese Government received from Russia the assurance that she would not interfere with Japanese interests in Korea.[1] This early use of the term *Outer* Mongolia in a treaty-text was due to Japan's unwillingness to admit that the whole of Mongolia should come within Russia's sphere of influence. The Japanese refused to mention Mongolia in an open treaty, because it would not have been " in accord with the treaty with China and might be interpreted in a sense unfavorable to Japan." [2] The Russian representative in Tokyo cited Viscount Hayashi as speaking of Mongolia as being outside the sphere of action of Japan and Japan as having no intention of opposing there the natural interests of Russia.[3] Nevertheless, the French representative, Gérard, heard the Japanese statesmen explain that what Japan had agreed to in this treaty were the " extreme limits of the concessions Japan was prepared to make." [4]

Japan's ally, Britain, was informed of the contents of the

[1] Ernest Batson Price, *The Russo-Japanese Treaties of 1907-1916 concerning Manchuria and Mongolia*, Baltimore, 1933, p. 118, Appendix B; text of convention translated from a photostat copy of the French original supplied by the Commissariat of Foreign Affairs, Moscow. Art. I concerns rights in Manchuria, Art. II Korea.

[2] *Ibid.*, p. 26; referring to Émile Laloy, *Les Documents Secrets des Archives du Ministère des Affaires Etrangères de Russie publiés par les Bolcheviques*, p. 26: telegram of M. Bakhmetov, Russian Minister in Tokyo to the Russian Ministry of Foreign Affairs, May 9, 1907.

[3] *Ibid.*

[4] *Ibid.*, p. 37; Gérard, Auguste, *Ma Mission au Japon*, Paris, 1919, pp. 19-20.

secret agreement as was Russia's ally, France. Germany did not know if there was a secret agreement, but suspected one in which Japan recognized Russia's special position in Outer Mongolia in return for Russia's acknowledgement of Japan's in Manchuria.[5] Hence, when the Japanese Ambassador informed Berlin in April 1912 of Japan's attitude toward the proposed loan to the new Chinese Government, which was to depend upon the respecting of Japan's right in Mongolia, the Wilhelmstrasse expressed its astonishment as nothing was known about any Japanese interests in Mongolia.[6] The German Ambassador in Tokyo was thereupon directed to inquire of the Japanese Government " whence Japan derived special rights in Mongolia which are unknown to us." Viscount Ushida, the Foreign Minister, answered that Japan claimed the same interests along the South Manchurian frontier with Mongolia as Russia did along her Mongolian frontier. He met the objection that Japan had no Mongolian frontier by pointing out that " she had large interests in Southern Manchuria." [7]

Indeed, opinions differed as to the exact limits of the Japanese and Russian zones of influence. " In order to avoid all cause of misunderstanding over their special interests in Manchuria and Mongolia," a secret Russo-Japanese convention in July 1912 fixed the meridian of Peking as the line of demarcation between the Japanese and the Russian zones.[8] This in a very rough way corresponded both to the frontier between Outer Mongolia and the Barga region in Manchuria, and to the line dividing Western Inner Mongolia (provinces of Chahar and Suiyuan) from Eastern Mongolia, which was later partitioned between Jehol (Jo-oda and Josoto Leagues) and the Manchurian provinces of Fengt'ien, Kirin and Heilungchiang (Jerim League).

[5] *G. P.*, Vol. 25, Pt. I, pp. 69, 70; also No. 8556, the Minister in Peking Count Rex to Chancellor Prince Buelow, December 7, 1907, p. 82.

[6] *G. P.*, Vol. 32, No. 11886, State Secretary Kiderlen to Chargé d'Affaires Kuehlmann, April 30, 1912, p. 307.

[7] *G. P.*, n. XX.

[8] Price, *op. cit.*, p. 117, Appendix D. Text of the Secret Convention; translated from a photostat copy of the French original, supplied by the Commissariat of Foreign Affairs, Moscow.

The material available as to Japan's attitude toward the declaration of independence of the Princes of Khalkha and the subsequent Russo-Mongolian treaty is extremely vague. Korostovets mentions some inquiry from the Japanese Government, after a Government declaration in the Duma, in which Japan politely reminded the Russian Government of the agreements of 1907 and 1909 with their mention of the maintenance of the status quo in these regions.[9]

The attitude of the Japanese press after the publication of the Russo-Mongolian agreement was remarkable. For some days there was general silence; it would have been unwise to welcome the step because it would have alienated Chinese opinion. It would have been equally inopportune, however, to have opposed it as this would have precluded Japan from taking similar action in Manchuria. With no hint from official channels, the press was left to its own devices and the general comment was that Russian action was understandable and could be explained by the circumstances.[10] When the German Ambassador tried in September 1912 to discuss the development in Mongolia with Viscount Ushida he responded in an indifferent voice that he himself was not well-informed about events there, but that it was quite possible that a lot of things were happening behind the scenes.[11] The Russian Ambassador in Tokyo is reported to have assured Japanese journalists after the conclusion of the Urga agreement " probably in order to diminish the importance of the event " that Russia was fully satisfied with what she had achieved and did not intend to proclaim a protectorate over Mongolia, even if the Mongols were to ask for it themselves." [12]

It is difficult to say what truth there is in the remark of a Soviet commentator that the prudent and reserved replies of the Russian Government to the Mongols' requests for support in their struggle against Chinese trade and capital before their

[9] Korostovetsz, p. 124.

[10] *G.P.*, Vol. 32, No. 11995, Ambassador in Tokyo Count Rex to Bethmann-Hollweg, November 14, 1912, p. 431.

[11] *G.P.*, same to the same, September 28, 1912, p. 426.

[12] Korostovets, p. 214.

declaration of independence was due to "their leering at Japan." [13] There were a few who took a far-sighted view of Japan's possible ambitions in that region even in 1911 and 1912. From the Russian side, one of Korostovets's main points in pressing on the Russian Foreign Ministry a more active policy in Outer Mongolia in July 1911 was that the refusal to take the lead in Khalkha would serve as "an encouragement to Japan, who will not hesitate to take our place." [14] Emperor William II commented on Sazonov's remark to the German Ambassador that Russia did not want to take Outer Mongolia, but only aimed at creating a buffer-state between Russia and China with a "Nonsense (Quatsch). They will have to take it anyhow, otherwise the Japanese will get there." [15] Another observer from Peking, however, the well-known journalist Putnam Weale, warned Russia that her forward policy in Outer Mongolia would certainly provoke Japan to advance on the Asian continent and finally into Mongolia itself. [16] This finds corroboration in the comment of the Japanese Minister in Peking to his American colleague in March 1913 that Russia's advance in Mongolia was followed in Japan with a fair amount of uneasiness. [17] And it is also borne out by the report of the German Minister in Peking at the same time that the representative of the Japanese Bank had remarked in conversation with the German Bank representative that Japan, having been until then in a very delicate position in regard to Mongolia because of her (Japan's) relations with Russia, would now be compelled to make a change in her attitude because of her commercial aims. The advance

[13] Popov, p. 8.

[14] Popov, p. 12, Korostovets to Sazonov in wire of July 30, 1911. See also Benckendorff, Vol. 1, report of Korostovets to Sazonov, November 3/16, 1910, p. 383, in which the former stresses the fact that Russia should take advantage of the relative liberty of action in Outer Mongolia permitted by the Russo-Japanese convention.

[15] *G. P.*, Vol. 32, p. 246.

[16] *The Daily Telegraph*, August 28, 1912, p. 6, "Russia and the Chinese Frontier, Future of Mongolia," from Peking, July 25.

[17] *G. P.*, Vol. 32, No. 12000. Minister in Peking to Bethmann-Hollweg, March 2, 1913, p. 437.

of the Russians in Mongolia was " a matter of grave concern " to Japanese policy.[18]

But the practical value of the Russo-Japanese convention was put to the test when the Mongols approached the Japanese on two occasions. When in 1912 Da-Lama, the pro-Chinese Minister of the Interior, attempted a journey to Japan, the Japanese Consul in Harbin adopted a most unfriendly attitude and made it impossible for him to proceed.[19] In the beginning of 1914 the Urga Living Buddha addressed a letter to the Emperor of Japan soliciting the assistance of the Japanese Government in Khalkha's struggle for Mongol unity, and asking him to send a Japanese diplomatic representative to Urga.[20] It was said that the Living Buddha had been inspired to send this message by the visit of a Japanese officer, Kodama, to Mongolia.[21] The Japanese Government categorically denied that Kodama's visit had any official character.[22] The Mongolian Foreign Minister, on the other hand, claimed that he had declared during his visit that if the Mongols were to grant certain trade and territorial rights and concessions, Japan would not be disinclined to take up the cause of the unification of all Mongols and their complete separation from China.[23]

The Hutukhtu's letter was transmitted by the Russian Government to the Japanese Government. Russia was thereby observing strictly, as the Russian Minister in Tokyo said to the Japanese Minister of Foreign Affairs, the spirit of the

[18] *G. P.*, p. 438.

[19] Korostovets, p. 255; also pp. 213-4.

[20] *K. A.*, Vol. 37, pp. 58-59, January 6/19, 1914, translation of Urga Living Buddha's letter to the Japanese Emperor; see also *Chin. Soc. and Pol. Sci. Rev.*, Vol. XVII, No. 1, April 1933, pp. 192-194.

[21] *K. A.*, report of Sazonov to the Tsar, January 6/19, 1914, p. 58; also the Living Buddha's letter itself: " When Mr. Kodama, an official of your country, recently arrived in our capital . . ."

[22] *K. A.*, the Russian Ambassador in Tokyo, Malevskii-Malevich, January 10/23, 1914, No. 4, p. 60; also *IBZI*, Vol. I, 1, No. 281, Sazonov to Miller, February 6/19, 1914, p. 267; *K. A.*, Vol. 37, Malevskii-Malevich, January 3/16, 1914, No. 2, p. 54.

[23] *IBZI*, Vol. II, p. 39, n. noted on November 20/December 3, 1913, by Badmajapov, a Buriat, a Russian subject, and brought to the attention of the Russian Government.

political agreements existing between the two countries.[24] The Japanese Government, having been acquainted with the contents of the letter by the Russian Minister, refused to accept it. The letter, in the words of the Japanese Foreign Minister, would have " put the Japanese Emperor in a dilemma "; moreover, it was not possible for him to accept a letter from a foreign ruler with whom Japan did not have diplomatic relations. The Russian Minister was asked to act as mediator and to return the letter unopened to the Urga Government.[25] The Japanese Government was, however, extremely anxious that its refusal should remain secret. The Russian Minister was twice urged by the Japanese Foreign Minister to keep the fact of the Hutukhtu's sending the message secret and was asked to take measures to prevent the Mongols from giving publicity to the incident. " Rumors as to the Hutukhtu's letter, if they get into the press, may provide pretexts for interpellations in Parliament. If this should be the case the Minister will be compelled to have recourse to a complete denial in order to avoid serious complications." [26] This attitude was, in fact, adopted by the Japanese Government when rumors about the letter began to circulate.[27] The Japanese Government, in the words of the Russian Ambassador, wanted to " avoid supplying the opposition with a new opportunity for reproaching Japanese diplomacy for its passivity and its servility toward us." [28] The Russian Foreign Minister rejoiced over the return of the letter and said that " by this act an end will be put to the intrigue designed to involve the Japanese Government in the affairs of Outer Mongolia." [29]

[24] *K. A.*, Vol. 37, telegram of Malevskii-Malevich of January 2/15, 1914, No. 1, p. 53; January 3/16, 1914, No. 2, pp. 53-54; esp. the same of January 5/18, 1914, No. 1, p. 56.

[25] *K. A.*, Malevskii-Malevich on January 2/15, 1914, No. 1, p. 53; also p. 55.

[26] *K. A.*, Malevskii-Malevich, January 10/23, 1914, No. 4, p. 60, and the detailed report of his conversations with the Japanese Minister of Foreign Affairs in despatch of January /18, 1914, esp. p. 57.

[27] *IBZI.*

[28] *K. A.*, telegram of Malevskii-Malevich of January 3/16, 1914, No. 2, p. 54, and end of long despatch of same of January 8/18, 1914, No. 1, p. 57.

[29] *K. A.*, Vol. 37, Sazonov to Malevskii-Malevich, January 5/18, 1914, No. 51, p. 54.

Shortly afterward, however, it became known that Major Tanaka, the Chief of Staff of the Japanese Division in Tientsin, intended to go to Urga. The Russian Minister to China feared that, though his Japanese colleague in Peking was hostile to the plan, the attempt might be repeated by another Japanese officer and this time without the Russian's knowledge.[30] The Russian Minister in Tokyo was thereupon instructed by Sazonov "to draw the attention of the Japanese Foreign Minister to the fact that journeys of Japanese military persons to Urga seem untimely, because it makes more difficult our task of persuading the Mongolian Government to renounce the idea of the reunion of Outer Mongolia with Inner Mongolia."[31] The Japanese Foreign Minister, professing ignorance of the whole affair to the Russian Ambassador, approved, at any rate, the negative attitude of the Japanese Minister in Peking.[32] A few months later, the Russian Diplomatic Agent in Urga interpreted the Mongolian project of an Outer and Inner Mongolia under the protection of Russia and Japan as a proof "that the Japanese are to a certain extent involved in the present anti-Russian mood in Urga."[33]

In July 1915, i. e., directly after the conclusion of the tripartite agreement of Kiakhta, it became known that a Japanese officer disguised as a pharmacist had conferred with the Inner Mongolian Prince Babojab and had promised him money and arms to gain the independence of Barga. Barga was expressly excluded from the territory of Outer Mongolia by the treaty of Kiakhta and a Sino-Russian agreement on Barga was concluded only in November 1915.[34] Prince Babojab had sent one of his officials with the Japanese to Japan to procure arms for his 7,000 troops for whom he received pay-

---

[30] *IBZI*, Vol. I, 1, p. 444, n. 2, letter of Krupenskii to Sazonov of February 14/27, 1914.

[31] *IBZI*, No. 440, Sazonov to Malevskii-Malevich, February 28/March 13, 1914, p. 444.

[32] *IBZI*, Vol. I, 2, No. 105, Malevskii-Malevich to Sazonov, March 14/27, 1914.

[33] *IBZI*, No. 131, Miller to Sazonov, May 18/31, 1914, p. 130.

[34] *IBZI*, Vol. II, 8, 1, No. 349, Krupenskii to Sazonov, July 6/19, 1915, p. 328; for Barga see Chapter II.

ment from the Mongolian Government.[35] It seems that Babojab aimed at a quasi-independent status for the territory over which his influence extended. The Russian Vice-Consul at Hailar thought it possible that Babojab together with other princes were aiming at a revolt " in which, apparently, the Japanese will participate." [36]

The fact remains, however, that the Japanese Government had never openly declared its approval of these not very numerous exploits of individual Japanese, mainly officers. It disclaimed them, though it had not the courage to do this openly for fear of the military clique. The aggressive anti-Chinese policy of Japan during the Great War was, on the other hand, welcomed by Russia in so far as it provided her with a means of exercising pressure on the Chinese delegation at Kiakhta. The declaration of the Russians during the discussions that they would break off negotiations would, in Sazonov's words, " in the present moment of complications with Japan produce favorable results." [37] And, indeed, the recalcitrant Chinese delegation received instructions to lessen their resistance and to conclude the treaty quickly.[38]

At the same time the Russian Minister in Tokyo, communicating to the Japanese Government the Russian view on the Twenty-one Demands, spoke of the Russian conviction that Japan would keep political treaties. " The parallelism of our policy and that of Japan in Manchuria and Mongolia gives us cause to assume that we shall give each other substantial assistance in the ensuring of our success, if we each state frankly and confidentially our intention in China." [39]

[35] *IBZI*, Vol. II, 8, 2, No. 129, Russian Vice-Consul in Hailar to the Russian Minister in Peking, Krupenskii, September 5/18, 1915, p. 672, and n. 2.

[36] *IBZI*, No. 899, same to the same, September 29/October 12, 1915, p. 792.

[37] *IBZI*, Vol. II, 7, 1, No. 364, Krupenskii to Sazonov, February 28/March 13, 1915, p. 333.

[38] *IBZI*, No. 118, Sazonov to Miller, January 20/February 2, 1915, p. 109, but cf. telegram of Krupenskii to Sazonov, November 9, 1916, No. 690, as cited in S. S., 1928, No. 5, Prof. R. Gladstern, *The Mongolian Policy of the Russian Provisional Government*, p. 166: " The Japanese here are trying to persuade the Chinese that the refusal of the Mongols (to sign the tripartite agreement) is caused by Russian intrigues."

[39] *IBZI*, No. 140, Malevskii-Malevich to Sazonov, January 23/February 5, 1915, p. 129.

In a speech in the Duma made at the end of July 1915, Sazonov was able, when referring to Russo-Japanese relations, to express the hope that " our present relations with Japan, having actually the character of an alliance, would be the starting point for a still closer understanding." The Russo-Japanese agreements which were concluded in 1916 took away nothing of the importance of the earlier agreements of 1907, 1909, and 1912, and constituted " a rapprochement even more binding than an entente cordiale and almost equal to an alliance for the maintenance of peace in the Far East." [40]

Japan's attitude toward Outer Mongolia in the days of Tsarist Russia, i. e., after the first Russo-Japanese agreement, was thus based on treaties which gave Outer Mongolia to Russia as a sphere of influence. We have knowledge of isolated attempts by Japanese militarists to make contact with the Urga Government.[41] These became more numerous with the downfall of Tsarist Russia as becomes clear from a message of the Russian diplomatic agent in Urga in the last days of the Provisional Government (September 1917) when Russia was unable to provide the Mongols with arms. " I am afraid," he wired, " that the Mongols will buy the arms from the Japanese, whose number has increased lately in Urga." [42] On the other hand, official attempts were never made by the Japanese Government; on the contrary, such overtures as there were came from the Mongolian Government and did not meet with any response. On the whole, therefore—and the impor-

---

[40] *IBZI*, Vol. II, 8, 2, p. 467, n. 1, speech of Sazonov of July 19/August 1, 1915; Victor A. Yakhontoff, *Russia and the Soviet Union in the Far East,* London, 1932, p. 64.

[41] For activities of Japanese officers in Outer Mongolia in the year 1911, see Hermann Consten, *Weideplatze der Mongolen, Im Reiche der Chalcha,* Berlin, 1919, Vol. 1, p. 209, and plate 50, opposite p. 192, showing Japanese visitors in the Russian Consulate in Uliassutai. For mentioning of earlier activities see *B. D.*, Vol. 4, p. 342, M. Poklevskii-Koriell, first Secretary at Russian Embassy in London to Sir C. Hardinge in July 1906; ". . . there were Japanese emissaries in Mongolia encouraging the Chinese authorities to tighten their hold over the administration, and that such a policy would inevitably end in a conflict with the Mongol Princes." For earlier Japanese economic activities in Mongolia (presumably chiefly in Inner Mongolia) see RJ, I Année, No. 7, June 15, 1911, p. 440.

[42] *S. S.*, telegram of diplomatic Agent in Mongolia of September 27, 1917, p. 166.

tance of this summary will become evident only when it is compared with that of the following section dealing with the Japanese attitude toward Outer Mongolia during the Sino-Japanese War—the attitude of the Japanese Government gave no cause for any serious apprehension in Urga or in St. Petersburg where attention was concentrated much more on Chinese aims in that region than on those of Japan.

B. Activity Between Wars

The Russian revolution and the creation of the Omsk Government of Admiral Kolchak brought with them Allied intervention in the Far East. Japanese intervention was more extensive than that of the other Allies, but here we are only concerned with its connections with Mongolian and, more particularly, Outer Mongolian affairs. The Japanese Government never denied the part it played in the history of Allied intervention, nor did it ever repudiate its support of Ataman Semenov, who was active not only in organizing anti-Bolshevik activities, but in creating a Pan-Mongolian movement and a new Mongolian State. Baron Shidehara, as one of the delegates at the Washington conference, felt it incumbent on him to read out a special statement concerning his Government's connection with Ataman Semenov, saying that while the other allies had severed connections with Semenov " the Japanese were reluctant to abandon their friends, whose efforts in the Allied cause they had originally encouraged," and that they had maintained for some time their connection with him. He added, however, that when it was found out that the assistance rendered to Semenov was likely to complicate the international situation in Siberia they had severed all relations with him and had not renewed them since that time.[43]

The material in our hands from the Russian side seems to confirm the statement of the Japanese that they were reluctant

---

[43] Cf. Conference on the Limitation of Armaments, Washington, November 12, 1921-February 6, 1922 (Washington 1922), 24th meeting, p. 1394 and esp. p. 1398, " concise statement " read by Baron Shidehara (Japan).

to encourage Semenov's attempts to gain their official backing
for his ambitions. But there is no doubt that Japanese officers,
and the support which they had promised to Semenov, played
an important part in the Pan-Mongolian movement. In March
1919 the Russian Minister in Peking, in a report to the Department of Foreign Affairs of the Omsk Government, referred to
Japanese agitation, especially among the Trans-Baikal Buriats,
which was fostering the idea of complete Mongolian unity;
Semenov's plan of creating a sort of buffer against Chinese
movements in the Northwest was " probably " not advanced
without Japanese influence.[44] In a conversation which the
Head of the Diplomatic Chancery of the Chief Executive of
the Omsk Government had with Semenov, the latter complained that the Mongols, who were aspiring to self-administration, " were harassed by the Japanese, who wished to subject
them to their exclusive influence." " Numerous Japanese
emissaries were active " but he (Semenov) had already
succeeded in making them lose all influence in Mongolia. He
threatened that if he were not permitted to direct the Mongolian movement, the Japanese would do it.[45] But the Russian
Minister in Peking considered him " to be more or less a tool
of foreign interests " and it was from the Japanese Ambassador
that he first heard about the conference of Mongols arranged
by Semenov in Dairen.[46] Outer Mongolia was not represented,
but there was a Japanese observer in the person of Major
Suzuki, who had been sent there by a Captain Kuroki. The
conference adopted a resolution for the creation of a Mongol
Government (which was to include Outer Mongolia within
its territory). It was also laid down that loans for the up-keep
of the army of this new government as well as for its other
expenses were to be obtained " from a foreign state " in return

[44] *N. V.*, Vol. II, Materials and Documents. Materials on the history of intervention, Japan's part in the Mongolian movement by A. F. S-ky, p. 592, report of
the Minister in Peking on March 19, 1919, to the 30th Department of Ministry of
Foreign Affairs, J. J. Sukin.

[45] *Ibid.*, pp. 592-93, report of the Head of the Diplomatic Chancery, etc., of April
2, 1919, file No. 625.

[46] *Ibid.*, p. 593, telegram of Minister in Peking of February 18, 1919, file No. 83.

for a guarantee of gold, silver, salt and other mineral wealth for a period of twenty years and the granting to this state of the right to build railways for an unlimited period. To all these deliberations Suzuki, the Japanese officer, listened in silence. Two participants of the conference were then sent to Captain Kuroki to report to him the decisions made. Kuroki said that he was greatly pleased by the work done by the assembly and that he would immediately leave for Tokyo to report the result and he promised full support from Japan. As to the status of the new state, at the conference it was said that Russia had been a friend of the Mongols, but that they were fully entitled to expect similar protection from Japan. The possibility of an international protectorate was also mentioned.[47]

In Tokyo, however, the Assistant Minister of Foreign Affairs denied to the Russian Ambassador that Japan had anything to do with the attempts to create a new Buriat-Mongol state. All Japanese military and civil servants had been ordered to keep aloof from this movement. The whole idea was not serious and was bound from the start to be unsuccessful.[48] This argument is acceptable as a reason for Japan's passivity since many of the promises made by Semenov to the assembled Mongols were nothing but his own invention and were not based on actual engagements made, so that the Mongols are said to have very soon lost confidence in him.[49]

The danger coming from Japanese military circles was, however, keenly felt by Baron Witte, at that time Russian Diplomatic Agent at Urga (in succession to Miller); he reported to the Omsk Government that internal differences between lamas and princes, with the possibility of a coup d'état, " might make it necessary to bring Japanese troops to Mongolia and that the preservation of order by Japanese would

---

[47] *Ibid.*, pp. 593-96, report of Minister in Peking, March 19, 1919, file No. 30.

[48] *Ibid.*, p. 596, telegram of Russian Minister in Tokyo, of March 12, 1919, file No. 83.

[49] *Ibid.*, p. 602, copy of report of Vice-Consul in Hailar of June 2, 1919, file No. 104, and telegram of Minister in Peking, June 7, 1919, No. 423.

undoubtedly have a one-sided character through which the whole adventure would be unsuccessful" from the Russian point of view.[50] The Omsk Government in a wire to Sazonov, their representative at the Paris Peace Conference, warned him that "Semenov is playing the game for Japan, for although the Japanese Government officially keeps aloof from this affair, Japanese military circles are interested to create conditions for a rising in the districts bordering our territory which would justify them in establishing Japanese troops—and their influence—in our territory for an indefinite time."[51]

When a delegation from the Mongolian Provisional Government—as it styled itself—landed at Yokohama and proceeded to Tokyo in order to get visas to go to Paris, they were given the cold shoulder not only by the British, French and American diplomats, but also by the Japanese Government. The latter went so far as to protest strongly against the sending of Mongolian delegates to the Peace Conference.[52] Captain Kuroki, who had supported the idea of a Mongolian state was replaced by Major Kurasawa, who was stationed at Chita.[53] But the Russian Vice-Consul at Hailar in May 1919 adds in his report that this new Japanese representative while protesting to Neisse Gegen, the nominal head of the provisional Mongolian Government, against the sending of a delegation to Tokyo and to the Peace Conference, nevertheless assured him that Japan would support the Mongolian Government with arms and also financially, but this only secretly.[54]

When, however, not much support, and in particular little of a financial character, was forthcoming, discontent among the Mongolian and Buriat leaders grew to such proportions that Semenov had to consent to a delegation being sent to Tokyo

[50] *Ibid.*, p. 597, report of Russian diplomatic agent in Mongolia to the Russian Minister in Peking, April 12, 1919.

[51] *Ibid.*, p. 598, Minister of Foreign Affairs of the Omsk Government to the Ambassador in Paris (Sazonov), March 28, 1919, file No. 444.

[52] *Ibid.*, p. 601, telegram of Minister in Tokyo, April 24, 1919, file No. 144.

[53] *Ibid.*, Annex to the report of Minister in China of May 6, 1919, file No. 19.

[54] *Ibid.*, p. 601, Annex to the report of Minister in China of May 6, 1919, file No. 19.

to secure a clarification of the attitude of Japan and other powers. This delegation, however, never started.[55]

Some months later it was reported that emissaries of Semenov had again approached Japan for support in his struggle against Bolshevism, and that one of his chief lieutenants, Malinovski, was negotiating with a Japanese firm " Sazto " for the purchase of rifles and had concluded an agreement for a loan with a Japanese bank in Korea. Semenov went to Mukden for a personal interview with Chang Tso-lin. The Japanese Consul also called on Chang Tso-lin, on which occasion he is said to have given him Japan's support for his becoming " the independent master of Eastern Mongolia and Southern Manchuria." It is also said that aid was promised to Semenov from Japan on similar conditions.[56]

The Chinese General Hsü, who was then sent for purposes of " pacification " to Urga was a member of the Anfu Club, an organization with obvious pro-Japanese sympathies. But " Little Hsü's " reign in Urga was too short-lived for us to be able to ascertain whether there was any direct Japanese influence on his policy. It seems difficult to go so far as to say that Japanese military circles, seeing that Semenov was not much use to them, tried to establish influence in Mongolia through General Hsü,[57] since the Chinese regime established by the latter was destroyed by Semenov's lieutenant, Baron Ungern Sternberg, who entered Urga—as we know also from a non-Russian observer, Major Dockray—with a bodyguard of forty Japanese and whose equipment, apart from some Italian machine-guns, was largely Japanese.[58] But it is contended that when in 1921 in the Civil War in China the influence of the Anfu Club in North China was broken General

[55] *Ibid.*, p. 602, telegram of Minister in Peking, June 7, 1919, file No. 423.

[56] *Ibid.*, pp. 602-603, telegram of Minister in Peking, September 2, 1919, file No. 119-63, and telegram of the same, September 6, 1919, file No. 129; and telegram of same, September 27, 1919.

[57] See *N. V.*, 1925, No. 8-9, " Mongolia and Japanese Imperialism " Shoizhelov, p. 199.

[58] See North China Herald, Vol. CXXXVIII, No. 2798, March 26, 1921, p. 793, col. 1. " Maj. Dockray's story of Urga " by Rodney Gilbert, Peking, March 17.

Hsü lost his usefulness to the Japanese and that they made use of the bands of which the " mad Baron's " army was composed. Documents which were found on Ungern Sternberg when he was captured seem to confirm that he was counting on substantial help from the Japanese,[59] though it must not be forgotten that he had somehow lost his sense of proportion, so that it seems impossible ever to ascertain to what extent his actions were based " on a well-prepared, wide political plan " not emanating from his own imagination but seriously supported by important Japanese officers.

Actually his policy might well have served the aims of those " Japanese representatives." While we have no actual proof that Semenov and Ungern were financed by Japanese circles, the comment on Semenov of an English officer who was a member of the British Military Mission seems appropriate when he says that in any case the presence of contingents of Japanese troops in the neighborhood of the scene of his activities " practically assured his safety." [60] While we may add for Ungern that the extension of his activities from Urga to Russian Siberia, without sufficient support and with treacherous Mongolian adherents, procured his fall.

We may, therefore, sum up these confused years in the history of Mongolia and Japanese influence on it by saying that we can discern a consistency in the method with which Japanese interests were pursued, in that Japanese officers still actively intervened, while the Japanese Government, though supporting Semenov for some time, never endorsed his Mongolian activities publicly and categorically denied any support. There is, however, the difference that the extent to which

---

[59] See *N. V.*, 1925, No. 8-9, p. 201, referring to the Journal " Peoples of the Far East," organ of the Far Eastern Secretariat, I. K. K. I., Irkutsk, 1921, No. 5, pp. 623-638; see also papers found on Ungern-Sternberg, published by the Special Delegation of the Far Eastern Republic to the U. S. A., Washington, 1922, and published by the same, memorandum on Japanese Intervention in the Russian Far East, Washington, 1922, 165 pp.

[60] Major Phelps Hodges, *Britmis. A Great Adventure of the War,* being an Account of Allied intervention in Siberia and of an escape across the Gobi to Peking, London, 1931, pp. 68-69.

Japanese officers participated was much greater than in former years. Their activities were not very successful, and it may be suggested that this was due to the incapacity and reluctance of the Japanese Government to lend them active support. Pressure from the Allies and the United States, as well as sound strategical reasons may have dictated this course; with Japanese soldiers engaged on the Pacific coast of Siberia and Japanese influence in the northern provinces of China and Eastern (Inner) Mongolia not yet sufficiently established, the position in the vast territory of Outer Mongolia would have been untenable.

The establishment of a Far Eastern Republic in place of the Soviet Government but with its consent and the results of the negotiations of the Washington Conference, particularly the Nine-Power Treaty binding the signatories to maintain the integrity of China, were generally considered as set-backs to Japanese ambitions. But neither Soviet Russia nor the Far Eastern Republic was a signatory to the Nine-Power Treaty, and while Japan did not make any treaty with the Far Eastern Republic, her commitments in the agreements with Russia of 1907-1916 could no longer be regarded as influencing her attitude towards Outer Mongolia, as the Soviets had declared all treaties concluded by the Tsarist Government null and void. There were frequent rumors that a secret political agreement had been concluded between Japan and Russia,[61] but later events made it highly improbable that such a convention ever eixsted, and it is clear that, if it did, it soon lost all practical value.

A few facts only can be mentioned to show the interest with which the Japanese followed Mongolian affairs up to their campaign in Manchuria in 1931-1933. It is perhaps not unremarkable that whereas the Russo-Japanese agreements definitely divided Mongolia into an Outer and Inner Mongolia, Japanese publications or pronouncements in post-war

---

[61] See *Russia, U. S. S. R.*, a complete handbook ed. by P. Maleskii-Malevich, New York, 1933, p. 324.

years use the general term " Mongolia." Therefore it is often
not clear whether Outer or Inner Mongolia is meant, but in
general it can be assumed that it is the latter as Japanese seem
to have been unable to establish much contact with the Outer
Mongols. A Soviet source cited for instance a Japanese newspaper, the " Harbin Nichi-Nichi " of July 1924 as expressing
Japan's strong desire to invest capital in Mongolia in order
to be able to exploit the natural riches of the country. The
Society for Asiatic Research (Adsia Tanken-Kio-Kai) is said
to have sent an expedition to Mongolia in September 1924,
led by the son of the former Prime Minister, Kiyoura, Keigo
ostensibly to conduct researches in the geological structure of
the country, but in reality to " reconnoiter " the political situation.[62] It is difficult, if not impossible, to check the truth of
these or similar reports. One may also be puzzled by the
problem of the authenticity of the Tanaka Memorial. The
Japanese Prime Minister, General Baron Giichi Tanaka (1863-
1929), who from 1918-1921 was Minister of War and in 1925
leader of the Seiyukai party, is said to have submitted to
the Emperor in 1927 a memorial in which he had set out in
detail the aims of Japan's foreign policy. During the Sino-
Japanese controversy before the League of Nations in 1931-32,
the Japanese delegate described it as a " forgery from beginning
to end." [63] Others think that " its genuineness is no longer
doubtful " [64] as nearly all the plans mentioned in this memorial
were later carried out. It is impossible to dispute this last
fact, and forgery or not, it seems important to know what
this document had to say about Japan's policy toward Outer
Mongolia. In the section devoted to Mongolia, it stated first
in a historical introduction that Mongolia had never been
Chinese territory but that Japan had unfortunately bound
herself at the Washington Conference to respect the sovereignty

[62] *N. V.*, 1925, Vol. 8-9, etc., pp. 203-204, referring to " Harbin Nichi-Nichi " of
September 7, 1924.
[63] Cf. Westel W. Willoughby, *The Sino-Japanese Controversy and the League of
Nations,* Baltimore, 1935, pp. 161-62.
[64] See Stepan Vostrotin, " Russia's Crisis in the Far East," in *The Slavonic Review,*
Vol. IV (1935-36), p. 112.

of China over this region. As to the policy to be pursued toward Outer and Inner Mongolia it advises that everywhere possible Japan should station her retired military officers to take a leading part in the princes' affairs. " After a large number of our people have moved into Outer and Inner Mongolia, we should then buy land at one-tenth of its worth and begin to cultivate rice where it is possible in order to relieve our food shortage. Where the land is not suitable for rice cultivation, we should develop it for cattle-raising and horse-breeding in order to replenish our military needs. The rest of the land could be devoted to the manufacture of canned goods which we might export to Europe and America. The fur and leather would also meet our needs. Once the opportunity comes, Outer and Inner Mongolia will be ours outright." [65]

C. MANCHUKUO POLICIES

Many of the aims of Japanese policy as enunciated in the Tanaka Memorial were realized by the creation of Manchukuo, including Manchuria and Jehol. The declaration of the establishment of the new Government of Manchukuo, dated March 1, 1932, spoke of the state as comprising " the territory of Manchuria and Mongolia." [66] The result of this was to confront Outer Mongolia with a new neighbor.

Within Manchukuo, the province which bordered on Outer Mongolia was the " autonomous " province of Hsingan, itself inhabited by Mongols. The setting apart of such a province, in such a manner, within the new state, in itself suggested the idea of a future unification of all Mongol territory under Japanese control and following a course of development agreeable to Japanese interests. For the Mongols this was a reminder of the earlier idea of Mongol unity centering in Outer Mongolia,

[65] For text of Tanaka Memorial see: " The Puppet State of Manchukuo," Shanghai, 1935, Appendix IV, pp. 204-238; partial text in *The Slavonic Review*, Vol. IV (1935-36), pp. 113-17.

[66] *Proclamations, Statements and Communications of the Manchukuo Government*, published by the Department of Foreign Affairs, Manchukuo Government, Series No. 1, October 1932, Hsinking, pp. 3-6.

and at the same time a challenge to the idea. To the Soviet Union, it must have appeared as an ominous step toward an attempt, long foreseen, to assert Japanese influence in Outer Mongolia.

Indeed, the new official interest of Japan in Outer Mongolia changed the whole aspect of Outer Mongolian diplomatic relations as well as of Soviet-Japanese relations. For, after the creation of Manchukuo by Japan, one of the chief points at issue between the U. S. S. R. and Japan was connected with Outer Mongolia. The Manchukuo-Mongolian frontier and the whole status of Outer Mongolia were in dispute between the two countries.

As to the frontier, the Japanese considered Lake Bui Nor as a part of Manchukuo and the Khalkha River as "the natural boundary between the two countries." [67] The Outer Mongolian maps (and apparently also Soviet maps), however, included the Khalkha River and Lake Bui Nor within the territory of the Mongolian People's Republic. Nevertheless, there seems to have been general agreement that the territory disputed was " a vast plain with patches of desert here and there " extending along the frontier between the two countries " and that " it is practically impossible to tell exactly where the frontier lies." [68]

It is important to note that the dispute between Manchukuo and the Monoglian People's Republic was not so much one of delimitation of frontiers, but was concerned mainly with the demands of Manchukuo to have a formally accredited Manchukuo agent with wide powers, virtually equivalent to diplomatic status, to protect Manchukuo interests in the Mongolian capital and to participate in the settlement of frontier incidents. Manchukuo went even further and asked to be permitted to maintain representatives, in addition to the repre-

[67] See *Japan Chronicle*, Kobe, March 28, 1935. " The Mongol Border Dispute. Maps at Variance." By Prof. Chuzo Yoshimura, Director of the Investigation Bureau of Zenrin-Kyokai.
[68] " Manchukuo's Foreign Relations," by Kanichi Narazakai, Chief of Bureau of Manchukuo General Intelligence (cf. *Who's Who in Japan, 1936-1937*, p. 323), in *Contemporary Japan*, Vol. V, No. 2, September 1936.

sentative in the capital, Ulan-Bator (Urga), in five other places in Outer Mongolia, of which three were near the frontier.[69] That would have meant that Manchukuo would have recognized the Mongolian People's Republic as an independent state and then recognition by Japan would have been only a matter of form.

Tokichi Tanaka, the Japanese Ambassador in Moscow from 1925 to 1930, had maintained contact with the Mongolian representative there, though this had ceased toward the closing years of his ambassadorship.[70] Hence, a passage written by him in 1932, when Vice-Minister of Foreign Affairs, makes very interesting reading. He says: " In my personal opinion Japan should accord recognition to the independent Mongolian Republic and formally enter into official relations with it. There can be nothing strange in treating a state as independent, when that independence has not been challenged either internally or externally for over a decade. I see no serious reason which will preclude either Japan from recognizing Mongolia, or Mongolia from accepting the recognition, unless the Northern giant should stand in the way, which, all things considered, is extremely unlikely," [71]—a prophecy which was not borne out by events.

When, however, during the alarming situation created by border incidents in the middle of 1935, the Mongolian Government refused to admit representatives sent to discuss the settlement of these incidents, the Japanese Military High Command in Manchukuo, which executed the policy of Japan in both civil and military matters, declared in October 1935 that the flat refusal of Outer Mongolia to exchange representatives conveyed the impression that her liberty of action was restricted by another agency. Therefore, Manchukuo could not consider Outer Mongolia to be a state in the usual

---

[69] *La Revue Nationale Chinoise,* February 1, 1936, p. 173; cf. also *T. O.,* No. 3 (9), July-September 1936, " Historical Lessons . . .," p. 77.

[70] See *Japan Chronicle,* Kobe, weekly edition, February 21, 1935.

[71] " Soviet Japanese Relations," *Contemporary Japan,* Vol. 1, No. 1, Tokyo, January 1932.

sense of the term. From this date forward Manchukuo would consider Outer Mongolia as a mysterious and dangerous zone adjacent to its own territory; and she would take the intiative in settling questions arising between the two countries, whether outstanding or subsequently arising.[72]

In the same month a spokesman of the Japanese Foreign Office expressed approval of the effort of the Manchukuo Government to open up Outer Mongolia. He said that Manchukuo " was now knocking at Outer Mongolia's door as Commodore Perry knocked at Japan's door in 1858," implying that the same result was inevitable.[73] As, however, the Mongolian People's Republic showed no signs of weakening in its resolve not to admit a diplomatic representatitve, the Manchukuo Government agreed to meet the Outer Mongols in a conference at the border town of Manchuli in order to discuss the border disputes. No result emerged from this conference, at which representatives of the Japanese army also took part, and which discussed frontier-demarcations and the creation of a joint commission to settle frontier incidents on the spot during a great part of the second half of the year 1935. It had to adjourn twice, the last time being in November 1935, because the delegates were unable to agree.[74]

When in March 1936 Stalin, in an interview, referred to Russia's attitude in case of an attack by Japan on Outer Mongolia, the Japanese Ambassador in Moscow was instructed by his Foreign Office to enquire what was the actual relationship between Russia and Outer Mongolia. Thereupon the fact was made known by the Russian Foreign Office that a Soviet-Mongolian Protocol of Mutual Assistance had been concluded.[75]

---

[72] *La Revue Nationale Chinoise*, February 1, 1936, p. 175; and *T. O.*, *op. cit.*

[73] *N. Y. Times*, October 22, 1935 (dispatch from Tokyo); *The Times*, London, July 25, 1935.

[74] As to the Manchuli Conference, a Japanese officer alleged that the Outer Mongolian delegation refused to take quarters in a hotel, remaining on board a train which, they said, had been provided for them by the Soviet Government at the request of their own Government. See article by Colonel M. Kanda, translated from *Ishin*, March 1936, in *Contemporary Opinions on Current Topics*, translated from Japanese Magazines, Journals, Government Bulletins, etc., Tokyo Information Bureau, No. 120, March 26, 1936.

[75] *The Times*, London, April 2, 1936.

Upon learning the terms of the protocol a spokesman of the Manchukuo Foreign Office, in a declaration to the press made at the beginning of April 1936, asserted that in view of the fact that Outer Mongolia was entirely secluded from all foreign countries, with the sole exception of Soviet Russia, the conclusion of such a mutual aid pact between Moscow and Ulan Bator was little short of the actual absorption of Outer Mongolia into the Soviet Union. Though that pact was called a "mutual assistance" instrument, it virtually constituted a military alliance between the two contracting parties, with Manchukuo as its objective. Thus, Manchukuo could not but feel serious concern in this matter; she could not remain indifferent toward such a state of affairs in view of the fact that she had a long, common frontier with Outer Mongolia, and also because she had ties of blood with this country. Finally, the spokesman claimed that Manchukuo took as much interest in Outer Mongolia as the Soviet Union, if not more. As far as that area was concerned Manchukuo was entitled to have at least an equal voice. It had also the right to obtain the same position in that area that Moscow had achieved.[76]

It is consistent with this view that in the beginning of May 1936, in his address to the Japanese Diet, Hachiro Arita, the Foreign Minister, reiterated the opinion that the Manchukuo-Outer Mongolian difficulties must not be settled by a Russo-Japanese arrangement, but by "direct negotiations" between the Manchukuo Government and the Government of the Mongolian People's Republic, which he hoped would result in an early solution of all questions and particularly in the exchange of representatives between Manchukuo and Outer Mongolia."[77]

That the Japanese were not satisfied with the control they exercised over the Mongol Province of Hsingan in Manchukuo and had feared intrigues between the political leaders of this

---

[76] *Japan Chronicle*, weekly edition, Kobe, April 16, 1936 (dispatch from Hsinking of April 6).

[77] *Contemporary Japan*, Vol. V, No. 1, June 1936, 69th Session of Japanese Diet, May 6, 1936, p. 154; also see Tokyo Dispatch in *The Times*, London, April 29, 1936.

region and those of Outer Mongolia, was illustrated by the reported shooting of four leading officials of Northern Hsingan in April 1936, for conspiring with the Outer Mongols during the Manchuli conference, and for aiming at the independence of the province.[78] The effect of this change of Japanese policy on the Manchukuo Mongols themselves is difficult to estimate. But it may be said that Japan was at first welcomed by them as a protector against Chinese exploitation and possible future domination by the Russian-influenced Government of Urga.

An additional important aspect of Japan's policy was her steady advance in Inner Mongolia, into the provinces of Chahar and Suiyuan. Prince Teh, one of the ablest of the Inner Mongolian Princes, had to yield to Japanese pressure and broke off relations with Nanking, forming an Autonomous Mongol Council. He was compelled to admit Japanese officers to serve on this.[79] Certain setbacks were at first experienced by Japanese troops because of the strong resistance they encountered in 1936 in Suiyuan.

These anti-Japanese successes, however, were only temporary and progress by the Japanese troops, supported by the Mongol Prince Teh and others, or aided by the acquiescence of the Mongol princes in Suiyuan, turned the tables in favor of complete Japanese dominance, particularly after the new operations which started in the second half of 1937. The capture of Kalgan, the gateway to the Mongolian plateau, the subjugation of Suiyuan and the seizure of the railway from Kalgan to Paotou, at no great distance from and running parallel to the Outer Mongolian border, and the creation of a new autonomous Government of Inner Mongolia, were milestones of Japan's success. The creation of this last under the auspices of the Kwantung army at the end of October 1937 foreshadowed a conflict between the two " independent " Mongol states, the

---

[78] *The Times,* London, April 22, 1936.

[79] See M. Arens, " Japanese Agression in Inner Mongolia " in *T. O.,* No. 4 (10), October-December 1936, pp. 138-146 and Owen Lattimore, " The Lines of Cleavage in Inner Mongolia " in *Pacific Affairs,* Vol. X, No. 2, June 1937, pp. 196-201.

10

Mongolian People's Republic, and the "Mongolian Autonomous Government "—as it had been named.[80]

It must be remembered too that Japan had evolved a Monroe Doctrine for Asia. General Araki, when Minister of War, wrote an article in 1932 in which he explained that Japan considered herself as the protector of other Asiatic races. Referring to the Mongolian People's Republic, he wrote that " Japan naturally deplores the existence of a tract of wild land, such as Mongolia, bordering on a region in which she has vital interests. She would like to have a Mongolia of the Orientals with peace and security for ever. It is out of the question that she should permit it to be invaded by a foreign power. There is every possibility that Mongolia may prove a greater barrier in the way of Japan's mission of peace and order than Manchuria has been. It is no idle boast to say that if anything obstructs Japan's mission of peace, we are ready to do away with it." [81]

A look at the map will show the strategic importance of Inner Mongolia as it "encloses Outer Mongolia on the east and south." [82] Together with Manchukuo, Japan might have been able to hem in Outer Mongolia, and this long and vulnerable frontier became a source of increased friction and menace, to Outer Mongolia as well as to Siberia. On the other hand the presence of the Outer Mongolian army on their flank was a constant threat to the Japanese, particularly if considered in conjunction with the Far Eastern army of Soviet Russia stationed on the frontiers of Manchukuo.

It is perhaps no exaggeration to say that Japanese strategy in World War II might have been different if the miniature war started by Japanese and Manchukuo troops in the Nomonkhon area near the Outer Mongolian frontier in 1939 had not resulted in severe defeat. As we have seen, border incidents

[80] For details of organization of this " Mongolian Autonomous Government," see the *North China Herald*, Vol. CCV, No. 3665, November 3, 1937, p. 166.

[81] *The Times*, London, October 4, 1932, p. 13, " Japanism " from Tokyo Correspondent, referring to Kaikosha (Army Club Magazine).

[82] Owen Lattimore, *The Mongols of Manchuria*, London, 1935, p. 31.

in that region were of long standing, but the intensity of the battles, including the use of aircraft and tanks, provided a new element. There is no evidence to show that the Mongols of Manchuria took this opportunity to revolt and thus to increase the difficulties of the Japanese. However, Japanese plans had certainly received a set-back which not only influenced their general policy toward Russia, but also their plans in Manchukuo. Their strategic railway construction had brought them close to the Outer Mongolian frontier at Wen Chuan (Arshan). It was intended to continue this railway northward so as to link up with the former Chinese Eastern Railway at Hailar, but the project was not carried out, possibly because such a line would have run too near the Outer Mongolian frontier and particularly near the Nomonkhon area, where the Mixed Border Commission, set up at the end of the fighting in September 1939, was making no progress because, as an official Japanese statement put it, of " technical difficulties unforeseen by both parties; and the approach of severe winter left no choice but to suspend the work." [83]

The main explanation of the delay, however, seems to have been that Russo-Japanese relations in general were at a critical stage at that time with the Japanese anxious not to provoke Russia in any way,[84] but yet unwilling to confirm officially certain Mongolian advances made in the disputed Nomonkhon area. This appears to be borne out by the fact that the Border Commission only resumed work following the conclusion of the Neutrality Pact between Japan and the U. S. S. R. of April 13, 1941. The latter created a *modus vivendi* between the two parties insofar as in a declaration attached to the pact Japan and the U. S. S. R. pledged themselves to respect " the territorial integrity and inviolability " of the Mongolian People's

---

[83] Announcement by the Board of Information, June 16, 1941 in *Contemporary Japan*, July 1941; p. 962. For original agreement of Nov. 19, 1939 between Molotov and Togo on the setting up of the mixed border commission see *Moscow News*, Nov. 20, 1939.

[84] *Nazi-Soviet Relations 1939-1941*, Department of State, Washington 1948, p. 301. Memorandum of conversation between Ribbentrop and Matsuoka, March 28, 1941.

Republic and of Manchukuo.[85] Work on the demarcation of the frontier was begun on June 27, 1941. All preliminary work "eliminating completely . . . technical difficulties" between the representatives of Manchukuo and the M. P. R. had been done at Chita,[86] on Russian territory, and the negotiations ended with the ratification of a Mongol-Manchukuo border demarcation agreement in May 1942, six months after Pearl Harbor.

The Japanese occupation of Manchuria and Inner Mongolia has left a legacy among the Mongols of these regions, the discussion of which falls outside our field. But we cannot refrain from adding that the recent history of Outer Mongolia might have been very different if Japanese strategy had turned northwest instead of south.

It seems curious today that not even after Russia had denounced the Neutrality Pact on April 5, 1945, did Japan suspect that Russia would enter the Far Eastern war. She became suspicious only when the Chinese Foreign Minister visited Moscow at the beginning of July 1945, when Japan tried desperately to arrange at the last moment [87] for Soviet mediation. It has also been said that Japan offered to make Manchuria a neutral zone, i. e. Japanese troops would be withdrawn while Russian troops would keep out.[88] Finally, two days after the first atomic bomb had fallen on Japan, Russia declared war on August 8, 1945, which was followed by the same declaration by the M. P. R. on August 10. Subsequent events culminating in the defeat of the Japanese-Manchukuo troops by Soviet-Mongolian forces [89] are described in a memorandum which the Mongols submitted to the Far Eastern Commission in Washington dated October 18, 1946. On the

[85] For text see Harriet L. Moore, *Soviet Far Eastern Policy*, 1931-1945, Princeton, N. J., 1945, pp. 200-1; also Frederick L. Schuman, *Soviet Policy at Home and Abroad*, London, 1948, pp. 408-9.

[86] *Contemporary Japan, op. cit.*, the original Molotov-Togo agreement specified, however that "the second half of the Commission's sittings will be held in the city of Harbin." *Moscow News, op. cit.*

[87] James F. Byrnes, *Speaking Frankly*, London, n. d., p. 211.

[88] M. Kato, *The Lost War*, New York, 1946, pp. 231-35.

[89] The Russians gave Japanese losses as 80,000 killed. *The Times*, London, September 11, 1945.

same day when the government of the Mongolian People's Republic requested of the Council of Foreign Ministers that they be permitted to have a representative on the Far Eastern Commission they claimed that since 1935 they had been " one of the bulwarks of peace in the Far East and an effective barrier against the extension of the aggressive designs of the Japanese imperialists in the interior of Asia." [90]

[90] *Soviet Monitor,* Oct. 25, 1946.

CHAPTER V

RELATIONS WITH OTHER POWERS

A. FRANCE, AN ALLY OF RUSSIA

HOW FAR Outer Mongolia was a bone of contention between Russia, China and Japan, whose attitudes we have been discussing until now, can only be seen by reviewing the policies of other powers. We have already seen that Tsarist Russia's attitude toward the recognition of China's suzerainty over Outer Mongolia was to a great extent conditioned by her respect for the Powers' policy of preserving the integrity of China. The attitude that occasioned least anxiety to St. Petersburg was that of France.

Gérard, French Minister in Peking from 1893 to 1897 and later Ambassador to Japan, wrote that his instructions from Paris stipulated that in all diplomatic action he was to undertake in Peking he was never to forget to cooperate with France's ally, Russia. "Since the interests of Russia in the Far East were wider and more important than ours, it was natural and necessary that she should be assured of our support and that the character of our alliance should be apparent to China herself, and to the Powers represented in Peking." Events in the Far East were to be the first test and the first demonstration of the Franco-Russian alliance.[1] If this was the position toward the close of the 19th century, still more was Franco-Russian collaboration a reality in 1911 and the years following.

At the beginning of November 1911 Isvolskii, the Russian Ambassador in Paris, sent to the Quai d'Orsay a note expressing the conviction of his government that the French Government would not lend any assistance to the efforts of the Chinese

---

[1] Gérard, Auguste, *Ma Mission en Chine*, 1894-1897, Paris, 1918, pp. XXII-XXIV; see for instance "Joint French-Russian Declaration on Policy in the Far East," 1902. *U. S. For. Rel. 1902*, p. 931.

Government to modify the existing administrative and military position in Mongolia, Manchuria, and Chinese Turkistan which would be detrimental to Russian interests.[2] Commenting on this, the French Ambassador in Constantinople expressed regret that the Far East seemed again to be Russia's chief preoccupation. This repetition of old mistakes, which in 1905 had had as bad results for France as for Russia, did not inspire him with any hope that " the attention of our ally " would be concentrated upon European affairs, which were the chief concern of France.[3] On the other hand the French Chargé d'Affaires in St. Petersburg perceived no inconvenience whatever in giving to Russia an engagement of the kind asked for by Isvolskii, although he claimed that, while France was totally disinterested in Mongolia and Chinese Turkistan, this was not the case with Manchuria.[4]

The official answer returned by de Selves, the French Minister for Foreign Affairs, early in 1912, confirmed the support of the French Government for all legitimate Russian rights and interests in Northern China, whether in North Manchuria or in Mongolia and Chinese Tukistan. " The policy which we have constantly pursued in this respect is a sure indication of the policy which we will adopt in the future in these regions which especially interest our allies." [5] However, in an instruction to the French Ambasador in St. Petersburg he added a warning that even if one recognized the legitimate ambitions of Russia one should not forget that, from the economic point of view, the historical tendency of international politics has been against the assertion of exclusive rights in particular territories by particular countries. This was shown in the case of Morocco, where France had to accept the prin-

[2] *DDF*, Tome 1, No. 18, p. 15, Isvolskii, Russian Ambassador in Paris to M. de Selves, Minister of Foreign Affairs, November 4, 1911.

[3] *DDF*, No. 279, p. 261, M. Bourpard, French Ambassador in Constantinople to M. de Selves, December 2, 1911.

[4] *DDF*, No. 322, p. 314, M. Panapien,. French Chargé d'Affaires in St. Petersburg to M. de Selves, December 8, 1911.

[5] *DDF*, No. 433, p. 441, M. de Selves to M. Isvolskii, January 4, 1912; also Isvolskii, Vol. 2, No. 185, p. 25.

ciple of equal rights for all. One might like or dislike this tendency, but Russia should not insist in marching against the " will of the world." [6]

In the discussions during the first half of 1912 over a reorganization loan, France supported the Russian demand that the loan should not be used by China to the detriment of Russian interests in Manchuria, Mongolia and Chinese Turkistan. The French representative in the Consortium of Four (American, British, French and German bank groups), Baron Hély d'Oissel, reassured the Russians by declaring that in the case of the Consortium engaging in activities hostile to Russian special interests, the French group would consider it a reason for severing all connection with it.[7] But the French Government refused to yield to Russian pressure—coming mainly from M. Isvolskii, the Russian Ambassador, and the Russo-Asiatic Bank—to join at once a new Russo-Japanese-Belgian group which the Russian Government intended to set up as a rival of the Consortium of Four, which would then have become an Anglo-German-American Group. " Such a combination," read the instructions of the Quai d'Orsay, " does not take account of French interests and is exclusively based on Russian interests." French interests, it was added, were considerable in southern China primarily because of her common frontier with French Indochina. France had given proof of her loyalty to her ally on many occasions and especially by persuading the other members of the Consortium to let the Russian group join them, which it (the Russian group) finally

---

[6] *DDF,* No. 448, pp. 459, 462, M. de Selves to M. Georges Louis, French Ambassador in St. Petersburg, January 9, 1912. Instructions; Draft of December 5, 1911, revised January 9, 1912. The following characterization of Mongolia is to be found at the end of the instructions, p. 463: " La Mongolie, extérieure à l'Empire, hostile, non colonisée et sous l'influence russe."

[7] Isvolskii, Vol. II, No. 232, Isvolskii to Sazonov, March 1/14, 1912, p. 66; also No. 178 Memorandum of the Russian Ministry of Foreign Affairs 1912, p. 17; No. 250, Sazonov to Isvolskii, March 24/April 6, 1912 (referring to Selves' promise of support, cf. No. 185 of January 4, 1912), p. 80: " Based on this promise of which I take note with greatest satisfaction, we have decided to participate in the Chinese Reorganisation Loan, convinced as we are that we can count on the support of France in eliminating those conditions of this loan which might be prejudicial to our interests."

did at the end of March 1912 with reservations concerning Manchuria, Mongolia and Chinese Turkistan.[8]

That Russian activities in the Far East generally, and particularly in Mongolia, were reviewed by France exclusively in the light of the Franco-Russian entente is evident from the attitude taken by Poincaré, then Minister of Foreign Affairs, when in November 1912 the Russo-Mongolian agreement of Urga was communicated to him by the Russians who, however, omitted to forward the commercial protocol concluded at the same time and mentioned in the second article of the political agreement. " Because of the absence of any French political or commercial interest in Mongolia " wrote Poincaré to the French Ambassador in St. Petersburg, " and because of our relations with Russia, we have actually no reason to reveal this omission, the more so because it can be advantageous not to know of stipulations which we should have difficulty in accepting if they were contrary to the universally accepted principle of commercial equality of nations in China." The French Ambassador was instructed to thank the Russian Government for this communication and to let them know that " according to their wishes " the French Government took notice of it. At the same time Poincaré enclosed for Sazonov's inspection the text of a note of protest from the Chinese Foreign Office (Wai Chiao Pu), which had been officially transmitted to him by the Chinese Legation in Paris, but added that he had left it unanswered.[9]

---

[8] *DDF*, Tome 1, No. 448, pp. 460-61; for pressure of France on Russia to participate in Four Power Consortium see *ibid.*. Tome II, No. 174, pp. 166-67, M. Poincaré to Chargé d'Affaires in St. Petersburg, March 8, 1912; cf. also the report of a conversation between Poincaré and Isvolskii of March 9, 1912 in No. 178, pp. 170-71. There is no other record of this conversation and the note bears the annotation: " Indications données par M. Paléologue." The editors of the Doc. Dipl. Fran. who obviously could not criticize the reliability of M. Paléologue, contrast this conversation, in which Poincaré is reported to have taken a very anti-Russian attitude, with a telegram published in Isvolskii, Vol. 2, p. 56, which like those referred to above reveals the critical but by no means hostile attitude of the French Government; see also No. 283 Note du Départment of March 31. drawn up by M. Berthelot. As to the agreement of the Russian Government to enter the Consortium see No. 307, Annex IV Aide-Mémoire, March 24/April 6, 1912, p. 320.

[9] *DDF*, Tome IV, No. 459, p. 471, M. Poincaré, Minister of Foreign Affairs to M. Georges Louis, November 12, 1912.

The Chinese Government addressed itself to Conty, the French Minister in Peking, for mediation, and the latter drafted a note in which the Chinese recognized the Russo-Mongolian agreement and declared that it did not violate their sovereign rights. In this note the relations of China to Mongolia were said to be the same as those of Turkey to Egypt. At first the Chinese were inclined to accept the note, but afterwards changed their minds.[10]

What actually happened was that President Yuan Shih-k'ai asked the French Minister to come to see him, and an interview took place on November 23, 1912. Conty, expecting that the subject of the discussion would be Mongolia, first went to consult his Russian colleague " as to what language he could use on this occasion without causing complications." He advised the President to enter into negotiations with Russia which would end in a recognition of the terms of the Russo-Mongolian agreement, though not necessarily in the recognition of the agreement itself. He then repeated the Russian demand that Chinese colonization and the stationing of Chinese troops in Mongolia should be prohibited.[11]

The French Minister in Peking came into direct contact with the Mongolian problem again when, in the middle of 1924, he received from the Mongolian Ministry of Foreign Affairs two identical letters, stating that Mongolia had declared her independence and had concluded a trade treaty with Russia. France was asked to enter into direct negotiations with the Mongolian Government and to send a consul to Urga to conclude a trade agreemnt.[12] But before reporting this official action on the part of the Mongolian Government to Paris, the French Minister made enquiries of his Russian colleague as to the Russian attitude in this matter. Thereupon the latter received elaborate instructions from Sazonov expressing the

[10] Korostovets, p. 211.

[11] *DDF*, Tome IV, No. 609, pp. 629-630, M. A. R. Conty, French Minister in Peking to M. Poincaré, December 2, 1912.

[12] *IBZI*, Vol. I, 3, No. 147, p. 137, The Russian Chargé d'Affaires in Peking (Grave) to the Russian Foreign Minister, June 2/May 20, 1914.

hope that the French Government would leave the communications of the Mongolian Government unanswered, behaving in the same way as it did when the Mongols made similar advances to the French Consul in Harbin and to the French Ambassador in St. Petersburg. The French Minister promised that he would pass on these presentations to the Quai d'Orsay and said that he supposed that his Government would take the same attitude as it had done in the past.[13]

In a word, the French Government never for one moment obstructed Tsarist Russia's Mongolian policy. On the contrary, on one or two occasions at least, the French Minister acted as an advocate of that policy to the Chinese Government.

No details are known of the French Government's attitude toward Soviet policy in Outer Mongolia. An official communiqué concerning the international status of Outer Mongolia was issued by the Soviet Government through its Paris Embassy in 1925. Franco-Russian relations became closer and closer, approaching the spirit if not the letter of the prewar cooperation. The French are reported—and there is no reason to doubt it—to have insisted upon their refusal to come to the aid of Russia in the event of a Far Eastern conflict. The text of the Franco-Russian Treaty of Mutual Assistance unmistakably refers only to unprovoked aggression " on the part of any European state." [14] Now it is evident that the Russians bound themselves to afford actual military assistance in Mon-

---

[13] *IBZI*, No. 154, pp. 142-143, The Assistant of the Russian Foreign Minister (Neratov) to Grave, June 4/May 22, 1914.

[14] League of Nations *Treaty Series*, Vol. CLXVII, 1936 (No. 3856-3882), No. 3881. France and Union of Soviet Soc. Rep. Treaty of Mutual Assistance, and Protocol of Signature, Signed at Paris, May 2, 1935. Original in French and Russian. English translation pp. 404-406, Art. 1 and Art. 2 on p. 404; see also *Revue Gén. de Droit Int. Publ.*, Vol. XLII, 1935, p. 650 and *The Bulletin of International News*, Vol. XI, No. 23, May 16, 1935, pp. 3-8, mainly p. 4; *ibid.*, Vol. XII, No. 16, February 22, 1936, p. 3: " It should be noted that the obligations of mutual assistance became operative only in the case of an unprovoked attack directly upon the European territory of France or Russia. . . ." For use of term alliance compare the words of M. Archimbaud, rapporteur of the budget of the Ministry of War, before the French Chamber of Deputies, Nov. 23, 1934: ". . . il y a entre la Russie et la France une union étroite—je ne prononce pas le mot d'alliance— . . .," see *Journal Officiel*, November 24, 1934, p. 2572, col. 1.

golia, by the Soviet-Mongolian Protocol, in a much stronger way than they ever did in Tsarist days. Obviously they did this because of Japanese and Manchukuo designs upon their neighbor, the Mongolian People's Republic. It is, therefore, worth while mentioning that the French Ambassador to Japan published at the end of October 1936, three months after relinquishing his post, a declaration in which he insisted that Japan, in spite of whatever may be the general opinion in the West, was in no way (" nullement ") guided by a desire for new conquests for herself or her protégé when aiming at the creation of a buffer zone around Manchukuo. " She wants only to consolidate what she has and what exists." [15] The inference which could be drawn from this reasoning, which, however, the French diplomat did not draw, was that Russia did not need to trouble unnecessarily about Japan's aims.

B. Great Britain: No Special Interests

An indirect reference to Mongolia appeared in the Anglo-Russian railway agreement of 1899 in which Great Britain engaged herself not to seek railway concessions north of the Great Wall either on her own acount or on behalf of her subjects. This region included not only Manchuria but also Mongolia and was greater than the British had originally suggested.

In the middle of 1906, during the negotiations for an Anglo-Russian agreement relating to Tibet, the British Foreign Office was asked by the Russians what it thought of their action in Mongolia. The reply was that, " as the result of carefully watching Russian activity there," the British Government felt that Russia contemplated some action in that region.[16] The Russians responded that they were very anxious for the main-

[15] *Le Temps*, October 25, 1936, p. 3, Declaration de M. Fernand Pila, ancien ambassadeur de France au Japan.

[16] *B. D.*, Vol. IV, No. 314, pp. 336-349, Memorandum on the Correspondence relating to the proposed Agreement between Great Britain and Russia on the subject of Mongolia, July 1906. (Conversation between Sir C. Hardinge and M. Poklevskii-Koriell, 1st Secretary at the Russian Embassy in London), p. 341.

tenance of the status quo in Mongolia, and enquired whether the British Government could agree to some formula compatible with the terms of the Japanese alliance. Sir Charles Hardinge, the Permanent Undersecretary, gave an assurance that the Anglo-Japanese Alliance was formed expressly for the maintenance of the status quo in Asia. But he pointed out that the Chinese could hardly be expected to give up their right to do what they liked in their own territory. The British Government could only lend its diplomatic assistance " to induce the Chinese Government to recognise the Russian frontier, and to abstain from any interference with it." The Japanese Government might assist in such a policy as well. Therefore " any proposals which the Rusian Government might make with reference to the status quo in Mongolia would receive the careful consideration of His Majesty's Government." [17]

Early in 1907 Isvolskii, then Foreign Minister, enquired of Sir Arthur Nicholson, the British Ambassador, whether the latter's Government would be disposed to make some reference to the maintenance of the status quo in Mongolia when the general basis of the agreement between the two countries had been settled. He suggested that it might be possible to state " the desire of the two Governments that no alterations should be introduced into the existing administrative system in Mongolia." [18] A short time later Sir Edward Grey mentioned this suggestion to the Japanese Ambassador in London, who denied that a similar proposal had come up during the Russo-Japanese negotiations.[19] Grey thought it advisable to lay down some formula " such as a promise to give our diplomatic support to the ensuring of security on the whole extent of the Chinese frontier." [20] In the " Mongolian Frontier Formula," which was then agreed upon, the two Governments promised each other

---

[17] *Ibid.*, p. 342 in conversation with Count Benckendorff, the Russian Ambassador in London.

[18] *Ibid.*, Sir A. Nicholson to F. O., January 5, 1907; see also Edit. Note p. 284, The Mongolian Frontier Formula.

[19] *Ibid.*, Sir Edward Grey to Mr. Lowther, March 7, 1907.

[20] *Ibid.*, Sir Edward Grey to Mr. Lowther, March 18, 1907.

support on the whole of the frontier in question.[21] A Russian enquiry as to whether the word " s'appuyer " implied both material and diplomatic support was answered by Grey in a letter to the British Ambassador in St. Petersburg, in unequivocal language: " That is not a place where we would give material support: ' s'appuyer ' must, therefore, be diplomatic support, good offices, or whatever other varieties of support there may be, given at Peking or where it would be useful. . . . The formula simply means that our influence will be used to prevent Russia being disturbed on the Chinese part of her frontiers." Or, as a telegraphic version ran: Great Britain " could not give armed support in such a place as the Mongolian frontier." [22]

The Russians continued for a while to consider the formula, but at the same time brought the negotiations with Japan to a successful conclusion. In May Hardinge told Nicholson that as they had heard nothing more from the Russians about the Mongolian proposal he thought that the matter had been forgotten, adding " I hope so." [23] As a matter of fact, Russia did not take up the question again for the reason given by Grey himself, when in August 1907 he attributed it to her having " succeeded in settling that with Japan. Our agreement with Russia would, therefore, relate only to Tibet, Afghanistan, and Persia." [24]

At the end of 1910 the subject of the respective interests of Great Britain in Tibet and Russia in Mongolia was mentioned again in a long report made by Korostovets, the Russian Minister in Peking. He contended that Russia would have to take measures to counter China's active economic and military

[21] Ibid., p. 285 (Enclosure in No. 262 a) The Mongolian Frontier Formula: " Les Gouvernments de la Grande Bretagne et de la Russie s'étant mutuellement engagés à respecter l'intégrité et l'indépendence de la Chine et animés du sincère désir de voir l'ordre et le développment pacifique se maintenir sur toute l'étendue de leurs frontières avec la Chine, s'engagent à s'appuyer mutuellement pour assurer la paix et la sécurité sur leurs frontières respectives."

[22] Ibid., Sir Edward Grey to Sir A. Nicholson, April 1, 1907. Telegram April 3, 1907.

[23] Ibid., p. 286, May 2, 1907.

[24] Ibid., p. 289, Sir Edward Grey to Sir C. MacDonald, August 14, 1907.

policy in Outer Mongolia. But before doing so it would be advisable to know whether England would look with favor upon Russia's action or support it by means of diplomatic pressure in Peking. The British Government had unequivocally expressed its opinion regarding administrative measures in Tibet and the presence of Chinese troops there. From her own experience Great Britain should realize that Russia had grounds for anxiety over China's projects, especially as Russia's Chinese frontiers, in contrast to those of Tibet and India, lay completely open and without natural protection. If England would recognize Mongolia as a Russian sphere of influence Russia could renounce all claims in Tibet, where she had unimportant interests. Korostovets thought that a proposal for an agreement on these lines would be favorably received in London, as the Tibetan situation, with the second flight of the Dalai Lama, seemed likely to be permanently critical. He suggested that the negotiations with the British Government could begin with a discussion of the question of scientific expeditions to Tibet.[25]

Sazonov thereupon enquired of Benckendorff, the Russian Ambassador in London, whether the Russian Government should postpone the communication of their assent to the proposal for the exclusion of scientific expeditions from Tibet until the British Government has acquiesced to certain demands relating to Mongolia. He also wished to know how far Russia could in general count on Britain's support in opposing China's Mongolian policy. Benckendorff, in replying to this enquiry, rejected the idea of using the question of scientific expeditions to Tibet in order to put pressure on Great Britain. The matter was far too unimportant to have any effect on British policy toward China in general, and he was afraid that Whitehall would not understand reference to it in this connection. Of course, Tibet played an important part in Anglo-Russian relations in the Far East, and the parallel between Russia's preferential rights in Mongolia and those of England in Tibet should be emphasized. However, he insisted on the importance

---

[25] Benckendorff, Vol. 1, pp. 382-383, The Minister in Peking to the Russian Foreign Minister, November 3/16, 1910.

of good relations between Russia and Great Britain on other questions, chiefly in connection with Persia. " Russian opinion in the question of the Bagdad railway will react upon the English attitude toward the Trans-Persian railway and, I believe, such a railway will rivet more than anything else British interests in Tibet to Russian interests in Mongolia." [26]

When in December 1911, after the proclamation of their independence by the Mongols, Korostovets tried to win Sazonov over to an active Russian policy in Outer Mongolia, he advanced as an argument the fact that not even Great Britain would be able to find there " so-called British interests." [27] That no difficulties were to be expected from Great Britain was well known to Sazonov with Korostovets' comment; only a few days before he had spoken to a French diplomat about the entente with Great Britain, of which he was an avowed supporter and which offered, in his view, a guarantee of Russia's Asiatic policy.[28]

In March 1912 Benckendorff submitted to Grey a memorandum setting forth Russia's demand for certain guarantees with respect to Mongolia and Manchuria. Grey's answer was couched in the following terms: " His Majesty's Government has not failed to take notice of the communication and they recognise Russia's right to take measures which may be necessary for the protection of her special rights and interests in North Manchuria, Mongolia and Western China as far as they follow from Russian treaties and agreements with China." [29]

[26] *Ibid.*, pp. 401-402, Sazonov to the Russian Ambassador in London, Count Benckendorff, November 27/December 10, 1910; p. 413, Benckendorff to Sazonov, December 7/10, 1910.

[27] Korostovetsz, p. 128.

[28] *DDF*, Vol. I, p. 283, No. 297, M. Beau, French Ambassador in Berne to M. de Selves, December 5, 1911, Conversation with Sazonov. Cf. also inquiry of M. de Selves addressed to M. Paul Cambon, French Ambassador in London, November 8, 1911 (No. 55): " Could you make inquiries about the British attitude towards the probable initiatives of Russia in these regions? Will the British Government, for example, permit the Russian Government to forbid China to modify the actual administrative and military status of these regions? Will they, consequently, refuse their consent to any Chinese loan to these regions contracted ouside of Russia? "

[29] Benckendorff, Vol. 2, No. 579, Benckendorff to Sazonov, March 16/29, 1912. See also Isvolskii, Vol. II, p. 53, No. 219; compare *U. S. For. Rel. 1912*, p. 76, The British Ambassador to the Acting Secretary of State, April 2, 1912.

But it was Grey's turn to introduce the topic of Mongolia during the visit of Sazonov to Balmoral in September 1912. He then tried to draw a parallel between England's position in Tibet and Russia's position in Mongolia.[30] But he encountered a strong disinclination on the part of the Russian Foreign Minister to admit that there was any resemblance between the two situations. On the contrary, Sazonov pointed out that England had obligations toward Russia with respect to Tibet under certain agreements, whereas the Russians had not entered into any engagements with England regarding Mongolia, where, moreover, the British had neither political nor economic interests. Sazonov adds in his report of this interview that Grey had apparently realized the strength of this argument and did not attempt to answer it. " For the purpose of the maintenance of friendly relations between us and England " Grey was acquainted, in general terms and very confidentially, with the nature of the mission of the State Counsellor Korostovets to Urga.[31] About a month after this meeting Grey was asked in the House of Commons whether the Russian Government had consulted the British Government before dispatching the Korostovets Mission to Mongolia " to dissuade the Mongols from their allegiance to China; and whether a mission for that purpose was a breach of international law and of all the treaties made for the preservation of the integrity of China? " Grey answered: " I am not aware that the object of the Russian Mission is what the Hon. Member states it to be. I have no reason to believe that it is intended to alter the status quo in Outer Mongolia." [32] After the conclusion of the Urga agreement the same member asked a question in which he implied

[30] Cf. also *G. P.*, Vol. 32, No. 11784, Ambassador in London Count Metternich to Chancellor Bethmann-Hollweg, February 7, 1912, p. 205, " Sir Edward Grey is of the opinion . . . that just as much as Mongolia was useful for Russia as a buffer-state so was Tibet for England."

[31] *K. A.*, Vol. 3, Report of Sazonov to the Tsar, pp. 22-23, also Isvolskii, Vol. II, No. 508, p. 295; for Grey's report: *B. D.*, Vol. IX, part 1, No. 803, p. 758; also *G. P.*, Vol. 32, No. 11899, note of the Director of the Disconto Gesellschaft, January 11, 1912, p. 328.

[32] House of Commons, *Parliamentary Debates*, Vol. 42, October 24, 1912, col. 2344.

that the British Government had consented to it; this Grey denied categorically.[33]

When in 1914 Britain desired to free herself from the restrictions placed upon her liberty of action in Tibet by the Anglo-Russian Convention of 1907, her ability was certainly impaired by the absence of any agreement with Russia with respect to Mongolia, which can be attributed mainly to her own conduct in 1907. Benckendorff, the Russian Ambassador in London, whose utterances carry additional weight because of the fact that he was more than once Grey's mouthpiece and the gifted and sympathetic intermediary between Grey and Sazonov,[34] reported to his Government in February that " in Tibet also conditions have changed; they change daily to China's advantage, and the English are bound hand and foot by the Convention (of 1907); but, in truth, what is Tibet to us, and how much more important it is to England than to us." [35] The Russian Minister in Peking believed that " the only compensation England could give us in return for our recognition of her freedom of action and of her privileged position in Tibet to which I could point would be the recognition of our exclusive sphere of influence in Northern Manchuria, Mongolia and Western China." [36]

The Imperial Ministry of Foreign Affairs, however, did not fall in with this view. Sazonov recalled that England had originally expressed her willingness to negotiate " on the basis of mutual recognition of Russia's preferential position in Mongolia and England's in Tibet," and that he had " refused such a basis of negotiations." A proposal put forward by the Ministry runs: " If the question of the revision of the Anglo-Russian agreement of 1907 regarding Tibet were raised, we could

---

[33] *Ibid.*, Vol. 44, November 28, 1912, col. 1457. In the same volume other parliamentary questions relating to Mongolia will be found, mainly asked by the same member (Mr. Grinnel), but also by Mr. George Lloyd (later Lord Lloyd), see col. 451-452, col. 2455; see also Vol. 46, January 9, 1913, col. 1346.

[34] *IBZI*, Vol. 1, 2, Preface of the Editor of the German Edition Prof. Hoetzsch, pp. III-IV.

[35] *Ibid.*, Vol. I, 1, p. 329, No. 398, Benckendorff to Sazonov, February 25/12 1914.

[36] *Ibid.*, No. 430, p. 430; also B. de Siebert, G. A. Schreiner, *Entente Diplomacy and the World War* (London, 1921), p. 42, February 26/March 11, 1914, no. 104.

demand a certain compensation for the virtual surrender of Tibet to the protectorate of England; we are sensible that this is the aim of England, therefore our demands would be serious." [37] But the possible concessions enumerated refer only to Afghanistan and Persia and ignore the Far Eastern situation. And these countries, with Tibet, are those to which Grey referred in August 1907, after having willingly removed Mongolia from the list of points to be covered by the Anglo-Russian agreement.

There was indeed, as the German Secretary of State wrote to the German Ambassador in London in April 1914, " no special talent of construction " necessary to imagine that the basis of negotiations between Russia and Great Britain would be a transaction in which the two recognized Mongolia and Tibet as their respective spheres of influence.[38] But this contemporary comment, as we can see today, over-simplified the matter to a considerable extent. A comparison between Mongolia and Tibet made to the German Ambassador by high officials of the British Foreign Office after the date of this letter seems worthy of note. Sir Arthur Nicholson, then Permanent Under-secretary of State for Foreign Affairs, and Sir W. Langley had nothing to say against considering Mongolia as a part of China. But they declared that Tibet did not belong, and had never belonged, to China.[39] Since this statement is historically untrue, the only explanation of it that can be offered is that it was an ingenious way of making it clear to the German Government that the affairs of Tibet were Britain's business and not that of China, let alone that of any other country, such as Germany.

There are two other matters besides this incident that link the affairs of Mongolia to those of Tibet. First, British demands in Tibet were certainly encouraged by Russia's success

---

[37] *Ibid.*, No. 384, p. 381. Note drawn up in the Ministry of Foreign Affairs of February 20/March 5, 1914. This draft is identical with Sazonov's letter.

[38] *G. P.*, Vol. 32, No. 12009, p. 447, April 5, 1914.

[39] *Ibid.*, No. 12010, The Ambassador in London, Prince Lichnowsky, to Chancellor von Bethmann-Hollweg, April 8, 1914.

in Mongolia and by the triviality of the resistance on the part of China encountered there. It may be remarked that a British note to the Chinese Government on the subject of Tibet, dated September 1912, was first published in the American press, apparently at the instigation of Russia, because the Russians were " at pains to dispel the odium attending their own actions in Mongolia by pointing to the similar plans of England in Tibet," and that they were " decidedly successful in this intention." [40] The treaty of Simla (1914) with its division of Tibet into Inner and Outer Tibet—which was later rejected by the Chinese Government—seems also to follow closely the Mongolian model.

The other point is that during the conference of Simla " the atmosphere was clouded," as Sir Charles Bell, the chief British delegate reports, by fears that Tibet and Mongolia had concluded a treaty of alliance. It was feared that such a treaty " was . . . likely to establish an ever-increasing Russian influence which could not fail to endanger British and Indian interests." And it was thought to be an indirect means whereby Russia was endeavoring to avoid the restrictions placed upon her as well as upon Great Britain by the agreement of 1907—to the effect that neither Government was to send representatives to Lhasa, nor to obtain concessions or other rights in Tibet. [41] However, these anxieties proved to be largely unfounded.

[40] *Ibid.*, No. 11990, p. 424, The German Minister in Peking to Bethmann-Hollweg, September 10, 1912; see also *U. S. For. Rel., 1912*, p. 86, The American Minister in Peking to the Secretary of State, August 31, 1912: " From the Foreign Office I learn that on the 17th instant the British minister presented a memorandum that recognises China's suzerainty, not sovereignty, over Tibet; objects to Chinese action during the last three years in interfering in the internal affairs of Tibet, declares this interference to be opposed to the spirit of the 1906 treaty, which demands joint action by Great Britain and China; and declares that unless China agrees to these demands the British Government cannot recognise the Republic and will forbid the entrance of Chinese into Tibet via India."

[41] Sir Charles Bell, *Tibet, Past and Present*, Oxford, 1924, pp. 229-30, p. 151. Art. III and Art. IV of the Russo-British Convention of 1907 said: " Art. III. The British and Russian Governments respectively engage not to send Representatives to Lhasa. Art. IV. The two H. C. P. engage neither to seek nor to obtain for themselves or their subjects, any concessions for railways, roads, telegraphs, and

It seems most probable that the attitude which the British Government took at the beginning of March 1914 in regard to British trade rights in Mongolia was also connected with the Tibetan problem and was meant as a sort of pressure on the Russian Government to make it more willing to agree to the contemplated change in Tibet. For whereas in May 1912 the British Minister in Peking, had reassured his Russian colleague with the words, " Now you can undoubtedly proceed to Western China and Outer Mongolia without anxiety," [42] an aide-memoire from the British Embassy in St. Petersburg to Sazonov went so far as to threaten Russia with her permanent " cauchemar " [43]—entry into direct relations with the Mongolian Government. This document ran: " His Majesty's Government propose, with the acquiescence of the Imperial Government, to instruct His Majesty's Minister at Peking to enter into negotiations with the Mongolian Government with a view to concluding an arrangement for securing fair terms and the maintenance of the open door for the British trade. The Russo-Mongolian Protocol, whilst giving no special privileges to Russian goods, secures to Russian subjects the right to import into Mongolia goods of any origin free of duty. H. M.'s Government desire to secure, under the guard of the Most-Favored Nation treatment, the same privileges for British subjects and their goods as those enjoyed by the subjects of Russia as well as an undertaking that no import, transit or other duties shall be imposed on the produce or manufacture of any part of H. M.'s territories which are not equally imposed on those of any foreign country." [44]

mines, or other rights in Tibet." See MacMurray, Vol. I, p. 677. Cf. House of Commons, *Parliamentary Debates*, Vol. LXIII, January 18, 1914, col. 1258-59, Question of Mr. George Lloyd (later Lord Lloyd; President of the Royal Central Asian Society, 1937-38).

[42] *Entente Policy and the World War, op. cit.*, p. 38, No. 32, The Russian Minister at Peking to the Russian Minister of Foreign Affairs, May 1/14, 1912.

[43] This phrase is borrowed from Bismarck's famous " cauchemar des coalitions."

[44] For original English text used see: *MOEI*, Ser. III, Tome I, No. 363, pp. 477-478, Memorandum of the British Embassy in St. Petersburg to the Russian Minister of Foreign Affairs, March 3/February 18, 1914; also (in German) in *IBZI*, I, 1, No. 363, p. 364.

The answer of the Russian Foreign Minister, presented as an aide-memoire two and a half months later, stated that the impression gained from the British document was that the claims of the British Government for trade with Mongolia were without precedent. Its words were: "'This is in direct contradiction to the principles which have been the basis of the trade agreements with China. The British Government asks for its sea-borne trade privileges which no other power, Russia not excluded, enjoys, neither in China proper nor in the territories which are under Chinese suzerainty. The Imperial Ministry ventures to hope that the British Government will be content with the conditions which the treaties with the Chinese Government create for British trade, and that it will cease to consider asking for more favorable treatment in Mongolia than Russia enjoys." [45]

In June 1914 Sir Edward Grey admitted in the House of Commons that "His Majesty's Government had been given to understand from private sources that the Mongolian Government would be prepared to welcome a British representative. There has, however, been no opportunity for the Mongolian Government to make an official communication of this nature." [46] It seems to be something of a coincidence that, at about the same time that Grey made this statement, the British Minister in Peking forwarded to his Government, without comment, an official letter from the Mongolian Ministry of Foreign Affairs, couched in terms similar to those of the letter received by the French Minister.[47]

The Great War which broke out in the summer of that year prevented any further discussion of the question of Mongolia between the allies, Russia and Great Britain.

In post-war years, attempts were made by British firms, up to that time practically unrepresented in Outer Mongolia, to

---

[45] Aide-Mémoire of the Russian Minister of Foreign Affairs to the British Ambassador in St. Petersburg, Buchanan, May 8/21, 1914. *IBZI*, I, 3, p. 44, No. 46; *MOEI*, Tome 3, Ser. III, No. 46 in original French.

[46] House of Commons, *Parliamentary Debates*, Vol. LXIII, June 16, 1914, cols. 903-04.

[47] *IBZI*, I, 3, p. 143, footnote, telegram from Grave of June 5, 1914.

take part in trade with that country. The British International Export Company began to buy and slaughter sheep from Mongolia and to export sheep skins to England and America. It established a slaughterhouse in Harbin and a factory where the skins were cured. Another British concern, Kaufman and Company, is said to have invested heavily in Outer Mongolia. Both firms, however, got little out of their endeavors and with the new regime in Outer Mongolia and the increasing influence of Soviet Russia soon had to close down altogether.[48]

Thus as regards post-war policy, apart from considerations of a general character, such as the denunciation by the Soviets of all treaties concluded by the Tsarist Government, and the reaffirmation of the principle of the integrity of China by the Washington Conference (at which, however, Russia was represented only by delegates of the Far Eastern Republic, acting as observers), nothing seems to indicate that any special interest in Mongolian affairs was evinced by Great Britain. But one curious incident may be mentioned, responsibility for its authenticity resting with Korostovets, who refers to it in his book. At the end of September 1925 the "Little Hural" of the Mongolian People's Republic decided to convoke the "Great Hural," in which all people of Mongolian origin were expected to participate. For this purpose a delegation was sent to Tibet. And "as was learned from Soviet sources" the British police (sic) in Tibet received instructions to prevent the entry of the delegation. It succeeded in entering Tibet illicitly, however, and wanted to proceed to Siam. The British Government saw Soviet machinations behind the journey and lodged a strong protest.[49] Now whether this account is regarded

---

[48] Larson, p. 251; W. Karamisheff, *Mongolia and Western China*, p. 201 and 204; for the pre-war years 1912-13 Perry-Ayscough and Otter-Barry write in their book, p. 137: "There are no English trading in Mongolia and but few merchants of any nationality other than Russian and Chinese." For undue stress on Anglo-Saxon interest see Dr. Friedrich Otto, *China: Wirtschaftspolitische Landeskunde,* Petermanns Mitteilungen, Ergänzungsheft No. 194, Gotha, 1927, p. 23.

[49] Korostovets, pp. 342-43. Cf. *IBZI*, I, 2, No. 233, The Russian General Consul in Simla to Neratov, April 16/3, 1914: ". . . one thing is certain that they (the British) will follow attentively the relations of Tibet with Sikkim. Nepal and Bhutan, but also those with China and with Mongolia."

as a fabrication or is actually accepted as an historical fact, it seems essential to recall, when seeking the clue to the British attitude in post-war years, that " the fantastic fear of Russia's marching into India "—as Sazonov called it [50]—which infected Anglo-Indian public opinion, was after the First World War, limited to a fear of communist propaganda in India and China. Although, from the strategic point of view, the chief fear in regard to India is for the Afghan frontier, Mongol-Tibetan relations have not been unimportant in British Indian and Far Eastern policy. Many of Britain's economic interests in China, including Manchuria, came to be threatened, in view of the foreign policy of her former ally, Japan. Hence it would be too much to expect that she should be especially interested in Outer Mongolia, which was never considered by her otherwise than in connection with Anglo-Russian relations.[51]

The view has been expressed that the British self-governing dominions, especially Australia, did not look with disfavor upon Japan's aggressive policy in the direction of the Asiatic continent, since it might distract her from looking with too much envy on the empty spaces of white Australia. This speculation

---

[50] *IBZI*, I, 1, p. 141, No. 152, Sazonov to Benckendorff, January 31/18, 1914.

[51] A Japanese view on British Far-Eastern policy may be cited here: " The fixed British policy in the Eastern Asia now is to mobilize the American and Russian influences against Japan. Under the present circumstances, Britain is by no means in a mood to change her policy against Japan even if the Japanese Government undertakes to cut down its military preparations and suspend its expansionist policy toward the continent, for she has been suffering more than any other nation on account of Japan's advance in foreign trade." Teiichi Muto, editorial writer of the *Tokyo Asahi*, translated from the March 1, 1937 issue of the *Gaiko Jiho* in *Contemporary Opinions on Current Topics* (*Tokyo*), mimeographed, no. 166, p. 2, March 4, 1937. See for British attitude: House of Commons, *Parliamentary Debates*, 1935-36, Vol. 310, March 19, 1936, col. 627, Viscount Cranborne, Under-Secretary of State for Foreign Affairs: " His Majesty's Government has never ceased to recognize Chinese suzerainty (sic) over Outer Mongolia." Compare also view expressed by "A Traveller in Central Asia" in an article in *The Times*, London, May 9, 1928, p. 17, passage headed "The British Interest." With special reference to Chinese Turkistan and Mongolia the author concludes: " Our view of the modern Russian interest in China . . . has given overmuch value to reports of Communist political activity. The true commercial voice has thus been unduly obscured." P. 18: "The . . . conclusion of the whole matter is that the decay in the hinterland of Chinese and British trade (which are bound up together) marches with the revival of Russian trade."

however served to show that a possible Russo-Japanese conflict in Outer Mongolia could not have been regarded with any degree of indifference by Great Britain, nor by Australia.

C. Germany: Active Interests

At the end of 1913 Sazonov, the Russian Foreign Minister, wrote to Kokovtsev,[52] the Russian Minister of Finance, that " in our relations with the Japanese, the French and the British Governments, our preferential position in Inner Mongolia is sufficiently recognised. . . . As to the German and American Governments, the same cannot be said." [53] Although this passage was concerned with possible railway construction only, and referred only to Inner Mongolia, it could also be applied to illustrate the difference between the attitude of Germany towards Outer Mongolia and the policy of the other powers mentioned.

Late in 1907 the Emperor William II, in a letter to Chancellor Prince Bülow, summarized Germany's Far Eastern policy in the words: " Our most important export interests . . . condition the continuance of China *as a whole*." [54] At the same time negotiations for a German-American guarantee of the integrity of China in the face of the plans of other powers for partition were begun. The German Minister in Peking believed that the protection that these two powers could offer to China ought to be limited to China proper and should exclude the outer provinces " in which we have comparatively little interest." [55] An extension to these provinces of German protection was thought to be impossible more particularly because Russia " had already been assured of certain advantages in Outer Mongolia and, in the event of disorders in China, would immediately be offered the whole of Mongolia and Eastern Turkistan by Japan, France and England. This would be the

[52] Korostovets, p. 268, Count Kokovtsev " who as it is known has been the chief advocate of the agreement with Mongolia." See also n. on his successor in office (69).

[53] *IBZI*, I, 1, Letter of January 2, 1914/December 20, 1913, p. 11.

[54] *G.P.*, Vol. 25, I, p. 88, December 30, 1907, No. 8557.

[55] *Ibid.*, p. 84, Count von Rex to Bülow, December 7, 1907, No. 8556.

way in which these powers would persuade Russia to play the part of passive spectator during the partition of China." [56] When the project of an alliance between Germany, the United States and China was abandoned—mainly because it was realized that it would have been difficult to gain the assent of the U. S. Senate—Bülow thought that China would prefer an exchange of notes between Germany and the United States to a treaty of alliance, because the latter would have had to be expressly limited to the eighteen provinces of China proper, and this would amount to a consent by treaty to give up the outer territories to the encroachment of third states. [57]

At the end of January 1912, during the revolution in China and shortly after the Mongolian declaration of independence, Germany admitted that these events gave her cause for grave anxiety. The Secretary of State for Foreign Affairs asked the French Ambassador in Berlin what was the nature of the incidents which were taking place in Mongolia. He said: " We are adversaries of the policy of spheres of influence and your interests, as well as those of England and the United States, are identical with ours. We want to preserve China as a whole, open to trade and to European trade, and we are against all designs which tend to a more or less disguised partition of China." [58] The Chancellor also impressed this view on the French Ambassador, insisting on Germany's commercial interest in the maintenance of the unity of China and of the open door. [59]

In the Consortium of Four, the German representatives were leading the opposition against the special conditions which Russia wanted to have attached to the Reorganization Loan. They rejected them on the ground that they were of a political character whereas the loan was a financial matter. [60] But at

---

[56] *Ibid.*

[57] *Ibid.*, Bülow to Rex, January 3, 1908, pp. 89-90, No. 8558.

[58] *DDF*, Vol. I, p. 514, No. 499, M. Jules Cambon, French Ambassador in Berlin, to M. Poincaré, Minister of Foreign Affairs, January 21, 1912.

[59] *Ibid.*, see also *G.P.*, Vol. 132, No. 11818. Note of the acting State Secretary of Foreign Affairs Zimmermann to Chancellor Bethmann-Hollweg, January 24, 1912, p. 251, " As to Russia, her action in Mongolia is without doubt *louche*."

[60] Isvolskii, Vol. II, No. 321, Isvolskii to Sazonov, May 28/June 8, 1912, p. 145.

guarantee the endurance of the existing Sino-German treaty stipulations." [63]

This correspondence took place, and the declaration in the Reichstag was made, while the Mongolian delegation was in St. Petersburg. A suggestion that the delegation should proceed to Berlin was rejected by the Wilhelmstrasse " as its reception would prejudice us in our attitude toward the agreement between Russia and China, which has not yet been officially communicated to us." [64] When the Mongols tried to get into contact with the foreign representatives in St. Petersburg, the German Ambassador was the only diplomat who held out any prospect of an audience, but this did not take place. [65]

Whereas in 1907 the German Minister in Peking had called the Outer Provinces of China regions in which Germany was " comparatively little interested," the German Ambassador in London was informed by the Wilhelmstrasse in April 1914 that it could not have escaped his notice that public opinion (sic) in Germany " disclosed a special interest " in the Outer Provinces, especially in Tibet and Mongolia. It was again emphasized that, although Germany's actual interests in Mongolia were small, and were next to nothing in Tibet, it was desirable that these regions should not develop into exclusive spheres of influence of particular powers, because this would prevent the participation of German enterprise in their exploitation in the future. A warning voice added that a possible division of Mongolia and Tibet into different spheres of influence would have an unfavorable effect not only on German economic interests, but also on Anglo-German relations in general. [66]

At the same time the Russians were somewhat disturbed by the news that the Chinese Government had projected, and had tried to raise, a Mongolian loan with the active aid of the German Minister in Peking. It was reported to the Russian

[63] *Ibid.*, p. 438.
[64] *Ibid.*, p. 443, No. 12007, the Provisional Secretary of State for Foreign Affairs, Zimmermann, to the Chargé d'Affaires in St. Petersburg, Freiherr von Lucius, November 22, 1913.
[65] Korostovets, p. 230.
[66] *G. P.*, Vol. 32, p. 445 and p. 447, No. 12009.

Prime Minister, as well as to the Russian Foreign Minister, that one of the principal conditions attached to the giving of this loan to the Mongols was that a branch of a Chinese Bank should be opened in Urga, and that this was to be a disguised private German bank.[67] Reports from Miller, the Russian Diplomatic Agent in Urga, that he feared the opening of a private Russian or foreign bank there caused the Tsar himself more than once to remark, at the bottom of the dispatches, that no time should be lost in opening the Mongolian National Bank.[68]

German trade interests in Outer Mongolia were principally represented by the firm of Biedermann of Leipzig, one of the largest fur houses. A German explorer, Hermann Consten, wrote in 1919 that he had devoted his prolonged stay in Khalkha to the advancement of German science and trade, despite the fact that he completely failed to get a hearing from the competent authorities in Germany.[69] However, as he records that he returned to Germany in 1914 after an absence of eight years, it seems probable that he refers to earlier periods and this would be consistent with our findings. But he refrains from giving us any particulars as to the means at his disposal to convince the German Government of the great economic services which Mongolia might render to the " Fatherland," nor of those which he himself might render or had already rendered in the same cause. Indeed, the only evidence of his activities which we could find was a record in the German Diplomatic Documents of a visit he paid to the German Foreign Office in November 1913 (i. e. directly after his return). He is described as " the informant of the Imperial General Consulate in Moscow for conditions in Mongolia," and he conveyed a request to visit Berlin from a Mongolian delegation, then in

[67] *IBZI,* I, 2, No. 146, The Russian Prime Minister to the Russian Foreign Minister, April 3/March 21, 1914, and Note on the Mongolian loan from China of March 30/17, 1914 (mainly point 3).

[68] *IBZI,* Vol. I, 1, p. 443, ad No. 439: " I repeat one must hurry with the opening of the bank." Zankope Selo, March 13/February 28, 1914.

[69] Consten, Vol. I, Preface, p. V. As to the firm of Biedermann Consten writes on p. 132 that this firm had an average turnover of 250,000 rubles.

St. Petersburg, which was refused by the German Foreign Office.[70]

During the Great War it was the Germans, the enemies of all the powers we have so far treated, who caused trouble on the eastern frontiers of Outer Mongolia. In the middle of 1915 two expeditions, one led by Colonel Pappenheim, the other by two naval officers, proceeded to Mongolia.[71] Pappenheim's expedition was wiped out by the fierce Mongolian Prince Babojab whose territory was not included in Outer Mongolia under the terms of the tripartite treaty of 1915, which fact, however, did not prevent the Mongolian Government in Urga from continuing to subsidize him and his " considerable force of about 7000 men." [72] The Tsar, on reading the report of the victory, inquired of his headquarters as to who this leader was whose success he so much admired.[73] The Russian Minister in Peking drew the attention of the Chinese Government to the other expedition and asked them to take measures to intercept it.[74] Sazonov, giving Bark, the Minister of Finance, information on these matters, said that he did not believe that Russia could altogether count on China's taking effective measures against the activity of German agents, the less so because they could escape the notice of the Chinese Government when entering Mongolia, because the latter province was outside the region to which effective government extended. The chief anxiety was lest these expeditions should approach the Chinese Eastern Railway.[75] Although no definite document seems to be available concerning the fate of this second German expedition, it seems hardly likely that it could have met an end very different from that of Colonel Pappenheim and his cavalrymen.

In post-war years, the only European country except Russia

---

[70] See above, n. 64.

[71] Consten, Vol. I, p. VII.

[72] *IBZI*, II, 8, 2, No. 129. The Russian Vice-Consul in Hailar to the Russian Minister in Peking, Krupenskii, September 5/18, 1915.

[73] *Ibid.*

[74] *IBZI*, II, 8, 1, p. 244, n. 4, tel. of Krupenskii of June 31/18, 1915.

[75] *Ibid.*, p. 224, No. 224, July 5/June 22, 1915.

which was successful in establishing even temporary relations with Outer Mongolia was Germany. It was on the suggestion of Count Brockdorf-Rantzau, the German Ambassador in Moscow, that a Mongolian trade delegation proceeded to Germany in 1925. From 1925 to 1926 a " Handels-delegation der Mongolei " existed in Berlin. Economic relations were almost exclusively confined to Germany, contact with France and Sweden being but transitory. But in Germany machinery was bought and experts were engaged. In the light of the fact that Germany's later trade was done almost entirely by barter, it is interesting to note that this was the first attempt she made at concluding a barter-trade agreement. The life of the delegation came to a sudden end because negotiations for the establishment of a Mongolian consulate in Berlin were begun.[76] In 1928 a German engineer employed by the Mongolian Government published in Germany a most valuable report on economic conditions in Outer Mongolia, confidential parts of which were submitted to the German Foreign Office.[77] And in 1926 there arrived in Berlin a so-called " Administration of Mongol Students in Germany and France," which stayed until 1930. Only a very few of the young Mongols were sent to France, most of them being educated in Germany. The expenses were borne by the Mongolian Government.[78] A German author stated in 1934 that the Mongolian People's

[76] This is based on personal information. But see also note in *Geopolitik*, V. Jahrgang, Heft 9, September 1928, p. 793, col. 2; *Zeitschrift der Gesellschaft für Erdkunde zu Berlin*, 1927, No. 7/8, footnote in note on map.

[77] Article on " Die wirtschaftlichen Verhältnisse in der Aeusseren Mongolei " by Diplom-Bergingenieur Fritz Weiske in *Osteuropa*, December 1928, pp. 149-165, being a report based on first-hand information.

[78] Roland Strasser, *The Mongolian Horde* (London, 1930), p. 116, containing the incorrect statement that the expenses were met by the German, French and Austrian Governments, whereas Austria had nothing to do with the mission and it was financially supported by the Mongolian Government only. Larson gives the following version of the Educational Mission: p. 241 ". . . recently a group (of young Mongols) refused to stop at Moscow and independently went to Berlin." Prof. Karl Haushofer comments in a book review in *Geopolitik*, December 1937, p. 144, ". . . Outer Mongolia which for some time seemed to lean so strongly politically and scientifically (politisch-wissentschaftlich) upon Germany which presented her once with a model school map." Again, it may be added, the Mongol Government paid for the maps.

Republic was maintaining a plenipotentiary in Berlin.[79] It has not been possible to ascertain from private [80] or official [81] sources if this was the case, but it seems highly unlikely.

A diplomatic incident seems to have occurred after the conclusion, at the end of 1925, of the Russo-German trade agreement—which stipulated that the most-favored-nation clause of the agreement should not apply " to those preferences which the USSR has accorded to Persia, Afghanistan and Mongolia." [82] It appears that the Chinese Government protested against this special mention of Mongolia, but that the German Government stated that this stipulation only took account of a de facto situation without prejudice to any of China's legal rights.[83]

Germany was again confronted with the question of the de facto situation when, in 1931, the first trial was made of a direct air-route from Berlin to Shanghai.[84] An airplane belonging to the Sino-German air company had to make a forced landing, and the two German pilots were arrested by the Mongols.[85] A relief plane, which went " to rescue the two

[79] Peter Kleist, *Die völkerrechtliche Anerkennung Sowjetrusslands*, Königsberg Pr. and Berlin, 1934, p. 105, issued by the Osteuropäische Forschungen by Prof. Otto Hoetzsch (also editor of the *IBZI*).

[80] A letter was addressed to Kleist in care of his publishers, but remained unanswered.

[81] A letter was addressed to the German Foreign Office and the following reply was received (October 1936): ". . . I inform you that unfortunately there is no possibility here of verifying the matters you mention."

[82] *Reichsgesetzablatt*, Part II, 1926, January 13, 1926. No. 1, p. 4, Article 6 (mainly point 3).

[83] *CYB*, 1928, p. 379 (footnote). We tried to check the accuracy of this information but have been unsuccessful. The answer of the German F. O. (see n. 81 above) refers also to this " matter."

[84] *Chinese Affairs*, No. 94-95, August 30, 1930, Details for the operation of the Sino-German Air Mail and Passenger Service, pp. 11-12. P. 12: " The cooperation is to operate the following air mail and passenger lines:

1. Shanghai to Berlin; via Nanking, Tientsin, Peiping, Manchuli, and Siberia;
2. *Shanghai to Berlin: via Nanking, Tientsin, Peiping, Kulun (Outer Mongolia) and Siberia;*
3. Shanghai to Berlin: via Nanking, Sinkiang, Kansu and Siberia."

See also *Jahrbuch der Deutschen Lufthansa*, 1931/32, p. 23.

[85] *Hansa Deutsche Nautische Zeitschrift*, Jahrgang 68 (1931), p. 1137, Number of July 18, 1931 under " Weekly Review "; see also p. 1329.

pilots," was shot down.[86] The pilots were committed to prison for five years for espionage. Newspapers reported that, because of political differences between Outer Mongolia and the authorities in Nanking, the latter were unable to procure their liberation.[87] The German authorities tried unceasingly to achieve this, but " their efforts met with great difficulties because of the complicated political circumstances in Outer Mongolia." [88] Apparently the release was eventually secured by means of official steps on the part of Germany in Moscow.[89] It has not been possible to ascertain whether or not these were in the form of a note of protest addressed to the Soviet Government. But it is hard to imagine any other step which would have had the desired effect. Representations to the Mongolian plenipotentiary in Moscow may be suggested as an alternative or supplementary means, but they are more likely to have been made by the Soviet Government than by the German Ambassador.

Although all preparatory work had been completed air communication between Germany and the Far East had not been established by 1935 " because of political difficulties." [90]

Outer Mongolia entered German foreign policy again when an offer of mediation between Russia and Japan was made by the German Foreign Minister Ribbentrop in November 1940; he said that " he knew that, in case of a non aggression pact, Japan would be willing to recognize the Russian sphere of influence in Outer Mongolia and Sinkiang, provided an understanding with China was reached." [91] And the German

[86] *Ibid.*, p. 1137; also *Frankfurter Zeitung*, July 20, 1931, No. 533, p. 2.

[87] *Frankfurter Zeitung*, July 9, 1931, No. 504, p. 2.

[88] *Ibid.*, Aug. 19, 1931, 1. Morgenbl., p. 1.

[89] *Ibid.*, Sept. 8, 1931, No. 680, p. 3: " The German fliers . . . are said to have been released thanks to steps taken officially (" von amtlicher Seite ")." See again answer of the German F. O., n. 81 above. A Chinese author has written that Berlin addressed a note of protest to Moscow; though this may be true, we were not able to check it; see C. Y. W. Meng in *La Politique de Pékin*, 23e Année, No. 18, May 2, 1936, p. 496 (from the *China Weekly Review*).

[90] *Zeitschrift des Vereins Deutscher Ingenieure* (V. D. I), Jahrgang 1935, article by E. Berendt, pp. 1307-10, mainly p. 1308.

[91] *Nazi-Soviet Relations 1939-1941*, Documents from the Archives of the German Foreign Office, Department of State, Washington, 1948, p. 251. Memorandum of the Final Conversation between Ribbentrop and Molotov on November 13, 1940.

11

Foreign Minister heard from the Japanese Foreign Minister in March 1941 that "without the good offices of Germany and without her strength there was no chance for Japan to mend Russo-Japanese relations completely."[92] Germany's war strategy did not envisage in time a coordinated German-Japanese-Manchukuo attack on Russia and Outer Mongolia. The Tripartite Pact (Germany-Japan-Italy) of September 1940 was concluded when Russia was still a neutral, and in the following months the possibility was even discussed of including Russia in the pact. Germany did actually conceal her plan of attacking Russia from her ally Japan, but the pressure she exercised on Japan in the summer of 1941 was of no avail.[93] Once Japan had started her campaigns in a different direction at the end of 1941, it was not possible for her to help Germany's Russian war directly, especially in its most critical stage at the end of 1942 and in 1943.[94] Her military alignments along the Soviet-Mongolian frontier may have hampered withdrawals of Russia's Far Eastern units to the Western front to some degree though they did not prevent them altogether; in the later stages of the war, however, the Kwantung army appears to have been no longer strong enough to launch any campaign which might have postponed the day of Germany's approaching military defeat.[95]

D. UNITED STATES, SWEDEN AND OTHERS:

INTERMITTENT INTERESTS

We have already referred to the Far Eastern entente between Germany and the United States. During this period, which is exactly contemporaneous with the terms of office of Presidents Theodore Roosevelt and Taft—from the time of

---

[92] *Ibid.*, p. 301. Memorandum of conversation between Ribbentrop and Matsuoka, March 28, 1941.

[93] United States, Department of State, *Bulletin*, 1948, I, 1041; United States, Office of the United States Chief of Counsel for Prosecution of Axis Criminality. Nazi Comspiracy and Aggression, Washington 1946, Vol. V, pp. 564-65; for pressure in November 1941 see *ibid.*, Vol. VII. pp. 160-61; for July 1942 see *ibid.*, Vol, V, p. 580.

[94] *Ibid.*, Vol. V, pp. 658-9.

[95] M. Kato, *The Lost War*, New York, 1946, p. 17.

Secretary of State Hay to that of Secretary of State Knox—
" the high sanction of the Open Door " was one of the major
principles of American foreign policy. This involved the payment of " continuous attention to the economic penetration
of Korea, Manchuria and Mongolia, thereby causing collision
with Russian enterprise." [96]

The only event which brought the United States into contact
with Mongolia was the refusal of the Russians in 1910 to
agree to the Chinchow railway project, and their suggestion
of an alternative line crossing Mongolia. This would have
connected the Peking-Kalgan line, via Urga and Kiakhta, with
the Trans-Siberian line.[97] Secretary Knox was confidentially
informed by the German Government, who were also invited
to subscribe to this scheme, that they would decline, because
China herself wanted to build a line across Mongolia with
Chinese capital. Quite apart from this, such a line would
not have been a profitable enterprise.[98] Nevertheless, Knox
instructed Rosen, the American Minister in Peking, to obtain
" the technical information necessary to form an intelligent
opinion " about the alternative Russian project.[99]

It is interesting to note that, unlike Great Britain or China,
the United States was bound neither by treaty, agreement nor
promise to respect Russia's railway interests north of the Great
Wall. But on the whole, as Bernstorff remarked, the Russian
proposal was given a " very friendly " reception by Knox.[100]

---

[96] Charles and Mary Beard, *The Rise of American Civilization*, Vol. II, p. 495
(London 1927; New York 1930).

[97] *U. S. For. Rel., 1910*, p. 109. Cf. also Anatol Kantorivitch, *Amerika v borbe
za kitai* (America in its struggle for China), Moscow 1935, pp. 191 and 229. The
necessary condition of the Russian project was that the stretch from Urga to
Kiakhta should be built by Russia only. (Circular letter to the Ambassadors,
Feb. 10, 1910, Fil. No. 1097.)

[98] *G.P.*, Vol. 32, p. 99, No. 11691, Schoen to Bernstorff, March 1, 1910.

[99] *U. S. For. Rel., 1910*, p. 264, Knox to Rosen, March 9, 1910. See Kantorovich,
op. cit., pp. 191 and 229. The Russian counter-project was officially supported by
the French Government, objections were made by England (Secret Wire of
Benckendorff, Feb. 27/March 12, 1910, Fil. No. 1098) and received cool reception
in Japan (Malevskii-Malevich to Isvolskii, Feb. 20, 1910 (Fil. No. 906). Against
this project even the Japanes press in China led a campaign (Korostovets to
Sazonov, April 12, 1910, Fil. No. 133).

[100] *G.P.*, Vol. 32, p. 108, Bernstorff to Schoen, April 20, 1910; *U. S. For Rel.*,

In March 1912 the American representative in Peking categorically declared to the Russian Chargé d'Affaires and to the British Minister that his instructions contained nothing which would cause him to attempt to thwart Russia's action in Mongolia or even to keep a watch on Russia's policy in any unfriendly manner.[101] And Knox, two months before the expiration of his term of office, remarked to Bernstorff that he thought that no special action could be undertaken in Mongolia. The only possibility was to outmaneuver the Russo-Mongolian Protocol if Russia were to put any demands to the United States concerning the Chinese question.[102]

However, American policy did not in these years follow the active lines taken in the Far East during the term of office of President Wilson and of his first Secretary of State, Bryan. The German Ambassador was instructed to sound the American Government as to its attitude toward the new situation in Mongolia. The argument of the German Foreign Office was this: the United States was the chief purchaser of the wool exported via Tientsin, and participated in the Mongolian trade by the import of textile goods, oils and grains; therefore it was to her interest to see that the pre-existing legal position was not altered to her disadvantage by the recognition of the special aims of Russia in the territory.[103] But when the German Ambassador inquired of the Secretary of State as to what was the attitude of the United States Government toward the Russo-Mongolian Protocol, an answer was at first postponed because the new Secretary of State had not yet found time to look into the matter, and no reference to it was ever made by him subsequently.[104]

1910, pp. 264-66. Memorandum to the Russian Embassy by the Department of State, Washington, April 18, 1919, p. 265: ". . . the American Government welcomes the principle of the proposal of the Imperial Government (as to a possible line from Kalgan to Kiakhta) for the special reason that it is happy to see therein the clearest expression of a reciprocal disposition on the part of the Russians to cooperate with the United States in jointly aiding China's railway and commercial development."

[101] See above n. 42.

[102] *G. P.*, Vol. 32, No. 11997, Bernstorff to Chancellor, Jan. 2, 1913.

[103] *Ibid.*, No. 12002, p. 439, Jagow to Bernstorff, March 24, 1913.

[104] *Ibid.*, footnote on p. 440, report of Bernstorff of April 17.

When W. W. Rockhill, the great American Far Eastern explorer and diplomat,[105] spent a short time in Urga in December 1913, the Russian Diplomatic Agent there had " an impression that Mr. Rockhill had a special mission from his Government." [106] Mr. Rockhill, however, in an interview a few months later, denied that his visit had any official political significance.[107] His tour was undertaken under the auspices of the American Asiatic Association. The results of his observations were published in the journal of the society; we are deprived of any supplementary information he might have been able to give as he died one year after his visit to Urga.[108] It is most likely that the attitude adopted by this " American diplomat of large experience " [109] while in Urga, was the personal expression of his " skill in Oriental diplomacy," [110] and owed nothing to any specific instructions from his Government. Rockhill was, in fact, very helpful to the Russians in explaining to the Mongol princes that they must have complete confidence in their friend Russia, whose advice they should follow strictly. Da Lama, the Minister of the Interior, was warned by him not to make any hasty decisions, as " what has been a province in the past cannot at once become an independent state." [111]   ,

It is difficult to detect many direct links after that time between American diplomacy and Outer Mongolia. In the years 1918-1922 a few connections seem to have been estab-

[105] Korostovets, on Rockhill p. 137. See also Obituaries in *Tung Pao,* Vol. XVI, Leide, 1915, pp. 160-64 with list of all his works; *Journal of the North China Branch of the Royal Asiatic Society,* 1914, Vol. XLV, pp. 117-19.

[106] *K. A.,* Vol. 37, p. 45, Miller to Sazonov, Dec. 29/16, 1913.

[107] *Journal of the American Asiatic Association,* May 1914 (Vol. XIV, No. 4), p. 110; reprint of an interview which originally appeared in the *Peking News.*

[108] *Ibid.,* pp. 102-09 " The Question of Outer Mongolia," compare *Dictionary of American Bibliography,* Vol. XVI, p. 67, London-New York 1935. It was not possible to get further information from the American Asiatic Association. Rockhill's papers are apparently in private hands.

[109] MacMurray, Vol. I, p. IX, Introductory note by James Brown Scott (Jan. 1921).

[110] *American Secretaries of State and their Diplomacy,* Vol. IX, Ph. C. Knox, Secretary of State by Herbert F. Wright, p. 334.

[111] See above n. 102, p. 44.

lished. From the American explorer Roy Chapman Andrews we know of two American officials who were at Urga for a short time in 1919—a Mr. Guptil who was representing the American Military Attaché and Mr. Price, Assistant Chinese Secretary to the American legation, who had come to Urga to establish communication with the American Consul in Irkutsk.[112] From a Soviet source we learn that before the Revolutionary Government of Mongolia asked the Soviet Government to intercede for them with the Chinese Government in September 1921, the American Consul in Kalgan, Mr. Sokobin, tried to obtain this mission for the American Government.[113] From another Soviet source, and this seems to be confirmed to some extent for the earlier 'twenties by some neutral sources, it appears that the American Consul regularly visited Urga to perform his duties there on behalf of American citizens.[114] The truth is that the American Consul at Kalgan was also the representative to whom other nationals addressed themselves in matters concerning travel in Outer Mongolia.[115] But after 1927 no travellers were allowed to visit Outer Mongolia, and there was no longer an American Consul at Kalgan.

The poverty of the material available bearing on the attitude of the United States toward Outer Mongolia may safely be attributed to the triviality of the economic, not to say political, interests in that territory. American firms trading there, the British-American Tobacco Company and a few others, closed down in the early 'twenties.[116] But that does

---

[112] Roy Chapman Andrews, *Across Mongolian Plains*, New York-London, 1921, p. 25.

[113] "SSR na Dalnyem Vostoke" by M. Galkovitch (SSR in the Far East) in *Meshdunararnaya Letopis* (*International Chronicle*) Moscow, N. 3, March 1925, p. 10.

[114] V. Durdenevskii, Narodni respubliki tsentralnoi Asii (Mongolska ta Tavinska) —The People's Republics of Central Asia (Mongolia and Tuva) in *S. S.*, p. 115, n. 1. Information partly confirmed by private information obtained from two American travellers.

[115] Korostovets, p. 336; Kalgan is not situated in Outer Mongolia; also personal information.

[116] Larson, *op. cit.*

not mean that events in the vicinity of Outer Mongolia were of no concern to American Far Eastern policy. And it would not be correct to say that the tendency of this policy was toward a withdrawal from the political and commercial arena of the Far East. A number of things, and chiefly the rapid development of American military strength in the Pacific did "not suggest any lessening of interest there." [117]

The connection which Sweden has had with Outer Mongolia is confined to the first years of the Mongolian People's Republic, during which Swedish Christian missionaries were stationed at Urga. The Swedish explorer Sven Hedin has given an account of the humanitarian work of the Swedish sisters in one of his books; he passed through Urga in 1923, on his way from Peking to Moscow.[118] But in 1925 the Mission came to a sudden end. It was accused of political activities prejudicial to the Mongolian Government, and had to leave the country.[119] A few Swedish engineers worked in Urga for some time, and a Swedish merchant, F. A. Larson, exercised considerable influence in Mongolia for many years and acted as mediator between Chinese and Mongols.[120] Thus the relations of Sweden to Mongolia were not of an official character, but were either contractual or humanitarian. The same can be said of another Scandinavian country, Denmark. A private telegraph line running through Mongolia from Russia to Peking was constructed and owned by the Danish Great Telegraph Company. A colony of Danes under the leadership of Dr. Krebs established an agricultural settlement in the northern part of Outer Mongolia which broke up, however, at the end of the 'twenties.[121]

---

[117] *N. Y. Times,* February 22, 1937, p. 16, editorial on " Our Far Eastern Front "; see also *The Japanese Chronicle,* Kobe, Weekly Ed., February 25, 1937, reproduction of editorial of February 17 on " America and the Orient," pp. 222-23. Refers mainly to *America's Stake in the Far East* by Miriam Farley, American Council of the Institute of Pacific Relations, 1936.

[118] Sven Hedin, *Von Peking nach Moskau* (Leipzig 1925), Chap. 5, p. 84, " The Swedish Sisters."

[119] Korostovets, p. 337; also personal information.

[120] Cf. Larson, *op. cit.* See also Sven Hedin, *op. cit.,* end of chapter on " The Swedish Sisters."

[121] H. Haslund-Christensen, *Tents in Mongolia.*

E. The Powers as a Whole

If we add Japan to the " other Powers," we realize that the situation before the Russian Revolution was comparatively simple. The Japanese, French and British Governments were unlikely to put any serious difficulties in the way of Russian designs in Outer Mongolia. The Franco-Russian alliance, the Anglo-Russian entente and agreements and, last but by no means least, the Russo-Japanese agreements which in 1916 practically amounted to a Russo-Japanese alliance,[122] were no scraps of paper but provided, besides other things, a guarantee for Russian policy in that region. It was therefore only natural that Russia should communicate to the representatives of these three Governments the text of a note of protest, dated Febuary 1911, addressed to the Chinese Government and relating to Mongolia, that she should inform the British and French Governments of the conclusion of the Russo-Japanese agreement, and that she should officially forward to the three Governments the text of the Russo-Mongolian agreement.[123] One of the reasons for the conclusion of this last agreement was the fear lest Republican China should offer to the powers special trading advantages in Mongolia.[124] And the " two unselfish powers "[125] believed to be very anxious to prevent Mongolia from becoming an exclusive economic sphere of Russia were Germany and the United States. Neither of these states was bound by any agreement whatever to take account of Russia's interests in the territory.

On the other hand, Germany and the United States were not isolated sponsors of the principle of the integrity of China as a whole, for all the powers were committed to this policy. None of them wished to agree to the violation of its respective trade treaties with China, which gave it the right of trading

[122] Cf. Chapter IV.
[123] Korostovets, p. 178; *G. P.*, Vol. 32, see above note 64: November 22, 1913, concerning the non-notification of the Russo-Chinese agreement.
[124] Korostovets, p. 132; see also Chapter III.
[125] *G. P.*, Vol. 32, No. 11686, p. 92, Bernstorff to Schoen.

with Mongolia as an integral part of China. Tsarist Russia had continually to beware of causing unnecessary discussions or difficulties by disregarding the trade rights of the powers. Stipulations concerning the payment of duty on the Russo-Chinese frontier, which were contemplated during the tripartite negotiations at Kiakhta, were not, according to the official Russian point of view, to be binding on the other foreign powers, for it was felt that, without bringing any benefit whatever, they would not only call forth the protest of the states concerned, but would also leave a feeling of dissatisfaction among them. It was for this reason that the " likin system " was provided for in the tripartite treaty for, as Sazonov wrote in the beginning of 1915, " it is difficult to find any other system of payment of duty suitable because, in matters touching the trade of foreigners, one must, in order to avoid their protests, consider Autonomous Outer Mongolia as a part of China." [126]

That Barga was not included in the territory of Outer Mongolia was partly due to the fact that the two towns, Hailar and Manchuli, were open to foreign trade, and their inclusion would have led to friction with the powers.[127]

In the Russo-Mongolian railway agreement the insertion of shipping rights on the seas and rivers among those reserved exclusively to Russia was omitted as it might have caused undesirable controversies with foreign powers.[128]

After the tripartite treaty of 1915 between Russia, China and Outer Mongolia, Autonomous Outer Mongolia was recognized as an integral part of China, so that the Powers were again faced with a comparatively clear situation.

But with the Russian revolution in 1917 and its repudiation

---

[126] *IBZI*, II, 7, 1, No. 54, January 21/8, 1915, Sazonov to Miller, p. 51.

[127] Korostovets, p. 133; also *IBZI.*, I, 7, note of the German editor, p. 459; see also in this connection the incorrect translation in the Chinese Social and Political Science Review of Krasny Arkhiv, Vol. 37, that Russia is not opposed to the restoration of Chinese *sovereignty* in Barga (instead of *suzerainty*).

[128] *IBZI*, I. 1. No. 10, Sazonov to Miller, January 15/2, 1914, p. 9.

of all treaties signed by Tsarist Russia followed first by the repudiation by China of the Kiakhta agreement in 1919, and then by the new Soviet-Mongolian agreement of 1921, and with the complete absence of any tripartite agreement since then, the situation became anything but clear. For the extraterritoriality of foreigners in Outer Mongolia was abolished and they ceased to have any legal status there.[129] Moreover, a state wishing to conclude a trade agreement with the Mongolian People's Government would find that this involved recognition of the situation created by the Russo-Mongolian agreement of 1921, necessitating opposition to the Chinese Government, which refused to recognize it.[130] The Russo-Chinese treaty of 1924 did not make the task of a state desiring to negotiate any easier, but political events have gone to show that those relations were of a temporary character.

Nevertheless, the part played by foreigners other than Russians, as long as the latter were not able " to take their place," is certainly worth mentioning as it was the beginning of what has now been continued by the Russians or by the Mongols themselves. In various ways, foreigners had played a role. The automobile transport Urga-Kiakhta was already in pre-war days in danger of falling into the hands of the Germans.[131] In 1918 the Chinese, who reopened their postal services in Outer Mongolia, were helped in the organization by Englishmen.[132] A Hungarian prisoner of war in Siberia, Geleta, who came to Mongolia in 1921, built a little electric power station (steam-driven) in Urga in 1923 which supplied the town with electricity.[133] Another foreigner, Gnadenberg, an Esthonian, who was formerly bailiff of a Russian estate in Siberia, came to Mongolia in 1920 and became forester in the service of the state in 1925. Others, who were engaged by the

---

[129] Korostovets, pp. 336-37.
[130] O. Mossdorf, " Das Mongolische Problem " in *Zeitschrift für Politik*, Vol. 14, 1925, p. 439.
[131] Popov, p. 11 referring to Bolaban, p. 15.
[132] Maiskii, p. 172.
[133] Forbath, *The New Mongolia*, London 1936.

Mongolian Trade delegation in Berlin, built a saw-mill at Iro (25 miles from Urga), and also a small factory in Urga with a new power-station, a foundry, a machine shop, a carpenter's shop and brick-factory. Among them were: Lieutenant S. von Montenon, a tractor-specialist and gentleman-farmer (German), Charles Gehring, a building engineer and expert in bricks (Swiss), S. Lindblom, metallurgist and chemist (Swede), R. Moeller, a mechanical engineer (German) and G. Berger, textile expert (German). A few foremen were engaged as well, one carpenter, Herr Chreisti (Swede), a mechanic Herr Broderius (German) and a smith, Herr Malmsten (Swede). Though these activities [134] should not be exaggerated, they played a part for a few years before coming to an abrupt end about 1930; today official Mongolian or Russian reports completely ignore the help given by these men and attribute all achievements in Outer Mongolia to the energy displayed by the Mongols or to the aid given by the Russians.

The citizens of the " other powers " were, therefore, able to benefit the Mongols to a certain extent by their experience and by their machinery. On the other hand, it cannot be said that the " other powers " have been able to make use of the commercial possibilities Mongolia offered.[135] Practically this was possible only in the two to three years (1919-21) of Chinese rule. Today trade possibilities in Mongolia are an academic question because of the state trade-monopoly (since 1930) and Soviet influence which tends as in Tsarist days to prevent Outer Mongolia from trading with other countries. The short-lived attempt of Germany at economic relations with the Mongolian People's Republic shows clearly the limits of such an enterprise. Through re-export from Russia, other

[134] Information for which I am indebted to Herr Ing. Sven Lindblom through Dr. E. Lindgren.

[135] Most interesting observations on Outer Mongolia's commercial possibilities in R. C. Andrews, *op. cit.*, pp. 178-79. The book of W. Karamisheff, *op. cit.*, should also be consulted in this connection.

countries, mainly Great Britain and the United States, obtain a part of Outer Mongolia's export in furs today.[136]

We have seen that there were a certain number of agreements between the Powers which to some extent afforded to Tsarist Russia a guarantee for her Outer Mongolian policy. In late years, however, the treaty link between Russia and Japan was of course broken by the war, and the treaty link between Great Britain and Japan was ended at the Washington Conference of 1921-22. It was for time to show whether the engagement entered into by the Powers "to respect the sovereignty, the independence, and the territorial and administrative integrity of China"[137] was to extend to Manchuria and Mongolia.   ,

And time has shown that with the exception of Japan,— Germany was not a signatory of the Nine-Power Treaty of Washington,—the powers did not violate the letter of the engagement, although they were unable or unwilling to defend it effectively.

Time has also shown that Russia, although not a signatory of the Nine-Power Treaty, in 1924 and again in 1936 recognized Outer Mongolia as an integral part of China. Thus all the Powers, including Germany—and, of course, Japan—respected the de jure situation in Outer Mongolia. The answer given by the British Prime Minister to a question asking whether, after the conclusion of the Soviet-Mongolian Protocol of Mutual Assistance, Outer Mongolia was to be considered as an independent state or as a part of the Chinese dominion contained the only possible legal interpretation of the position to be given by a state politically unconcerned in Mongolian affairs. He said: "His Majesty's Government continues to regard Outer Mongolia as under Chinese suzerainty; and since

---

[136] See Ryshik in *Planovoe Khozyaistvo* (Planned Economy) No. 6, 1936, p. 181 and 185. The value of exported furs in 1934 formed 15.1 percent of the total export of the Mongolian People's Republic. Furs take fourth place, after cattle, wool and raw skins.

[137] Art. I of the Nine Power Treaty, text in *Treaties and Agreements with China*, 1919-29, Washington 1927.

the conclusion of the Protocol of 12th March the Soviet Government have declared that in their view the Sino-Soviet treaty of May 1924, in which Outer Mongolia was recognized as an integral part of the Chinese Republic, is not infringed by the Protocol and retains its force." [138]

In one word, France, Great Britain, and the United States had no interests which could bring them into contact with the situation arising from the de facto existence of the Mongolian People's Republic, nor has its de jure recognition by China in 1946 appeared to affect their attitudes.

[138] House of Commons, *Parliamentary Debates*, Vol. 312, No. 83, May 11, 1936, col. 5.

CHAPTER VI

THE PRESENT POSITION OF MONGOLIA

THE QUESTION of the "to be or not to be" of Outer Mongolia in the community of nations meets today with a somewhat less ambiguous answer than it encountered up to the beginning of 1946. Until that time the international position of Outer Mongolia had for decades escaped a clear legal definition. The comment made in 1900 by the Russian Minister of the Interior that "in intercourse with Asiatic States the principles of international law are not completely applicable "[1] has been particularly true of Outer Mongolia and it was rather a puzzle to understand why Soviet Russia should have recognized China's "sovereignty" over an "independent" Mongolia, whereas Tsarist Russia was only prepared to concede to China "suzerainty" over an "autonomous" Mongolia.

The only clear definition of status had been in the tripartite Agreement of Kiakhta of 1915, but this operated in practice for only two years, after which the legal position became very confused. We must summarize this position briefly from the point of view of each country separately if we are to appreciate the advance or limited advance achieved today.

First, from the viewpoint of Outer Mongolia itself, the Mongolian People's Republic has considered itself an independent state since 1924. The constitution adopted at that time declared that Mongolia must "coordinate its foreign policy with the interests and fundamental aims of small oppressed nations and the revolutionary workers of the whole world." A note which reads curiously in a constitutional document adds that "nevertheless as circumstances demand, the possibility of entering into foreign relations with various foreign powers is not excluded, provided however that any attempt against the Mongolian People's Republic will meet with decisive

[1] Cited by *Grumm-G.*, Vol. II, p. 791.

resistance in all circumstances." It was also stated that it was the function of the supreme organ of the Mongolian People's Republic to represent the Republic in international relations, to conduct diplomatic relations, and to conclude political and commercial and other treaties with other powers and to modify the frontiers of the Mongol State; to declare war and conclude peace, and to ratify international treaties.[2] Few changes were made in this system by the new constitution of 1940.[3]

Before January 1946 this independence was recognized only by the U.S.S.R., in the anomalous fashion described in Chapter II, and the Mongolian People's Republic had no treaty or official relations with any other state except for the Republic of Tannu Tuva before its absorption into the Soviet Union in 1945, and for a Trade Delegation established in Germany for a brief period in 1925-27.[4] In January 1946 China also recognized her independence, and today she is " striving to develop her foreign relations in accordance with the increasing needs of the Mongolian People's Republic for the establishment of political and economic relations with other countries." [5]

The Russian position is still that which was expressed in a statement made by the Soviet Embassy in Paris in January 1925, on instructions from Moscow:

The Mongolian People's Republic is attached to the Soviet Union by bonds of close friendship as the government of the Union has repeatedly served as the intermediary between China and Mongolia for the settlement of questions between the two countries. The Mongolian's People's Republic is an independent state and not part of the USSR.[6]

Three general agreements concluded by the Soviet Union with Outer Mongolia have been published. The first, in 1921,

[2] *CYB*, 1928, p. 383; also *British and Foreign State Papers*, 1931, vol. CXXXIV, London, 1936, p. 1225.

[3] See Reply from the representative of the Mongolian People's Republic to the questionnaire of the Committee on the Admission of New Members received August 28, 1946; *United Nations, Security Council, Official Records*, First Year: Second Series, Supplement No. 4, esp. pp. 127-8.

[4] Cf. Chapter II and V, C.

[5] Cf. n. 3 above, p. 127, Answer to Question 2.

[6] *Le Temps*, Jan. 9, 1925.

established friendly relations between the R. S. F. S. R. and the Mongolian Revolutionary Government. The second, in 1936, between the government of the U. S. S. R. and the Mongolian People's Republic guaranteed mutual assistance in case of attack. The third agreement was the Treaty of Friendship and Mutual Assistance, together with an Agreement on Economic and Cultural Collaboration, which was signed in Moscow on February 27, 1946.[7]

On the other hand Soviet Russia twice recognized China's sovereignty over Outer Mongolia and her status as an integral part of the Chinese Republic, once in a Russo-Chinese agreement of 1924 and another time in a note of April 1936 by Litvinov, then Soviet Commissar for Foreign Affairs. Not unlike the pre-1914 Government of India's attitude toward China's suzerainty over Tibet, Soviet Russia's attitude toward China's sovereignty over Outer Mongolia must have been that it was a " constitutional fiction." [8]

This position has now been clarified by the exchange of notes on the independence of the Mongolian People's Republic attached to the Sino-Soviet Treaty of August 14, 1945. In this the Soviet Government " declares on its part that it will respect the state of independence and territorial integrity of the Mongolian People's Republic (Outer Mongolia) ." In addition, the Chinese Government's intention to "recognize the independence of Outer Mongolia in her existing boundaries " is acknowledged.[9] The phrase " in her existing boundaries " is significant, since it implies that Russia would not consider that an attempt to include other Mongol territory in the Mongolian People's Republic was compatible with her security and her good relations with China.[10]

China insisted on her sovereignty in Outer Mongolia until 1945 and refused to recognize any agreements concluded by

---

[7] Full text in *Soviet News* (London), March 1, 1946, pp. 1-2.

[8] Sir Francis Younghusband, *India and Tibet*, London, 1910, p. 77.

[9] Full text in *Soviet News,* Aug. 28, 1945, p. 5; also in Harriet L. Moore, *Soviet Far Eastern Policy, 1931-45*, Princeton, 1945, p. 277.

[10] Cf. my article " Russia's Position in the Far East," in the *Contemporary Review*, Oct. 1945, p. 213.

the latter with Soviet Russia. It was always difficult to see how China would extricate herself from this legally tenable but practically untenable position. A face saving formula was found, however, in the exchange of notes of August 14, 1945, wherein the Chinese government declared for the first time that it would " recognize the independence of Outer Mongolia in her existing boundaries," " if a plebiscite of the people of Outer Mongolia confirms this desire." This plebiscite was held in January 1946, with official Chinese witnesses present, after which full recognition was granted.

During the discussions before the Security Council of the United Nations in the summer of 1946 the Chinese representative thought that he " might have given the impression that my government was opposed to the application of the Mongolian People's Republic for admission to the United Nations. This was not the case—we are now happy to receive the replies from the Mongolian People's Republic, which we hope will remove whatever doubts we have entertained," [11] and added later " as far as the Chinese delegation is concerned we are prepared to support the application."

By the summer of 1947, however, when the application was again considered, China had reversed her position on the grounds of " an armed invasion of her province of Sinkiang by the applicant State, with attempts to seize territory in the Peitashan region there," and that therefore " She has not shown herself to be a peace-loving State. Whereas the Chinese Delegation had merely doubts as to her qualification for membership before, it has now come to believe she does not possess it. For this reason it is not possible to give her support as last year." [12]

---

[11] *United Nations, Security Council, Official Records,* First Year, Second Series, No. 4, 53rd Meeting, August 16, 1946, p. 51. But the Chinese delegate added at the 56th Meeting on August 29, 1946; " When I say we are satisfied, that is not tantamount to any endorsement of all the answers contained in his statement, especially the historical part "; *ibid.,* No. 5, p. 90.

[12] *United Nations Document* S/C, 2/SR, 18-29 July 1947, p. 89. The Chinese and Russian versions of this border dispute are given in Annex A and Annex B of this document and also in S/P. V. 186, Aug. 18, 1947, pp. 66-80 and S/479, Aug. 11, 1947, pp. 8-12 and pp. 41-46.

By other interested powers Outer Mongolia was always considered under Chinese sovereignty. In the words of the British Under Secretary for Foreign Affairs in 1936, " His Majesty's Government has never ceased to recognize Chinese suzerainty over Outer Mongolia." [13] Consequently, according to the President of the Board of Trade, exports of British goods to Outer Mongolia were included in the item " China." [14] Similarly in statistical or other works of international bodies such as the League of Nations the Mongolian People's Republic was classified as a part of China.[15] The claim of a Soviet author that, at the International Statistical Conference at Geneva in 1928, the Soviet Union tried to obtain the recognition of the Mongolian People's Republic by other powers is an overstatement.[16] Actually the Soviet delegate only protested that political considerations of the " capitalist " participants seemed to frustrate a universal system of statistics.[17]

Since there has now been a legal change of status the other powers can no longer recognize the sovereignty of China in Outer Mongolia. But as long as they themselves are not willing to assume diplomatic relations with the Mongolian People's Republic they are under no obligation to recognize the independence of Outer Mongolia, nor would they automatically do so if the Mongolian People's Republic were to become a member of the United Nations. Many works of reference continue to ignore the existence of the Mongolian People's Republic as an independent state.[18]

---

[13] House of Commons, *Parliamentary Debates,* 1935-36, Vol. 310, March 19, 1936, col. 627, Viscount Cranborne. Cf. Chapter V, n. 134.

[14] *Ibid.,* March 17, 1936, col. 221.

[15] This is progress compared with the heading "Mongolia comprising Inner Mongolia and Outer or North-Western Mongolia (Urga etc.) " to be found in the List of Countries on p. 319, item 42 of the League of Nations Economic and Financial Questions, 1928, II, 52, International Conference relating to Economic Statistics, November 26-December 14, 1928.

[16] Prof. V. Durdenevskii, " Narodni Respubliki Tsentralnoi Asii (Mongolska ta Tuvinska) " in *S. S.,* 1929, No. 3, p. 114.

[17] As in n. 15 above, pp. 97-8.

[18] E. g. *The Political Handbook of the World,* edited by Walter H. Mallory, Council on Foreign Relations, New York, has for the first time a very brief reference to the M. P. R. in its 1948 edition, p. 212.

In the summer of 1946 when the application of the Mongolian People's Republic for membership came before the Security Council of the United Nations, it was the only case among a number of other applications in which a number of delegates "felt the available information . . . inadequate." Representatives of the United States, Australia, Egypt, the Netherlands and the United Kingdom made it clear that the "available information was not sufficient to show the Mongolian People's Republic was capable of fulfilling the obligations under the Charter and expressed the desire for further information which would clarify some points." [19]

Accordingly the Acting Secretary General of the United Nations, A. Sobelov, sent a telegram to the Minister of Foreign Affairs of the Mongolian People's Republic. Since the questions asked him may set a precedent as to the information required in order to be admitted to the United Nations, we give the full text here:

" 1. What is the present extent of Mongolia's foreign relations including political, economic, social and cultural?

2. What is the attitude of the Mongolian Government regarding the development of her foreign relations and in particular the exchange of diplomatic or consular representatives?

3. What countries other than the Soviet Union and China have hitherto proposed to enter into diplomatic or consular exchanges with the Mongolian People's Republic, and what replies have been given?

4. It would also assist the Committee if it could be given more detailed information regarding:

    (a) The Constitution of the Mongolian People's Republic and other pertinent facts relating to its system of government and the conduct of its foreign relations.

    (b) The budget, particularly the appropriation in respect to international affairs.

The asking of these questions is not in any way an expression of opinion by the Committee on the Mongolian People's Republic's application." [20]

---

[19] *United Nations, Supplement No. 4, Security Council, Official Records,* First Year: Second Series, p. 66.

[20] *Ibid.,* Appendix 12, p. 123.

The answers of the Mongolian People's Republic's Government, which arrived after some delay, were laid before the Security Council when it met toward the end of August 1946.[21] Whether or not they were considered satisfactory was not decided on legal grounds nor even on political grounds directly concerned with the problem at stake, but on the unwillingness of those sitting at the Security Council's table to reach an equitable compromise. The original Chinese suggestion to postpone consideration of the application for one year [22] was replaced by the United States' proposal to postpone the voting "until the next occasion when the Security Council shall have to consider applications for membership in the United Nations." [23] From the moment, however, when it became clear that the Soviet delegation was unwilling to permit any delay, the issue was decided. Two permanent members (U. S. A. and U. K.) voted against admission, as did the Netherlands; Egypt and Australia abstained from voting, but the number of member-states voting in favor was substantial: Brazil, China, France, Mexico, Poland and the Soviet Union. From the fact that nobody has yet suggested that Brazil, China, France or Mexico are Soviet satellites, it can be deduced that they were satisfied with the information available. Only the abstaining Egyptian delegation still considered "that until now they have not at their disposal sufficient information. . . ." [24] No other speeches were made directly preceding the voting.

Earlier on the same day the British representative had suggested that the fact that they "have been in diplomatic relations with only two other countries . . . shows that they have not yet gained experience in international affairs sufficinetly to equip them to play a proper part in the international work of the United Nations." [25] It is interesting to note that the British representative was the only one who rather pointedly continued to refer to " the Outer Mongolian Govern-

---

[21] *Ibid.*, addendum to Appendix 12, pp. 124-30.

[22] *Ibid.*, p. 64.

[23] *Ibid.*, First Year: Second Series, No. 5, 56th and 57th Meetings, Aug. 29, 1946, p. 86.

[24] *Ibid.*, p. 138.   [25] *Ibid.*, p. 90.

ment or Republic " whereas all other delegates used the official translated designation—Mongolian People's Republic.

In July 1947 the Committee on the Admission of New Members reexamined the application and in August it was again rejected by the Security Council. This time Poland, Syria and the U.S.S.R. voted in favor of admission, China; the United Kingdom and the United States voted against it, and Australia, Belgium, Brazil, Columbia and France abstained from voting.[26] The only new considerations discussed were contained in memoranda presented by the Chinese and U.S.S.R. representatives concerning the border incidents of June 1947 which have already been referred to as taking place in the Peitashan area along the Sinkiang-Mongolian border. The Chinese claimed that the Peitashan post which the Mongols attacked was more than 200 kilometers inside the Sinkiang border and the Russians claimed that it was 15 kilometers from the frontier on the Mongol side. Each representative referred to official maps to substantiate his claim.[27]

The Chinese used these border incidents as an excuse for reversing their position, but other nations explained their attitudes on other grounds. Australia, Belgium, Brazil, Columbia, the United Kingdom and the United States all stressed the insufficiency of available information. The United States representative said that his government " had yet to receive information which convinced it that the Mongolian People's Republic was in fact an independent State," and the representative of Australia pointed out that " a criterion of sovereignty was that the government of a State should be solely responsible for its foreign affairs. The Australian Government had no evidence that the Mongolian Government fulfilled that condition, since it had established diplomatic relations only with the U.S.S.R." The committee discussion indicates that the only real criterion was the relation of the Mongolian People's Republic to the Soviet Union.[28]

[26] *United Nations Document* S/P.V. 186, Aug. 1947, pp. 77-80.
[27] See n. 12 above.
[28] *United Nations Document* S/479, Aug. 11, 1947, p. 12.

As for the disputed border, if it is true that Chinese maps and Russian and Mongolian maps which were considered official by each side at the time of the Sino-Soviet Pact in 1945 differed by as much as 200 kilometers, the question arises why, at that time, neither side requested the appointment of a border commission to settle the exact position of the boundary.

Some light is thrown on this question by Christopher Rand, an American newspaper correspondent who visited Sinkiang in 1947. Mr. Rand was told by a Chinese who was in Moscow at the time the pact was signed that no map delineating the border was attached to the treaty simply because they were working under great pressure and considered Manchurian problems far more urgent than Mongolian ones. Most of the inhabitants of the Peitashan area are neither Chinese nor Mongols but Kazakhs. At the time of the treaty they were getting help from the Mongols and considered their territory, practically at least, as part of Mongolia. In the last few years, however, they have transferred their loyalty to the Chinese who have been arming and subsidizing them. Both sides undoubtedly consider the Kazakhs unstable and could not count on the outcome of a local plebiscite. Since this unsettled frontier has already led to armed conflicts, in June 1947 and again in February 1948, and may do so again it seems obvious that either a Sino-Mongolian or a United Nations commission should be appointed to effect a legal settlement.

The Mongols have had little opportunity in recent history to voice their views abroad and it is regrettable that the opportunity to have a delegation regularly a part of an international assembly was denied to them when their application for admission to the United Nations was rejected. Mongols have never considered themselves a part of the Soviet Union and would welcome contacts with the outside world. Edgar Snow, after interviewing Mongols in Moscow in 1943, reported that " young Mongols—aspire to see their country emerge from its seclusion (You to visit Ulan Bator and I to visit America)." [29]

[29] Edgar Snow, *People on Our Side*, New York, 1944.

the bottom of the German opposition were fundamental differences from the Russians as to the policy in China as laid down by each side at the meeting between the two monarchs and their statesmen (Bethman-Hollweg and Sazonov) at Baltischport at the end of June 1912. Germany saw in China a market with great possibilities in the future. She did not wish therefore for the disintegration of this great empire. A large loan would have enabled the Chinese Government to overcome the difficulties with which it was faced.[61]

Germany continued to insist on the policy thus outlined. Therefore the Russo-Mongolian agreement, and especially the Commercial Protocol which accompanied it, caused the German Foreign office to instruct the German Minister to China to fortify the Chinese Government in its resistance to the recognition of this treaty, and to urge it to open Mongolia to foreign trade on the basis of the Urga agreement.[62]

In his instructions and memoranda, and in a declaration to the Reichstag, von Jagow, the Foreign Secretary, asserted Germany's right to trade with Mongolia on the basis of Article 50 of the trade treaty with China of September 2, 1861. " We are now in a position to claim for ourselves all rights in Mongolia which have been conceded to Russia under the Treaty of St. Petersburg, 1881." He added that the fact that Germany had not previously taken advantage of her " legal powers " at all, or at least only to a small extent, did not alter the position. But he pointed out that this would not be so if China were to recognize the independence of Mongolia or if she were to admit the special claims of Russia set out in the Urga Protocol. Therefore he wrote, " It seems desirable, in order to make possible a further development of our economic interests in the future, that there should continue to be a constitutional relationship between Mongolia and China, which would also

[61] *Ibid.*, No. 366, Sazonov to Isvolskii, June 25/July 8, 1912, pp. 179-180.
[62] *G. P.*, Vol. 32, p. 439, No. 12001, the Secretary of State of Foreign Affairs von Jagow to the Minister von Haxthausen, March 24, 1913. See also Note of the Under-Secretary of State in the Foreign Office, Zimmerman, pp. 441-45, December 1, 1913; declaration in the Reichstag by Jagow, December 9, 1913, for text Schultheiss' Europ. Geschichtskalender, 1913, p. 403 (Munich, 1915).

Mr. Serge M. Wolff, talking with two Mongols at the Soviet Embassy in London during their brief stay on the occasion of a Youth Congress at the end of 1945, found them very responsive to his visit.

On October 18, 1946, the Government of the Mongolian People's Republic addressed a request to the Council of Foreign Ministers that they be permitted to have a representative in the Far Eastern Commission.[30] It based its argument on the decision of the Moscow Conference which envisaged the possibility of broadening the Commission " by the addition of representatives of other United Nations in the Far East or having territories therein." Since Mongolia's application for admission to the United Nations was refused, the legal basis of the claim seems somewhat slender, but the argument is similar to that contained in the first application for admission to the U. N. Reference is made to the Mongolian People's Republic as " one of the bulwarks of peace in the Far East and an effective barrier against the extension of the aggressive designs of the Japanese imperialists on the interior of Asia, and of their seizure of the western and northern parts of China and territories of the Soviet Union." The claim that they have performed this function since 1921 may be somewhat exaggerated. The note, however, is on firmer ground when it recounts the engagements against the Japanese since 1935 and refers to active military participation following the Mongolian declaration of war on Japan on August 10, 1945.

On the same day the Government of the Mongolian People's Republic addressed to the Chairman of the Far Eastern Commission, Major-General Frank McCoy, in Washington, a message signed by Marshal Choibalsang, setting forth its claims to reparations from Japan. Since this note contains a detailed description of the engagements with Japan as seen from the Mongol side, it may be useful to record part of it here:

On January 24, 1935, Japanese troops attacked a Mongolian frontier outpost in the area of Buir Nor Khalkin-Sume. The men of the frontier

---

[30] *Soviet Monitor*, Oct. 25, 1946.

outpost were slaughtered as the buildings burnt down. On February 17 of the same year, the Japanese stationed their own frontier outposts in Mongolian territory they had seized.

In 1936 they launched an armed attack in the Bulun-Dersu sector in the same area on a large scale, putting into action planes and motorized and armored troops.

Besides, between January 24, 1935 and March 31, 1936 Japanese troops on eight occasions invaded districts of the Mongolian People's Republic with forces ranging from a platoon to a battalion, not counting numerous attacks with smaller groups of 10-15 men each.

In 1935 and 1936 the Mongolian army lost 233 men not counting civilian casualties while the material damage to the War Ministry of the Mongolian People's Republic is estimated at more than 11 million tughriks.

In 1939, before the start of the offensive of the Japanese army against Mongolia, between January and May, the command of the Kwantung army on seventeen occasions staged armed attacks on the Khalkhin-Gol area.

On May 11, 1939, an army group under Lieut. Gen. of the Japanese army, Kamatsubara, crossed the frontier of the Mongolian People's Republic in the area of Khalkhin-Gol river pressing back frontier units and launched an offensive supported by armored units and aircraft.

On May 22, in the same year, violent fighting flared up in the Khalkhin-Gol area, as a result of which the Japanese seized the locality called Noman-hon-Bure-Obo.

On June 22, 120 Japanese planes flew across the Mongolian frontier and started bombing Mongolian rear areas including the administration center of the Driu-Tumen region and the town of Tamtsak.

On June 24, 60 planes flew over Mongolian territory. By order of the commander of the Kwantung army, General Ueda, dated July 20, and of the commander of the 23rd Division, General Kamatsubara, dated July 30, 1939, Japanese troops launched a general offensive against the Mongolian People's Republic. It was only after violent battles on land and in the air, which lasted two months, that, at the close of August 1939, Mongolian troops, aided by units of the Red Army of the U.S.S.R., repelled the attacks. The Government of the Mongolian People's Republic in conformity with the protocol on mutual assistance of March 12, 1936, routed and finally ejected the Japanese troops from Mongolia.

In the Khalkhin-Gol battles the Mongolian army lost 1,131 men while the material damage inflicted by the Japanese army upon the Mongolian People's Republic is estimated at more than 60 million tughriks.

The Mongolian People's Republic has made its contribution to the coming cause of the United Nations by declaring war on Japan on August 10, 1945, and by taking part with its armed forces in the final crushing of Japan.

At this concluding phase of Japan's debacle, the Mongolian army suffered 675 casualties, and material damage estimated at more than 249 million tughriks.

Thus, as a result of Japanese aggression against the Mongolian People's Republic the total casualties of the Mongolian army in the period from 1935-1945 were 2,039 men. Material damage caused to the Mongolian People's Republic by Japanese aggression amounts to 321,983,000 tughriks.

. . . The Government of the Mongolian People's Republic proclaims its right to and firmly hopes to receive, a commensurate share of reparations from Japan, as well as indemnification of the material damage caused by Japan to the Mongolian People's Republic.[31]

At this stage it was perhaps not necessary for the Government of the Mongolian People's Republic to explain in detail how the sum of nearly 322 million tughriks material damage was arrived at and whether the material damage included items not strictly falling under this definition. The recital of military operations in 1945 is somewhat colorless. The special feature of the Mongolian troops was its mechanized cavalry. The mobility of the Mongolian army can be seen from the report that in ten days its mechanized cavalry units covered 950 km. in a raid.[32] The Mongolian cavalry took part in the surprise blow in the south in the general direction of Kalgan aiming at Liaotung Gulf.

The Mongolian troops had to cross the waterless Chahar desert and this approach surprised the Japanese; but if the Japanese had studied the direction the Chinese commanders chose in the fifteenth and seventeenth centuries via Darigangga, which they did not take by mere chance, they would have been able to envisage a possible attack in the reverse direction.[33] We have explained in Chapter I the favorable conditions obtaining in this frontier part of the Mongolian People's Republic because of the good grazing for cattle, so that since for the Chinese Darigangga was a natural base of one of the shortest routes from interior China to central Khalkha, so it became

---

[31] *Ibid.*

[32] *Pravda,* July 11, 1946.

[33] V. N. Kazakevich, " Materialy kistorii kitaiskikh voglunijkh expeditss v Mongoliu " (Materials on the History of Chinese Military Expeditions to Mongolia) in *Zapiski Kollagei Vostokvedoi,* II, 3, Leningrad. 1933, p. 159.

for the Mongolian troops a natural base of one of the shortest roads from Mongolia to Kalgan and Jehol.

The other maneuver started at Dalai Nor (in the Barga district). " The Mongolian troops," read a Red Star despatch, " showed great skill in maneuvering in difficult climatic conditions on a terrain particularly unfavorable for big movement. These desert areas are almost completely devoid of settlements. As the maneuvers took place in immense spaces the units proceeded in separate directions. Great skill in orientation was needed to keep strictly to the routes and reach assigned points." [34]

The mobility of the Mongolian cavalry was also shown in the operations connected with the approaches to Jehol which were under the command of Marshal Choibalsang who captured the town and thence moved swiftly towards Liaotung Gulf. It is not unusual for Mongolian cavalrymen to cover 700 kilometers in a week. Their horses are changed on the road. Generally every Mongolian soldier has two horses; he rides one and leads the other. The natural training and the excellent condition of the horses make it possible for a Mongolian cavalry unit to cover fifty or more kilometers in a day. Training given by Red Army officers and collaboration with Red Army mechanized troops on previous occasions have given the Mongols experience in the tactics of modern warfare: [35] in addition, at the beginning of 1945 talks were given by Red Army men at various centers in Mongolia on the Soviet military achievements in the war against Germany.[36]

To get a Mongolian army into reasonable shape at all must have been a difficult undertaking. The short reference contained in the report of the Central Asiatic Expedition of the American Museum of Natural History of the 1920's gives us a glimpse into the organizational, and also political, difficulties:

Late in the afternoon we saw about two hundred Mongol recruits being drilled by Buriat officers, at a village of five or six yurts. As we neared

---

[34] Despatch by Major Petrov, Moscow Radio, Aug. 25, 1945.

[35] *Ibid.*

[36] *Soviet Monitor*, Feb. 23, 1945.

them they formed in a double rank and stood stiffly to attention. A more ludicrous sight can hardly be imagined, for they had clothes of every description and the huge boots with pointed up-turned toes did not lend themselves to dignity when the wearer was on the ground. We were told that this was a concentration camp for men of the district who had been drafted into the army. They are given preliminary instruction at this first camp and then later at another where the recruits are more advanced. Later still they get to Urga to receive training under Russian officers. They remain in Urga for several months and are required to return every year for a stated period of training. Lamas and ' black Mongols ' alike are taken, and we heard continual complaints from the natives throughout the country that there were not enough men left to look after the herds properly.[37]

Official information available shows that the duration of compulsory military service is three years.[38] Edgar Snow's estimate of the strength of the Mongolian army in 1944 was 80,000 men " which seems quite large for a country with a comparatively small population." [39] Army units are either central or territorial, but apparently only the central units are organized on the model of a regular army. The commander-in-chief is also the Minister for War, while the General Staff is also the Ministry for War, and all brigades, regiments, and " polit-sections " are subordinate to it. There is also a military school and an air training school. The territorial units are the garrisons of various points in the aimaks. During their service the recruits learn also to read and write and " grow to under-stand politics," i. e., are politically indoctrinated. Sometimes also they learn a trade. We read that thirty percent of the army belong to the Mongolian People's Party and fifty percent to the Youth Organization.[40]

As in Tsarist days, much of the training of Mongol recruits is done by Buriat-Mongol officers. As Maiskii observed,[41] the Buriats were never very popular with the Mongols who considered them traitors to their historic tradition because they

[37] R. C. Andrews, *The New Conquest of Central Asia*, New York, 1932, p. 246.
[38] B. Perlin, *Mongolska Narodnaya Respublika, Moscow*, 1941, p. 52.
[39] Edgar Snow, *op. cit.*, p. 198.
[40] See n. 38 above.
[41] Maiskii, p. 94.

had fallen under foreign influence. Since they are generally more intelligent than the Mongols,[42] and, as in Tsarist days were useful intermediaries from the Russian point of view,[43] the impact of their presence can be felt in the entire administration of the Mongolian People's Republic.[44] It is unlikely that as military instructors they are very popular with the Mongols for, as we can read in the report of the Central Asiatic Expedition of the 1920's " I know of no more insolent type of human being than a Buriat in possession of a little authority." [45]

The political implications of the Mongolian cavalry " freeing brother Mongolians in Barga and Inner Mongolia " " from the Japanese yoke " [6] are manifold, but, since no details are available we refrain from speculation. A touching scene, however, appeared in the film recording the Mongolian advance into Inner Mongolia:

> In a small village in Inner Mongolia a troupe of army singers and dancers gave a concert for the local inhabitants. The small square which the performers had chosen for their " stage " was literally beseiged by a dense crowd. Gaunt and ragged herdsmen, lamas in their long black robes, and indescribably dirty and scabby children elbowed each other in the effort to get nearer to the platform to get at least a peep at these jolly, well-clothed and well-fed soldiers. Their lively dancing, agile acrobatics and jolly shafts of humor were met with vociferous acclamation. The contrast between the performers and the audience was astonishing.[47]

The political conclusion drawn is that " the troupe's tour of the villages in the newly liberated country inhabited by

[42] See discussion after Sir Charles Bell's lecture on " The Struggle for Mongolia," Journal of the *Royal Central Asian Society*, Vol. XXIV, Jan. 1937 (Part 1, p. 69).

[43] Korostovets, p. 244: " I could not do without the Buirats because from earliest days they have been the intermediaries between us and the Mongols."; also the *Chinese Recorder and Missionary Journal*, Vol. V (Shanghai 1874), p. 69 " Russians and Buriats live together on good terms, eating and sleeping together. The Buriats learn the Russian tongue, go to Russian schools, know what the Russians know . . ."; also John F. Baddeley, *Russia, Mongolia, China*, London, 1919, p. 7ii.

[44] There are numerous references confirming this fact in R. C. Andrews, *op. cit.*; cf. also Chapter I on Darigangga.

[45] R. C. Andrews, *op. cit.*, p. 246.

[46] Moscow Radio (in English), July 11, 1946. See also *Pravda*, July 11, 1946.

[47] M. Markov, " In the Mongolian People's Republic " in *New Times*, Moscow, Jan. 15, 1946, p. 31.

their kinsmen, was a striking illustration of what twenty-five years of independence have given the Mongolian people." [48]

As we have discussed the internal affairs of Outer Mongolia in previous chapters, we shall not examine them in detail now. A summary of them here, however, might help in gauging Outer Mongolia's international position today. In general, we may say that Outer Mongolia has radically changed its political life and is on the way toward transforming its economic and cultural structure. Four stages may be discerned. From 1921 to 1925 the princes and high lamas resisted the suppression of feudalism more or less openly. From 1925 to 1928, the new revolutionaries, having gained the ascendancy, had in turn to consolidate themselves against the reaction of the partially dispossessed ruling class and against attempts to restore feudal privileges, allied with the usury capital of the Chinese trading interests which had once dominated Outer Mongolia economically. From 1929 to 1932 it was evident that the forces of the old ruling class had been spent. In this period there was attempted a hasty socialization of Mongol economy, which was too grandiose in conception and which provoked resistance in the form of a general slaughter of livestock by private owners to avoid the loss of their private wealth, and also in the form of popular risings in which remnants of the old nobility and senior members of the lama hierarchy were also implicated. The Government then inaugurated the fourth period, which still continues, in which due account is taken of the fact that a feudal country cannot in one day be converted to a collectivist economy and society. [49]

In its attempt to change the social structure of the country the M.P.R. government had to deal with a population in which almost half the males, including the shabinar, were lamas. After the death of the Hutukhtu in 1924 the first fundamental change was the law of 1926 concerning the separation of religion from the state. A special tax was levied on all lamas of military age (i.e. under forty-eight); a decree was

[48] *Ibid.*
[49] Doksom, p. 85.

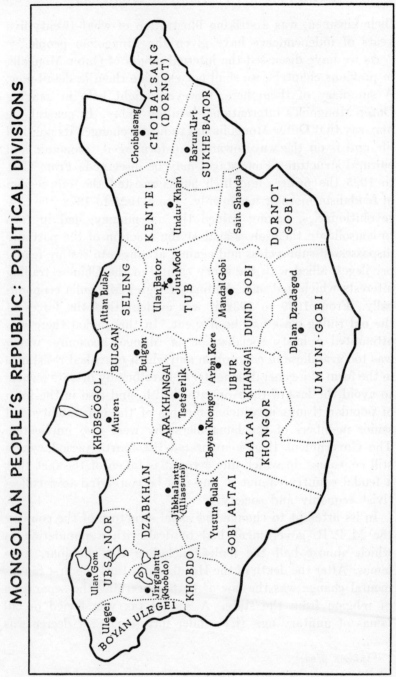

MONGOLIAN PEOPLE'S REPUBLIC: POLITICAL DIVISIONS

CHOIBALSANG (DORNOT)

Choibalsang

Barun-Urt

SUKHE-BATOR

KENTEI

Undur Khan

Sain Shanda

DORNOT GOBI

SELENG

UlanBator
JunMod

TUB

Mandal Gobi

DUND GOBI

Altan Bulak

BULGAN

Bulgan

Arbai Kere

UBUR

Dalan Dzadagad

U MUNI-GOBI

KHÖBSÖGOL

Muren

ARA-KHANGAI

Tsetserlik

BayanKhongor

BAYAN KHANGAI

KHONGOR

Jibkhalantu (Uliassutaj)

DZABKHAN

Yusun Bulak

GOBI ALTAI

Ulan Gom

UBSA-NOR

Jirgalantu (Khobdo)

KHOBDO

Ulegei

BOYAN ULEGEI

300

passed in 1930 prohibiting the monasteries from accepting boys under eighteen; and a decree in 1936 forbade the two eldest sons in a family to become lamas.[50] These measures have brought about a considerable reduction in the number of lamas. Dependable figures cannot be obtained, but a Japanese source,[51] basing itself on a Soviet journal (*Bezboshnik*, The Atheist, date not given) lists the number of lamas in 1917 as 117,000, in 1928 as 95,000, in 1932 as 82,000, and in 1938 as 80,000. The same source refers sceptically to a speech by Premier Choibalsang in April 1939 in which he was alleged to have said that there were no more lamas in Outer Mongolia. However the Wallace party in 1944 observed a lama temple and monastery functioning in Ulan Bator.[52]

Administratively considerable changes have been made. The new administration of districts was introduced in 1925-26, abolishing the hoshuns.[53] The primary unit is the bag, made up of from 30 to 100 households. The original four aimaks were divided into thirteen well defined territories, which have since been increased to eighteen. The subdivision of the aimak is the somon, of which there were 322 in 1946. Most of the somons have fixed centers but the administrations of the bags move with the nomad population. It is thus difficult to estimate their exact number, but Perlin gives it as between 1900 and 2000.[54] The table on page 302 gives the names, areas, and capitals of the eighteen aimaks as they were listed in 1946.[55]

Certain limitations are imposed upon Outer Mongolia's development by her geography. Of her immense territory only a small area can be cultivated. To make Outer Mongolia to any great extent an agricultural country seems impossible and attempts have hitherto not been successful. The observation

---

[50] Ryshik, p. 177.

[51] A Japanese View of Outer Mongolia, p. 48.

[52] John N. Hazard in *Pacific Affairs*, June 1948, p. 168. Tsapkin, p. 59, mentions that most lamas are absorbed into socially useful work, but says nothing about their present number.

[53] Doksom, p. 85.

[54] Perlin, p. 38.   [55] Murzaev, p. 20.

		Area in Thousands of Sq. Km.	Number of Somons	Aimak Capital
1.	Boyan-ulegei	46	12	Ulegei
2.	Khobdo	73	14	Khobdo (old name) Jirgalantu (new ")
3.	Ubsa-nor	72	16	Ulan-gom
4.	Dsabkhan	90	23	Uliassutai (old name) Jibkhalantu (new ")
5.	Gobi-Altai	126	18	Yusung-bulak
6.	Bayan-khongor	116	20	Bayan-Khongor
7.	Khöbsögol	102	23	Muren
8.	Ara-khangai	47	23	Tsetserlik
9.	Ubur-khangai	69	23	Arbai-kere
10.	Umuni-gobi	156	12	Dalan-Dzadagad
11.	Dund-gobi	79	18	Mandal-gobi
12.	Dornot-gobi	101	17	Sain-shanda
13.	Bulgan	48	17	Bulgan
14.	Tub	78	23	Jun-mod
15.	Seleng	48	10	Altan-bulak
16.	Kentei	89	21	Undur-khan
17.	Choibalsang *or* Dornot	120	17	Choibalsang
18.	Sükhe Bator	71	15	Barun-urt
		1,531	322	

of I. Maiskii in 1921 that " in Autonomous Mongolia there is no future for agriculture " [56] does, however, not represent the policy adopted by the Mongolian Government in recent years. Agriculture is encouraged especially in those regions where Chinese formerly cultivated the land. Thus Mongols who do some farming are freed from taxes for three years on the income derived from farming. They are also given the best districts available for farming, forf which they need not pay.[57] As for the development of industry, small electricity plants, work-shops, printing presses, wool washing plants, and shoe-factories have been erected, but there seems to be no point in industrializing a country whose main economy has always been cattle-breeding, whose population is small and whose proximity to Russia enables it to get from there all necessary manufactures. A thorough exploitation of the natural resources in

[56] Maiskii, pp. 230, 237. Also *SSE*, Vol. 3, p. 520.
[57] Ryshik, " Khozyaistvennoye i kulturnoye stroitelstvo Mongolskoi narodnoi Respubliki " in *Planovoye Khozyaistvo*, No. 6, 1936, p. 180.

minerals will only be possible when geological expeditions have made greater progress in their investigations (there is, for instance, coal in many parts of the country, generally brown coal of low quality and largely mixed with phosphorus). A certain relative progress in industry is indicated by some figures, which should be accepted with the necessary caution. We are told that in 1927 the total capital invested in industry amounted to 318,000 tughriks, in 1931 to 3,260,000 tughriks and in 1941 to 64,000,000 tughriks. Whereas in 1927 there were only about 500 workers employed in industry the majority of whom were Chinese, the figures for 1934 speak of over 3,000 workers 90 percent of whom were Mongols and in 1945 there were said to be 50,000 employees in industry and public services.[58]

While there are natural limits set to the development of agriculture and industry, there seems still much scope for the improvement of animal husbandry and recent figures indicate that some progress has already been made in this direction.[59]

Taking a long range view it is conceivable that Outer Mongolia, which participated in world trade in the course of the nineteenth and early twentieth centuries but which has been cut off from it since 1930, will sooner or later take its place again. This may depend not only on the requirements of the Soviet Union, especially as regards food, but also the development of the livestock industry where the possibilities are still enormous. To a more limited extent this also applies to the fur trade. The rate of advance would be speeded up considerably, and the good will of the Mongols secured, if countries more able to than the war exhausted Soviet Union would supply machinery and other goods.

In 1921 Dr. Sun Yat-sen had the vision to write:

Argentine is now the greatest source of the world's meat supply, while the Mongolian pasture is not yet developed owing to the lack of transportation facilities. As Argentine has superseded the United States in supplying

[58] *Ibid.*, p. 182. *SSE*, pp. 525, 526. Tsapkin, p. 78.
[59] *SSE*, p. 532. Ryshik, pp. 179, 180.

12

the world with meat, so the Mongolian pasture will some day take the place of Argentina, when railways are developed and cattle raising is scientifically improved. Thus the construction of railroads in this vast food-producing region is an urgent necessity as a means of relieving the world from food shortage.[60]

The railway construction which Sun Yat-sen envisaged has not yet been understaken, except for the line from Choibalsang to the Trans-Siberian Railway and the other short spurs described in Chapter II, and would probably not be justified without a large increase in export trade, but the technical possibilities of such trade are increasing and new road construction is being undertaken.

In brief, once the " go ahead " is given the opportunity will be open to Outer Mongolia to link her economy to the industries of Manchuria and Northern China and this will give her access to the sea which Russia has successfully forestalled ever since the nineteenth century. The importance Mongolia's cattle exports could then gain for China we can only gauge if we relate it to China's future industrialization program. The present meatless diet of the average Chinese stands in the way of producing a modern and efficient labor force,[61] and the proximity of Mongolia compared to the other available sources of supply makes it the most economical source of meat supply for China.

It is a simplification to say that a change of attitude by Russia and the lessening of her grip on Outer Mongolia are the only keys which will open the closed doors of that country. Isolated it is, but not in any way insulated from the happenings of Asia. If earlier history did not show this in clear outline, the events between 1931 and 1945 have proved it to the satisfaction at least of all students of Asiatic affairs. The answer to the question: " How long will Russia consider Outer Mongolia's rôle mainly from the point of view of protecting her position in Manchuria and Korea? " depends a great deal on

[60] Sun Yat Sen, *The International Development of China*, p. 123.
[61] Charles H. Behre, Jr. and Kung Ping Wang, " China's Mineral Wealth," in *Foreign Affairs*, Oct. 1914, p. 137.

the development of Chinese internal affairs and United States policy towards them, as well as toward Japan and the American-controlled part of Korea, all of which throw " shadows numberless " on the already unilluminated area of Outer Mongolia.

APPENDICES

BIBLIOGRAPHY

NOTE. This bibliography does not claim to cover the whole field of publications concerning Outer Mongolia. It is, however, as far as we are able to ascertain, the most complete and up to date one concerning the period dealt with. No mention has been made of articles of news-value only, though they will be found in the notes. Neither have books mentioned in footnotes only to substantiate minor points been mentioned again. For a good bibliography of books and articles covering the whole field of Mongolia (geography, history, explorations, etc.) recourse should be had to the *Bibliotheca Sinica, Dictionnaire Bibliographique des ouvrages relatifs à l'Empire Chinois* par Henri Cordier, Deuxième édition, Vol. IV, Paris, 1907-08. Cols. 2760-2802 and Supplément, Paris, 1922, Cols., 4284-4300; also to the published Subject-Index of the British Museum under the heading Mongolia, though this is not very satisfactory for post-1918 years. More recent is the full bibliography of Russian books and articles on all aspects of Mongolian affairs: E. N. *Yakovleva, Bibliografiya Mongolskoi Narodnoi Respubliki*, Moscow, 1935. A useful, though not extensive bibliography can also be found in Dr. Hugo Knoepfmacher's *Outer Mongolia, A Selection of References*, New York, The New York Public Library, 1944.

I. *Official Documents and Diplomatic Archives:*

(a) *China (and Outer Mongolia)*

Ulozhenie Kitaiskoi Palaty vneshnykh snoshenii (The Regulations of the Chinese Board of Foreign Relations), translated from the Manchu by Stefan Lipovtsov, 2 Vols., St. Petersburg, 1828.

Treaties and Agreements with and concerning China, 1894-1919, compiled and edited by John V. A. MacMurray, New York, 1921.

Outer Mongolia. Treaties and Agreements, Washington, D. C., 1921 (39 pp.).

Treaties and Agreements with and concerning China, 1919-1929, Washington, 1929.

The three last mentioned works are published by the Carnegie Endowment for International Peace.

(b) *Russia*

Sbornik dogovorov i drugikh dokumentov po istorii mezhdunarodnykh otnoshenii na dalnem vostoke, 1844-1925 (Collection of agreements and other documents from the history of international relations in the Far East), edited by Prof. E. D. Grimm, Moscow, 1927.

Oranzhevaya Kniga (Orange Book), Ministerstvo Inostrannykh Del (Ministry of Foreign Affairs); Sbornik diplomaticheskikh dokumentov po Mongolskomu voprosu (23 Avgusta 1912 g.—2 Noya-brya 1912 g); (Collection of Diplomatic Documents concerning the Mongolian question, August 23, 1912—November 2, 1913), St. Petersburg, 1914.

Krasny i Arkiv (Red Archives), Vol. 37, *Tsarskaya Rossiya i Mon-goliya 1913-14gg.* (Tsarist Russia and Mongolia 1913-1914), pp. 15-68.

> An English but not always adequate translation of this important collection is available in *The Chinese Social and Political Science Review*, Vol. XVI, No. 4, January 1933 and Vol. XVII, No. 1, April 1933.

Benckendorff, *Graf Benckendorffs Diplomatischer Schriftwechsel.* Neue stark vermehrte Auflage der diplomatischen Aktenstücke zur Geschichte der Ententepolitik der Vorkriegsjahre, 3 vols., Berlin-Leipzig 1928, edited by B. von Siebert.

Isvolski, *Der Diplomatische Schriftwechsel Iswolskis, 1911-1914.* Aus den Geheimakten des russichen Staatsarchivs, im Auftrag des deutschen Auswärtigen Amtes in deutscher Uebersetzung heraus-gegeben von Friedrich von Stieve, 3 vols., Berlin, 1924.

Mezhdunarodnye otnosheniya v epokhu imperializma 1878-1914.

> Compare with item that follows. The Russian source has been consulted only in order to check up certain points and while citing the original version of despatches in English and French. Vols. 18 & 19 of Series II (4 vols. in all) which appeared at the end of 1938 have been consulted in the Russian only. They contain material already partly published in Benckendorff, Popov, Shoizelov.

Die Internationalen Beziehungen im Zeitalter des Imperialismus. Dokumente aus den Archiven der zaristischen und provisorischen Regierung. Authorized translation into German, edited by Prof. Otto Hoetzsch, Vol. I, (i), Vol. II, 8-2, Berlin, 1931-1936 and Vol. III, I (i), Berlin, 1939.

> The last volume, published in 1939, contains some of the material published in Vol. 18, 1 of Series II; but due to war conditions it was not obtainable until after the end of hos-tilities in Europe and it has not been consulted.

Vneshnyaya Torgovlya Soyuza SSR Statobzor. (Statistical Survey of the External Trade of the Soviet Union). Moscow.

Statistika Vneshnei Torgovli (Glavnoe tamozhennoe Pravlenie SSSR). (Statistics of External Trade.—Chief Customs Depart-ment of the U.S.S.R.), Moscow.

(c) *Great Britain*

British Documents on the Origin of the War, 1894-1914, edited by G. P. Gooch and Harold Temperley H. M. Stationery Office), London, 1926-1938. Especially Vols. IV and X (Part II).

Parliamentary Debates (Official Report), 5th series. Especially Vols. for 1914 and 1935-36.

British Parliamentary Command Papers. Especially China, No. 3, 1912.

British and Foreign State Papers. For treaty texts, texts of constitutions, etc., e. g., Mongolian Constitution of 1924, Vol. CXXXIV, London, 1936.

(d) *France*

Documents Diplomatiques Français, 1871-1914, Paris, 1929 *et seq.,* 3me série.

(e) *Germany*

Die Grosse Politik der Europäischen Kabinette 1871-1914. Sammlung der diplomatischen Akten des auswärtigen Amtes. Im Auftrage des auswärtigen Amtes, edited by Johannes Lepsius, Albrecht Mendelssohn-Bartholdy, Friedrich Thimme, Berlin, 1922-1926. Especially Vol. 32, but also Vol. 25.

(f) *U. S. A.*

U. S. Foreign Relations. Papers relating to the Foreign Relations of the United States, Washington. Especially Vols. for 1910, 1912 and 1918.

II. *General References*:

In Russian: Sibirskaya Sovetskaya Entsiklopediya (Siberian Soviet Encyclopedia), Vol. 3: " The Mongolian People's Republic," pp. 508-42, Chief Editor B. Z. Shumyatskii, Moscow; West-Siberian Dept. Ogiz, 1932.

> Of special importance. Most objective of all Soviet accounts.

Bolshaya Sovetskaya Entsiklopediya (Great Soviet Encyclopedia), Vol. 40; " The Mongolian People's Republic," cols. 68-69, Moscow, 1938.

Malaya Sovetskaya Entsiklopediya (Small Soviet Encyclopedia), Vol. 5: " The Mongolian People's Republic," cols. 338-44, Chief Editor N. L. Meshcheryakov, Moscow, 1930.

In English: Handbooks prepared under the direction of the Historical Section of the Foreign Office, No. 68: *Mongolia* (H. M. Stationery Office), 24 pp., London, 1920.

Encyclopaedia Britannica: 11th (and 13th) Edition, Vol. 18, pp. 711-12. Prince P. A. Kropotkin: " Mongolia." 14th Edition: Vol. 15, pp. 707-11. Prof. P. M. Roxby: " Mongolia."

China Year Book:
1914: Lt. Binsteed, " Mongolia," pp. 609-43.
1933: Owen Lattimore, " Mongolia," pp. 191-201.
1939: Owen Lattimore, " Mongolia," pp. 454-461.

In French: Géographie Universelle. Tome XIII: " Haute Asie " par Fr. Grenard. " La Mongolie," pp. 248-86, Paris, 1929.

Dictionnaire Diplomatique, ed. by Académie diplomatique internationale, Vol. II: B. Nikitine, " Mongolia," pp. 141-48. Paris, *n. d.*

III. *Books, Pamphlets, Articles, Speeches,* etc.:
(asterisk *—of special importance)

In Chinese:

* Prof. C. F. Chang. " Recollections of the Outer Mongolian Question " in *Tu Li P'ing Lun* (Independent Critic), April 26, 1936, pp. 3-8.

* T. L. Hsü, " Some doubtful points concerning ' The Recollections of the Outer Mongolian Question '," *ibid.,* May 31, 1936, pp. 3-8.

* Prof. C. F. Chang, A reply to Mr. Hsü's article, *ibid.,* June 7, 1936, pp. 3-12.

T. L. Hsü, " Rediscussion of the Abolition of the Outer Mongolian Autonomous Regime," *ibid.,* July 12, 1936, pp. 5-14.

Prof. C. F. Chang, Answer to above article, *ibid.,* pp. 14-15.

In Russian:

* A. P. Boloban, *Mongolia v eye sovremennom torgovoe-konomicheskom otnoshenii* (Mongolia in its contemporary trade and economic relations).
Was not accessible, but cited in Grumm-Grzhimailo (see below) and in other works.

* M. Bogolepov and M. Sobolev, *Ocherki russko-mongolskoi torgovli* (sketches of Russian-Mongolian trade), Tomsk, 1911.

E. Breiter, " Denezhnaya reforma i narodnoe khozyaistvo Mongolii " (Monetary reform and the national economy of Mongolia) in *Novyi Vostok* (The New East), 1929, 25, pp. 127-46.

* Doksom, " Istoricheskie uroki 15 let revolyutsii " (Historical Lessons of Fifteen Years of Revolution). Report by Doksom, Chairman of the Little Hural, and short report of Amor (Prime Minister) at the 21st Jubilee Session of the Little Hural at Ulan Bator, in *Tikhii Okean* (Pacific Ocean), No. 3 (9), Moscow, July-September 1936, pp. 63-94.

* Gendung, " Iz doklada premierministra MNR Genruna VII velikomu khuralu " (Extract from the Report of the Prime Minister of the Mongol People's Republic, Gendun, to the Seventh Great Hural, in *Tikhii Okean,* No. 1 (3), January-March 1935, pp. 250-67.

Georgy Konstantinovich Gins, *Mongolskaya gosudarstvennost i pravo v ikh istoricheskom razvitii* (The Mongolian state and law in their historical development), 55 pp., Harbin, 1932 (with a summary in English).

* G. E. Grumm-Grzhimailo, *Zapadnaya Mongoliya i Urgankhaiskii Krai* (Western Mongolia and the Urianghai Region), Vol. I, St.

Petersburg, 1914; Vol. 2, Leningrad, 1926; a historical sketch of these countries in connection with the history of Central Asia, Vol. 3, part 1, Leningrad, 1926; Vol. 3, parts 2-4, Leningrad, 1930. The 1926 volumes of this great work are edited by the Science Committee of the Mongol People's Republic.

J. Genkin, " Dva syezda mongolskoi narodnoi partii " (Two Congresses of the People's Party in Mongolia) in *Novyi Vostok*, 1926, 12, pp. 184-95.

A. Kallinikov, *Revolyutsionnaya Mongoliya* (Revolutionary Mongolia), Publication of Sovremennaya Geographiya, Chief Editor I. Maiskii, Moscow, 1925.

* " Aratskoe revolyutsionnoe dvizhenie v doavtonomnoi Mongolii " (Arat Revolutionary movements in pre-autonomous Mongolia) in *Revolyutsionnyi Vostok* (Revolutionary East), 1934, No. 5, pp. 137-56 and No. 6, pp. 43-64.

* " Agrarian Relations and Anti-Feudal Agrarian Revolution in Mongolia," Chapter 3 of: A. Mineev et al, *Agrarny vopros na vostoke* (The Agrarian Question in the East), Moscow, 1933.

D. Kashintsev, " Chuiskii trakt v Mongolii " (The Chuisk highway in Mongolia) in *Novyi Vostok*, 1925, 8-9, pp. 133-43.

V. A. Kazakevitch, *Poyezdka v Darigangu* (Journey to Darigangga). Materialy Komissii po issledovaniyu Mongolskoi i Tannu-Tuvinskoi narodnykh respublik i Buryat-Mongolskoi ASSR, No. 5; with map. Leningrad, 1930.

N. Khalkin, " The Stages of the Development of the Mongol People's Republic " in *Pravda* (Truth), Moscow, April 8, 1936, p. 2.
See also under Viktorov.

J. Kushelov, *Mongolia i Mongolskii vopros* (Mongolia and the Mongolian question). With the cooperation of the " Society of Friends of Military Science," St. Petersburg, 1912.

* I. Maiskii, *Sovremennaya Mongoliya* (Otchet Mongolskoi ekspeditsii snaryazhennoi irkutskoi kontoroi Vserossiiskogo Tsentralnogo soyuza potrebitelnykh obshchestv " Tsentrosoyuz "). (Contemporary Mongolia.—Report of the Mongolian Expedition organized by the Irkutsk Office of the All-Russian Central Union of Consumer's Societies " Tsentrosoyuz "), Irkutsk, 1921. " Mongolia " in *Novyi Vostok*, 1922, I, pp. 152-83.

M. Markov, " 25th Anniversary of the Mongolian People's Republic " in *Pravda*, Moscow, July 11, 1946, p. 3.

V. Maslennikov, " K Mongolskomu voprosu " (About the Mongolian Question), in *Mirovoe Khozyaistvo i Mirovaya Politika* (World Politics and Economics), Moscow, May 1936, pp. 77-78.

* *Moskovskaya Torgovaya Evpeditsiya v Mongoliyu* (Moscow Commercial Expedition to Mongolia), Moscow, 1912.

E. M. Murzaev, *Mongolskaya Narodnaya Respublika, fisiko-geograficheskoe opisanie*. (Mongolian People's Republic, a physical geographical description) published by the Institute of Geography of the Academy of Sciences of the U. S. S. R., Moscow, Ogiz, 1948. A companion volume, *Mongolskaya Narodnaya Respublika, strana, lyudi, khozyaistvo* (MPR., Land, Peoples, Economy) Geographical Society of the U. S. S. R., Leningrad, 1947, has not been available.

* Baron B. E. Nolde, " Mezhdunarodnoye polozheniye Mongolii (The international situation of Mongolia) in *Pravda* (Law), 1915, No. 34, Cols. 2153-68 and No. 35, Cols. 2217-31.

> Baron Nolde was the legal advisor of the Ministry of Foreign Affairs, St. Petersburg. Different parts of this article will be found cited in Korostovets' book (see German column) pp. 272-5 and 279-80, and in Grumm-Grzhimailo's book (see above), Vol. II (1926), p. 749 and esp. pp. 758-59.

Y. V. Obruchev, " Bolshe vnimaniya chuiskomu traktu " (More attention to the Chuisk Highway) in *Novyi Vostok*, 1925, 8-9, pp. 125-32.

N. Pennskii, " Ekonomicheskie vzaimootnosheniya SSSR s Mongoliei " (Economic relations of the USSR with Mongolia), *ibid.*, 1925, 10-11, pp. 163-72.

B. Perlin, *Mongolskaya Narodnaya Respublika* (The Mongolian People's Republic), Moscow, 1941.

* A. Popov, " Tsarskaya Rossia i Mongoliya v 1913-1914 gg." (Tsarist Russia and Mongolia in 1913-1914), Foreword to the Collection of Documents in *Krasnyi Arkhiv*, Vol. 37, 1929, pp. 3-14.

> Based on documents from 1905-1911. Not included in the English translation of the documents for 1913-1914 in *The Chinese Social and Political Science Review*.

* A. M. Pozdnyeev, *Mongoliya i Mongoly. Rezultaty Poyedzki v Mongoliyu ispolnennoi v 1892-1893* (Mongolia and the Mongols. Results of a trip to Mongolia made in 1892-1893); 2 vols., St. Petersburg, 1896-8.

* A. Rish, " Mongoliya na strazhe svoei nezavisimosti " (Mongolia guarding her independence) in *Tikhi Okean*, No. 4 (6), October-December 1935, pp. 98-112.

* B. A. Romanov, *Rossiya v Manchzhurii* (Russia in Manchuria), 1892-1906, Leningrad, 1928.

* Ya. Ryshik, " Khozyaistvennoe i kulturnoe stroitelstvo Mongolskoi narodnoi respubliki " (Economic and cultural reconstruction of the Mongolian People's Republic) in *Planovoie Khozyaistvo* (Planned Economy) No. 6, 1936, pp. 169-90.

T. Ryskulov, " Velikii Khuruldan Mongolii " (The Great Khuruldan of Mongolia) in *Novyi Vostok*, 1925, 8-9, pp. 215-29.

* A. F. S-ky (Speranski), " Materialy k istoriyu interventsii. Rol Yaponii v panmongolskom dvizhenii " (Materials on the history of intervention. Japan's part in the Pan-Mongolian movement), *ibid.*, No. 2, 1922, pp. 591-603.

D. Shambolon, " Kak ne sleduet stavit vopros o natsionalnom samo-opredelenii Mongolii " (How one should not put the question of the national self-determination of Mongolia) in *Revolyutsionnyi Vostok*, 1928, No. 3, pp. 235-40.

> The article of Rinchino—to which this article is an answer and which was published in a preceding number of this journal—was not available. Rinchino himself refers to his pamphlet " The Prospects of the Mongolian Revolution " at the 3rd Party Congress—cf. *Mongolia, Yesterday and Today* in *English Column*.

B. Shlezinger, " Chastnyi Kapital v Mongolii " (Private capital in Mongolia) in *Novyi Vostok*, 1929, 26-27, pp. 91-104.

* S. Shoizhelov, " Mongoliya i yaponskii imperializm " (Mongolia and Japanese Imperialism), *ibid.*, 1925, 8-9, pp. 199-205.

> * " Avtonomicheskoe dvizhenie Mongolii i tsarskaya Rossiya " (The autonomous movement of Mongolia and Tsarist Russia), *ibid.*, 1926, 13-14, pp. 351-63.

" Perelomnyi moment v istorii natsionalno-osvoboditelnogo dviz-heniya v Mongolii " (The critical period in the history of the national emancipation movement in Mongolia), *ibid.*, 1925, 10-11, pp. 203-11.

V. Tomilin, *Mongoliya i eyo sovremennoye snacheniye dlya Rossii* (Mongolia and its contemporary importance for Russia), Moscow, 1913.

N. V. Tsapkin, *Mongolskaya Narodnaya Respublika* (The Mongolian People's Republic), Ogiz, Gospolitizdat, Moscow. 1948. 112 pp. Statistical data to 1947 and an outline of the 1948 Five Year Plan.

N. N. Tugarinov, " Byudzhet Mongolskoi Narodnoi Respubliki " (The budget of the Mongolian People's Republic) in *Novyi Vostok*, 1926, 15, pp. 169-77.

> " Denezhnoe obrashshenie Mongolii " (Monetary circulation in Mongolia), *ibid.*, 1928, No. 20-21, pp. 241-57.

S. Viktorov and N. Khalkin, *Mongolskaya Narodnaya Respublika* (The Mongolian People's Republic), Moscow, 1936.

Vl. Vilenskii (Sibirikov), *Sovremennaya Mongolia* (Contemporary Mongolia), Published by " Proletary," 1925.

* B. Ya. Vladimirtsov, *Obshchestvennyi stroi Mongolov.-Mongolskii kochevoi feodalizm* (The Social Structure of the Mongols.-Mongol Nomad Feudalism), Leningrad, 1934.

> " Buddism v Tibete i Mongolii " (Buddhism in Tibet and Mongolia). Lecture delivered on September 31, 1919. Peters-burg, 1919.

L. Zolottarev, " Denezhnaya reforma v Mongolii " (Monetary Reform in Mongolia), in *Novyi Vostok*, 1926, No. 13-14, pp. 234-36.

* " The Mongolian People's Republic " in *Sputnik Agitatora*, No. 23, December 1945.

In Ukrainian:

* Prof. V. Durdenevskii, "Narodni Respubliiki Tsentralnoi Azii " (Mongolska ta Tuvinska) (The People's Republics of Central Asia.—Mongolia and Tuva), in *Skhidnii Svit* (The World of the Orient), 1929, No. 3 (9), pp. 97-116.

* Prof. A. Gladsberg, " 1917 rik u Mongolii " (The year 1917 in Mongolia), *ibid.*, No. 1, 1927, pp. 91-119.
  "Mongolska politika timtchasovoho rossiyskoho uriadu " (The Mongolian policy of the Provisional Russian Government), *ibid.*, 1928, No. 5, pp. 154-71.

In English:

Roy Chapman Andrews, *The New Conquest of Central Asia.* Narrative of the explorations of the Central Asiatic Expedition in Mongolia and China, 1921-1930, pp. 678, New York, 1932.
Across Mongolian Plains, New York-London, 1921.

* John F. Baddeley, *Russia, Mongolia, China,*—being some Record of the Relations between them from the beginning of the XVIIth Century to the Death of the Tsar Alexei Mikailocich A.D. 1602-1676. Given mainly in the form of narratives by the envoys sent by the Russian Tsars to the Kalmuk and Mongol Khans and Princes and to the Emperors of China. With introductions, historical and geographical, and a series of maps showing the progress of geographical knowledge in regard to Northern Asia during the XVIth, XVIIth, and early XVIIIth Centuries. Texts taken especially from Manuscripts in the Moscow Foreign Office Archives. Two Volumes, London, 1919.
  In a review of this valuable book in *Zapiski Kollegii Vostokovedov* (Memoirs of the College of Orientalists), Tom I, 1925, Leningrad, pp. 542-51, Vl. Kotvich says rightly that it contains far more than is revealed by the title.

Sir Charles Bell, " The Struggle for Mongolia," in the *Journal of the Royal Central Asian Society*, January 1937, Vol. XXIV, Part 1).
  The Mongolian situation as viewed from Tibet.
Tibet, Past and Present, Oxford, 1924.

T. A. Bisson, " Outer Mongolia. A new danger zone in the Far East," in *Foreign Policy Reports*, Vol. XI, No. 19, November 20, 1935, pp. 226-36.

H. S. Brunnert and V. V. Hagelstrom, *Present Day Political Organization of China* (revised by N. Th. Kolessoff), Shanghai, 1912.

Beatrix Bulstrode (Mrs. E. M. Gull), *A Tour in Mongolia*, London, 1920.

Tsi Chu Chen, *China's Frontier Problems.*
>Typewritten manuscript. Thesis for London University, 1936. Almost the only presentation of the Chinese position but based on meager sources.

* Douglas Carruthers, *Unknown Mongolia,* 2 vols., London, 1913.

Violet Conolly, *Soviet Economic Policy in the East,* London, 1933.

Ladislaus Forbath, *The New Mongolia;* as related by Joseph Galeta, translated from the Hungarian by Lawrence Wolfe, London, 1936.
>Interesting account, but does not throw much light on the situation from the political point of view. Appeared 1934; originally in Hungarian; also in German in 1937.

Gerard M. Friters, " The Prelude to Outer Mongolian Independence," in *Pacific Affairs,* Vol. X, No. 2, June, 1937, pp. 168-89. " The Development of Outer Mongolian Independence," *ibid.,* No. 3, September 1937, pp. 315-36.
>Should be compared with Klévanski's (see French section) and Makerov's (see German section) studies written about the same time. See also Philip Grierson, *Books on Soviet Russia, 1917-1942,* London, 1943, p. 290.
>*The International Position of Outer Mongolia.* A contribution to Russia's and Japan's Policies in the Far East, Dijon 1939.
>" Soviet's Eastern Defenses " in *The Daily Telegraph and Morning Post,* London, June 24, 1942, p. 4.
>" Russia's Position in the Far East " in *The Contemporary Review,* October 1945, pp. 208-13.

James Gilmore, *Among the Mongols,* London, 1888.
>*More about the Mongols,* London, 1893.

John N. Hazard, " The Constitution of the Mongol People's Republic and Soviet Influences," *Pacific Affairs,* New York, June 1948, pp. 162-107.

Huc and Gabet, *Travels in Tartary, Tibet and China, 1844-46.*
>Translated by William Hazlitt, 2 Vols., London, 1928.

H. Haslund-Christensen, *Tents in Mongolia,* London-New York, 1934.
>*Men and Gods in Mongolia,* London-New York, 1935.

Pao Chao Hsieh, *The Government of China (1644-1911),* Johns Hopkins University. Studies in Historical and Political Science. New Series, No. 3, Baltimore, 1925.

W. Karamisheff, *Mongolia and Western China, Social and Economic Study,* Tientsin, 1925.
>*Economic Map of Outer Mongolia.* Drawings by P. Mezenzeff. Issued by Librarie Française, Tientsin, 1925.

F. A. Larson, *Larson, Duke of Mongolia,* Boston, 1930.

* Owen Lattimore, " The Unknown Frontier of Manchuria " in *Foreign Affairs,* Vol. 11, Jan. 1933.
>*The Mongols of Manchuria,* New York, 1934, London, 1935.

" Prince, Priest and Herdsman in Mongolia," in *Pacific Affairs,* Vol. VIII, No. 1, March 1935, pp. 35-47.

" On the Wickedness of Being Nomads," in *Asia,* Vol. 35, Oct. 1935.

" Russo-Japanese Relations," in *International Affairs,* Vol. XV, No. 4, July-August 1936, pp. 525-42.

" The Historical Setting of Inner Mongolian Nationalism " in *Pacific Affairs,* Vol. IX, No. 3, September 1936, pp. 388-405.

" Mongols of the Chinese Border " in *The Geographical Magazine,* Vol. VI, No. 5, March 1938, pp. 327-44.

" The Geographical Factor in Mongol History " in *Geographical Journal,* January 1938, pp. 1-20.

* *Inner Asian Frontiers of China,* London, New York, 1940.

* *Mongol Journeys,* New York-London, 1941.

Solution in Asia, Boston, 1945.

Situation in Asia, Boston, 1949.

" The Outer Mongolian Horizon " in *Foreign Affairs,* July 1946, pp. 648-60.

Eleanor Lattimore, " Report on Outer Mongolia " in *Far Eastern Survey,* November 6, 1946, pp. 337-40.

> Parts of the December 1945 *Sputnik Agitatora* (cf. end of Russian column) are mentioned for purposes of information only since no critical analysis is entered into.

Ma Ho-t'ien, *Chinese Agent in Mongolia,* translated by John De Francis, Baltimore, 1949.

I. Maisky (Maiskii), " Russia's Foreign Policy " in *The Challenge to Democracy* (Speeches delivered to the Liberal Summer School), London, 1936, esp. 59-62; " U. S. S. R. and Outer Mongolia."

> An interpretation by the then Soviet Ambassador at the Court of St. James (the author of *Sovremennaya Mongolia*).

Fedor S. Mansvetov, " Tsarist and Soviet Policy in the Far East " in *Foreign Affairs,* July 1934, pp. 654-63.

" Strategic Mongolia " in *Asia and the Americas,* April 1945, pp. 202-5.

" Inside Outer Mongolia," *ibid.,* May 1945, pp. 244-47.

" Russia and China in Outer Mongolia " in *Foreign Affairs,* October 1945, pp. 143-52.

* *Mongolia, Yesterday and Today,* Tientsin Press, 69 pp., n. d.

> This purports to be a verbatim report of the 3rd Congress of the Mongolian People's Party in August 1924. The translation from the Russian was made by Mr. Attree who during the intervention period was attached to the British Military Mission in Siberia and afterwards resided in Urga for a considerable period. I was not able to check whether the manuscript available in the Hoover War Library called " The 3rd Assembly of the Mongolian People's Party," Urga, English translation by F. Attree, 95 pp. is identical with the above.

Neither was I able to consult the manuscript obtainable at the same place called " New Mongolia," being the report of the 1st Great Assembly (Khuruldan) of the Mongolian People's Party at Ulan Bator, November 1924, English translation by F. Attree, 168 pp.

Illarion G. Matveev, " Mongolia," in *Foreign Commerce Weekly* (U. S. Department of Commerce), Vol. XV, No. 4, April 22, 1944, pp. 6-11.

Yasuo Mishima and Tomio Goto, *A Japanese View of Outer Mongolia*; being a condensed translation of *The Outer Mongolian People's Republic*. Translated and summarized from the Japanese by Andrew J. Grajdanzev. International Secretariat, Institute of Pacific Relations, New York, 1942, mimeographed. Must be read with caution.

Moore, Harriet L., *Soviet Far Eastern Policy, 1931-1945*, Princeton, 1945.

W. J. Oudendyk, " Soviet Policy in the Far East," in *International Affairs*, Vol. XV, No. 6, November-December 1936, pp. 824-45.

Leo Pasvolsky, *Russia in the Far East*, New York, 1922.

* H. G. C. Perry-Ascough and R. B. Otter-Barry, *With the Russians in Mongolia*; with a preface by the Right Hon. Sir Claude Macdonald, London, 1914.

G. D. R. Phillips, *Russia, Japan and Mongolia*, London, 1942. A journalistic account.

R. T. Pollard, *China's Foreign Relations, 1919-1931*, New York, 1933.

Ernest Batson Price, *The Russo-Japanese Treaties of 1907-1916 concerning Manchuria and Mongolia*. Baltimore, 1933.

N. M. Rivo Riabukhin, *The Story of Baron Ungern-Sternberg*. Told by his Staff Physician.
  A typed manuscript in the Hoover War Library. Not consulted.

V. A. Riasanovsky, *Customary Law of the Mongol Tribes*, Harbin, 1929.
  * *Fundamental Principles of Mongol Law*, Tientsin, 1937.

H. D. Robinson, " Mongolia, its Trade Routes and Trends." *U. S. Commerce Reports*, No. 1, January 6, 1930.

* W. W. Rockhill, " The Dalai Lamas of Lhasa and their relations with the Manchu Emperors of China 1644-1908," in *T'oung Pao* ou Archives concernant l'Histoire, les Langues, la Géographie et l'Ethnographie de l'Asie Orientale, Vol. XI, Lcide, 1910, pp. 1-104.
  * " The Question of Outer Mongolia," in *Journal of the American Asiatic Association*, May 1914 (Vol. XIV, No. 4, pp. 102-9), and in *The Far Eastern Review* (Shanghai), June 1915, pp. 1-11.

George N. Roerich, *Trails to Inmost Asia,* New Haven, 1931.
Interesting account of Tibet-Mongol Relations and of Ja-
Lama.

I. I. Serebrennikov, " A Soviet Satellite: Outer Mongolia Today," in
Foreign Affairs (New York), Vol. 9, No. 3, April 1931, pp. 510-15.

Edgar Snow, *People on Our Side,* New York, 1944.

Anna Louise Strong, *China's Millions,* London, 1936.

Tennyson Tan, *The Political Status of Mongolia,* Shanghai, 1932.
Representative of a certain type of monographs written by
Chinese on this question.

Sir Eric Teichman, " Mongolia and Her Overlords," in *The Geographical Magazine,* Vol. VI, No. 5, March 1938, pp. 321-26.

Henry A. Wallace, *Soviet Asia Mission,* New York, 1946.

K. S. Weigh, *Russo-Chinese Diplomacy,* Shanghai, 1928.

E. T. Williams, " The Treaty of Kiachta," in *American Journal of
International Law,* Vol. 10, 1916, pp. 798-808.

Serge M. Wolff, " The People's Republic of Mongolia," in *The Con-
temporary Review,* March 1929, pp. 362-68.
" Mongols in Western Europe," in *Man,* A Record of Anthrop-
ological Science, Vol. XLV, March-April 1945, pp. 41-42.
* " Mongol Delegations in Western Europe (1925-1929) " in
Journal of the Royal Central Asian Society, July-October
1945, pp. 289-98 and January 1946, pp. 75-92.
Mr. Wolff was Secretary to the Mongol Trade Delegation to
Berlin 1925-26 and subsequently to the Mongolian Educational
Mission. See also last item in German column.

W., " The Soviet Mongol Protocol of Mutual Assistance," in *The
Contemporary Review,* July 1936, pp. 67-75.

Victor A. Yakhontov, *Russia and the Soviet Union in the Far East,*
New York, 1931.
" Mongolia: Target or Screen? " in *Pacific Affairs,* Vol. IX, No.
1, March 1936, pp. 13-23.

In French:

Le P. Pierre Hoang, " Mélanges sur l'Administration," in *Variétés
sinologiques,* No. 21, Shanghai, 1902.

A. Houyet, " Les Traités asiatiques de la Russie des Soviets et la
question russo-sino-mongole," in *Bulletin de la Societé Belge
d'Études Coloniales,* XXIX, No. 7-8. July-August 1922, pp. 393-
443, No. 9-10, September-October, 1922, pp. 469-524.
Length suggests more than the articles actually contain.

Georges Klévanski, " La politique russe en Mongolie de 1881-1915,"
in *La Revue du Pacifique,* 16me Année, No. 1, January 1937, pp.

16-38, No. 2, February 1937, pp. 79-102, No. 3, March 1937, pp. 133-159.
> This journal has apparently ceased publication and thus this study was not completed. It is a chronogically arranged narrative based on the same materials as this book, but the Orange Book has not been consulted.

F. Lévine, *La Mongolie, Historique, Géographique, Politique*, Paris, 1937.
> Based only on *Krasny Archiv*, Vol. 37 and recent Russian periodicals.

B. Nikitine, *La Mongolie. Sociétés d'études et d'informations économiques* (Mémoires et documents), October 1930, p. 31.
> " Le Status internationale de la Mongolie," in *Revue des sciences politiques*, 54 t., pp. 590-609, 1931.
> " Les Relations Russo-Japanaises en Extrême Orient." Supplément au Bulletin quotidien, April 1936; Société d'Études et Économiques, Paris (mimeographed).
> " Le statut international de la Mongolie " in *Académie Diplomatique Internationale*, 11e Année, No. 1, 1937, Séances et Travaux, pp. 1-8.

* *La Revue Jaune*, Bruxelles: Agence d'Extrême Orient, 1911-12. Directeur: K. Wang.
> This semi-official Chinese publication is generally overlooked. Korostovets and Strupp (see German column) refer to it.

Le P. Dr. R. Verbrugge, " Les Confins Sino-Mongols," in *Bulletin de la Société Belge d'Études Coloniales*, XX, No. 1, January 1913, pp. 1-51, No. 2, February 1913, pp. 176-216.
> " Hinterland Mongol," *ibid.*, XXIX, Nos. 3-4, March-April 1922, pp. 99-168, No. 5-6, May-June 1922, pp. 221-77.
> " Les Déserts spécialement étudiés en Mongolie," *ibid.*, 31e Année, Nos. 11-12, November-December 1924, pp. 551-74.

In German:

Curt Alinge, *Mongolische Gesetze.* (Leipziger rechtswissenschaftl. Studien). Heft 87, Leipzig, 1934.
> A dissertation. The author lived in Urga for several years and was employed by the Mongol Government.

Rudolf Asmis, *Als Wirtschaftspionier in Russisch Asien*, Berlin, 1924.
> See Chapter V, pp. 52-99: " In der Mongolei."

Walter Bosshard, *Kühles Grasland Mongolei.* Zauber und Schönheit der Steppe. Berlin, 1938.
> Account of travelling in Inner Mongolia. Some information on Japanese activities.

* Georg Cleinow, *Neu-Sibirien* (Sib-krai), Eine Studie zum Aufmarsch der Sowjetmacht in Asien, Berlin, 1928. esp. Part II: Die russ. Chin. Beziehungen in der Mongolei, pp. 69-124.

* Hermann Consten, *Weideplätze der Mongolen. Im Reiche der Chalcha.* 2 vols. Berlin 1919 and 1920.

> An interesting work, but doubtful whether always reliable. The author does not acknowledge the many Russian books on which his account is based to a considerable extent. On author see Chapter VI.

O. Franke, *Die Grossmächte in Ostasien von 1894-1914.* Ein Beitrag zur Vorgeschichte des Krieges, Hamburg, 1923.

> A good study, but by now out of date because of new material available. Franke refers to the Orange Book.

Sven Hedin, *Von Peking nach Moskau,* Leipzig, 1925.

* Isschi-Dordji, " Die heutige Mongolei, II: Kulturelle Aufbauarbeit in der Mongolei," in *Osteuropa,* 4. Jahrg. Heft 6, March 1929, pp. 401-9.

R. Klaus, " Die Mongolische Volksrepublik " in *Jahrbuch der Weltpolitik,* Berlin, 1944, pp. 74-5.

> In spite of minor inaccuracies, the information is well put together and includes some statistics up to 1939 which are identical with those given in the Japanese book on the Mongolian People's Republic (see English column).

* Iwan Jakovlewitsch Korostovets, *Von Cinggis Khan bis zur Sowjetrepublik*; eine kurze Geschichte der Mongolei unter Berücksichtigung der neuesten Zeit unter Mitwirkung von Erich Hauer, Berlin, 1926.

> Based mainly on author's diaries as Russian Minister in Peking and later as Envoy to the Mongols.

G. Lange, *Politische Geographie der Nebenländer von China ausschliesslich der Mandschurei.*

> A dissertation for the University of Königsberg, 1932.

Werner Leimbach, *Landeskunde von Tuwa; Das Gebiet des Jenissei-Oberlaufes*; Petermanns Mitteilungen—Ergänzungsheft No. 222, Gotha, 1936 (with maps).

> A valuable piece of research.

A. N. Makarov, " Die Rechsstellung der Aeusseren Mongolei in ihrer historischen Entwicklung " in *Zeitschrift für ausländisches öffentliches Recht und Völkerrecht,* Bd. VII, May 1937, pp. 313-44.

> Author consulted Orange Book besides the other diplomatic archives available. Cf. note following Friters (English column).

K. A. Merisno, *Itinerarien und Landschaftsprofile J. G. Granös aus Uranhai (Tannu-Tuwa) und der Nordmongolei.* Mit Vorwort und einleitenden Text von J. G. Granö etc. Societas Geographica Fenniae, Acta Geographica, 6, Helsinki-Helsingsford, 1938.

Otto Mossdorf, " Das mongolische Problem " in *Zeitschrift für Politik,* Vol. II, 1925, pp. 425-39.

" Chinas entfremdete Aussenländer " in *Ostasiatische Rundschau,* 13. Jahrg., No. 3, February 1, 1932, pp. 50-1.

Friedrich Otte, *China: Wirtschaftspolitische Landeskunde,* Petermanns Mitteilungen Ergänzungsheft No. 194, Gotha 1927.

Hermann Poerzgen, " Zwischen Moskau und Ulan-Bator. Der Bolschewismus in der Mongolei " in *Frankfurter Zeitung,* Sunday, June 12, 1938, No. 294-5, p. 5.

* Dashi Sampilon, *Eine kurze Abhandlung über die mongolische Schafzucht und die Aussichten ihrer Entwicklung.* Translated from the Russian by Serge M. Wolff, Typescript, 1925 (33 foolscap pages).
    " Die moderne Mongolei " in *Deutsche Allgemeine Zeitung,* February 7, 1926, with illustrated supplement.
    An interview with Sampilon, the then Mongolian Minister of Economic Affairs.

Dietrich Schäfer, " Kommunistische Propaganda in der Mongolei " in *Zeitschrift für Geopolitik,* Vol. 53, 1938.

Sowjetwirtschaft und Aussenhandel. Edited by the Trade delegation of the U. S. S. R. in Germany.

K. Strupp, " Der Konflikt zwischen Russland and China vom Frühjahr 1911 " in Beiheft II in Vol. V of *Zeitschrift für Völkerrecht und Bundesstaatsrecht.*
    A dissertation for the University of Breslau in 1911. By no means original and mainly based on *La Revue Jaune.*

Erich Thiel, *Verkehrsgeographie von Russisch-Asien,* Osteuropäische Forschung, Neue Folge, Band 17, Königsberg-Berlin, 1934.
    Esp. pp. 197-201: " Die Wege in die Mongolei."

Thilo v. Thotha, " Die Mongolei. Eine militärisch-geographische Skizze " in *Petermanns Geographische Mitteilungen,* 1912, II, pp. 365-68.

Rudolf Walter, " Fernöstliche Probleme: I. Die Aussenmongolei " in *Eurpäische Revue,* January 1938, pp. 21-28.
    Mongolien im Ringen der Mächte, Berlin, 1941.
    Mentioned in *Jahrbuch für Auswärtige Politik* (ed. Friedrich Berber), Berlin, 1943, p. 426. Attempts of friends in 1946 to track down this book in Berlin were unsuccessful.

Bernard Waurik, " Auf der Suche nach dem neuen ' Lebenden Buddha.' Das Ende der weltlichen Herrschaft der mongolischen Kirchenfürsten " in *Berliner Tageblatt,* Sunday, September 14, 1924, No. 438, I, Beiblatt (dated from Urga in August).
    " Die heutige Mongolei I. Preface to a series of articles (Ischi-Dordji, Weiske) in *Osteuropa,* 4. Jahrg. Heft 3, December 1928, pp. 147-8.
    The therein promised longer article on the political situation by Waurik himself never appeared.

* Fritz Weiske, " Die Wirtschaftlichen Verhältnisse in der Aeusseren Mongolei," *ibid.,* pp. 149-65.
    The author was for a time employed by the Mongol Government.

* Serge M. Wolff, " Die Volksrepublik der Mongolei " in *Geopolitik* V. Jahrg. Heft 9, September 1928, pp. 755-69.
> Compare with English column. In view of the position held at that time by the author, the article may be said to have at least a semi-official character.

NOTE: " VESTNIK AKADEMII NAUK SSSR," No. 4-5, mentions that the following treatises were completed by the Pacific Institute in Moscow: " The Economic and Cultural Development of the Mongolian People's Republic " (Prof. I. N. Ustyuzhainov) and " Inner Mongolia and China " (the history of Sino-Mongolian relations from 1911 to 1947). Several attempts to obtain these studies have been unsuccessful.

GLOSSARY OF MONGOL TERMS

This glossary contains the Mongol words used in the text. There is no generally accepted system of transliterating Mongol into English. The system used in the text as well as on the maps is in general that adopted by the U. S. Army Map Service because of its simplicity and logic.

aimak	tribe, administrative unit, territory. Formerly there were six aimaks, of which four were in Khalkha. At present there are eighteen.
airak	fermented milk, kumis.
ara	behind, north, northern.
arat	people, common people. This word is important in the political vocabulary of the M. P. R. A number of important terms derive from it, such as arat-un erketei (democratic), arat erke (democracy), arat erke-in ulus (republic) and arat-tumen (the masses).
arul	hard dry cheese
bulak	spring
bag	community. Primary administrative unit in the M. P. R. made up of 30-100 households.
bodo	tax unit of cattle
bogdo	holy
Bogdo Gegen	title of the Hutukhtu of Urga, frequently translated as Living Buddha. Another form used to describe his political and religious position after 1911 is Bogdo Jebtsun Damba Hutukhtu Khan.
Buriat	name of a Mongol people living near Lake Baikal.
byslak	curds
chagan, tsagan	white
Da Kuriyen	great enclosure, i. e. the great monastery. The monastery district of Urga.
Dalai Lama	the supreme religious and political figure in Tibet.
dogoilong	circular. A group of conspirators.
ezegai	dried curd
gegen	enlightened, clear, holy, holy man. Title of ecclesiastical dignitaries, Many hutukhtus received the title of gegen from the Chinese government.
gobi	desert
gol	small river
gutul	Mongolian top-boots.
hoshun	banner, standard. Administrative unit of the aimak, recently abolished.

hubilgan	incarnation. Designation of incarnated ecclesiastical dignitaries often called Living Buddhas.
hural	meeting. The Little Hural and the Great Hural in the constitution of the M. P. R. correspond to the Russian soviets (councils).
hutukhtu	holy, sublime. Title of higher ecclesiastical dignitaries.
jassak	tribute in kind
Kalgan	the town (from Khalaga, gate, barrier) through which Mongols entered China.
Khalkha	shield, protection. Tribe of northern Mongolia occupying all but the western part of Outer Mongolia. The territory occupied by the Khalkha people.
khan, khagan	ruler, prince
Chingghis (Jenghis, Genghis) Khan	founder of the Mongol Empire in the thirteenth century.
khanate	principality. Under the Manchus the khanates received the name aimak.
Khanggai	a mountain chain in Outer Mongolia. A territory with fertile soil, forested mountains and many lakes and streams.
khainok	a cross between ordinary cattle and yak
khara	black
khorin	score. A small administrative unit.
Kuriyen	enclosure, monastery
lama	priest of the Lama Buddhist church.
mungge	Mongol coin, 100 to the tughrik.
muren	large river
nor, nur, nuur	lake
noyan	prince
Oirat	western Mongols, called Kalmuks by Russians
ola, ula, uula	mountain
otom	cross between khainok and either cattle or yak
sarlik	yak
shabi	pupil, disciple, novice, servant of monastery
shabinar	plural of shabi. Serfs belonging to monasteries.
shara	yellow
somon	arrow. Subdivision of aimak. There were 322 somons in 1946.
taiji	Mongol noble claiming descent from Jenghis Khan.
tarbaga	marmot
tughrik	currency unit in M. P. R.

Ulan Bator	Red Hero. M.P.R.'s name for Urga, the capital of the M.P.R.
Uliassutai	Place of Poplar Trees. Town in western Mongolia renamed Jirgalantu by the M.P.R.
ulus, ulas	community, people, nation, country. This forms part of the name translated " Mongolian People's Republic. Bughut Nairamdukho Monggol Arat Ulus, literally " all in agreement Mongol People's Country."
Urga	former name (in Russian and Western literature only) of capital of Outer Mongolia
Uriangha	territory northwest of Outer Mongolia, renamed Tannu Tuva and now the Tuvinian Autonomous Region of the U.S.S.R.
urum	a thick cream formed by heating milk over a slow fire while cream is rising
usa, usu	water, river

APPENDIX 2

CONSTITUTION (FUNDAMENTAL LAW) OF THE MONGOL PEOPLE'S REPUBLIC [1]

Ulan-Bator, June 30, 1940

CHAPTER I

SOCIAL ORGANIZATION

Article 1

The Mongol People's Republic is an independent state of workers (Arat cattle raisers, workers, and intelligentsia), who have annihilated the imperialistic and feudal yoke, ensuring a noncapitalistic approach to the development of the country to pave the way to socialism in the future.

Article 2

The Khurals of Arat workers, which came into being as a result of the overthrow of the feudal order and the seizure of political power by the people, the abolition of privilege and arbitrary law, the political and economic subjugation and exploitattion, which were inflicted upon the broad masses of the Arats by the feudal overlords (khans, vans, guns, taidzhis, khutukhta, and khubilgans)—constitute the political foundation of the Mongol People's Republic.

Article 3

In the Mongol People's Republic all power belongs to the urban and rural workers as represented by the workers' Khurals.

Article 4

The development of the Mongol People's Republic along noncapitalistic lines and the transition in the future to socialism are guaranteed by the achievement, in accordance with the state plan, of reforms in the economic, cultural, and social life of the Mongol People's Republic, that is: by assistance on the part of the state, in every way possible, toward the development and improvement of the Arat labor economy, by assistance on the part of the state to the voluntary and collective organizations of Arat workers, by the development of a network of stations for mowing machines drawn by horses, by the development in the country of cattle raising, industry, transport and communications.

The development of the national economy of the Mongol People's Republic is being carried out with the aim of increasing the public wealth,

[1] From *Soviet Press Translations*, Vol. III, No. 1, Jan. 1, 1948. Translated from *Sovietskoe Gosudarstvo i Pravo* (Soviet Government and Law), No. 8, August 1947, pp. 36-50.

of steadily improving the material welfare and the cultural level of the working people, of consolidating national independence and the defense capacity of the country.

Article 5

All the land and its natural resources, the forests, the waters, and all the wealth contained therein, the factories, mills, mines, gold production, the railroad, automobile, water and air transport, means of communication, banks, mowing machine stations, and state enterprises are state property, that is, they belong to the people as a whole.

Private ownership of the above is forbidden.

Article 6

The right of citizens to private ownership of cattle, agricultural implements and other tools of production, raw material, manufactured products, dwelling houses and outhouses, yurts, and household articles, incomes and savings, as well as the right of inheritance of private property, is protected by law.

Article 7

Public enterprises in the cooperative organizations and the Arat associations, together with their equipment and stock, their manufactured products, as well as their voluntarily socialized property, cattle, agricultural implements, and public buildings, constitute public ownership of these cooperative organizations and Arat associations.

Article 8

The land, being state property, that is, the common property of the people, is given free of charge to citizens as well as to voluntary associations of workers for use as pastures and agricultural tracts.

Article 9

Honest and conscientious labor is the basis of the development of the people's economy, of the consolidation of the defensive capacity, and of the further growth of the well-being of the workers of the Mongol People's Republic, and is the honorable duty of every able-bodied citizen.

CHAPTER II

THE ORGANIZATION OF THE STATE

Article 10

The jurisdiction of the Mongol People's Republic, as represented by its highest organs of authority and organs of government, extends to:

(a) Representation of the Mongol People's Republic in international relations; the conclusion and ratification of treaties with other states.

(b) General control over the domestic policy of the Mongol People's Republic and the development of its economic and cultural life.

(c) The organization of defense, control over the armed forces, and the preservatiton of the independence of the Mongol People's Republic.

(d) The fixing and alteration of state boundaries.

(e) Questions of war and peace.

(f) Control over the observance of the Constitution.

(g) Establishment of the administrative divisions of the Republic.

(h) The guarantee of the political, economic, and cultural development of the people who inhabit the Mongol People's Republic, in accordance with their national peculiarities.

(i) Foreign trade on the basis of a state monopoly, and control over the system of domestic trade.

(j) Maintenance of the security of the state, of order, and the rights of citizens.

(k) Approval of the national economic plan.

(l) Control over the monetary and credit system, approval of the state budget, and the establishment of taxes, levies, and revenues.

(m) Administration of state banks, industries, agricultural and trade enterprises, and institutions.

(n) Organization of the state, as well as of social insurance.

(o) Conclusion and approval of foreign loans and the issue of domestic loans.

(p) Control of transport and the organs of communications.

(q) Organization of the protection and exploitation of the natural resources of the country and the establishment of regulations for the use of the land, pastures, forests, waters, and the wealth contained therein.

(r) Organization and administration of the development of cattle raising and agriculture.

(s) Establishment of a system of weights and measures.

(t) Organization of the state inventory, accounts, and statistics.

(u) Administration of dwelling houses and communal economy, of construction and public utilities in the cities and of road construction in the country.

(v) Administration of national education and culture, public health, scientific, and physical culture organizations.

(w) Organization of court organs and of the organs of the Procurators.

(x) Award of orders, certificates of merit, and the conferring of honorable titles of the Mongol People's Republic.

(y) Legislation concerning citizenship in the Mongol People's Republic.

(z) Issuance of regulations concerning amnesty and pardon.

Article 11

The Mongol People's Republic consists of aimaks: the Central, Kentei, Eastern, East-Gobi, South-Gobi, Uburkhangai, Arakhangai, Dzapkhyn, Kokdos, Khubsugul, Bulgan, Selengin, Ubsanur, and the city of Ulan-Bator.[2]

[2] At the 24th session of the Little Khural of the Mongol People's Republic (February 1941) it was decided that: "In connection with the formation of the Bain-Ulegei and Gobi-Altai aimaks to revise Article 11 of the Constitution of the Mongol People's Republic as follows:

"Article 11. The Mongol People's Republic consists of aimaks: the Central, Kentei, Eastern, East-Gobi, South-Gobi, Uburkhangai, Arakhangai, Gobi-Altai, Dzapkhyn, Kobdos, Bain-Ulegei, Khubsugul, Bulgan, Ubsanur, Selengin, and the city of Ulan-Bator."

Article 12

The aimaks are divided for administrative purposes into somons. The somons, in their turn, are divided into bags. The city of Ulan-Bator is divided into khorons, and the khorons into khorins.

Chapter III

THE GREAT PEOPLE'S KHURAL

Article 13

The highest organ of state authority of the Mongol People's Republic is the Great People's Khural.

Article 14

The Great People's Khural is comprised of deputies of the urban workers, the aimaks and the armed forces of the People's Revolutionary Army, elected by the urban and aimak Khurals, on the basis of one deputy for every 1,500 of the population.

Article 15

The Great People's Khural is convened by the Little Khural once in three years. Special (extraordinary) sessions of the Great People's Khural are convened at the discretion of the Little Khural, or upon the demand of the local organs of authority representing not less than one-third of the entire population.

Article 16

The exclusive jurisdiction of the Great People's Khural extends to:

(a) Approval and revision of the Constitution (Fundamental Law) of the Mongol People's Republic.

(b) Establishment of basic principles and measures in the sphere of foreign and domestic policy.

(c) Election of members of the Little Khural.

Article 17

In the interval between sessions of the Great People's Khural, the highest authority in the Mongol People's Republic is vested in the Little Khural.

CHAPTER **IV**

THE LITTLE KHURAL AND THE PRESIDIUM OF THE LITTLE KHURAL

Article 18

The Little Khural is elected by the Great Khural for a term of three years, on the basis of one member for every 10,000 of the population.

Article 19

The jurisdiction of the Little Khural extends to::

(a) Convocation of the Great People's Khural.

(b) Formation of the Council of Ministers, confirmation of the newly organized Ministries, or the reorganization of existing Ministries and the central organs of the state administration.

(c) Annulment, whenever necessary, of the decisions and orders of the Council of Ministers.

(d) Confirmation of laws and regulations adopted by the Presidium of the Little Khural in the interval between the sessions of the Little Khural.

(e) Examination and confirmation of the state budget.

(f) Receiving the reports of the Presidium of the Little Khural and the Council of Ministers, and the examination of questions of state, economic, and cultural development.

(g) Election of the Supreme Court of the Mongol People's Republic.

(h) Appointment of the Procurator of the Mongol People's Republic.

Article 20

Regular sessions of the Little Khural are convened once a year. Special, extraordinary sessions may be convened by the Presidium of the Little Khural at its discretion, as well as upon the demand of not less than one-third of the members of the Little Khural.

Article 21

For the conduct of current business, the Little Khural elects from its own members a Presidium consisting of seven members: a President, Vice-President, Secretary, and four members.

Article 22

The Presidium of the Little Khural, in the interval between the sessions of the Little Khural, is the highest organ of state authority.

Article 23

The Presidium of the Little Khural:

(a) Exercises control over the putting into effect of the Constitution of the Mongol People's Republic and the carrying out of the decisions of the Great People's Khural and the Little Khural.

(b) Convenes sessions of the Little Khural.

(c) Passes new laws, subject to the subsequent confirmation of the Little Khural; interprets existing laws.

(d) Suspends, when it deems necessary, the decisions of the Council of Ministers and submits proposals for their annulment for the confirmation of the Little Khural.

(e) Appoints and removes Ministers from their duties upon representation of the Chairman of the Council of Ministers, subject to the subsequent confirmation of the Little Khural.

(f) Makes decisions as to amnesty and exercises the right of pardon.

(g) Awards decorations and certificates of merit of the Mongol People's Republic, and confers titles of honor.

(h) Receives the credentials and letters of recall of diplomatic representatives accredited to it by foreign states.

(i) Appoints and recalls plenipotentiary representatives of the Mongol People's Republic to foreign states.

(j) Ratifies treaties and agreements with other states.

(k) In the interval between the sessions of the Little Khural proclaims a state of war, in the event of an armed attack on the Mongol People's Republic, and likewise whenever necessary to fulfill international treaty obligations concerning mutual defense against aggression.

(l) Orders general or partial mobilization.

(m) Exercises control over admission to citizenship in the Mongol People's Republic.

(n) Annuls, when it deems necessary, the decisions of local Khurals.

Article 24

The Presidium of the Little Khural is accountable to the Little Khural for all its activities.

Article 25

The President of the Presidium of the Little Khural presides over the Little Khural and exercises jurisdiction over its internal organization.

Article 26

The members of the Little Khural may not be prosecuted or arrested without consent of the Little Khural, and during the interval between sessions of the Little Khural—without the consent of the Presidium of the Little Khural.

CHAPTER V

THE COUNCIL OF MINISTERS OF THE MONGOL PEOPLE'S REPUBLIC

Article 27

The highest executive and administrative organ of state authority of the Mongol People's Republic is the Council of Ministers of the Mongol People's Republic.

Article 28

The Council of Ministers of the Mongol People's Republic is responsible for its activities to the Great People's Khural and to the Little Khural, and in the interval between sessions of the latter, to the Presidium of the Little Khural.

Article 29

The Council of Ministers of the Mongol People's Republic issues decrees and orders on the basis and in pursuance of existing laws, and supervises their execution.

Article 30

Decrees and orders of the Council of Ministers of the Mongol People's Republic are binding throughout the territory of the Mongol People's Republic.

Article 31

The Council of Ministers of the Mongol People's Republic:

(a) Coordinates and directs the work of the Ministers of the Mongol People's Republic and other agencies under its jurisdiction.

(b) Adopts measures for the carrying out of the national economic plan, state and local budgets, taxes, and the credit system.

(c) Exercises general guidance in respect to relations with foreign states.

(d) Exercises general supervision over defense and the building up of the armed forces of the country, and likewise determines the annual contingent of citizens to be called up for military service.

(e) Adopts measures for the maintenance of public order, for the protection of the interests of the state, and for the safeguarding of the personal and property rights of citizens.

(f) Directly supervises and controls the work of the aimak and Ulan-Bator autonomous institutions and other local Khurals and their Presidiums.

(g) Revises and annuls orders, instructions, and decrees of the agencies directly subordinate to the Council of Ministers, the Ministers, and the local organs of authority.

(h) Sets up, when it deems necessary, central administrative agencies under the Council of Ministers of the Mongol People's Republic to deal with economic and cultural development.

(i) Approves patterns and issues the permit for the preparation of the state seal for the use of organs and institutions of the government.

Article 32

The Council of Ministers of the Mongol People's Republic is appointed by the Little Khural and consists of:

The Chairman of the Council of Ministers of the Mongol People's Republic.

The Vice-Chairman of the Council of Ministers of the Mongol People's Republic.

The head of the Commission on State Planning, Inventory and Control.

The Ministers of the Mongol People's Republic.

Article 33

The following Ministries are functioning in the Mongol People's Republic:

War	Finance
Foreign Affairs	Domestic Affairs
Cattle Raising and Agriculture	Education
Industry and Construction	Public Health
Transport	Justice
Trade	

Article 34

Directly subordinate to the Council of Ministers of the Mongol People's Republic are:

(a) The Commission on Planning, Inventory, and Control

(b) The Commission on Communications

(c) The Committee on the Arts

(d) The Committee on Science

(e) The State Publishing House [3]

---

[3] At the 24th session of the Little Khural of the Mongol People's Republic (February 1941) it was decided: "In view of the elimination of the Handicrafts Industrial Union from the Ministry of Industry and Construction, and the organization of the Central Council of the Handicrafts Industrial Cooperative, directly subordinate to the Council of Ministers, to revise Article 34 of the Constitution (Fundamental Law) of the Mongol People's Republic, as follows:

"Article 34. Directly subordinate to the Council of Ministers of the Mongol People's Republic are: (a) The Commission on Planning, Inventory, and Control; (b) The Commission on Communications; (c) The Committee on the Arts; (d) The Committee on Science; (e) The State Publishing House; (f) The Central Council of the Handicrafts Industrial Cooperative."

Article 35

The Ministers and Chairmen of the central agencies of the Mongol People's Republic each direct a corresponding branch of state administration and assume full responsibility for it before the Council of Ministers.

Article 36

The Ministers of the Mongol People's Republic and Chairmen of the central government agencies, within the limits of their competence, issue orders and instructions, and also supervise their execution. Orders and instructions are issued on the basis of, and in conformity with, the existing laws, decrees, and orders of the Council of Ministers of the Mongol People's Republic.

CHAPTER VI

LOCAL ORGANS OF STATE AUTHORITY

Article 37

The highest organs of authority in the aimaks, in Ulan-Bator, in the somons, khorons, khorins, and bags are the Khurals of Arat workers.

Article 38

The aimak, somon, and khoron Khurals, as well as the Khural of the city of Ulan-Bator, are composed of deputies in conformity with the below-mentioned Khurals, which are elected on the basis of: in the city of Ulan-Bator, one deputy for every 200 of the population; in the aimaks, one deputy for every 400 of the population; in the somons and khorans, one deputy for every 50 of the population. The bag and khorin Khurals are composed of all citizens of the bag and khorin who have the right to vote.

Article 39

Regular sessions of the aimak Khurals of workers, and of the Khural of workers of the city of Ulan-Bator, are convened once in three years. Regular sessions of the somon, khoron, bag, and khorin Khurals of workers are convened once a year. Special sessions of the workers' Khurals are convened upon the demand of not less than half of all the voters of the aimak, somon, bag, khoron, or khorin, or upon the demand of not less than two-thirds of the members of the elected Khural, and also upon the recommendation of the Presidium of the Little Khural of the Mongol People's Republic.

Article 40

The aimak, somon, khoron, khorin, and bag Khurals, as well as the Khural of the city of Ulan-Bator, receive the reports of the organs of administration subordinate to them, and conduct elections of local organs of administration and of deputies to the above-mentioned Khurals.

Article 41

In the interval between sessions of the Khurals of the aimaks and the city of Ulan-Bator, the highest organs of authority in the aimaks and in the city of Ulan-Bator are the Little Khurals, elected by the workers' Khurals of the aimaks and the city of Ulan-Bator for a term of three years, on the basis of one deputy for every 1,000 of the population.

Article 42

The Khurals of the aimaks and of the city of Ulan-Bator are convened twice a year.

Article 43

For the conduct of current business, the Little Khurals of the aimaks and the city of Ulan-Bator elect from their own members a Presidium of from 7 to 13 persons, consisting of: a Chairman, Vice-Chairman, and members.

Article 44

The executive and administrative organs of the somon, khoron, bag, and khorin Khurals of workers elect local, self-governing bodies of from three to 13 persons, each consisting of: a Chairman, a Secretary, and members of the self-governing body, for a term of one year. The Chairman of the self-governing bodies direct all the business, convene sessions of the self-governing bodies, and preside over them.

Article 45

The Little Khurals of the aimaks and of the city of Ulan-Bator and their Presidiums, as well as the somon and khoron self-governing bodies:

(a) Direct cultural-political and economic development in their territories.

(b) Draw up the local budget.

(c) Direct the work of the organs of administration subordinate to them.

(d) Ensure the maintenance of public order, the observance of the laws and protection of the rights of the citizens.

(e) Annul the decrees and orders of the below-mentioned organs of authority, in the event that they are at variance with the laws of the Mongol People's Republic.

Article 46

The Little Khurals of the aimaks and of the city of Ulan-Bator and their Presidiums, the somon, khoron, bag, and khorin self-governing bodies, pass resolutions and give orders, within the limits of the powers vested in them by the laws of the Mongol People's Republic.

Article 47

The Presidiums of the Little Khurals of the aimaks, and of the city of Ulan-Bator, as well as of the somon, khoron, bag, and khorin self-governing bodies, are directly accountable to their Khurals, elected by the workers, and to the above-mentioned organs of administration.

Article 48

The Presidiums of the Little Khurals of the aimaks and of the city of Ulan-Bator have the following departments:

Cattle Raising and Agriculture   Education
Finance   War
Public Health

CHAPTER VII

THE COURTS AND THE PROCURATOR'S OFFICE

Article 49

In the Mongol People's Republic justice is administered by the Supreme Court of the Republic, by the city court of Ulan-Bator, by the aimak courts, and by the district people's courts.

Article 50

Judicial proceedings in all the courts are conducted by permanent judges, with the participation of People's assessors, with the exception of cases specially provided for by law.

Article 51

The Supreme Court of the Mongol People's Republic is the highest judicial organ. The Supreme Court is charged with the supervision of the judicial activities of all the judicial organs of the Mongol People's Republic. The Supreme Court directly tries the most important cases submitted to its consideration by the Procurator of the Republic, and likewise reviews complaints and protests, in the capacity of a court of appeal and supervision, of cases tried by the courts mentioned below.

Article 52

The Chairman and members of the Supreme Court and the special courts are elected by the Little Khural of the Mongol People's Republic for a term of four years.

Article 53

The city, aimak, and district people's courts are elected by the city and aimak Little Khurals for a term of three years.

Article 54

Judicial proceedings are conducted in the Mongol language, persons unfamiliar with the language being ensured an opportunity to become fully acquainted wtih the proceedings through an interpreter, and likewise the right to use their own language in court.

13

Article 55

In all courts, cases are heard in public, the accused being guaranteed the right to be defended by Counsel. Closed judicial sessions are permitted in cases specially provided for by law.

Article 56

Judges are independent and are subject only to the law.

Article 57

Supreme supervisory power over the strict execution of the laws by all the Ministries, central organs and agencies subordinate to them, as well as by the public servants and citizens of the Mongol People's Republic, is vested in the Procurator of the Republic.

Article 58

The Procurator of the Mongol People's Republic is appointed by the Little Khural for a term of five years.

Article 59

In the cities, somons, and bags, the Procurator's power is exercised by the city and aimak procurators, who are appointed by the Procurator of the Mongol People's Republic for a term of four years.

Article 60

Local procurators exercise their functions independently of any local organs whatsoever, being subordinate solely to the Procurator of the Republic.

CHAPTER VIII

THE BUDGET OF THE MONGOL PEOPLE'S REPUBLIC

Article 61

The entire financial policy of the Mongol People's Republic is directed toward the betterment and well-being of the broad masses of workers, the decisive restriction and dislodging of the exploiting elements and, at the same time, the strengthening by every possible means of the authority of the workers, as well as the independence and defensive capacity of the country.

Article 62

Government revenues and expenditures of the Mongol People's Republic are combined in the over-all state budget.

Article 63

The state budget is prepared by the Ministry of Finance and examined by the Council of Ministers. The budget as approved by the Council of Ministers is subject to the confirmation of the Little Khural of the Mongol People's Republic.

Article 64

The Little Khural of the Mongol People's Republic elects the budget committee, which reports to the Little Khural its conclusions on the state budget of the Mongol People's Republic.

Article 65

There can be no disbursement whatsoever of state funds, unless it is provided for by the state budget, or unless such expenditure is authorized by a special decree of the Presidium of the Little Khural or the Council of Ministers. The funds provided for by the state budget are expended solely in accordance with their direct allocation, within the limits of the established estimates.

Article 66

The Little Khural distributes the revenues among the state and local budgets.

Article 67

Laws regarding taxes and levies are passed by the Presidium of the Little Khural, subject to the subsequent confirmation of the Little Khural of the Mongol People's Republic. No other organs of authority have any right whatsoever to introduce taxes and levies.

Article 68

Somon estimates of revenues and expenditures are confirmed by the Little Khural of the aimak or its Presidium, the estimates of the khorons— by the Little Khural of the city of Ulan-Bator or its Presidium, aimak estimates and the estimates of the city of Ulan-Bator—by the Presidium of the Little Khural of the Mongol People's Republic.

Article 69

The report on the execution of the state budget, after its examination by the Council of Ministers, is approved by the Little Khural of the Mongol People's Republic.

CHAPTER IX

THE ELECTORAL SYSTEM OF THE MONGOL PEOPLE'S REPUBLIC

Article 70

Elections of all organs of authority are conducted in the Khural by voice vote. Each member of the Khural may nominate candidates for membership in the executive organs and candidates as deputies for the above-mentioned Khurals. The name of each candidate nominated must be submitted for discussion in the Khural prior to the voting. Each member of the Khural is guaranteed the right of free expression *for* or *against* the candidate nominated. Candidates who have received a simple majority of votes are considered elected.

Article 71

All citizens of the Mongol People's Republic who have reached the age of eighteen have the right to participate in elections and to be elected, irrespective of their sex, nationality, religion, education, nomadic or settled mode of life, and property status, with the exception only of exploiters who hire workers for profit, usurers, former khutukhta, khubilgans, higher Lamas, active dzasak and nadzasak, khans, vans, beili, beisi, guns, and also those who have had slaves and cruelly oppressed their slaves, government officials, who managed the khoshun and shabin institutions, influential shamans, active participants in the White Army and counter-revolutionary uprisings, as well as the insane and persons convicted by the court, whose sentence includes deprivation of electoral rights.[4]

[4] See the new text of Article 7, adopted by the Presidium of the Little Khural of the Mongol People's Republic on September 28, 1944 (Appendix).

Article 72

In elections all voters have equal rights; each voter has one vote. Members of the armed forces have the right to participate in the elections on an equal footing with all citizens.

Article 73

Women have the right to elect and be elected on equal terms with men.

Article 74

For the conduct of elections, central and local electoral commissions are appointed, which act in accordance with instructions and regulations approved by the Presidium of the Little Khural.

CHAPTER X

FUNDAMENTAL RIGHTS AND DUTIES OF CITIZENS

Article 75

The Constitution of the Mongol People's Republic consolidates the right won by the people to free use of pastures, in order to promote the greater development of cattle raising, as well as the application by the citizens of their knowledge and labor in all branches of state, economic, and cultural development.

Article 76

Citizens of the Mongol People's Republic have the right to rest. This right is ensured by the reduction of the working day to 8 hours for employees and workers, the institution of annual vacations with full pay for workers and employees, and the provision of theaters, clubs, sanatoriums, and rest homes for the accommodation of the working people.

Article 77

Citizens of the Mongol People's Republic have the right to education. This right is ensured by education free of charge, by the development of a network of schools, technical schools, and by instruction in schools in the native language.

Article 78

Citizens of the Mongol People's Republic and hired laborers have the right to material assistance in old age, as well as in the event of illness and loss of the capacity to work. This right is ensured by a system of social insurance for workers and employees at the expense of the state or employer, free medical service for the working people, and the development of a network of health resorts.

Article 79

All citizens of the Mongol People's Republic, irrespective of their nationality, have equal rights in all spheres of the state, economic, cultural, and socio-political life of the country. All direct or indirect restrictions on the rights of citizens, the manifestation of imperialistic chauvinism, discrimination, and propaganda on nationalistic grounds, are punishable by law.

Article 80

Women in the Mongol People's Republic are accorded equal rights with all spheres of economic, state, cultural and socio-political life. The opportunity to exercise these rights is ensured by granting women equal rights with men in regard to work, rest, social insurance, education, state protection of the interests of the mother and child, and by granting hired women prematernity leave with full pay.

Interference, in any way whatsoever, with the emancipation and equal rights of women, that is: marrying them off before they have become of age, taking them in marriage, giving or receiving ransom for the bride, polygamy, preventing them from attending school, or from participating in the economic, state, cultural, and socio-political life, etc., is punishable by law.

Article 81

In the Mongol People's Republic religion is separated from the state and the school. Citizens of the Mongol People's Republic have freedom of religion and of antireligious propaganda.

Article 82

In conformity with the interests of the workers, and in order to develop the organizational initiative and political activity of the working masses, citizens of the Mongol People's Republic are ensured the right to unite in public organizations: trade unions, cooperative associations, youth organizations, sport and defense organizations, cultural, technical, and scientific societies; and the most active and politically-conscious citizens in the ranks of the workers, Arat workers, and intelligentsia, are united in the Mongol People's Revolutionary Party, which is the vanguard of the working people in their struggle to strengthen and develop the country along noncapitalistic lines into a party which is the foremost nucleus of all organizations of workers, both public and state.

Article 83

Every citizen of the Mongol People's Republic has the right freely to submit written or oral complaints or declarations against the unlawful acts of the organs of authority, or against individual officials in the corresponding organs of the government and administration, up to the very highest. All organs of authority and officials are obligated to examine forthwith the declarations and complaints submitted, and to give the complainant a reply bearing upon the declaration or complaint.

Article 84

All citizens of the Mongol People's Republic have the right to move about freely, and to select a place of residence.

Article 85

In conformity with the interests of the workers, and in order to develop and strengthen the state system of the Mongol People's Republic, citizens of the Mongol People's Republic are guaranteed by law:

(1) Freedom of speech
(2) Freedom of the press
(3) Freedom of assembly and meetings
(4) Freedom of street processions and demonstrations.

Article 86

Citizens of the Mongol People's Republic are guaranteed inviolability of the person. No person may be placed under arrest, except by decision of a court or with the sanction of a procurator.

Article 87

The inviolability of the homes of citizens and privacy of correspondence are protected by law.

Article 88

The Mongol People's Republic affords the right of asylum to foreign citizens persecuted for defending the interests of the workers, or for their struggle for national liberation.

Article 89

It is the duty of every citizen of the Mongol People's Republic to abide by the Constitution (Fundamental Law) of the Mongol People's Republic, to observe the laws, to maintain labor discipline, to promote in every way possible the economic, cultural, and political development of the country, and to perform their public duties honestly.

Article 90

Compulsory military service is the law of the land. Military service in the Mongol People's Revolutionary Army is obligatory for citizens of the Mongol People's Republic.

Article 91

The defense of the motherland is the sacred duty of every citizen of the Mongol People's Republic. Treason to the motherland—the violation of the oath of allegiance, desertion to the enemy, impairment of the military power of the state, and espionage—is punishable as the most heinous of crimes.

CHAPTER XI

ARMS, FLAG, CAPITAL

Article 92

The State Emblem of the Mongol People's Republic consists of a circle, in which is depicted an Arat with a lariat in his hands, galloping on horseback toward the sun.

Inside the circle is depicted a typical Mongol landscape (a forested steppe, a desert, mountains).

Around the edge of the circle, which is framed in green, on two sides there are depicted in small circles the heads of a sheep, a cow, a camel, and a goat. At the base of the circle is the ornament " Alkha " in one line.

In the center of the upper part of the circle is a five-pointed star. At the base of the circle is a bunch of greens tied with a ribbon, with the inscription " The Mongol People's Republic."

Article 93

The flag of the Mongol People's Republic consists of a red cloth with the State Emblem depicted in the center, and the inscription on either side " Mongol People's Republic."

Article 94

The capital of the Mongol People's Republic is Ulan-Bator.

CHAPTER XII

PROCEDURE FOR AMENDING THE CONSTITUTION OF THE MONGOL PEOPLE'S REPUBLIC

Article 95

The Constitution of the Mongol People's Republic is amended only by the decision of the Great People's Khural, adopted by not less than a two-thirds majority vote.

DESCRIPTION OF THE EMBLEM OF THE MONGOL PEOPLE'S REPUBLIC

The State Emblem of the Mongol People's Republic consists of a circle, in which is depicted an Arat with a lariat in his right hand, galloping against the background of a summer landscape representative of all parts of Mongolia (mountains, forest, steppe, desert) on a brown horse in the direction of the rising sun.

Around the rim of the circle, which is framed in green, on two sides there are depicted in small circles the heads of a sheep, a cow, a camel, and a goat.

In the upper part of the circle is the ornament " Alkha " in one line. In the center of the upper part of the circle is a five-pointed star, one point of which protrudes slightly beyond the circle. At the base of the circle are bunches of greens tied with a red ribbon, with the inscription " The Mongol People's Republic."

The clothing of the Arat consists of a blue Mongol robe and a white Mongol lambskin cap, the upper part of which is covered with a brown material; the cap rises to a peak (Dzhinsa) and the strings of the cap are flying behind. The gutul (boots) are black with a band of variegated embroidery around the top.

The rider's saddle is red with silver ornamentation (the edge).

The gulem (wing) of the saddle is of brown leather with a band of embroidery around the edge.

The animals depicted are of Mongol pedigree and their colors are as follows: the horse is brown, with white spots on the legs above the pastern, and with a star on the forehead; the sheep is white and the horns are curled; the cow is red and the horns are bent inward; the camel is chestnut; the goat is steel grey and the horns are bent slightly backward.

Opposite the hind hoofs of the horse, in an oval, is placed the cow, and beneath it is the goat; opposite the front hoofs is the sheep, and beneath it is the camel. The tips of the bunches of greens are just visible beyond the cow and the sheep.

The description of the landscape is as follows: the sun is half visible beyond the distant dark-blue mountains, the peaks of which are covered with eternal snow; below an orange-colored mountain is depicted, then a forest and a green steppe which gradually changes to a desert, sparsely covered with grass; the sky above the landscape is blue, becoming overcast toward the rim of the circle.

THE CONFERRING OF ELECTORAL RIGHTS UPON PERSONS DEPRIVED OF THESE RIGHTS BY ARTICLE 71 OF THE CONSTITUTION OF THE MONGOL PEOPLE'S REPUBLIC

Decree of the Presidium of the Little Khural of the Mongol People's Republic

With a view to the further expansion of democracy to all citizens of the Mongol People's Republic, and also with the subject of strengthening the people's revolutionary order in our country and the development of the political consciousness and activity of the working people, taking into consideration in this connection that:

(a) Whereas persons deprived of electoral rights do not represent at the present time an organized force in opposition to the people's revolutionary order, and do not constitute a threat to its existence, especially since their number in the Republic is insignificant and amounts only to 0.08 percent of the entire population of the Mongol People's Republic;

(b) Whereas the overwhelming majority of persons deprived of electoral rights have for more than the past ten years been occupied in useful public work and in reality are workers;

(c) Whereas, in depriving individual citizens of their electoral rights, local organs of authority have in many cases acted without due consideration, as a result of which the interests of the Arat workers were injured;

Therefore, the Presidium of the Little Khural of the Mongol People's Republic decrees:

1. That electoral rights be granted to all those citizens of the Mongol People's Republic heretofore deprived of these rights by Article 71 of the Constitution of the Mongol People's Republic, with the exception of the insane, and persons deprived of political rights by the court, which will promote the further strengthening of the people's revolutionary order.

2. That Article 71 of the Constitution (Fundamental Law) of the Mongol People's Republic be amended to read as follows:

" Article 71. All citizens of the Mongol People's Republic, who have reached the age of eighteen, have the right to participate in elections and to be elected, irrespective of their sex, nationality, religion, education, nomadic or settled mode of life, and property status, with the exception of the insane and persons convicted by the court, whose sentence includes deprivation of electoral rights."

That the changes indicated be submitted for approval to the regular session of the Little Khural of the Mongol People's Republic and the regular session of the Great People's Khural of the Mongol People's Republic.

President of the Presidium of the
Little Khural of the MPR

BUMA TSENDE

Secretary of the Presidium of the
Little Khural of the MPR

BAIR

September 28, 1944
City of Ulan-Bator

SOME MONGOL PERSONALITIES

Amursana	Prince of the Kalmuks (Oirats) in Western Mongolia in the middle of the 18th century. After fights with other aspirants to leadership, he led the struggle against the Chinese. He had to flee to Siberia where he died. He was reputed to have sworn an oath on his flight to Russia, after he failed in his revolt against the Manchus, to come back and liberate Mongolia. He has become a legendary figure. (see also Ja Lama).
Ayushi	Leader of the Dogoilong movement in the south of the Jasaktu Khan Aimak about 1905. Considered one of the veterans of the Mongolian revolution and of the M. P. R. Had rank of Bagin-Darga (Village Elder).
Jebtsun Damba Hutukhtu	Living Buddha of Urga. Born in Tibet and considered the 23rd incarnation (8th in Mongolia) of a pupil of Buddha; from the family of an official in the Government of the Dalai Lama. Lived in Urga after 1874. Proclaimed Khan of Mongolia in December 1911—temporal ruler up to November 1921 when an agreement was signed between him and the new Mongolian Government restricting his powers to religious matters. Died in June 1924. Last incarnation allowed. An important political influence between 1911 and 1921.
Taiji Toktokho	from South Gorlos Banner of eastern Mongolia. Head of a group of " bandits " according to the Chinese, forerunner of " liberation fighters " according to Soviet sources. Fled from China to Russia. Offered his services to the Mongolian Government at the end of 1911. Received the title of Gung and later Beise and became head of the bodyguard of the Hutukhtu of Urga. Executed in 1922 in the " Bodo conspiracy."
Agwang Dorjiev	a Buriat from Transbaikalia. He acted on behalf of the Dalai Lama of Tibet (whether properly authorized or not is doubtful) in concluding the Tibet-Mongolia Treaty of January 1913 at Urga.
Ja Lama (also transliterated as Chal Lama or Dja Lama)	Ja Lama is the popular name of Dambi-Danzan, a Kalmuk reputed to have had a perfect knowledge of Mongolian and Russian. Posed as a wandering lama after 1890 and agitated against the Chinese. He proclaimed himself the grandson of Amursana (see above) and was welcomed as his incarnation. He

styled himself Hutukhtu. Was arrested by Russians (as a " Russian subject ") in 1914 and transported to Siberia. Returned to Mongolia in 1918, and greeted as a martyr. Founded a hoshun of his own in Western Mongolia. Agitated against new Mongolian regime. Murdered by emissary of Urga Government in 1924.

Prince Palta
(P'a Wang)

A leader of the Western Mongols. His mother was Chinese and he was educated in Japan. In 1911 he refused to unite the (Chinese) Altai district, of which he was Governor between 1911 and 1914, with Autonomous Mongolia. He concluded a temporary agreement with Russian Consul Kusminski on the cessation of hostilities between Chinese and Mongols at Shara Sume in December 1913.

Prince Udai
(Otai, Wut'ai)

Fled from Jasakto Wang Banner of Inner Mongolia to join the new Mongolian Government in 1911-12. Member of the Mongol delegation to St. Petersburg in December 1913.

Sain Noyan Khan

One of the most powerful hereditary rulers of Outer Mongolia. Prime Minister from February 1914 to 1919. A most able negotiator. Poisoned in 1919.

Da Lama
(Pontsok Dorji)

Minister of the Interior in the first Mongolian Government. Though a high dignitary of the Lama Church, he was an enemy of Lamaism and of the autocracy of the Princes. Anti-Russian. Executed in the " pro-Chinese " Bodo conspiracy in 1922.

Tsereng Dorji

First an official in the Foreign Ministry of the autonomous government after 1911-12. Had a remarkable political career for he also had a leading government position during the regimes of " Little Hsü," Ungern Sternberg and in the M. P. R. Foreign Minister and later, Prime Minister in the M. P. R. until his death in 1929.

Prince Handa Dorji

of Tushetu Khan Aimak. Member of the Mongolian delegation to St. Petersburg in 1911. Foreign Minister in the first Mongolian Government in 1911.

Dalai Wang
(Gombo Surung)

Minister of War in the first Mongolian Government. One of the hereditary rulers of Outer Mongolia.

Tushetu Khan

Finance Minister in the first Mongolian Government.

Namsarai Wang

of Tushetu Khan Aimak. Minister of Justice in the first Mongolian Government. Pro-Russian.

Tsetsen Khan

One of the hereditary rulers of Outer Mongolia. Minister of the Interior in first revolutionary Government in 1921-22.

Lama Bodo — Formerly a clerk in the Russian Consulate General in Urga. Prime Minister of first revolutionary Government in 1921-22. Executed in September 1922 as leader of a pro-Chinese plot.

Sukhe Bator — Born 1893; died 1923. Leader of Mongolian Revolutionary Army. War Minister in first revolutionary government. Details of career in Owen Lattimore's introduction to this book.

Danzan (Dansan Horlo) — One of the founders of the revolutionary party. In first revolutionary government he was Minister of Finance. After the fall of Bodo he became Commander-in-Chief of the Army. After the death of the Hutukhtu of Urga in 1924 he was accused of organizing a plot against the newly proclaimed republic and he was executed in July 1924.

Amor — Deputy Prime Minister in the second half of the 1920's. President of the Little Hural in the middle 1930's. There are numerous references to a published report of his in this book. " Liquidated " toward the end of the 1930's.

Gendung — President of the Little Hural in the second half of the 1920's. Prime Minister in the middle of the 1930's. There are several references to a long published report of his in this book. " Liquidated " toward the end of the 1930's.

Doksom — Prime Minister in the middle of the 1930's. There are references to a published report of his in this book.

Choibalsang — An influential member of the Mongolian People's Party since 1921 and successor to Sukhe Bator (see above). Foreign Minister in 1931. Prime Minister and Marshal. Details of career in Owen Lattimore's introduction to this book.

Some members of the Mongolian Trade Delegation and Education Mission in Germany 1925-29:

Dashi Sampilon — A Buriat. A graduate of the Petrovsko-Razumovskaya Agricultural Academy. Once a counsellor of the Mongolian Legation in Moscow. Chief of the Tarde Delegation. Later Minister of Economic Affairs. " Liquidated."

Shilon K. Hurlatt — Probably originated from Barga. Arrested some years ago.

Erdeni Batukhan — A Buriat. Minister of Education in the middle 1920's.

Ishi Dorji   Born in Urga. A teacher by profession. See also his article in Bibliography. No longer in M. P. R.

Gombojab   Of the Mongolian Scientific Committee (founded in 1921). Of noble descent. " Liquidated " as a " wrecker."

Persons in the Government of the M.P.R.[1]
(as of December 1948)

President of the Presidium of the Little Hural:	*Bumatsende*
Vice-President of the Presidium of the Little Hural:	*Yangjima*
Chairman of the Council of Ministers (Prime Minister) and Foreign Minister:	(Marshal) *Choibalsang*
Deputy Prime Minister (and head of the Mongolian Trade Delegation in Moscow, Dec. 1948):	*Lubsang*
Deputy Foreign Minister:	*Jamosurung*
Vice-Chairman of the Council of Ministers:	*Tsedenbal* [2]
Mongolian Minister to the U. S. S. R.:	*N. Idamjab* (since April 8, 1946) (Predecessor: Sambu)
Soviet Minister to the M. P. R.:	*Prikhodov* (Predecessor: I. A. Ivanov)[3]

---

[1] *Sources: Soviet News*, published by the Press Department of the Soviet Embassy in London, esp. the numbers of Oct. 20 and 27, Nov. 10, Dec. 13, 1948; also *Soviet Monitor*, August 4, 1946).

[2] Also: Secretary General of the Central Committee of the M. R. People's Revolutionary Party (*Moscow Radio*, Sept. 4, 1945, 21.05: Tass information for Soviet Provincial Press).

[3] No other country has a diplomatic representative in the M. P. R. A Tass report of October 16, 1948 from Ulan Bator carries an announcement as to the establishment of diplomatic relations between the M. P. R. and the Korean People's Democratic Republic (Northern Korea).

SHORT CHRONOLOGY OF EVENTS

1688	Mongol Princes assemble at Dolon Nor and leave the decision as to whether to affiliate with Russia or the Manchu Emperor to the Hutukhtu of Urga. The latter decides in favor of the Manchus.
1689	Russo-Chinese treaty (first treaty between China and a European State).
1691	The Princes of Khalkha swear allegiance to Emperor K'ang Hsi at Dolon Nor.
1719	Manchu restrictive decrees issued, depriving Mongol nobles of the right to enter into independent relations with neighboring powers.
1727	Russo-Chinese Treaty of Kiakhta establishing frontier demarcations, etc.
1757	Final conquest of Western Mongolia by Ch'ien Lung.
1860	Russo-Chinese Treaty of Peking.
1860	Establishment of first Russian trading firm in Urga.
1861	Opening of first Russian Consulate in Urga.
1864	Russo-Chinese Protocol of Chuguchak.
1878	Jungaria united with Sinkiang Province.
1881	Russo-Chinese Treaty of St. Petersburg (giving Russia the right to open consulates in Mongolia).
1904	Dalai Lama of Tibet flees to Urga (British expedition to Tibet).
1904-05	Russo-Japanese War ends in Russia's defeat and a more cautious policy in the Far East.
1905-11	New Chinese policy of active interference and economic penetration in Outer Mongolia.
1905	Mongols apply to Russian Consul in Urga for " advice and protection."
1907 (July)	Secret Russo-Japanese Convention recognizing special interest of Russia in Outer Mongolia. Altai district separated from the Khobdo district of Outer Mongolia.
1910	Hutukhtu of Urga appeals to Russia. Mongols oppose measures proposed by Peking Government.
1911(Spring)	China adopts most intransigent attitude concerning the renewal of the Treaty of St. Petersburg of 1881 withholding from Russia permission to open a consulate at Khobdo.
(July)	Delegation of Outer Mongolian princes in St. Petersburg asks for Russian protection.

(Autumn)	Increasing disorders in China.
(November)	Outer Mongolian (Khalkha) princes declare their independence and proclaim Hutukhtu of Urga as Ruler of Mongolia.
1912 (January)	End of Manchu Dynasty. Proclamation of Chinese Republic.
(Beginning)	Mongol tribes of Urianghai, Barga and a few of Inner Mongolia declare their allegiance to Urga.
(April 13)	Russian Foreign Minister gives Russian Duma reasons for not recognizing the independence of Outer Mongolia.
(July)	Russo-Japanese secret convention recognizing the meridian of Peking as dividing their spheres of interest.
(August)	Khobdo taken by Mongols and Chinese ousted from Western Mongolia.
(November 3)	Russo-Mongolian agreement concluded in Urga signifying Russian support for Mongolian autonomy, but not supporting Outer Mongolian claims on Urianghai, Barga, or parts of Inner Mongolia.
1913 (January)	Mongolian-Tibetan Treaty. Russia gives loan of two million roubles to Mongolian Government.
(November 5)	Russo-Chinese Declaration recognizing Outer Mongolian autonomy.
(November)	Mongolian Prime Minister arrives in St. Petersburg to ask for further financial help.
1914 (January)	Urga Hutukhtu sends letter to Emperor of Japan asking for help in struggle for Mongol unity and for a Japanese representative in Urga. Japan refuses to accept the letter.
(May)	French, British, German and U. S. Ministers in Peking receive letters from Mongolian Minister of Foreign Affairs informing them of the establishment of Mongolian independence and conditions of treaty of commerce with Russia.
(July)	Russo-Mongol Loan and Arms agreements.
(September)	Russo-Mongol Railway and Telegraph agreements.
1915 (June)	Tripartite Treaty of Kiakhta between Russia, China and Outer Mongolia recognizing autonomy of Outer Mongolia and China's suzerainty.
(November)	Russo-Chinese agreement on Barga.
1917 (February-September)	Fall of Tsarist regime. Provisional Government. Russian representatives and agents isolated.

(October)	Bolshevik Revolution. New regime denounces all "imperialist" treaties and rights derived from them.
1919 (November 22)	Cancellation of autonomy of Outer Mongolia by President of Chinese Republic. General Hsü in Urga.
1920-22	Existence of Far Eastern Republic in Siberia, independent of Soviet Russia.
1921 (February)	Urga taken by White Russian forces under Baron Ungern Sternberg.
(March)	Provisional Revolutionary Mongol Government proclaimed at Kiakhta.
(June 22)	Baron Ungern Sternberg defeated and captured.
(July)	Mongolian People's Revolutionary and Soviet troops enter Urga. Outer Mongolia again declared independent.
(August)	Mopping up operations with the assistance of Soviet troops. Appeal of the Provisional Revolutionary Government to Government of R.S.F.S.R. not to withdraw troops.
(November 5)	Soviet-Mongolian Treaty of Friendship concluded in Moscow.
(November)	Soviet Government recognizes independence of Urianghai (Tanna Tuva) after having crushed attempt by old Mongol official class in Urianghai to effect unity with Outer Mongolia.
1922 (April)	Mongolian Prime Minister Bodo and fifteen other officials shot, accused of Chinese connections.
(May)	Chinese protest against Soviet-Mongolian relationship (followed by other protests).
1923	Establishment of Buriat Mongol Autonomous S.S.R.
1924 (May 31)	Soviet-Chinese agreement on Outer Mongolia recognizing China's sovereignty over Outer Mongolia and promising withdrawal of Soviet troops.
(June)	Mongol Industrial and Commercial Bank (with monopoly status) founded.
(July)	Death of Hutukhtu of Urga (no new incarnation permitted).
(August)	Danzan, Commander-in-Chief of the Mongolian Army, arrested and shot during 3rd session of the Mongolian People's Revolutionary Party. Mongolian People's Republic proclaimed.
(November)	Text of Constitution of M.P.R. approved by the first Great Huruldan of the M.P.R. Soviet-Mongolian Bank agreement and Telegraph convention.

1925 (Beginning)	Soviet-Mongolian exchange of notes concerning withdrawal of Soviet troops from Outer Mongolia.
1925-28	Attempts to consolidate new regime. Revival of " right wing " forces.
1925-26	Mongolian Trade Delegation in Berlin.
1926-29	Mongolian Educational Mission in Berlin.
1926	M. P. R. and Tanna Tuva Republic sign a treaty.
1927	Tanaka Memorial to Japanese Emperor expounding (among other objectives) Japanese aims in Mongolia.
1928	Chinese Government divides Inner Mongolia into the three provinces of Chahar, Suiyuan and Ningshia.
(August)	Young Barga party attempts to retrieve autonomy of Barga—suppressed by Chinese troops.
1929-32	" Left-wing " attempts at a hasty socialization of Mongolian economy.
1929 (End)	Soviet Russia intervenes with troops in Barga.
1930	Soviet-Mongolian convention on animal diseases and sanitation signed.
1931-32	Japan invades Manchuria. Creation of Manchukuo gives Soviet Russia and Outer Mongolia a new neighbor.
1932-33	Reckless socialization program replaced by more moderate policy.
1934	Mongolian Prime Minister Gendung visits Moscow. Soviet-Mongolian agreements signed: on currency exchange rates, on Soviet-Mongol trade, for the delivery of goods to Mongols on preferential terms of gold, on joint companies, on terms of employment of Soviet workers.
1935 (Middle)	Border Incidents on Mongolian-Manchukuo frontier. M. P. R. Government refuses to admit Manchukuo representatives.
(November 25)	Mongol-Manchukuo Joint Commission at Manchuli for settling frontier incidents breaks down.
(December)	New border incidents near Buir Nor. M. P. R. Government files strong protest to Changchun authorities.
1936 (March 12)	Soviet-Mongol Protocol of Mutual Assistance. Soviet troops again in Outer Mongolia.
(April)	Four leading officials of the northern division of the autonomous Mongol province of Hsingan in Manchukuo executed for having conspired with the Outer Mongolian representatives during the Manchuli Conference, and for aiming at the independence of Northern Hsingan.

(November)	Anti-Comintern Pact between Japan and Germany.
1937 (July 7)	Japan begins attack on North China.
(August)	Demid, Commander-in-Chief of the Mongolian Army, dies from poisoning in the train on his way to Moscow.
(October)	Formation by Japanese of Federative Autonomous Government of Inner Mongolia.
1938 (Beginning)	Japanese occupy greater part of Inner Mongolia (Chahar and Suiyuan).
1939 (May 11)	Fighting starts on the Monoglian-Manchukuo border (in the Nomonhan district, east of Buir Nor).
(June)	Tanks and airplanes participate in battle between Soviet-Mongol and Japanese-Manchukuo troops. Implementation of Soviet-Mongol Mutual Assistance Pact of 1936.
(September 16)	Truce effected and Mongol-Manchukuo border commission set up.
1939-40 (September-March)	Border Commission makes no progress.
1940	New Constitution of Mongolian People's Republic.
1941 (April 13)	Declaration attached to Soviet-Japanese Neutrality Pact pledging respect of territorial integrity and inviolability of Manchukuo and of M. P. R.
(May 28)	Mongolian-Manchukuo Border Commission reassembles at Chita and decides to begin work of demarcation on June 27.
(December 7)	Japan declares war against the United States, Great Britain and British Dominions.
(December 8)	Manchukuo declares war on United States.
1942 (May)	Ratification of Mongol-Manchukuo border demarcation.
(July)	Mongolian People's Republic celebrates 21st anniversary of its founding.
(December 7)	Prime Minister of M. P. R., Choibalsang, arrives in Moscow.
1943 (November 20)	Mongolian trade delegation headed by Deputy Prime Minister arrives in Moscow.
1944 (or 1945)	People's Republic of Tannu-Tuva becomes Tuvinian Autonomous Republic of U. S. S. R.
1944	Soviet protest against Chinese attack on some Kazakhs who had fled from Sinkiang to Outer Mongolia. Denial by Chinese Government.
(November 25)	Mongol trade delegation arrives in Moscow.
1945 (April 5)	U. S. S. R. denounces Pact of Neutrality with Japan.
(July 5)	Stalin receives Marshal Choibalsang.

(August 6)	United States fliers drop atomic bomb on Hiroshima, Japan.
(August 8)	U. S. S. R. declares war on Japan. United States fliers drop atomic bomb on Nagasaki, Japan.
(August 9)	Soviet forces launch drive into Manchuria.
(August 10)	M. P. R. declares war on Japan.
(August 14)	Japan surrenders unconditionally to Allies.
(August 14)	Treaty of Friendship and Alliance between U. S. S. R. and Chinese Republic. Exchange of notes regarding Outer Mongolia in which Chinese Government agrees to a plebiscite of the people of Outer Mongolia regarding the independence of Outer Mongolia.
(August)	Chinese Communist forces occupy Chahar and Jehol.
(September 25)	Little Hural Presidium of M. P. R. decides on holding of plebiscite.
(October 20)	Plebiscite is held in M. P. R. on independence issue.
1946 (January 5)	China recognizes independence of Outer Mongolia.
(February 13)	Establishment of diplomatic relations between Chinese Republic and M. P. R. agreed upon, but not subsequently realized.
(February 27)	Soviet-Mongol Treaty of Friendship and Mutual Assistance and Agreement on Economic and Cultural Collaboration concluded.
(June 24)	Application of M. P. R. for membership in United Nations.
(August 6)	Application for membership of M. P. R. before Security Council. Decision postponed.
(End of August)	M. P. R. Government answers questionnaire sent by the Acting Secretary General of U. N.
(August 29)	Security Council rejects application for membership (China votes in favor).
(October 18)	M. P. R. requests Council of Foreign Ministers to allow them a representative in Far Eastern Commission.
1947 (June)	Mongol-Chinese border incidents in the Peitashan (Baitik Bogda) area along Sinkiang-Mongolian frontier. Chinese and Mongolian protests and counter-protests.
(August)	Security Council of U. N. again rejects application for membership of M. P. R. (China votes against admission.)
1948 (January)	Five Year Plan published in Ulan Bator.
(February)	Renewed Chinese-Mongolian incidents in Peitashan area.
(December)	Mongolian Trade Delegation arrives in Moscow.

INDEX

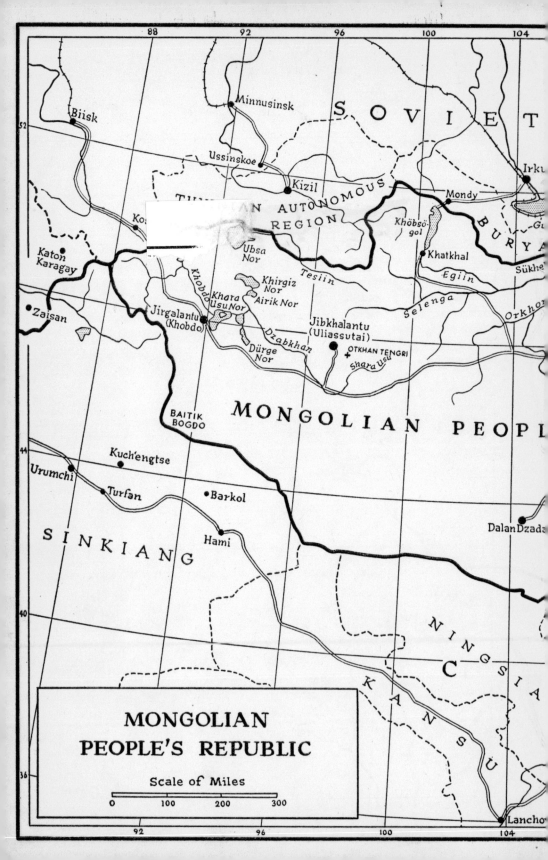

MONGOLIAN PEOPLE'S REPUBLIC

Scale of Miles

0   100   200   300